SWITCH, DEBARGE, MOTOWN & ME

SWITCH, DEBARGE, MOTOWN & ME

Gregory Williams

Switch Entertainment Book Publishing
Northridge, California

SWITCH, DEBARGE, MOTOWN & ME

Published by:

Switch Entertainment Book Publishing

switchentertainmentworld2@yahoo.com

Gregory Williams, Publisher / Editorial Director
Yvonne Rose/Quality Press.info, Book Packager

DEDICATION

This book is dedicated to my family, whether by blood or by love and to my true friends who I cherish beyond all measure.

To my mom (R.I.P.) for loving me unconditionally from day one of my life, till the last day of her own; to my for real "ride-or-die" brother Art (R.I.P.) who traveled by my side from my birth until he left his earthly bonds. My loving and missing you two has no end.

To my brothers, Garrett and Troyce, and my sisters, Crystal and Collette. To my Aunt Ruby Hickman and uncles James, Thomas, Elvin, Oscar, all of whom took leave of this life in recent years, this one is for you! Rest in peace all!

To my only biological child Autumn Rayne Williams; You'll never know how much U mean to me. To my many nieces and nephews, my love for you is endless!

To my living siblings, Skip, Hazel, Michael, "Gerry", Ed and Michelle, to my uncles Albert, Sylvester, Ronnie and my aunts Vera and Claudia, all of whom I consider my immediate family; To my BFF Cynthia Horner; my friend and brother of forty-plus years, Tommy Upshaw; to my adopted sister Maureen StCyr, I can't help but love you all!

i

To my brothers in Switch, Phillip Ingram, Tommy DeBarge, Eddie Fluellen, Jody Sims, Michael McGloiry, Akili Nickson and each of the others who passed through these ranks as an interim Switch member, I thank each of you for knowing how to make magic and doing the hell out of it at my side! To Darnell Wyrick and my White Heat brothers, Jessie T.C. Brown, Stanley Brown, Tony "Mutley" Jordan, David D Herrin and Pie, we made great music, became men, learned so much and had big fun together! *To Yvonne Rose for bringing the magic to my first book publishing journey.* To Aurelia Johnson, Judith Cassis, Mysti Day, Kambon Obayani and Mikey Skelton, I thank each of you for your support, encouragement and assist with the completion of this book."

To all the girls I've loved before, just know,… I never stopped!

And finally, this book is dedicated in loving memory to my dear brother Bobby DeBarge who left this earthly plain far too soon. We struck out on a mission to conquer the music world in our early teens, side by side and did just that, leaving behind magic that will last forever. I love you, miss you and pray you're finally at peace from the unjust hand life dealt to you!   Gone but never forgotten and through our music you will remain in the hearts and minds of all who, knew you, loved you and were touched by your incredible gifts of music.

ACKNOWLEDGEMENTS

My profound thanks to each of the awesome folks named in my telling and the few my mind failed to mention (but my heart will never forget), for sharing and contributing to this awesome journey called my life!

CONTENTS

Dedication i

Acknowledgements iii

Contents.. v

Foreword vii

Chapter 1: Mansfield to Motown 1

Chapter 2: And so, It began…..................................... 28

Chapter 3: School Daze 59

Chapter 4: Bobby and I 122

Chapter 5: My Nightclub Life.................................... 145

Chapter 6: 1971/TMG's/Grand Valley........................ 174

Chapter 7: White's L.A. 203

Chapter 8: Bye Bye Grand Raggedy; For Good! 268

Chapter 9: SWITCH, MOTOWN and ME.................... 304

Chapter 10: Contracts Signed & Moving to Montague.............. 343

Chapter 11: Lankershim--Bobby & Latoya.................. 381

Chapter 12: First Base with Free-Base 419

Chapter 13: Caribou Ranch 438

Chapter 14: Beginning of The End..459

Chapter 15: Let's Tour (finally) 481

Chapter 16: Switch V 524

Chapter 17: Leaving Motown...539

About the Author...546

FOREWORD

The SWITCH story and Gregory Williams story are intertwined as both entities are one in the same. Gregory Williams founded the band in Grand Rapids, Michigan, which was a hotbed for undiscovered talent. The young vocalist/musician always had his heart set on a career in the music business and after a few false starts, headed to Hollywood where dreams often come true.

The story of meeting superstar Jermaine Jackson in an elevator in the building which housed Motown Records is a heartfelt story that always brings a smile to faces. After all, how often would a would-be artist meet a person in an elevator who was actually a recording artist and the son-in-law of Berry Gordy Jr.

It was fate that brought Gregory Williams and his bandmate, drummer Jody Sims, in contact with someone who could break through the usual red tape. As Gregory and Jody hummed during the short elevator ride, Jackson, whose curiosity was piqued by their ingenuity, accepted the only cassette tape of Switch's music.

As the story goes, Switch got the coveted deal and although the band became an instant success and were heartthrobs in the iconic publication Right On!, there were pitfalls and challenges that seemed insurmountable.

This book takes its readers on a musical journey where the quest of following one's dreams can sometimes take an abysmal dive. But perseverance and tenacity can eventually right the wrongs. The Switch story is an amazing shake-your-head page turner that will fill eyes with tears, hearts with joy. There will never be a story like Switch, DeBarge, Motown & Me. Not ever.

- Cynthia Horner,
  Publisher/Editor-In-Chief, Right On! Magazine and
  Right On! Digital

Chapter 1

Mansfield to Motown

First Class / Hot Ice

It was January 17, 1977. I was twenty-two-years-old, Jody Sims was twenty-six. Together, we flew first-class from Columbus Ohio, in route to Los Angeles, eating filet-mignon and drinking free in-flight Chivas Regal with Coca Cola backs. Not that there had been many flights before this, but this was my first time in first class, and I was enjoying the best flight I had taken in my life thus far. And just as it was for me on another fateful date of February 21, 1973, the day Bobby DeBarge and I left Grand Rapids on a flight to Phoenix to join the TNT Flashers four years earlier, it was the middle of winter in the Midwest. Michigan and Ohio, as was most of that part of the country, were covered with knee deep snow and record-breaking cold. Again, the perfect time to get the hell out of dodge!

Upon Jody's and my arrival in L.A., Darnell Wyrick, my dear friend since the late 1960's and the person who brought me into White Heat, and his girlfriend Linda Dix picked us up at the airport and took us to their apartment in Hollywood. Unknown to Jody and me at the time, this apartment was around the corner from Hitsville USA, our soon to be home, Motown Records' L.A. recording studio. This is where Jody, Switch and I would wind up learning, growing and damn-near living with various new label mates like Stevie Wonder, Marvin Gaye, Smokey Robinson, Diana Ross, and The Commodores. We'd also work with producers Jeffery Bowen, Hal Davis, James Carmichael and many other "then" Motown great artists, producers, arrangers, engineers, studio traffic and personnel, including, of course, Switch's mentor and soon-to-be manager, Jermaine Jackson.

Darnell and Linda's small one-bedroom apartment sat in a cul de sac. It was clean, cozy and a welcome pit stop on Jody's and my way to fame without fortune, but onto a paycheck and our own apartments and lives. After dumping our bags on the floor, where we would also be sleeping, Jody and I immediately took a walk with Darnell and Linda to get our bearings on California soil once again and to familiarize ourselves with our new surroundings. As we walked, the four of us caught up on what had been happening in our lives since we'd last seen each other about a year before.

Among other things we discussed what each of us knew about what was going on with the other ex-White Heat members. It was late when we made it back to the apartment and after providing Jody and me bedding, Darnell and Linda quickly headed to bed to rest up for work in the morning. Jody and I, tired but too excited about being back in California to go to sleep, continued to talk. Having such a good time flying first class, one or the other of us suggested we name the group First Class. We played back and forth with that name while continuing to talk and before falling asleep we agreed that First Class was it.

The next morning, we took turns showering, taking the rollers out of our then permed heads, got dressed, finished grooming and called Phillip Ingram, Tommy DeBarge and Melvin "MC" Clark at the house back in Mansfield to let them know we had arrived. We told them they should all go back home if money got too tight while Jody and I sought out a record deal here in L.A. They agreed. Before ending that call, I asked M.C. to call Arnie Hayes after work to update him about where things were with Jody and me in L.A. After that call, with our cassette in hand, we hit the pavement and headed for our old haunt, Hollywood Blvd.

We rode the bus some, but mostly walked around checking out some of the places we used to frequent when we lived there as White Heat. Not much had changed in our two-year absence. The House of Pies and Johnny's Steak House assuredly had not changed and among other things Jody and I checked in on and confirmed Betty and Wayne still managed White Heat's old home, Howards Weekly Hotel!

We walked Hollywood Blvd. from La Brea to Vine and back, going in and out of the different open-front stores and restaurants, over almost every star on the Hollywood Walk of Fame. For little more than the next week this was our daily routine. With little to no money except the cash sent to us by our girlfriends, Jody and I had to be creative with the few bucks we had to work with.

Spending time at a few different coffee shops, we discussed how we would conquer Hollywood and get that record deal. We devised this "free meal" scam and would run it on the House of Pies every weekday until we finally got busted. It worked like this; one or the other of us would go in, be seated, order from the menu and soon after, begin to eat breakfast while the other waited or walked around for a few minutes more. In about the length of time for the meal to be served and almost eaten and the check to be delivered, the one of us outside would enter the restaurant, join the other, sit and order food. After the second food order was served the first one would casually leave the restaurant, taking their check with them. Once the second of us was finished eating, he would take his check to the register, pay for his meal only and leave with both having gotten full. This ritual continued, until one day this Asian waitress got wind of what we had been doing and guess who got confronted and busted?

You guessed right. Me! She waited till Jody had left the restaurant and ran up to me yelling in a thick Asian accent.

"Where you flin check?" Flin meaning friend. "Where you flin check?"

"Lady I don't know. Didn't he pay it on his way out?" I asked.

"No, no. Ebrey day you do dis. Where you flin check? She yelled.

"You do dis ebrey, Ebrey day!"

By this time, I swear, every eye in the place was looking at me and the manager was swiftly approaching as I slunk down a little under my table. Before he reached us, she was yelling to him, "He steals. He steals beltfuls!" Turning back to me, "Where he flin check?" In translation, beltfuls was breakfast and flin was friend.

Now I would have died laughing were it not me being persecuted and having to be serious while denying any knowledge of what she was accusing me of. I remained calm so the police wouldn't be called. Needless to say, while Jody waited for me down the block, I was banned from the House of Pies and that was the end of Jody's and my "free" meals at the House of Pies. After that ordeal, we continued to hit Hollywood Blvd's shops and restaurants discussing our record deal.

We talked and looked around, walking miles and remembering Hollywood. After a couple hours, we looked up and we were standing in front of the RCA Records building at 6590 Sunset. Even though the White Heat album was recorded for and released by RCA, neither of us had ever set foot in it before. Jody and I decided to walk in and check out the building.

Walking into the lobby, we noticed the directory and saw the name Don Burkheimer, division vice president of RCA. Well, we knew him from Barry and Glodean White's wedding reception where White Heat performed, and also another event we were allowed to attend. As Jody and I talked and remembered more, we decided we would see if he would listen to our tape and maybe give us a deal. We walked into his office and approached the receptionist; giving her our names and RCA history and told her we were there to see Mr. Burkheimer. She offered us a seat and placed a call from her switchboard. In short order we were directed to Mr. Burkheimer's office and asked his assistant to see him. Mr. Burkheimer just happened to be coming in the door and not knowing anything about us, told us to follow him into his office.

"Mr. Berkheimer, I'm Jody Sims."

"And I'm Greg Williams.

"And I hope you remember us as members of your and Barry White's act White Heat," Jody added.

"Of course, I remember White Heat, Jody, Greg" he said as he shook both of our hands. Then I said,

"We now have a new group called First Class and we have this cassette we'd like for you to hear."

He looked at us, smiled and held out his hand saying, "You know I thought White Heat was a really good group. We were pretty upset over here when Barry pulled you guys and the other's out from our deal."

Bewildered by his comment, I handed him the demo tape and he walked over and popped it in his cassette player, as Jody and I looked at each other surprised by what he had just said about Barry White. In the mean-time Mr. Berkheimer popped in the tape, listened to the first three songs, stopped it and said,

"Hey guys, the music is good, but I don't hear a hit. Your band does have talent though, so if you have anything else in the future come back, my door is always open." It was clear that this meeting was over as he extended his hand, shaking both of ours.

Jody and I thanked him as we left his office feeling rejected yet appreciative that he even took the time to see us without an appointment, because that stuff didn't happen back then, and it doesn't happen now with record executives of his stature. Yet, this impromptu meeting goes to show that our journey was blessed from the beginning. Even so, we were angry to learn that Barry White had pulled his whole company from RCA, dropped us, his other acts and other than the release letter he sent which ultimately broke White Heat up, he never sent us our artist or songwriter contracts or even a royalty statement, so Jody and I decided that we needed to find a lawyer who would help us sue the shit out of Barry White and that's exactly what we went and did right after leaving Mr. Berkheimer and RCA Records! Or so we thought when we found Mr. Kirk Lawson, attorney at law a couple of blocks away in a building we would later find out was the home of Motown Records. Yes, after the unplanned, unreal meeting we had just completed with Don Berkheimer of RCA Records, we somehow found ourselves in this building, on the twentieth floor, in the office of Mr. Lawson discussing our forthcoming law suit with Barry White and back out in the lobby in a matter of a few short minutes, impatiently waiting on an elevator to get us started on that long walk home.

Having just suffered our second major letdown of the day, we pressed the elevator button again and again and waited for what was the longest five minutes in history. Finally, the bell rang, the doors opened, we stepped in and they closed behind us. There were already a couple of people in this car, so Jody and I didn't really speak much on the way down. After stopping at the next couple of floors to additional passengers, the doors again opened and Jermaine Jackson, with his very pregnant wife Hazel Gordy Jackson entered. Immediately knowing who they were, Jody and I smiled at them and they returned the smiles and without a word passing between us, but we all nodded in acknowledgement of each other.

Jermaine & Hazel Jackson

As we rode down in silence the elevator continued to fill with passengers, with a few getting off until it stopped on the fifth floor, which is where the Jacksons got off. They again smiled at us as they made their exit and disappeared. Clearly excited at what had just taken place in this elevator, while enduring more stops as folks enter and exit, Jody and I repeatedly looked at each other and without a choice, continued our ride down to the first floor.

Once the elevator finally stopped and emptied on the first-floor, I can't recall who spoke first but one of us said to the other, "We should have given them our tape." Filled with the adrenaline of the moment and anxiety about the opportunity we might have just missed, Jody and I quickly jumped back into the same elevator and pushed the button to the fifth floor, which unknown to us, was a parking garage. Once there, we jumped out and ran down this corridor to the parking structure and there Jermaine and Hazel were, sitting in their car with him behind the wheel. They had stopped in the exit lane and were looking for a cassette to play on the ride home, as Jermaine had said. We quickly told them who we were and that we were trying to connect with someone who could help us with our music. Being so caught up in that moment, without hesitation I gave them our only cassette while Jody gave them our contact information, which Jermaine accepted.

We then thanked them for their time and let them get on their way. As we too began to walk away, we noticed them pop our cassette in their player before driving off. Jody and I were floating, hoping, praying, thanking God and believing something wonderful had happened to our lives this day, and we were right! Man, what started out so crazy turned out so right. After Jody and I made it back to the first floor and back out onto the street, heading to get something to eat with the twenty dollars Mr. Lawson had loaned us, it dawned on us that we had given the Jackson's our only tape. I remember saying "Yeah Jody, but we had to do that. We couldn't miss that moment."

"I know that's right, Greg!" Jody exclaimed. "Tomorrow we can call Tom at the studio in Ohio and have him send another one."

Still filled with adrenaline, excitement and serious hunger, we found a little, cheap coffee shop down on Vine Street and went in. This place was small but clean, with a few customers inside; so, Jody and I went in, ordered our food and talked about this insane day we had been living. We must have spent hours there talking and reordering coffee because when we finally looked up, it was now dark outside; so, we paid our check and continued to dream about what might be next as we headed back to Darnell and Linda's. When we got there, without taking time to catch our breath, we immediately filled Darnell in on our crazy day. We talked about the possibility of Jermaine and Hazel calling us back, till bedtime. After pink rolling up our hair, it was Jody's turn to sleep on the couch, so I took the floor; but tonight, it was really cool because I somehow knew it wouldn't be long now.

Upon waking up the next morning I sensed a promising day ahead. With Darnell and Linda off to work, I, then Jody awoke to get cleaned up and start our new, normal Hollywood day. From yesterday's thoughts we began to discuss who we should try to see today until it hit us like a ton of bricks, hell! We don't have a tape! "I guess that whole thing with meeting Jermaine Jackson of the Jackson Five and his real pregnant wife Hazel Gordy Jackson, Berry Gordy's daughter, really happened yesterday, huh, Greg?" Jody asked.

The two of us shared a giant, hopeful laugh and as in disbelief, we began a total playback of the events of our yesterday.

As the sunlight had left for the day and another Cali winter night was upon us so, with the few dollars we had bummed off of Kirk Lawson, we decided we'd walk down on Santa Monica Boulevard and grab a bite. As we were ready and about to leave the phone rang, so I answered it.

"Ha-ha-hello, ca-ca-can I s-s-speak to Greg and Jody?"

"Yes, this is Greg." I said, hoping this call was from who I thought it was and sure enough.

"Hi. It's Jermaine. Ha-a how are you guys?" Before I could respond he continued with "Ha-hay-hazel and I, liiiiiike, you ga-guys tape. That song called *Can This Be* is a smash."

As Jody was yelling hi to him through the phone I was thanking him for liking our tape.

Jermaine then asked, "Wa-Wa-What you gagaguyzz u-up to?"

"Were not up to anything Jermaine. About to go out for something to eat," said Jody.

"Ma-ma-my wife Ha-Hazel's in labor and I'm here waiting at the hospital do you, do-do you guys wanna come ddadown here? Can you guys come-come down here so we can-can ta-ta-talk?"

11

I wanted to scream Hell Yeah, but since he didn't really know me yet, I decided to contain myself and ask, "Where are you at? Jody and I will be there as soon as we can, just tell us where it is."

He told us Cedars-Sinai Hospital in West Hollywood and that was all I needed to hear, so I told him we would get there soon. After hanging up, Jody and I got the address of the hospital from Linda, called to get the correct bus route and directions and hurried over there.

From Darnell and Linda's front door to the Cedar's maternity lobby took us just short of an hour. We were directed to the maternity ward, where Jermaine was sitting in the waiting room alone, watching the television. As soon as he saw us walk in, he stood up to shake our hands, looking very happy to see us.

"Hi-hi guys. Thanks for coming down here," he said. "Hazel's in there having the baby so the doctor sent me out here. We-wa-wa-we- listened to your tape all the way home last night an-an and we-e l-l-like it. While we were still shaking his hand, Jody and I thanked him for liking the tape, for calling us back and for asking us to come and hang with him here at the hospital.

Jermaine had this broad smile on his face and asked "What-what do y'all want me-me to do-o?"

"If you can help us, we want a deal," Jody quickly blurted out.

"Ha-Ha-Hazel and I ar-re, starting a-a company in Motown called Ya-Ya-Young Folks. You guys ca can be, our fi-i-i-rst act ok? Wha-wa-wa- what do you-uo you guys call yourself?"

12

"First Class," Jody proudly stated, to which I nodded in agreement.

From there we talked for at least two hours. As we got acquainted, we talked about birthdays, our ages, our zodiac sign, about the band, how we got to L.A. And he told us a lot about Hazel and himself, his family and more about Hazel's and his new venture.

We'd been talking for a good while when Jackie, Tito and Marlon arrived. Jermaine introduced us and told them we were part of a band he and Hazel might be working with. The brothers shook our hands and encouraged our working with their brother and his wife as our conversation grew branches. I remember how elated I was because these were the coolest people I'd ever met. Not that I've ever been star struck; but here I was, spending time with four-fifths of the world-famous Jackson Five and true to their public image they were nice and down-to-earth folks.

After a while Jody and I tried to leave, feeling this was a family moment, but they engaged us even more. Within an hour of their arrival, Michael and Randy arrived and they too joined in the conversation. Soon after that, Jody and I excused ourselves, and we all shook hands and said goodbye. Once back on the street, Jody and I jumped in the air screaming and danced all the way to Darnell and Linda's home where we were staying.

I had taken for granted that Darnell would be with us in the new band, but I soon learned otherwise. Darnell and Linda both worked days, so he didn't really have the time to hang out with Jody and me; so, when we finally made the time to discuss things further, we sat down and put him up on where things were at and going. After everything had been said, Darnell shared his concerns about Motown's negative reputation and said how he wouldn't want to put his musical career in their hands should they offer a deal. I immediately understood and accepted what he was saying, because all of us had heard the negative stories about Motown throughout the years. But personally, I have never bought into rumor in any walk of life and didn't seek out Motown for a deal; but the way this chance meeting occurred, I knew it was an act of God and a possibility that I wasn't about to walk away from.

My faith and optimism were in control and I could only see I could win if I signed with this company. Before now I had never considered Motown in my dreams of having a record deal. I can't say I had not considered it because of the negative things I had heard or because I considered it out of reach. Anyway, Darnell then told us that Bernd Lichters had contacted him and asked him to be the leader of a band, Hot Ice and under that name he would sign a deal with Polygram Records Germany and release the White Heat/TNT Flasher recordings that I had suggested he pay for and take from the studio shelf in Ohio. I then agreed to go back into the studio with Jody, Darnell and Bernd to finish production on that material.

Even though I accepted Darnell's pass on Motown and subsequently Switch, I was somewhat hurt and disappointed because after basically growing up together, being in local bands, being college roommates and his getting me into TNT Flashers/White Heat, I always knew Darnell and I would make it in music together. Although not in Mansfield from the start of this new band, I knew once I had gotten things off the ground, he would be a part. See from what I knew, he and I had like-minds when it came to diligence, responsibility and overall leadership. I knew that we would be at each other's side. But I would soon come to learn even the best laid plans are subject to change, especially when there are elements beyond your control.

Having not spoken to the guys since the day we arrived nearly two weeks ago, Jody and I placed a call to them back in Ohio, but the phone had been disconnected. We tried to reach Arnie but there was no answer at his home either, so I made a call to the Ingram home to find that Phillip was there. Once he came to the phone, I told him about our meeting Jermaine and how we had given him our tape, and again I assured Phillip that we were gonna get a deal. I was surprised when Phillip told me that after they had run out of food and the heat in the house was about to be shut off, M.C. had gone back to Grand Rapids while he and Tommy had come to Akron a couple of days earlier and would be living with his family while I worked things out in L.A.

Although Bunny DeBarge and Mutley volunteered to come to Mansfield and take Tommy back to Grand Rapids, he told them no. He had told Phillip much about his home life, including about the physical, sexual and emotional abuse he suffered for years, and how he really didn't want to go back there, so Phillip asked his parents if Tommy could stay with them for a little while, till I called for both of them; and they kindly agreed after telling Tommy that he would have to be responsible and work for his keep just like Phillip would. Once again, I was appreciative for the Ingrams. Phillip yelled for Tommy to pick up the downstairs phone so Jody and I could talk with both of them.

While waiting for Tommy to pick up, Phillip added, "Hey Greg, Eddie is out of the hospital and ready to come, but there is no change in Reggie's condition."

I chimed in, "That's good news about Eddie. Let me have his number and the hospital number for Reggie Manley; and if he's allowed to accept calls and I'll call him and Eddie." Phillip gave me the number, as Tommy happily picked up the phone and joined in the chat.

Tommy immediately started stuttering like Arnie to which all of us burst out in laughter. I jokingly scolded Tommy for doing that, and Jody got in asking how Tommy was holding up and repeating what we had just told Phillip. We then told them that they could get ready to come soon, said our last words, and hung up the phone. We then called M.C. who had been back in Grand Rapids for a week or so and had gotten back into his old routine awaiting my call.

Once he answered the phone, not knowing who was calling, I asked laughing, "You ready to roll Baba??"

"Hey Baby. I been waiting for this call, ha, ha, ha! I don't care what you got just get me outta this muthafucka." He laughed.

"Help is on the way M.C., Jody and I met with Jermaine Jackson today and I know something's about to happen, so hold on a little longer."

After M.C. proceeded to tell me what was happening on the Grand Rapids music scene and complain about being buried in waist high snow, we soon got off of the phone. Jody and I couldn't sit still from happiness. We went back out and walked around Hollywood for a while before returning home for the night, elated over the fact that we were gonna get this record deal.

Hazel had the baby, Jermaine Jr., that night and Jermaine called us the next day too elated that he had a son. He again asked if we could meet him, so we joined him and just hung out, getting to know each other at Poinsettia Park, which was directly across the street from Hitsville USA, Motown's Hollywood recording studio which coincidentally was only three blocks from Darnell and Linda's apartment where we were staying.

Unknown to Jody and me at the time, this was where Switch would wind up recording most of our first and second albums. We wound up hooking up with Jermaine a few more days over that next week at the basketball courts where we'd see folks like Marvin Gaye, The Commodores and various other noted musicians, producers and music executives. After the next week or so, once Hazel got back into the swing of things, we met at Motown offices with Jermaine to discuss in depth what we envisioned for the group and to make plans as to how we would put everything together. Jermaine informed Jody and me that they, he, Hazel and others, whom we would later come to know included Berry Gordy, wanted to see and hear who and what we were and what we can do; and there would be others at Motown, such as folks from creative and legal we should meet with to discuss other questions and possible concerns.

Jermaine asked if we would be willing to do a showcase at Motown's expense. Of course, our response was an immediate and excited YES! As the days rolled on Jermaine,

Hazel, Jody and I met at Young Folks offices more frequently. We would either be hanging, going to Poinsettia Park, Hitsville USA while maybe the Commodores, Smokey or someone else might be recording, and even just going out for lunch or dinner. While up at Motown, Jody and I were allowed to go to the mailroom and get free albums, and promotional items, i.e. posters, tee shirts, caps, etc. of Motown artists. We could even back order product like (Rare Earth, Isley Brothers, Stevie Wonder, etc.) which was stored in the Motown warehouse as long as we picked it up within a week of its arrival in the mailroom.

Jody and I met Tom DePierro during our first few visits in the Motown building. At that time, Tom was holding down the jobs of running Motown's mail room and single-handedly tracking Motown's Disco airplay around the world as the Disco boom was just taking off. In the midst of maintaining his other responsibilities he was assigned to show Jody and me around the company. The sixteenth, seventeenth and eighteenth floors housed various departments, i.e. A&R, publishing, legal/business affairs, promotional, marketing, and mail. For a while Tom became our favorite stop, while up at Motown; and later, he started to visit and hang out with us at the house. Neither Jody nor I was aware that Tom was gay, as he carried himself in a way that never exposed us to his sexual preferences, until after the guys arrived. Actually, it was Bobby who blatantly told all of us that Tom was gay, which didn't really make a difference anyway.

After things got initiated between Jody and me with Motown, anytime we would come up to the company, they would allow us to make as many long-distance phone calls as we wanted. In our not being used to this kind of phone access in years and access to new music, of course we took advantage of these amenities. We would call our moms and other family members, girlfriends -including Jody's two girlfriends, to thank them again for buying our plane tickets to L.A.

Our main calls were to Phillip, Tommy and M.C. to keep them encouraged and to find out how they were preparing for their journey here to L.A. We also obtained and provided Hazel with information to send Greyhound bus tickets to Ohio and to Grand Rapids to M.C. who'd gone back home. Although I repeatedly called Arnie, I hadn't caught up with him yet, but I didn't think he was avoiding my calls, I just thought he was busy; and I didn't have a way to leave a number for him to call me back, so I kept calling Ohio again and again. As persistence usually pays, after more than a week of calling, I finally did reach Arnie real late one night, waking him up.

"Arnie, what's happening man I've been calling you all week. Like I promised, we got a deal man!"

"Re-re-really man?" He asked. "Tha-thatt's-s-s gre-gre-gre gr-gr-great Greg."

"Man, Jody and I met Jermaine Jackson and his wife Hazel, you know Berry Gordy's daughter, Hazel; and their talking about getting us a deal with Motown. They're sending bus tickets for all of you to come out here so we can do a showcase and get signed."

I heard Arnie breathing into the phone, but now he said nothing. I thought he was trying to get his thoughts together to keep from stuttering.

"Th-th-that's really goo-goo-good news Gr-Gr ahh, Greg. I'm-m-m ha- ha-happy for you guys, but Sue and I talked about it an an-an-an-and I'm not coming."

"What Arnie? You're not coming? You're not coming now or not at all?" I asked trying not to sound like I was in a panic, which after hearing this, I'm close.

"No ma-ma-ma-man. I-ai-ai-ai-a —"

I cut him off saying, "But Arnie, we got the deal man. I've been hangin' with Jermaine Jackson from the Jackson Five, man; and Motown wouldn't be sending you tickets if they weren't serious."

"I ca-ca-cain't co-co-come. I'm sorry, Greg bu-bu-bu-bu-but I' I-I'm not coming."

"Really man," I added, now getting angry. "Ok Arnie. I got it, but you're really losing out. You take care, man."

I hung up the phone. I understood but still couldn't believe what I was hearing. What I had to accept. Here I had basically built this group around Arnie's life. Moving to Mansfield because it was Arnie's hometown and so he wouldn't have to leave his family or drive up and down the Ohio freeways in all of that snow, ice and bitter cold. Writing songs that would fit his voice and style of keyboard playing and catering to his schedule for band and vocal rehearsals. *This dirty muthafucka!* I thought to myself, once it set in that he really wasn't coming. He could have told me this shit before I left Ohio, chasing this dream and saved me the grief that was now staring me in the face.

After that, I wouldn't speak with Arnie again till thirty-four years later. In my mind, Arnie's refusal to come put me in the worst dilemma I'd ever faced. We now had a pending contract with Motown and no lead vocalist and principal keyboardist. I'd written songs and molded the band for multiple vocalists, with someone who could sing in a high falsetto, and do duos with Phillip, and now I had no one. I tried to give Arnie a few days and reached out to him again, to no avail. However, in communicating back and forth with M.C., Phillip, Tommy and Eddie who were preparing to catch the Greyhound bus in route to Los Angeles, time was staring me in the face and my choices were limited.

When I thought about it, the one immediate option I had to replace Arnie presented serious problems. I didn't want to deal with the pain, chaos and destruction that came along with solution number one. Before he left for Youngstown, Jody and I pondered over what could be done if Arnie didn't change his mind, which actually, he never did, so we kept the impending change in band personnel to ourselves and let the existing plans move forward, knowing we would definitely find a solution.

As fate would have it and as if he had read my mind, Jody again brought up Bobby. I had to admit to myself and to Jody, "I too was thinking about him, but I can't get past the drug addiction and other personal hell that comes with him. Let's see if Arnie comes around before it's too late or cross the "Bobby-bridge" only if we have to, Jody," I concluded.

Jody agreed and we changed the subject, talking about his trip to Youngstown and what I would be doing while waiting for him and the fellas to get here. One day with nothing to do, I decided to take a walk down Hollywood Blvd. and got distracted by the strong smell of incense which coming out of this head shop I had seen but never ventured into. So, I walked in and started looking around. This place was big, and it contained any kind of drug paraphernalia one could imagine, from various pipes, bongs, roach clips, cigarette papers, Persian rugs and lots of other things I had never seen.

While checking out the black light room which was filled with posters, strobe lights and lots more, I thought I heard my name called over the loud psychedelic music, but I immediately wrote it off as me hearing stuff. But in less than a minute I hear my name again much clearer and closer than before, so I turned in the direction of the voice to find Revie, my old card playing friend from the White Heat days. Caught off guard by this happy surprise we began to talk. He informed me that he was the manager of this place since a few months after we'd last seen each other. Revie and I had become good friends in nineteen seventy-three and remained friends until White Heat made our trek back to Ohio.

He and I spent a few minutes talking about good times at Howard's Weekly, but the store began to fill up and he had to go. He made me promise if I could to come back for his seven-pm break to join him for dinner and get caught up on what's been happening since our last Tonk game two years ago, which I agreed to do.

I met Revie promptly at seven and we walked about one and a half blocks down to Johnny's Steak House, where most of White Heat members used to congregate and eat at least once a week. Once in and seated, Revie and I immediately began filling each other in on the cast of characters we used to hang out and play cards with. He asked about my brother Art as I got him up to speed on what happened to White Heat, with me and my life, including my new band and my possibly signing with Motown Records, about which he was excited to hear.

As we enjoyed our dinner and chatted about each other's lives, Revie told me the short story of how he wound up managing the head shop; then, as if the light bulb came on over his head he said, "Hey man, I have an idea, how would you like to work here with me while waiting to see if the record contract would come through? At least we can get in a good Tonk game now and then."

I was a little caught off guard, but without a second thought I said yes and started working the next day; and this is how I spent my days while waiting for the fellas to arrive for our new life at Motown Records. Fortunately, Revie made out the work schedule, so anytime I had a meeting with Motown he would have someone cover for me and I could make up the time later.

One day, Jody and I were called for an initial meeting with Motown's head of legal, Lee Young. During that meeting, among other things, it was suggested that Jody and I be signed as artist, songwriter and producer contracts, and create our own production company where we could sign the rest of the group to us. Thereby, if we chose we could give the group members money from the advance Jody and I received. Jody and I instantly passed on that suggestion explaining that all band members were in this together. From where I stood, that's how it would be from beginning till end. Once it was decided to move things forward, at the urging of Jermaine and Hazel, Motown moved Jody and me into a hotel, allocated us weekly per diem and sent bus tickets for the other guys to come to L.A.

Before things got too hectic, Jody decided that now would be the best time to relocate his wife and young son to California before the other band members arrived. So, he flew back to Youngstown Ohio and prepared for that move while I was checked into the Holiday Inn on Highland Ave in Hollywood. While waiting for the guys to finally arrive and the showcase to happen, Jermaine and I started hanging more frequently. His main protégé, at that time, was Michael McGloiry and they were together much of the time working on music for Jermaine's forthcoming solo album; so, he would sometimes pick me up or I would meet them at the studio, since it was also located in Hollywood, not too far from my hotel.

Even though he was busy and more often than not playful, I sensed a certain loneliness in Jermaine. His brothers had left Motown in 1976 and although he had contact and even got to see them from time to time during that period, the close bond was obviously broken, due to the different paths they were now on. I picked up that he missed the comradery of his brothers and McGloiry and I, and later Switch somewhat filled the void.

At that time Jermaine had no idea what fun and craziness he was in for once he started hanging with the fellas who would soon become known as Switch. A week or so after checking into the Holiday Inn, I ran into Lenny Williams, ex lead singer for Tower of Power in the hotel lobby. He was also at the Holiday Inn as a guest of Motown while negotiating and about to sign his deal with the label. As I had learned and performed the horns to "What is Hip?" many times before, I immediately knew who Lenny was. I introduced myself and he and I became instant friends from that moment.

During our chat, we exchanged room numbers and began to call each other just to check in. We wound up breaking bread most days and got to know each other while both dealing back and forth at Motown. We would discuss music, family and life in general over those few short weeks before my fellas would arrive from the mid-west. Now, Jody had already returned to Ohio to get his wife and son, leaving me alone in L.A. I had started working at the head shop and would now have money coming in from there and my weekly per diem from Motown.

When I wasn't working, I mostly hung with Lenny, Jermaine and McGloiry until my new bandmates made it out here. After they left Ohio, it took the guys five days to get to L.A. Once they arrived and had checked into the Holiday Inn with me, I knew I had to make a serious decision because we still didn't have a lead singer and Jermaine and Hazel and Motown would want to hear the band soon.

I waited a few days till everyone was situated and getting past the awestruck daze of actually being in Hollywood; till one afternoon, Jody and I called all the guys into the room, except Tommy, who was talking on the phone because I'd told him my thoughts first.

"Guys, Arnie's not coming. I called him when I called you guys and various times since, only to finally be told that he isn't coming; so, we're left with no choice, I'm gonna call Bobby DeBarge and see if he can come. They did not know the extent of my reluctance and concerns, but they did know that I had some kind of problem with what I had decided must be done. Eddie did not even know Bobby at that time, but Phillip and MC certainly did. Since MC came to L.A. from Grand Rapids, I asked had he seen Bobby before he left. He said he hadn't, but he knew from mutual friends that Bobby was battling drugs again. This time he was strung out on heroin.

Although Tommy and M.C. were very aware of the places Bobby's antics could take you, Phillip & Eddie looked worried and later told me of their concern in having two individuals in the group who'd suffered, like Bobby and Tommy; and he remembered what Tommy had told him about certain issues with Bobby. After talking with the fellas and returning to Tommy's room, I heard him on the phone talking to Etterlene. I patiently waited while Tommy talked and then understanding that the context of the conversation had changed soon after. Tommy passed me the phone, Bobby was on the other end.

"What's happening, Bobby?" I said in my upbeat but serious voice. "I'm sure Tommy has told you about Jody and me hooking up with Motown. If you want to come, I'll have them send you a ticket, but you have to be off drugs when you get here because I won't let drugs destroy the band."

Bobby started to cry.

"Man, I knew you wouldn't forget me. No matter what these niggas out here said, like always I knew you wouldn't forget me, Greg." He said through his trembling voice as he tried to regain his composure, "If I can get out of here I promise, I'm through with drugs Greg. I promise I'll get clean and stay clean when I get there with you guys."

"You promise Bobby? No more drugs?"

"I promise Greg. I'm just wasting away here. You know what it's like in this muthafucka. Just git me outta here, man. I won't let you down." And that's the way it was between Bobby and me. Always! Our differences would surface but we'd always find a way to never let them stop us from coming together through our love of music and our love for each other.

But still, in my not having the luxury of time to find a better replacement for Arnie, in my knowing better than all of the guys except Tommy about the often volatile and disruptive nature that Bobby displayed and subjected others to. Also, in knowing what I was about to bring into our new group, our pending signing with Motown Records and our possible musical journey together I insightfully told them, "This journey is not going to last long so we better ride it for all its worth."

That's how I am and have always been with folks I love since my early consciousness of being Gregory Williams, no matter what the cost. And man, let me tell you about some of the cost, wins and serious losses.

Chapter 2

And so, It began….

Williams Clan (left to right) Greg, Gerry, Hazel, Art, Mattie, Eddie

I guess I also learned from the start that, the less money you have, the less options you get at anything. My family really didn't have any money and due to my limited options, there were a couple things that I was born with, which stuck, and I learned to work with and make something good of them such as common sense, self-respect, kindness and music. From the way I really see it, I didn't choose any of those gifts. Especially music, it chose me and shaped and molded my life from the minute I could hear or make a sound.

To my mom and siblings, I was a winey kid because I couldn't drink milk due to a lactose intolerance, so I loudly and dramatically made that known to all. That too was something that took my mom awhile to discover and I used to have frequent nose bleeds from around age 3 till age 10. As soon as she adjusted to a kid who couldn't hold down milk and had serious nosebleeds and made the adjustments to both, she was cool, and I was even cooler.

In my early years I came to know both my parents' thoughts were largely consumed with music because it was an integral element in both their lives and subsequently mine. I later read somewhere that the thoughts of parents are absorbed by the child in the womb and then manifested in the child's life. In my case I found that to be true when it came to music. My dad, though sometimes visible through infrequent random visits, was absent from my life till we became friends in my mid-twenties.

For all intents and purposes William Charles Gray, or Willie C as everyone called him, was a charming, tall, heavy-set, brown skinned man with a bright smile, deep dimples, "good hair" and eyes that twinkled, which I am told I got from him. Although he was said to be able to charm the skin off of a snake, I don't think he ever really did. Now charm a woman out of her drawers, well that's another thing because from what little I witnessed over the years, women were all over him and let's not forget, I'm here. From what I knew, my dad was pretty intelligent for a guy with no more than a high school education and a talented tenor saxophone player to boot.

While coming up, the few times when I was around him, I took note that he could articulate on any subject discussed, he knew how to fix and make things work and he could tell you how and when you were feeling something, then he could tell you why. He came into my mom's life straight out of Greenwood, Mississippi when they we both sixteen years old. They instantly became high school sweethearts, but I didn't arrive until roughly three years after they met. Being left by his mom, who was fourteen when she had him, to be raised by his grandmother, Willie C grew up to be a grounded, somewhat strong and somewhat responsible man.

The reason my description includes the adjective somewhat is because I was not the beneficiary of his strong or responsible attributes with the exception of his paying his court ordered child support on time, but what I was aware of, once I came into the age of reason, was the fact that Willie C did his best to take care of his wife and the children he raised till he died, in 1992 of a fatal heart attack due to his life long fight with diabetes. But more directly, from the stress of trying to take care of his wife, his children, the ones who lived under his roof, his mother and a host of other folk which did not include me, my older brother Garrett and all of our baby sister Michelle. The later 3 of us all had different moms than our other siblings and would later in life have each other.

My mom, Mattie Williams, a very attractive brown-skinned woman stands five feet seven inches tall with a head full of thick black good hair. She too is a smart woman, even without that high school diploma. She is caring, outspoken in many matters but more so humble to a fault in others, which

I certainly took hold of and kept on my way into this world. Above all else she loved her five children and her family.

She too was very talented and through her youth and early years of her adulthood, she was the lead singer of an acapella gospel group The Jewels of Harmony who were a group to be reckoned with as powerhouse vocalist throughout Midwest churches and beyond. They would often rehearse in our living room - mom, my play aunts Cesther, Samella and Claretta - and she always sang around the house. Though at home she would play and sing to gospel and secular records publicly she would only sing for the lord.

During those early years my mom was also a card player, a very lucky one. She and Fanny, another of my play aunts and mom's close friend since childhood, would frequently hold card games in the many apartments we moved in and out of over the years; and as the house, the person hosting the games, she would make decent money which afforded us things, including clothes, food, toys and a few other modern items that made life easier.

As little guys, my older brother Art and I would sometimes hide and watch the grown folk laugh, drink, gamble, and dance to the music that was always playing and have fun. And of course, after many years of exposure, we followed in those footsteps, doing all of the above. My mom was number two in a family of eleven children from which nine were blessed with musical talents. From my earliest memories, my uncles James and Thomas played the trombone with James being a virtuoso, uncles Elvin and Albert were lead vocalist in one group or another, if I'm correct my uncle Oscar played trombone also for a short while. My aunt Vera played the clarinet, uncle Sylvester played trumpet, while every one of them could and did sing well, which I came to know years later was one of many talents inherited by nine of the 11 Williams siblings.

Williams Clan (left to right) Oscar, Vera, Ruby, Mattie, Thomas, Elvin, Albert, Sylvester. Claudia, Dora, James Sr., James Jr., Ronnie

There was so much sound going in the house and so many people that my cousin, Willie "Squeaky" Edwards and I, would go into the closet and sing this song, "Johnny got his nose open (da da da da da da da), Johnny got his nose open (da da da da da da da), Johnny got his nose open wide as can be, Johnny is a fool you see."

Squeaky, his sisters Sandy and Nira were my closest cousins, till they moved away to Detroit when Squeaky and I were eleven or twelve years old. Although my flesh and blood cousin, for years I had a secret crush on Sandy, but I kept it to myself, from her and everyone else. Good thing we were cousins because neither of us would have ever crossed that family line anyway. What all of us had to do was free up that music inside of us and respond to everything around as family; and as kids and at a tender age Squeaky and I claimed the music for life. I think that's where his nick name comes from, him trying to make music as a baby.

There were many of us, as back in that time seemed most families were large with lots of children. Between the Williams, my maternal relatives, the Edwards and the Jennings, we had a whole lot of immediate family surrounding each other, not to mention the extended relatives in and out of Grand Rapids. The Edwards children: Ethyl, Sam, Willie, Sylvester "Sonny", Earl, Audrey and Erma are the offspring of my grandmother's sister, Blanch and her husband Aubrey, who also raised my cousin Henry "Pop" Wilson who was the son of Ethyl, while the Jennings children: Jester, Ivory Jr., Mae Francis, Dean, Gloria, David, Martha, Ruby and Willie are offspring of my grandfather's younger brother Ivory Sr. and his wife Mary.

All big beautiful families with strong parental and Christian leadership whose children had no choice but to get an education and to grow up with home training and good grounding among other positive attributes. These people made me strong. These people made me proud. These people I will love and respect always, for they too are me.

During this time, the Williams home was actually two homes on Hall Street, on the south east side of Grand Rapids, Michigan. Most of my early and pre-teen years, mom, my brothers Art, Gerry and Eddie and our sister Hazel lived in one house and my grandparent's house where Granddad, Mother, my uncles and aunts lived, was two doors down the street. I grew between both houses of music, family and love. My maternal grandmother, affectionately known as mother, was half Negro and half Black Foot Indian and she had a very light complexion with red undertones, which was the total opposite of my aunt Blanch who was dark like me and through my life was my grandmother's only living sibling.

Mother, a devout Christian woman, all of the years I'd known her, was tall, standing about five feet nine or ten, slightly taller than my grandfather. She was an intelligent, blunt, outspoken woman with a sense of humor, who could be rather charming when she chose to be. '

My grandfather, James Williams Sr., also a Christian who was born the child of former slaves, was a small built man who stood about five feet, ten inches tall, was a moderately attractive, very dark-skinned man. His weight averaged around one hundred, forty pounds throughout most of my years of knowing him. Although he could read and write well he had no formal education beyond sixth grade, with the exception of the things he would teach himself; and from what I was told, he was always filled with wisdom beyond his years and had common sense of the ages. I too came to know his sense of humor, which appeared when he wasn't too tired from working so hard or too consumed in thought to let it break through. He lived a fairly average life as a hardworking man.

During my early years, my grandfather was living with the family and was clearly head of the household, but he always worked a lot, as would any responsible husband and father of 11 children, and everybody knew Mother was in charge of the household. She loved most music, but Nat King

Cole and his voice was probably the first I heard singing because she played his music all the time, and most of us kids could be heard singing along with her.

Mother loved music and didn't mind all that practicing in the house, because she believed children had to be involved in something. In all of my memories she was loving and kind but if you didn't do what you were supposed to, she would definitely discipline you. Her way of treating people and looking at the world derived from these principles: always put God first and "never throw a stone, hide your hand" and "don't ever half do nothing." She'd repeat these sayings to me a lot when I was a child and I learned what she meant.

These sayings have determined everything I've done in life. The message was clear though, to not only my mom, but also to all her brothers who worked, had families and all did well in school. Retrospectively, these were my examples and I followed the Williams because as best they could, they stepped up for Art and me in the absence of our dads.

The Williams men were and are some dapper sharp dressers and they were always clean. They got that from my grandparents as both like to dress and stay well-groomed. My grandfather worked hard to take care of his family and instilled in his sons these ideas: be responsible and accountable, always keep your shoes shined, your hair combed, mouth fresh, hands cleaned with no ash showing, keep wax out your ears, your clothes clean and ironed, with clean and no holey underwear, take care of your children, your home, your family, keep money in your pocket and always be extra clean when you go to spend money. There was another ideal which he lived by that was instilled in his children, grandchildren and now their children, "never half do nothing!"

My grandfather, James Williams Sr., I'm sure was where our, my family's intense level of humbleness and accepting spirit comes from. I say our, because I have witnessed these traits pass down through the generations. My mom, not knowing that it could ultimately prove harmful to me on my journey to be somebody, also imposed and enforced that thought process on each of her children, not knowing its interpretation would become a hindrance to all but one of her offspring.

I also note with some of my adventurous uncles, cousins and siblings, these traits are simply a part of who they are where, with a few including myself, these two traits in particular have become too humbling. As for me trying to maintain in the ruthless uncaring world of entertainment more specifically, in the music industry, there is no room for the soft and considerate as you will be eaten alive by most, simply trying to get ahead, including those you once thought were your friends and/or were just like you. I would come to learn that if you don't speak your mind, people misunderstand and often take your reserve attributes as a weakness or sign of limited intelligence for which they will prey upon.

Yes, Mother ran the house, but while Granddad was there, he definitely ran the family. He affectionately worked his sons and loved his daughters. The love he had for his sons was shown in the support and pride he displayed in all their accomplishments. He was also a firm believer in family and any of his children who fought each other had to deal with him. He used to say, "Greg, family is the most important thing you've got, so cherish it and look out for each other."

Once at a family gathering, Art and I, who were teens at the time, had a disagreement and we started fighting. Granddad stopped the fight and whipped both of us right in front of everyone. One of my uncles had the nerve to say something and he turned to him. "You want some of this strap (his belt), get in line."

My uncle backed off. He'd also tell me to always pronounce my words correctly because "the way you speak will determine how people perceive you." He'd read the newspaper aloud and have me repeat words, which were difficult. I'd repeat the words aloud and I was always pleased because he was pleased with me. He instilled discipline in me, as he did his sons, and the idea I represented the family in every way and at all times. This is from a man who was raised during the worst segregation in the U.S, who hadn't finished elementary school and was the first generation out of slavery! He was a well-rounded man who I also watched cook various dishes, a passion I cherish today.

He used to cook this dish called "Kush". You take day old cornbread and crumble it into a frying pan, then add onion, salt and black pepper, a little oil and you let it cook, almost like you're frying it, but you don't let it fry. I used to cook it for my brothers and sisters, and it was a hit.

I could easily see my grandfather's teachings in the family because, during that time, there were so many large families in that neighborhood and one among these were the Belchers. They were always feuding with the Williams. Now and then, we'd go as a family, men and women, no matter how small, everybody would pick someone from the other family, and we'd go to blows as a family against theirs. When the battle was over, who'd ever gotten his or her butt whipped would be laughed at by everybody. I always made sure I wasn't being laughed at by anyone. I learned loyalty and responsibility, at an early age, from these encounters and they've stayed with me all my life.

My mom and grandparents were also adamant about respect for your elders and everyone gave those older folks their props all the time. As I grew in this life, to this day, I'd often wished that teaching had a slight variation, which I now teach my own child to respect those elders who respect you and respect themselves. At least that should save my daughter some grief throughout her life journey. As my own daughter is to me and her mom, I am the only child of the union of my mom and dad, and my dad never lived with us. And though they were aware that he had his own family, my mother's family still accepted him because he always gave financial support and tried to see me from time to time.

Among the many jobs my dad held down to take care of his wife Annette and their 5 children over the years, he was a radio dispatcher for the C&O railroad and for the various Cab companies of Grand Rapids. For a time, he was also a deputy for Kent County Sheriff's department, and he continued to drive cab through all of those years as a second job to the various others he undertook. After getting married, his sax playing days came second and even third to his family. His children: William aka "Skip," Collette aka Wendy, Crystal aka Princess, Troyce and Michael, my stepmother's biological son and my dad's adopted son.

Michael was raised as my dad's flesh and blood and all of them were simply my brothers and sisters. I was the big brother to each of them and to my immediate siblings who were born to my mom, with the exception of Art who is sixteen months older than me. There were no steps, no halves, just brothers and sisters. I grew up with the understanding that I was the oldest of my dad's children; but years later I found out that I have an older brother, Garrett Riley, who was born and raised in Mississippi by his mom.

Garrett was born when my dad turned 16 years old. Also, the year my dad, who was raised by his grandmother, moved to Grand Rapids to live with his own biological mother. I finally met and spent a few days with Garrett and his wife Ruby in 1998 when they came to California to visit his sisters who live roughly 3 hours from me in Northern California. Over latter years, after my dad had told me about Garrett, we vowed to make a trip down south to see Garret and his family, but my dad passed away before we could make that happen.

I also found out I had another half-sister, 14 years younger than me, in 1981when Switch performed in Grand Rapids. I remember my dad bringing this cute little teenager back stage after the show. One look at her and I knew her face looked too much like the face I saw in the mirror every day for us not to be related. And since I was too young to have a kid her age, she had to be this baby sister I had once heard about. My dad introduced Michelle to me, and she jumped me, hugged me and would not let me go. We fell in love with each other that day and haven't let go since.

Including Garrett, who was my father's first and oldest child, we were each hated or strongly disliked by our stepmother and were after-thoughts to our dad. I still haven't figured out what we were to our paternal grandmother, but to the eight of us, we were, are and always will be brothers and sisters and best friends.

Although my dad had sporadically spent a few hours with me throughout my early years, I became most aware of his presence most when I was ten, in 1964 during a time where I sold The Grand Rapids Times, our city's only Black newspaper. I had found an application form inside the paper, cut it out, filled in my name and address, without anyone's help. I later received my papers, was provided a small route in my neighborhood and told anyone and everyone who asked that I was going to be an entertainer, which I had proclaimed from age six.

One day I opened the Grand Rapids Times and found my father's picture inside in their weekly feature, musician of the week. I proudly walked around selling my newspaper and pointed out to everyone, "This is my daddy!" featured inside. I finished my route, went to mother's house, washed up as soon as I entered the house and walked into the living room. I saw my dad sitting there. I wasn't a shy child. Frankly, I was talkative and active. I froze though, when seeing him and a sense of wondering pride churned within me.

He called me over and gave me a hug. I sat there and watched him talking to the men in my family. He was clean, his shoes shined, and his nails were clean and manicured, his stingy brim hat sat on his knee, not a hair was out of place and he smelled good. I sat among the men observing them talking to him and as he rose to leave, he called me over again, touched me on the head, gave me three dollars and told me to always do as my mother said. I put the money in my pocket and held onto it. It connected him and me; and I put the three dollars under my pillow, touching it that night before I slept.

It would be a while before I'd see him again as once, maybe twice a year he would come calling to see the family and check on his son. A few years later, my Uncle Thomas was taking me from my grandparents' home to my mom one evening after school. We happened to be passing this place called Barnett's Bar, and for some reason he told me we had to stop in for a minute. As we walked in we were greeted by the sound of live music. He sat me in a seat close to the door and told me to sit there and he would get me a coke from the bar across the room. I said I would, but I really didn't see him walk away because immediately upon walking into the place I focused on the music coming from the stage in the back of the club.

As my eyes adjusted to the dark I began to make out the faces of the musicians, and to my surprise there stood my dad with his saxophone in his hands and strapped around his neck. As the band practiced and each player took a solo, I heard my father play saxophone for the first time. Taking in these wonderful sounds, I closed my eyes. I felt as if every note was meant for me. I shut my eyes, hearing and feeling those notes making a beautiful Tulip with petals open inside my head. Opening my eyes as the music stopped, I looked around. My uncle was gone from sight, but I could see my dad, the band members and a few other bar customers. Holding his saxophone, my dad walked over to me with a broad smile on his face. As he sat down, I touched his horn, it was warm. He put his hand on top of my head turning my face to his and asked

"I hear you like to sing?"

"Yeah, I do."

He looked down at me and I glowed inside because his suit was a shiny light blue material and the gold of his saxophone caught a light gold strip I hadn't noticed before, in the material.

"Do you want to play and instrument too?"

I stared at the pearl keys on his horn.

"Yes."

"Which one?"

"A saxophone"

He chuckled as he took his hand from my head. His hands were soft and strong.

"Well alright then. I have to play again, and I bet you have to do your homework. I'll see you soon."

Standing, and looking down at me, I saw my eyes were his eyes and we both had a wide-mouthed smile with a gap in our teeth. He patted me on the head, and I touched his hand, feeling the veins. Out of nowhere, my uncle's hand on my shoulder told me it was time to go and I turned as we left, watching my dad walk back up on the band stand; and I heard him say to one of the musicians, "That's my son, Greg."

Tom kept his hand on my shoulder, and we hummed Jackie Wilson's "Lonely Teardrops" as we walked to my house. During this time, I was filled with a sense of myself because of my job as a paperboy, accepting the responsibility of my route and living what I'd been taught by my grandparents, mom and uncles. I sang as I walked my route selling papers and I remember marveling at my voice echoing off the houses and the street. Besides humming melodies from the few instrumental songs, I would randomly hear, early Motown and Staxx music was just hitting the airwaves and I sang "What Becomes of the Broken Hearted", "Hold on I'm Coming", "Ain't That Peculiar" and all the music I heard on Randy's at night, or on WLAV, the top forty stations because Grand Rapids didn't have a black station.

I grew up knowing that Grand Rapids was and still is a small racist town, which even now has no black radio station, so back then popular songs by Ray Charles, Tennessee Ernie Ford, Sam Cooke and The Righteous Brothers were some of the tunes I sang as I moved around in my neighborhood. Sometimes at home I would sing along with my older uncles and even then, I could harmonize and hear all the vocal parts clearly. I had a childhood crush on the music, and it was returning my affection by giving me a voice to do its bidding.

Harmonizing with my friends, I walked to school hearing songs float in my head. Learning the words to songs, from records and writing them down came easy to me because Granddad always checked-up on how well I could read, and having my uncles and aunts, who were like my older siblings, help me read even faster since everything they learned they taught to me.

Because of the gap between my teeth, I grew up with a heavy lisp, which meant when talking and singing my "s" sounds came out as "th" sounds. I was a little apprehensive when I first thought about saying and singing certain words but the music inside was determined to be heard and most times I was singing without warning, so even I knew something had to be done. I wound up taking speech class in school, second through fourth grade, which helped me correct my tongue around my gap. From time to time, even now that old lisp sneaks out to remind me that ain't nothing over till it's over.

My love of reading was born at that time and mom's, Granddad's and Mother's teachings always seemed to present themselves. I distinctly recall in the fourth grade, being mischievous. I'd written "Josie is made out of sticks" on the wall in the cloakroom because she was so skinny. I got caught. They knew it was me because only a few students in the class could write like I could. Being called to the principal's office, I was nervous, but I wasn't going to lie and hide my head. I admitted to what I'd done, and the principal gave me a couple of swats on my butt with that big wooden paddle with the giant nail holes in it.

Another time in that same class I was accused again, this time of writing in and tearing pages from some classroom books. I told the truth and said I didn't do it but was sent home anyway. My mom asked me did I do it and I said no. She believed me and contacted the school in my defense, got the whole thing straightened out and that was the end of it. They eventually caught the real culprit and Mr. McMillan, the principal came to me.

"Greg, I'm sorry. I didn't think you did it because you're a good kid and you're truthful. I just had to wait until we found out who did."

He was in my corner after that and singled me out for school monitor, other activities and privileges.

I sold him the *Times* from my paper route and expanded my route because he lived in a different neighborhood where the more affluent black people lived. I marveled at the houses and lawns, and how everyone spoke the way I did. Seeing his neighborhood expanded my view of the world and I saw how, in his area, people didn't sing on the corners, there were no drunks on the street, and you didn't hear loud music coming from the homes, like where I lived. One day I'd come from collecting the money from my route, singing, courting the music, and feeling full of the worlds I'd crossed.

There was Campau Park, where you could hear do wops cascading off the trees, watch the guys shooting craps, dominos and card games, and along Division Street you could smell fried fish, chicken, hear juke boxes playing the latest songs and watch the big cars move five miles per hour down the street; the drivers leaned to the right, and their hands with matching rings and watches, were hanging out the windows.

There was the principal's neighborhood where I'd been offered pie, an apple, or something to eat at almost every house I'd stopped at and on my street, Ray Charles played in one home, The Righteous Brothers in another and Sam Cooke crooned from our apartment.

I made it home, went inside and my mom was sitting on the sofa.

As I began to tell her about the things I'd seen on my route while putting my daily collections in my coffee can, mom said, "Greg, I need to use your paper money because we have to get some food in this house."

I saw her eyebrows were pulled together in worry.

"Okay mom. But I have to give them the money for the papers by Monday or they'll take my route away."

"I'll give it back to you. "

I gave her my money.

"Watch Hazel and Gerry (my younger sister and brother), I'll be right back."

She left and returned with groceries and we all ate together. We went to church the next day and there was no mention of the money. I went to school on Monday and upon returning home, with my day at school and paying back the Times money on my mind. I waited for mom to give me the money, but she didn't mention it. So just as she was about to go somewhere I stopped her and said, "Mom, I have to take the money to the Times by four or they'll take my route."

She touched me on the chin with her fingertips.

"I'm sorry Greg, but I don't have it now. I'll give it to you later."

"But mom."

"I'm sorry. Now come let's go to mother's house. I have to go to work."

I went to mother's house and when my mom had left, went to the Times office. The man, Mr. Bankston, didn't want to hear any stories and I lost my route because I didn't have their money.

I dragged myself to mother's house and buried my head in her lap, crying. She waited until I'd finished, then raised my head so I could see her face.

"I know how much you loved your paper route and you did a good thing by getting it on your own. And, I can see how you feel losing it. But son, sometimes in life you have to sacrifice to help those you love. Your mother needed that money to keep you all eating, so it helped everybody. I know it hurts but try and understand. It may not make much sense now, but it will when and as you get older. Now go wash your face and hands and come eat."

I did as I was told, ate, and asked permission to go to my house for a minute. Entering my home, I went into the kitchen and opened the cabinets. There was the government issued powdered eggs, spam, butter and the cans of food we'd been given. I looked around at our house. It was clean, small, the furniture simple, but old and taken care of very well. I had heard kids talk about other kids whose family was on ADC (Aid to Dependent Children), but I had never connected it to me. I was only a little boy, but I became aware of my poverty, we were on Welfare, poor and mom was alone with five children.

I began to watch my mom. Her almond eyes, the rich red undertone in her cocoa skin, her long slim limbs and the delicacy of her touch. I could feel her sadness, at times even through the laughter. It was a fragile pain and her tears eked from the corner of each eye, which she wiped away quickly, not wanting us to see. A hum would come from her, and sometimes I'd hear traces of the song, trouble in mind, I'm blue, but I won't be blue no more. She'd sit by the window looking out onto the street, not knowing I was watching her from the bedroom where we all slept.

I wanted to help her, to do something. I recall, watching her at that moment, her tears being my tears, the color of blue, surrounding her like a shroud and enveloping me, and I made up my mind that she wouldn't ever have to worry about me, and I wouldn't ever be a burden to her. I would never do anything to make her frown, her mouth pulled together in a line of disappointment. And, I would not make any woman grown with the weight of heartbreak, like my mom.

The lyrics to songs spoke to me from then onward and I paid close attention to what they said about love and life, now knowing what they meant. I really heard Jimmy Ruffin and "What Becomes of the Broken Hearted." I was grabbed by Smokey, not only because of the lyrics of life and love, but also because music had a hold on me, and it wasn't going to let me go because I had fallen in love with it and we were doing a slow drag that was about to turn into a bop.

Singing was my outlet and I let my voice ring all the time. Mr. Joseph McMillan, the principal who's apologized to me and, Mr. Ray Hopkins who became one of my favorite teachers, saw the creative light shining in me and provided avenues for it to glow. They put me in charge of the mimeograph machine, showed me how to make, create and copy the "weekly bulletin" for everyone and allowed me to write little sayings, draw pictures and distribute them to all the students in my school.

The Grand Rapids school system was full of supportive black and white teachers who carefully monitored the progress of its students and provided opportunities for our gifts to shine, whenever they could. I was a determined little kid, always moving, singing, talking, reading, having discussions with anyone who'd engage me and although I'd tell anyone who'd listen I was going to be an entertainer, I was mostly a listener. From adolescence well into my teens I would love to sit around and listen to those older than me talk, laugh and tell stories about their good and bad experiences. Most of the time, if their conversations weren't too private or too adult, and as long as I didn't say anything, I was left alone and not sent away with "go play with the other kids."

In school, I wrote plays for various classes and grades, one I acted in when I was nine and had a fake cigarette, which I feigned smoking and was later told by a teacher not to do it again. I sang in talent shows, all of which I won, I was my class monitor and I was always called on by the principal to do little chores, like helping with office work and showing new students the dos and don'ts, the wheres and whys of Sheldon School. Retrospectively, I think Mr. McMillan knew I had no father in my home, and like the black community at that time, believed that any child was everyone's child.

They now use the term, It Takes a Village. However, in the late fifties and early sixties, that was the norm and we all knew it. It was the attitude of care and love for community, which prompted black professionals to organize talent shows in the community, include the children in social organizations like the Masons step/marching troops and the Drum and Bugle Corps (both of which I was a member) and keep programs in the schools, which directed all the lives of the people closest to me as I developed.

Sheldon elementary, as with most public schools of that time, had a music program for all the kids. Although I wasn't supposed to know, my teacher, Mr. Hopkins, had a relationship with Ms. Ross, my music teacher who really tried to help black kids. They were a mixed couple in the mid-sixties, and everyone knew it. On one of my rare moments spent with my dad, we talked about the instrument he was playing in that picture that the *Grand Rapids Times* had used in his 'musician of the week' profile. He told me it was a Tenor saxophone and it was from the woodwind family of horn instruments. I remember him taking his out of its case and playing a few scales and even part of a jazz song that I had never heard, and I immediately fell in love with the sound of that horn. I remember later telling him "I want to learn to play that horn."

If you really do, when they offer music class again in your school, tell the music teachers, you want to learn the clarinet, which in school, you'll have to learn before they'll put you on a saxophone," he told me.

Well I don't really remember if one or two years had passed between that conversation and the opportunity for me to play an instrument arose but when asked, I confused what came before the "net" part of the horn and when Miss Ross asked me what instrument I wanted to play, I heard clarinet or cornet and I mistakenly said a cornet. Another part of my confusion was my uncle Sylvester, four years older than I, played trumpet and I'd hear him practicing around my mother's house. Though he was a few years older, I tried to run with him, and I admired him. He already played first chair in the orchestra at school. So, I was given a cornet mouthpiece, which I took home and began to learn it.

When I finally connected my mouthpiece to the right horn I was already hooked on playing what I had been learning, so I was a cornet player from that moment. I've often thought it was not only the mistake I made, but also destiny which took me to the cornet, then trumpet. I actually heard a clear sound out of it the first time I put the horn to my mouth, just like Louis Armstrong, who said he got a sound the first time he played the horn.

This is remarkable because it's very difficult to get a sound from a brass instrument, due to the embouchure or better yet, the way a horn player applies his/her mouth to the instrument. You have to tighten your lips, your ass, diaphragm and your lip muscles have to develop to get a tone. I put the horn to my mouth, made my mouth into a line like they said and blew from deep in my stomach. My teeth vibrated and Ms. Ross's back straightened. She smiled and that was all I needed. I moved the first valve, another sound emerged. It was a sensation I'd never felt before and I wanted to hold on to it. They let me take the mouthpiece home and I walked from school, to home, blowing all the way.

Sometime over that weekend I walked into Mother's house and heard my Uncle James' honey-toned trombone-running notes. He was an army veteran who'd (like many Negro soldiers) been used by the military for experiments, similar to the Tuskegee experiments and he now lived at the VA hospital in Battle Creek, Michigan. What had taken him over the edge of sanity was the experimental mind drugs he was subjected to over time. One day, during an airplane training jump his parachute didn't open and he lost it. He came home periodically and mostly stayed in his room practicing the trombone. He'd emerge after hours, perspiring, cradling his horn and he'd sit, drinking his wine and sing "Rambling Rose", by Nat King Cole, man did he have a beautiful voice.

Having the cornet mouthpiece in my pocket and seeing how I could only get a few notes from the horn, I heard all the sounds coming from that trombone and wanted to make music like my uncle James. He stopped for a minute and a five-note phrase snapped my head up and to the right, it was my aunt Vera practicing her Clarinet.

I was turned around by arpeggios coming from a trumpet down the hall and I knew it was uncle Sylvester practicing his horn. He played first trumpet in the school orchestra. Being led by his sound and the notes, I opened his door and found him standing, his music stand facing the door, along with his back and he read the notes on the paper. I took note of his wide legged stance, his back straight but arched, shoulders square and the horn held in a straight line. Pulling out my mouthpiece I blew as hard as possible. My uncle didn't stop until he'd finished reading to the bottom of the page, turned it and wiping the perspiration from his forehead, turned to me.

"You selected a cornet huh? I started with one. This is a trumpet. The metal's harder. Come here and let me show you how to blow correctly so you don't hurt your lips. Stand straight with your head up, hold the horn up, tighten your butt, but blow from here."

He touched my diaphragm.

"Now, place the mouthpiece lightly to your lips and don't pucker up your mouth."

I did as he said and got a light clear sound.

"You see? You don't have to blow hard to get a good tone. You can control your sound with the amount of air you blow into the horn". He took his mouthpiece from the horn, placed my mouthpiece into the trumpet and showed me the fingerings for the C scale, telling me the notes as I played. He then took out his beginners' book and showed me the lines. "The notes on the lines are E, G, B, D and F. Every Good Boy Does Fine. The name on the lines between them are F, A, C and E. Face. Here's how you blow them."

Putting the horn to his mouth, he blew the notes and then handed me the horn, showing me the fingering. I had watched how he moved his fingers where he placed them and how he shaped his sound. I didn't say anything, but I knew before he showed me and played the notes exactly as he did, duplicating his sound. He chuckled.

"That's my sound, not yours. You have your own sound inside. Now I have to practice." Gently taking his horn, he went back to practicing. I stood next to him watching everything he did. However, I was confused because I couldn't connect the notes to what was on the paper yet. As the days went by, I played on the mouthpiece, seeing my fingers move on the horn and hearing the different sounds until my mom told me she'd heard enough. I was going to be an entertainer, I had found by dance partner and we were going to party.

Jeanie Ross was my fourth-grade music teacher and she (and later Mr. Charles "Chuck" Wade my Drum and Bugle Corp leader), was very instrumental in me playing the horn. I asked her about the different notes as soon as music class started, and she explained to me the different beats for each note. She didn't have to tell me more than once. This was 1964, in the height of the civil rights movement in America. One year later Malcolm X would be killed. I wasn't really aware of him prior to his death, but did learn a lot about him in the coming years; and even later than that I learned that my brother Art's best friend. Steve Jones and his sister Debbie were the nephew and niece of Malcolm.

I did know about Dr. Martin Luther King though. He was like a savior in the minds of most black folks. What stood out for me, at that time was, even though she was white, my teacher had serious pride in Dr. King, who'd been crucial to civil rights for all, the voting rights act being passed and so much more for all people. I remember my own sadness when he too was assassinated some three years after Malcolm.

Anyway, back to Miss Ross. As should be with teacher to pupil, she and I had bonded with her teaching me how to define and read music on the page, so practicing was a joy for me from that point and onward. At home I would practice so much until my mom, brothers and sister would complain about the noise until my mom would tell me she too had enough. So, I would then go outside and try to play softly, not! I played until the neighbors came outside and told me to "cut that shit out", but that too didn't matter. I read from the beginner's book at school during recess, in class when I'd finished my work before anyone else, during music class and at home because I had a two-hour time space before anyone got home. My pattern was to first play all the lessons I'd learn, multiple times, then the new pages in the book, marking any parts I found difficult, and then listen to the big stereo and play along with all the records in the house with horns.

I'd only been playing about one year when I formed my first band, The Hot Five, after Louis Armstrong's band. I'd seen Louis Armstrong on the Ed Sullivan show and he amazed me with the way he entertained the crowd and played his horn. I'd never seen a trumpeter lead before and watching him opened the door for me. I listened to his music whenever and wherever I could find it. I practiced to it and I got myself a handkerchief, learned how to sing with a gravelly voice and started learning his music. Anyway, Hot Five played in talent shows, at school, at social gatherings and anywhere we could. It was through Hot Five that I first learned how to arrange and organize a group or band. I could hear the harmonies I wanted, the arrangements and how each horn would play off the other.

Later, I was first chair in the school orchestra for my grade and Mr. Wade had made me a standout in the Drum and Bugle Corps brass section. We read, marched, strutted, twirled out horns and stepped with the drums at games, assemblies and any official occasion which happened. Music created a world for me, and I lived within sound and everything which sprang from it. Little projects and opportunities in all walks of life would always show up front and center. And I rose to each occasion because I was determined to do better, to be better with each undertaking.

I turned being a kid who liked to read into a kid who could read, write, teach, narrate and tutor anyone with a desire to understand words and the magic they possess. I turned being a hungry kid, a kid who would cook dishes for his younger brothers, sister and relatives including my Aunt Claudia and Uncle Ronnie, into becoming a master chef by age sixteen. No matter what was in the cabinets and the fridge, Greg could make a meal to die for. These and other abilities I would carry throughout my life and I became noted for being able to read, write and negotiate contracts backwards and forward as the need arose and I too was noted for turning skinny girlfriends into a trail of happy fat women with my meals.

Even in my preteens I could see times were hard because my mom still carried that eyes drawn together look, worry. I'd sometimes see her open the refrigerator and sigh at the government products then turn and look at all of us, her eyes full. I knew my dad paid child support because I'd heard my uncles discussing it when talking about my mom, Mattie. Mom's singing group, The Jewels of Harmony, made little money and my mom wanted more materially for us. We never wanted for food or clothes and we were always clean and well kept, but being a Williams, her aims were higher than just surviving.

Love and companionship, I understood even at such a young age, was the key to her happiness, and was the note which if played correctly, could change the situation and provide what mom wanted. Her pain was my anguish and I was determined to not be another source of hurt for her. By this time mom, my siblings and I had moved around a lot causing us to repeatedly go to different schools, leave old friends and make new ones often.

Art, my older brother watched mom and internalized her feelings, without verbalizing anything. I'd see his moon eyes turn red and liquid and then he'd leave home.

He started spending time, days away from home when we were young, often at his 15-year-old girlfriend's, house and no punishment or scolding would stop him. As a teen, Art was long and wiry. He could sing a little, but he didn't. He could play a trumpet a little, but he didn't. He could dance his ass off which he did a lot, but he didn't take it anywhere. He could fight and rebel, and even fought in the local golden glove tournaments a few times but he didn't pursue that either. What he did was hang out in the streets where all the bad boys and street people congregated. He often carried a small pistol, which he flashed to let those who thought he was "too light to fight, too thin to win" know that he never walked alone. He would sometimes make quick decisions which he would later regret.

He was only one and a half years older than me and I was seen by most as the big brother, while he grew up in a reality I didn't know. His training ground was the streets and his teachers were the hoods who hung out there. He sometimes brought our mom money, like the head of a household does. See, Art's father, a so-called minister, was never there for him. He, Reverend Isaiah Snell or known to most as "Preacher", was a loud animated, big chested man with a gift of gab, a winning smile and a boisterous laugh that shook the walls wherever he went. He wore neon suits, yes even back then and was a self-proclaimed prophet. He carried a bible and a couple of dream books and people came to him for information about what their dreams meant and what number to play. He made me, Hazel and Gerry feel special, loved, appreciated... but not Art.

Seeing Art hurt, hurt me and made me more determined to succeed so that I could help him, and it started something which still lingers today, feeling as if I need to carry and help everyone. This feeling became clear to me, when I became the older brother and I noticed how my mom would turn to me for help with the others, as early in life I had exhibited a responsible character.

Chapter 3

School Daze

The "Me Nobody Knows" rehearsal (Me and Pantheah Barrows)

Curtis Mayfield and the Impressions sang It's Alright and I knew they were right because I had my music. I was twelve and I'd developed from playing in the Drum and Bugle Corp, to the junior high school band; and I was reading every Readers Digest, pamphlet, brochure, book, newspaper, magazine and all else I could get my hands on. Mr. Murphy was the music teacher; and around Grand Rapids, the upheaval and cultural pride taking place among black people manifested itself in the interest black professionals showed in the youth.

In Grand Rapids I remember only a few marches and demonstrations, but what stands out, at that time, is the way teachers and parents invested in the youth. There were talent shows featuring local young talent, youth organizations, skating clubs, dancing clubs, theatre groups, science clubs, speech contests; and the teachers at school stayed on top of all the youth, encouraging the gifts and talents the young people had been given.

During this time, we lived at the bottom of the hill on Paris Street across Pleasant Ave. Art had befriended Steve Jones, who turned out to be Malcolm X's nephew. We lived where we wanted, and I noticed an air of happiness in my mother. I think there was an accompaniment of love playing in her heart because she'd met someone who'd soon become my stepfather, Mr. LT Frazier. However, in those days, before he became part of our lives, it was she and her children on those evenings, telling the world we had something to say. Even then, I knew who and what was good and what wasn't. It was a blessing my music had given me, a natural ear for sound, harmony and musical ideas. I also figured out that I had another friend in words through reading. Music, words and family was what I lived for, and I was only twelve.

My high school days were full of music, playing in the band and reading everything I could reach musically and by using literature. Sitting first chair in the band provided me the opportunity to play all different types of music. It's funny how I never, at least in my mind, competed for first chair; but once I made it, I was proud to be there. See for some reason competition never entered my heart or my mind, as I was only trying to get better at everything I would do and with every breath I took. So, I really appreciated when someone, anyone else, could do something good. It didn't matter if they were younger or older, black or white, experienced or a beginner, I would be excited by their talent, support their efforts and openly compliment the good thing they had done.

Being the musically hungry opportunist and charmer that I was, I waited patiently for the moment that I would have the whole class of music students to myself. I'd organize the band into different parts and have everyone play all the popular music, especially James Brown, when Mr. Murphy left the room. I liked to have the tubas and baritone saxophones playing the bass parts, the woodwind section, tenor and alto saxophones, clarinets and flutes keeping the rhythm with the brass, trumpets and trombones on top, playing the melody with the drums hitting a syncopated funk.

Mr. Murphy would come back into the room, noticeably holding back a laugh and shout "Williams, I know it was you. Get out! You make all of these people stop doing what I instructed, to do what you want. Get out!" He'd make me leave the room for a few minutes to show he was still in charge, then allow me back into the class, giving me a wink. Mr. Murphy was typical of the black professionals at that time, they looked for ways to maximize and encourage talent in the youth. Mr. Murphy, seeing I had this ability, allowed me to organize the band and play popular music during half time at the football games and pep rallies.

Grand Rapids didn't have a black radio station and therefore we heard pop top forty all day and the black radio station WLAC, which we heard at "1510 on your AM dial, all the way from Nashville Tennessee" at night. On WLAC, many of the groups which got airplay were from Stax or Motown Records; and Booker T and the MG's, and the Temps were the groups which touched my ear. I could hear their five-part harmony and I memorized many of Curtis Mayfield's lyrics and sang them. I had developed a practice schedule for afterschool and weekends, which allowed me to stay close to my music. In various current magazines I'd run across, I found applications and joined various record clubs, which provided all kind of music and albums to all its members. I started using different names or different spelling to my own name on the applications to get records free because I had no money to pay for them. I'd order from six to a dozen of them at a time and have them come to my house through the mail. Over time, I built myself quite a collection. I really didn't see that as stealing, until some years later!

I learned all the words and all the songs from every album and could play them note for note. One day I was practicing to one of the songs, and I noticed when the trumpeter took a solo, he played little phrases from other songs. I listened again and then tried to do it myself, playing little songs within songs and copying the solos on each record; so, I picked up licks from each soloist, learned them in every key and applied them to every song I knew. I then started practicing these licks and songs in the keys of the music I was reading. Doing this took me all over the trumpet and I developed the ability to play every song in any key and I could immediately hear the song's key, as soon as it began. This is how my ear developed even more, since singing from age four and performing since my kindergarten play; my gifts were teased daily.

I had to stop blowing my horn when my mom came home because she didn't want to hear me practicing that thing most of the time. I would then go outside and practice until one of the neighbors would start shouting. Playing outside also assisted in my development because, in order to hear myself clearly, I had to blow hard, with a lot of control. This helped to develop my tone and I could soon hear myself clearly. I passed my ninth year playing in the orchestra, the band, practicing at home and knowing I'd become closer to something more than anything else in my life; music filled me with ecstasy.

Right now, my social circle, though broad, began to take a different road than ever before; and I also learned a whole lot more about life. I remember when Kerri-Ann Newman tried hard to introduce me to sex. That didn't work with her, but it would work with someone else in my near future. I remember taking my first drink of alcohol and I remember when Billy Lyle introduced me to weed, so my party was just beginning. Although I refused to miss my music, literature and civics classes, I began to skip school and hang out. There were the crap games at Friendly's Hamburger joint, occasional skip parties at a few friends' houses and there was my sexual tryst with Betty or Crystal, and maybe someone new who had heard me sing or play and got curious.

One of my main skip partners was Floyd Mayweather Sr. in our teens, besides entering talent and even dance competitions, Floyd began sharpening his skills as a fighter, while I continued to move on in music and entertainment. He was just starting to train and box in the local Golden Glove Tournaments, then eventually became a boxing champion welterweight contender; while on the other hand, I was moving from group to group, band to band. Although I once tried smoking weed in these early teens, I really didn't do much drinking or smoking, as most of the folks I was surrounded by. This too, was not a William's trait. My uncles, aunts and extended family as a whole, with the exception of a cousin or two, are good Christian people and for the few exceptions, drink or drugs did not ultimately rule or ruin their lives; so, I grew up knowing that was also not a way that I would go.

Through these early teens, my life was changing in leaps and bounds due to my exposure while playing in bars and clubs. While I once felt restricted by the music because in grade school, in the Drum and Bugle Corps, and even in high school band you had to stick to what was on the page; but now, playing R&B and jazz opened my heart, mind and soul to a whole new world of music and I wanted to play free and create from the new sounds that were consuming me. I was hearing sounds in my head, even at such an early stage; and after learning to read and play the music at school, I found it limiting. So, around the tenth grade, I stopped reading, but continued to sharpen my ear and imagination. Other parts of me began to wake up or take on a whole new meaning, as I noticed hair growing in places on my body that had always been bald; certain scents that used to only smell like the Ivory soap we always used to wash and bathe with; and I noticed I wanted to hang with specific girls, much more than I ever had. I met Crystal Vallington at South High School, when I was fourteen. She was honey-colored with long legs, a juicy butt, short hair, which stopped at the base of her neck, a beautiful smile and a hearty laugh. I was first attracted to her eyes and there was an air of melancholia about her, which touched something in me. It was that thing inside of me since I was a kid of wanting to help women first, and others second.

Our explorations of each other was intense, but she was a little bashful at first. We tried to make love, but I couldn't penetrate her. I remember how we held each other, moving, trying, working our bodies into each other, until finally it happened. Although I had fumbled experimenting with a couple of girls before, Crystal was my first. It wasn't long before we would skip school and have sex nearly every weekday. One day, after making love, while lying in each other's arms, Crystal told me her six pack guzzlin' stepfather had been fondling and rubbing on her. "Fooled around with her" is what she said. I learned that was the source of her melancholia and what I wanted to protect in her. However, I felt defenseless because there was nothing I could do.

Later she told me her stepfather started to have sex with her whenever he could catch her alone. Though I pleaded with her to tell, over and over, I never understood why she couldn't tell her mom. She didn't even tell her when he started taking her over to the next-door neighbor's and letting him have sex with Crystal for money. She'd hold me and tell me how she felt dirty all the time and she didn't want me to touch her after her father or the neighbor had been with her.

I knew her brother and I 'd look at her stepfather who was friendly and often funny.

Once, I, Crystal and a small group of our friends were having a skip party at her house and he came home early, and I was hiding in the upstairs closet while she and her brothers went downstairs to talk to their dad. We waited for a minute, then jumped off the second-floor balcony and ran. The next time I came over he called me to the family room where he always sat in his recliner.

"Hey Greg, the next time you all have a skip party over here, you should come downstairs and leave through the door you came in. I was sitting here the other day, having my beer. I look up and see these niggas flying past that dining room window. And, as long as I've lived, I didn't know niggas could fly. Ha, ha, ha. Now I don't want to see no more flying niggas around here so next time use the stairs and the front door."

He laughed, thinking it was funny and I forced a smile, wanting to hurt him and make him a flying nigger for what he was doing to Crystal. Her and my relationship continued for what then seemed a forever; when actually it was less than two years before we broke up. She eventually slept with another guy we knew, so I had to fire her. I left that relationship brokenhearted, but I still had my music, so I moved on! Yes, with my heart and my horn in my hands, I moved on.

I learned a life lesson from Crystal and her dad's circumstances, that remains with me to this day. I must constantly remind myself that people who feel bad about themselves, can never feel good about being with you or anyone else for long. They distrust whatever beauty you see in them and they will most likely sabotage a relationship or anything good happening to them because they don't believe they are worthy of or deserve anything good.

During the time I was coming into my own as a musician there were four black clubs/bars which had frequent live entertainment in Grand Rapids. The American Legion, Gussy Wussies, The Franklin Bar and The Golden Glow. Of these clubs, The Golden Glow had a jam session every Saturday from 4-7 and anyone could sit in, if you could really play or sing. NO SLOUCHES. I was Fourteen, I'd heard about the jam session and one day I decided to go and try my luck at getting in, since I legally wasn't old enough. I got there around 3:30 because I wanted to see what they were doing, and granddad had instilled in me to always be on time; and if you want to do something, it's best to arrive early. The bouncer stopped me when I first tried to enter.

"Boy, what you doing here?'

I raised my horn case. "I'm coming to the jam session."

"You ain't old enough to be in here." he said.

"But my dad might already be in here. We 're supposed to meet here and sit in together." I lied.

"Who's your dad? What's his name?"

"Willie C Gray," I said.

He scratched his head. "Wait here and don't try to run up inside."

I saw him go inside and talk to a man inside who followed him back to the door.

As they approached, the man began to smile. "You Willie Gray's son?"

I puffed out my chest. "Yes, sir."

"Okay you can come inside, but he ain't here yet, so don't be tryin' to be drinking in here because I'm about to be losing my license and you about what fourteen, fifteen?"

I deepened my voice. "I'm fourteen-and-a-half."

Both men laughed.

"Okay, fourteen-and-a-half Williams. You too young to be drinking; so again, don't try it. And if you can't play, you ain't gone be on that stage long no way, because these are some serious musicians. Now you go sit over there in the corner until things get started and don't you move. You hear me, Williams?"

"Yes sir."

I sat in the corner, pulled out my trumpet and playing very low, warmed up to the song that was playing on the juke box. It was Twine Time and I knew every lick and note. I played along and when I looked up the bar owner was smiling at me. After warming up about fifteen minutes, waiting for the jam session to start, I looked up and saw someone from behind the bar motioning for me to come over. I looked closer and it was my paternal grandmother. She pushed a coke in front of me when I got to the bar.

"Greg, I just walked in and Bill told me you were in here somewhere. What you trying to do?" She asked.

I'm meeting a couple of my friends here. We're gonna sit in with the band."

She laughed and then asked. "Can you play that thing?"

Feeling cocky I said, "Grandma Aggie, I'm real good on this thing."

She laughed again, saying, "ok, we'll see. Now, I don't have to tell you this is the only thing you'll be drinking in here, do I?"

I fingered my horn. "Not at all."

"Alright then. You gone on back over there and I'll be watching you." She smiled at me.

Walking back to my seat, I thought about how she'd often been somewhat distant with me. Visiting her was never really pleasant because she was nice to my father's other children, and indifferent with me. I remember one afternoon a year or so back, I went down to Barnet's bar with Skip and our younger sisters Collette and Crystal, which they told me was ok during the day and only if there wasn't a lot of people in there. After arriving and looking in the window to see if it was safe to go in, we did. Our grandmother immediately saw us and called us over. After saying hi, in a way that clearly meant "what the hell are you kids doing here?" She dug in her purse and gave each of us fifty cents then said, "now y'all need to get on away from me, I'm busy."

The others took the money and quickly ran to the pinball machines, but I hesitated, hoping for a little more than a shallow hi. She looked up at me, then asked, "Why are you still here, didn't you hear what I said? I'll see y'all in a little while." It really hurt my feelings because that time, I had just walked in and hadn't even had a chance to say hello. Plus, I had only gone with them to finally have a minute to get to know more about her. But in my confusing respect for my elders and speaking up for myself, I said nothing else and walked away from the bar. I never told her, my mom, my dad or anyone else how insulted I was by this act. I never told anyone how brokenhearted I was over her general lack of consideration and concern for me; for who I was supposed to be to her, or for my wellbeing, period.

I gave my fifty cents to one of my siblings and left the bar. I went home and told my mother I was never going back there again, and I didn't. I found out later, from a family member, when my grandmother found out that my mom was pregnant, she made my dad enlist in the army to prevent him from marrying my mom. Once my dad returned from the service, his mother immediately urged him to marry Annette, my step-mom who I came to call the evil step bitch. She didn't like me. Although both my parents had clearly moved on from each other, I'm sure she still felt threatened by my mom.

From our first encounter she made it a point to be nasty and verbally abusive to me (as I would find years later that she felt the same about my dad's other two children who came from other mothers) and had no problem making it clear that she didn't want me coming to her house, so I rarely went there over the years.

Each of her children were totally aware, concerned and perplexed, as I too was by her dislike for me; but they spoke out against it to her and made sure that her issues did not come between us. We were children, we loved each other, and I was simply their big brother. Years later, through Fanny, my mom's lifelong best friend, I came to know that my evil step bitch hated my mom because in high school, my mom would kick her ass on a whim because they simply didn't like each other.

Anyway, I sat down and turning my back to her, played quietly to every song played on the juke box until I saw the musicians coming in and setting up. The club owner talked to each of them, pointing at me. There was a house rhythm section of bass guitar, drums, piano, lead guitar, with about three musicians for each instrument - two saxophonist, two trumpeters and two vocalists, all grown men ten years older than I.

The last musician to walk in was a saxophonist not more than twenty. The other musicians glanced at each other when we he took out his horn and the other two saxophonists stepped off the stage, packed up their horns, and left. When all the musicians stepped onto the stage, I stepped up. The singer called out "Knock on Wood" by Eddie Floyd, the drummer counted it off, everyone started playing and I was right with them. The singer finished the verses, the guitar player took his solo, and the saxophone player lowered the microphone and he cut loose.

You could hear a mouse pee in the club; and as he finished his solo, he played a line from a song I'd learned from Wes Montgomery. He ended on a high note and I hit the same note, finished the phrase and launched into my solo, feeling deep inside the beat. Before I could finish, another trumpet player, much older than me stepped to the microphone and played some phrases then turned to me, laughing. I knew it was a challenge; so I leaned back, played his phrase back at him backwards, added about six notes and looked back at him; he wiped his mouth and cut loose with about eight notes; and I matched him by double-timing the notes, going from the top of my horn to the bottom, and ended by hitting a high note I'd learned from listening to a Louis Armstrong record. He tried to play a couple of notes, but I played a winding phrase and he put his horn down, laughing. People in the club said 'oooooh' while clapping approvingly. The other trumpeter didn't solo, and the band went back to the song and finished.

"I heard the drummer say to the bassist. "Did you hear that young muthafucka. He just cut the shit out of a grown man. Who is that little nigga? Green Onions, let's see what he can do."

We launched into "Green Onions" by Booker T. and the M. G's and I was right on top of it. This time, only the saxophone and I soloed. We traded riffs back and forth, chasing each other, playing melody after melody, speaking a language I'd only spoken to myself and the horn. Playing background, we harmonized, added touches of color behind the vocalist and accented what the pianist and guitar were doing. We played that day for three hours without taking a break and at the end of the jam session the musicians came up to me.

"Boy, what's your name?"

"Greg Williams"

"How old are you?"

"Fourteen-and-a-half."

They all laughed again.

"You talking a lot of shit on that horn. Come on back next week and give us your number, so if we need a horn we can call you. You didn't tell me you're Willie Gray's boy. That's where you got it from. That Willie can blow a little."

"You are Willie Gray's boy, ain't you?"

"Yes, sir, I am."

"You two young niggas know each other?"

"No"

"Greg Williams, this is Wilton Machen. Y'all got yourself a horn section."

"Man, you got magic coming out of that trumpet," Mache said.

"If that's so, you're the one who made the rabbit jump out of the hat," I added.

We laughed and shook hands, and it was the beginning of a profound, lifelong friendship. After that, it was on with us, learning, teaching and playing those horns side by side for the next five or so years. Mâché was just what a fourteen-year-old trumpet player needed. He was a philosopher, studied eastern religions, thoroughly knew astrology, and was a vegetarian and health advocate. At the time, he didn't smoke cigarettes or drink alcohol, exercised regularly, and was an avid chess player.

Mache read incessantly, was always abreast of contemporary events and opened my eyes to musical worlds I had never explored. Mache always wore a smile and was forever kind and considerate to everyone he encountered. He shared his knowledge of life with all who cared to listen. Among other things he reintroduced me to Miles Davis, Lee Morgan, Freddy Hubbard who really caught my ear, and the language of jazz. He'd point out to me what each horn was doing, how to resolve a phrase, play passing phrases.

I believe I knew harmonies from birth, and how playing less often says more than playing a lot, something my dad introduced me to that day as I watched and heard him rehearse. I'd get called during the week when the trumpeter couldn't make it because he had the regular gig at the club. I made about twenty dollars a night, which was a fortune for a fourteen-year-old boy, at that time.

Mache helped me with the basic structure of jazz, which I knew, but didn't realize I knew because when I'd played jazz, it was usually by myself most of the time. There was a two to two-and-a-half-hour window, when no one was at home except me and my horn. I'd sit in front of mom's stereo and practice to every song on every record I could get my hands on. But when I got with Mache, we'd play the licks in the background, then go to the bridge, play the vamp, then stretch out on our own, exchanging riffs.

Playing in the clubs opened another world for me. I saw the musical world from the inside and with all its intricacies. Early on, the older musicians wouldn't let me drink, but they would let me gamble and ninety nine percent of the time, I'd win. A couple of the older guys would watch over me and tell me when it was time to go. By the time I was fifteen, I was a regular at the jam sessions. The more I sat in the more other, older musicians showed their respect when the session was ending by asking, "Hey youngster, you comin' back next week?"

Of course, nothing could keep me from getting back there next Saturday. As I frequented the jam sessions Mache and I wound up either being and/or running all other horn players who joined us onstage. I remember he asked me if I wanted to play a weekend with a few of the older guys. I, of course, jumped at that opportunity. Soon after, there I was playing weekend gigs which were mostly gotten for us by Ed Honeycutt, a local guitar player and band leader.

I remember the day I was on stage at the Glow and my dad had slipped in just as it was my turn to take a solo. I didn't see him because the music had me, but once I finished I felt someone tug at my shirt bottom from the side of the stage. I looked down and it was my dad. I was about to come down off of the stage, but he motioned no. I read his lips saying "after," so I rejoined Mache, throwing a horn lick at him and catching what he threw back. As we continued, I saw what resembled joy on my dad's face as he watched me on stage. I can't be sure, because I wasn't around him enough to know his likes or dislikes, so I was actually guessing. Maybe even hoping a little, but in reality, for whatever reasons, I wasn't allowed into his life; I just didn't fit.

From what I had come to know, he'd always attempted to balance all his worlds, his wife and other children, his chick on the side, music, an 8 to5 plus a part-time job, and he never reached his main goal in life, which was to be a saxophonist. I learned a few things about his life but always from a distance. From time to time he tried to pull a reentry but only for fleeting moments. There was a time during my early teens, he had heard that I was skipping school. After coming to my mom's house looking for me and finding me outside, he approached me telling me what had been told and saying that he wasn't going to have it, and if I continued he would have to punish me.

"Where the hell is this coming from?" I thought to myself. This guy ain't never been there for me, other than to pay the state of Michigan those child support payments; and all of a sudden, my father wants to play dad because he had

75

heard from someone who knew nothing of his and my, lack thereof, over the years.

For most of my teen years, my father lived very near me and yet he wasn't involved in my life, at all. My step father, Mr. Frazier, in some ways tried to be a father to my younger brothers; but in reality, the closest I had to a real father was my grandfather, my uncles, and a couple of my teachers like Joseph McMillen and Ray Hopkins.

During this period, I wanted and sought out more musical education and outlets, which prompted my uncle Sylvester Williams, who is three years older than I, our cousin David Jennings, and our close friend Nate Thomas to start singing together; and soon after formed a vocal, stepping group. Now, both Sylvester's and David's fathers were brothers, aged respectively; so, our family was entwined, and often together at church and family gatherings. Things just came together as David and Nate hung out together; and Sylvester and I were always around each other, and after being at other's family members' homes, the four of us became good friends.

Knowing that we could all sing at the drop of a dime, we started singing at most of the gatherings and at some point we decided to form a group. We quickly discovered that each of us had our own unique vocal qualities and abilities and all of us could sing lead; so that's how we began as a group with four lead vocalists, not unlike the Temptations; with Sylvester filling the first tenor slot, Nate more alto than not, David holding down the baritone and me getting in where I fit in from alto to bass vocals. From the start, we fell into those vocal positions and they worked, so we just went with them some days.

In deciding that we would become a serious group, we pondered a few names and finally decided on the name The Patterns. Because of my ongoing quick wit, as with most of the bands I either started or was in from day one, I believe I actually came up with the name; but I won't swear to it, as I'm not totally sure, and I won't intentionally rob anyone of their just due. Fortunately, all four of us had similar interests and lived within miles of each other; so besides becoming a singing group, we also became close as friends.

Each of us had varied weight and body shapes, but were all roughly the same height and completion, chocolate, with me being the darkest. For the most part we came from like upbringings, fearing God, mama's voice and daddy's belt, and not necessarily in that order. I was the youngest of the four, yet for the most part, other than David's silliness and warped sense of humor, I kept everyone laughing with witty quips and anecdotes, and I always had good ideas and respected input.

While most of our peers and even my brother Art were doing stupid things including drugs and getting into trouble with the law, the four of us did none of the above. With the exception of my moments of youthful insanity, none of us ever took to even the smallest criminal behavior; and as for drugs, we were all exposed in one way or another, but Nate and David did not smoke or drink at all; Sylvester might hit a joint on a rare occasion, but he too did nothing. And although I had experimented with weed and alcohol once or twice in my young life, at most, I really didn't care for any of that stuff, so I too stayed away. The four of us kept each other together and we were too busy becoming a serious group to stray and get caught up. through the majority of our existence,

The Patterns were a four-man group, but a few times over our few years there were others whom we allowed in as group members. But only for short periods. Of the interim members, including my aunt Ruby and two others, but nobody lasted long enough to really matter and or make a difference. Now Ruby was my mom's and Sylvester's younger sister. She was by far the best vocalist of all of our extended members, but she would never stick with it for one reason or another.

Ruby could and did sing, dance and perform well, as a group member. She also outlasted the other two short-term members; but again, she was in one minute and out the next, so when she mentioned leaving us a third time, we decided enough, gave her an ultimatum and that was the end of that story. The four of us were inseparable and impenetrable on and off of the stage. Our own mothers, or anyone else for that matter rarely saw one of us without seeing the other three and that's the way we remained for a long time to come.

Now the beginnings of the Patterns were post segregation in the US but pre-bussing in the Grand Rapids Public School System; so, all of us attended different grades at South High School until the school board broke up the Black school. Now each of us were bussed to different parts of the city so we would get together immediately after school to practice and just hang together. Each of us made time for our individual families and our girlfriends; but first and foremost, The Patterns were friends, we were relatives, we were brothers, we were one. Early on, we did more practicing and preparing than actual live performing; but as we got better, we kept open for opportunities to get up on stage, and finally one came along.

Finally, our first chance to show the public and our family and friends what we had been working diligently on for months came, when the student council at South High School, where all four of us were students, announced it was to start an annual talent show and would be holding auditions the following week. This announcement quickly became the talk of the entire school that day; so, when the four of us got together that afternoon, that was all we could talk about.

Acknowledging that the opportunity to show the world who we were and what we could do had finally come. We practiced even harder that week, impatiently waiting for the day of the South High School Talent Show auditions. The day had finally come; so, immediately after school, the four of us got together and lined up outside of the auditorium with the rest of the future stars waiting for the doors to open to sign up for the auditions. The wait seemed forever, though in actuality, it really lasted about fifteen minutes before the doors flew opened and anxious wannabes with various sized entourages rushed inside to sign up or get a seat to watch the circus.

Once inside, we put our name on the list, were given a sheet with the rules, regulations and instructions and we took seats down front and waited. The auditions soon began, and the Patterns sat quietly watching those who would be our competition do their thing. Actually, most of those who auditioned were really good, but nobody would outdo the Patterns.

After impatiently waiting about forty minutes to hear our name, the moment finally came. From the second we stepped out on the stage, it was on. We broke out singing the R&B/Gospel version of the song "Born Free". Our harmonies and steps were so tight you couldn't cut em with a knife and by the time we got the chorus, the girls in the audience jumped to their feet and began to scream, many of them forgetting about the act they came with. I also heard some of the fellas in the audience, and even the other acts, yelling through the overwhelming applause when we finished our second song. We were on fire and before we could make it offstage, needless to say, we were picked to be in the actual show. We stuck around as the others auditioned, but we knew we were a hit and no one in the show and much of the audience let us leave without knowing we had kicked ass.

After that, word spread around the school and around town about us and we were all on cloud nine over the positive feedback we were getting; but we also knew that our work was just beginning, if we wanted to win that talent show. Over the coming weeks, we rehearsed extra hard, learning two new songs, perfecting our harmonies, our steps (choreography) and our overall stage presence.

I recall one of the bigger issues for us at the time was what we would wear. Having never performed as a group before, we did not have stage costumes or even a specific look; so, after various discussions, we decided and agreed a look similar to the premier male singing groups of the day like The Temptations, The Intruders and various others. Coming from basically poor families and still being high school students, we did not have money to have costumes made or money to even outright buy clothes, so our options were almost nonexistent, till Sylvester came up with the idea,

"We can always rent Tuxedos."

"Yeah, but I ain't even got no money to do that," I chimed in.

"Neither do we," David said pointing back and forth at Nate, then himself.

"But that ain't never stopped nothing." He laughed.

Nate too spoke up

"Yeah man, so we'll find ways to get the money for all of us."

We all agreed, began to laugh and moved on, as if all of our problems in life had just been solved. We made a big production out of seeking out the right place to get Tuxedos and soon after began our journey downtown to Sheldon Formal Wear to see what they had that might work for us. We found the perfect ensemble and got fitted one at a time, while the others watched and made jokes. Once we confirmed that no one else would be renting the same ensemble the day we were to pick up ours, fittings were complete, and the customer service rep tallied up the cost per outfit. We sealed the deal and happily left the shop making our way home, walking, talking, laughing and singing all , the way home. That's the way we were back then. We were kids in young men's bodies and as long as we could figure it out and work on it together, no problem was too big.

Needless to say, we somehow got the money to rent the Tuxedos along with shirts, accessories and even matching

Patent Leather shoes. Our Tuxedo jackets were white with a white satin leaf pattern sprinkled throughout with wide black satin, lapels, the usual black pants with the one-half inch black satin stripe up the side accessorized with black satin bow ties and cummerbunds.

Our instructions for the talent show clearly stated that there would be no dressing rooms available so we would have to arrive in full stage costumes. With me living one block over from the school, we all got dressed at my house and walked around that long corner to the school auditorium, which was at the end of the building. Damn, we looked good and we knew it as neighborhood folk began to walk up beside us, or they yelled compliments to us from the houses and from passing cars as we made our way to the auditorium.

Judging from the number of cars now on the street and in the parking lot and the amount of folks waiting in line for the box office to open, we could see this place was gonna be packed. All of us were totally pumped up as we made our way to the talent entrance at the side door of the auditorium. Although the South High School Talent Show consisted of mostly Gospel and R&B solo singers and singing groups, there were two pianists and a saxophonist.

There were also Go-Go dancers and even solo dancers, one of which was Floyd Mayweather, Sr. emulating James Brown, and he was the baddest James Brown imitation of anyone in Grand Rapids; and he wasn't shy about getting on the stage showing off his stuff while his sister Elouise danced. There was also a classical pianist, a little girl about eleven years old on solo flute, and a solo saxophonist playing Shotgun by Junior Walker.

The Judges consisted of the assistant principal, a few teachers and black city dignitaries, and a couple of music professionals from neighboring inner-city schools. As folks were filing into the auditorium from the front, side and stage entrances, one by one the entertainers for the evening were signing in and being given programs for the night's event. For inner city kids, almost everyone standing in line was dressed to do business on that stage. From our and other acts' rented costumes and those wearing Sunday best church clothes, to those which looked as if they had stolen dining room curtains turned them into homemade outfits just for this show, everybody including the Patterns were looking damn good and ready to tear up the stage.

Once checked off of the list, we were escorted backstage to the holding area where the shows participants were gathered. This room was filled with excitement as the room was gradually filling up and various acts were warming up, while waiting for the show to begin and their names to be called. After a few minutes, one of the production assistants approached us to confirm that we were all together, and to show us where we could get water and minimal refreshments while we waited. She then opened up the event program to confirm that we knew we would be going on closer to the end of the show.

At that information, we all became a little tense while Sylvester asked, "why are we being held to the end?" The girl quickly chimed in, "Oh, please don't get upset. Everybody's talking about how great you guys sing and dance, so it was decided not to put you on too early, so that you would have a full house, as well as the judge's undivided attention. I can't

83

tell you the rest, but it's good ok?" Puzzled and excited at the same time, each of us looked at each other, as she walked away.

As act after act went on and off the stage, we stayed together watching and talking and watching some more, until we were finally hailed over by the production assistant. She pulled us around her in a huddle and said, "You guys are on after this act, ok?"

"Yes!" we all said in unison then headed back to the area we had been hanging out in to wait just a little while longer.

Feeling a little nervous, I listened as Nate and Sylvester called out the key parts and dance steps to give special attention. As the wait lingered on a bit more, I considered the outcome of our performance. Although we had seen quite a few acts perform up to now and a couple of really good singing groups, I still knew none of them had anything on us; but in my normal reserved personality, I didn't dare think that we would win, but that 'do or die' moment had finally come as I saw the last act exit the stage and was slowly hearing the MC prepare the audience for our arrival. Again, Sylvester, David, Nate and I grouped into a huddle and said a quick prayer, ending just in time to hear the MC yell. "Ladies and gentlemen, as they take the stage, The Patterns."

We then let go of each other's hands and through the sounds of shrieks and loud applause, take the stage we did! Now, in my having been a performer in front of audiences off and on since age five, where I sang in my kindergarten

Christmas play and through age nine as the trumpet playing band leader of the Hot Five, I was always comfortable in front of an audience; but this time it was different.

This time, I was as much of a support player as I was a leader and I had others counting on me to be precise when adding my one-fourth to make a brilliant whole and that's what I did. We all did. From the first note of the first song to the last note of the last song, we sang and performed three songs which we put down exactly as we had rehearsed. Each of us moved about the stage with grace, speed and perfect execution from lead to background vocalist and from front man to support player, we were tight.

By the time we got to mid-show the whole audience were on their feet, singing and swaying and applauding with each dazzling occurrence we'd hit them with. By the end of our performance we had rocked that house. Yeah, we had kicked ass and we knew it. As we exited the stage, the music faded out and the applause accompanied by chants for an encore grew to a thunderous level. While this was happening, the MC called and insisted that we return to the stage to take a second bow, which we nervously yet happily did and again exited the stage. Coming off the stage we were met with congratulatory yells, hugs, fives and pats on the back from the acts, production personnel and others who were backstage as we made our way outside to the stage loading docks.

Finally, alone we yelled, laughed and patted ourselves on the backs for simply making it through the show without anyone freezing up or messing up. In the midst of our verbal playback of our own performance we decided to go out into the audience to catch the last few performances, so we went through backstage and around to the side stairs and into the side orchestra seats. Unbeknown to us, we must have been spotted because while the little girl was playing her flute, girls from the audience began to surround us and make a fuss over us, so much so that it was causing a disruption in the girl's performance.

Sylvester somehow got all of our attention, motioned for us to get backstage, so each of us began our fight to break free of those girls and made our way back up those stairs with the help of the security officers. From stage right, we watched the rest of the show, while anxiously waiting for the competition to end and the judging to begin. Finally the MC announced a short intermission, so the judges could tally their votes as "Just My Imagination" by The Temptations began to play over the loud speakers, followed by other R&B hits. The four of us milled around backstage for which seemed like forever, complimenting and congratulating many of the other acts on their performances, until we heard the music die down and the MC announce, "The Judges have finished voting. Please take your seats," which the audience took no time doing.

With bated breath, we listened as the fourth, third and even second place winners were called and awarded their respective prizes. Being somewhat surprised at not having heard our name in the previous winners, I held my breath until the MC announced, "the first-place winners of the South High School talent show are… The Patterns!"

All of a sudden, the four of us were rocked by the screams and applause that surrounded us from front, back left and right. Once hit by the MC's proclamation, we jumped up and down as we were summoned to center stage by the MC who was holding and extending the first-place trophy toward the four of us. Yes, the Patterns had arrived! We were proclaimed the best of the best in the South High School

Talent Show and unbeknown to us we would soon hold a similar position throughout all of Grand Rapids and Western Michigan talent. Now all of us took pride in our victory and may have even boasted a little about it, but for the most part we remained humble, took things in stride and focused on that next mountain to climb.

After that, beside all of the new friends and girlfriends trying to hang with us, we continued to practice and focus on what was next, a few new performance possibilities came up. With the success of our first big show, of course we wanted to do more, but I didn't have money to rent costumes or for transportation, so we had to pass up on those.

We did do a couple of small shows at other schools, which helped us perfect our performance and get our name out there a little more. With the South High win under our belt and the word spreading about this new singing group, promoters, event coordinators and nightclub owners began to approach us with offers for paying gigs.

It was now the late 1960's and the then local music scene for Blacks, which seemed ever-evolving, overflowed with talent, including: Gospel, Jazz, R&B, the beginnings of Funk, and even Classical and Country musicians and vocalists. And although Grand Rapids offered little to no musical outlets for the then negro youth, we made a way out of 'no way' to make music. And because there was so much local talent, you had to be good to get noticed.

Of the local R&B acts of that era, there were various acts like Family Brown, who were at the top of the heap and could sing their asses off; The Green Brothers, which featured younger brother Al Green, who sang gospel; The TMG's, whose members included my ex-girlfriend's brother Darnell Wyrick who played saxophone; The Topics aka The People's Choice; The Black Aces of Soul, with whom I later joined on trumpet for a few months and included my close, lifelong friends, Pantheah Barrows and Rodney Trotter.

Greg Williams (1971)

Of the up and coming, there was Young Blood and Captain Crunch and the Funky Bunch. The latter was a spring board for my friend Jeffery Daniel, who also found fame as a founding member of Solar Records' act, Shalamar.

With these serious post-talent-show offers came a responsibility to learn and take care of business, which Sylvester was eager to take on; so, Nate, David and I watched, backed him up and even participated in the business decisions. But we trusted him to make things work, and he did.

If we were going to do any of these shows, we would now need a band to work with us. After considering a few local bands, we realized that it would be best to create our own. Now, among the folks who performed in the South High Talent Show, we were congratulated back stage by Sherman Riley, a good keyboard player, who David knew from church.

Later, when we decided to look for musicians for our new band, David went to Sherman and asked if he would like to play for us and help pull together a few other musicians to make up a full band. Sherman enthusiastically agreed and together we sought out players who agreed to join us, including Larry Rhodes (bass), Calvin Welch (bongos and percussion), Basie Cunnings (drums), Sherman Riley and Vicki Upton (Keyboards), Butch Cook (Lead Guitar), Siri Ross, (rhythm guitar), Jerry Wade and Shelly Banister (tenor saxes) with Sylvester and myself on trumpets. Once assembled, this new self-contained version of The Patterns was born.

The Patterns Performance (1971) (Sylvester, me & Nate)

Within a few weeks of group-band rehearsals, we were ready and took our first gig at a black-owned bar in Grand

Rapids called the Club Rivera. The Patterns and our band would get calls to play various clubs and events throughout Western Michigan, over the next couple of years. Some time after the South High School Talent show, along came the opportunity to perform at another large talent show; and after much coaxing from our friends and families, The Patterns confidently entered the All City Talent Show, which was to be held at Aquinas Catholic College.

With this talent show, the stakes were higher than the South High talent show because, the show's organizers and production staff came largely from city government programs and it was promoted on a much larger scale than our first talent show. The call for talent was actually statewide and there were no ethnic boundaries for entrants. All of the performing arts were accepted with very few excluded entrants, so this third annual event was respected and attended by folks throughout the state of Michigan and surrounding borders like Canada, Indiana and Illinois.

Now we would have to compete with some of Grand Rapids and surrounding West Michigan areas' best acts. Although this show would boast a wider variety of talented performers from all genres and areas of entertainment, once again it would be dominated with musical acts and singers from adjoining Midwest states and were considered to be the best. The participants ranged from a classical pianist, a jazz quartet and other instrumental acts of various configurations. There were poets, jugglers, dramatic readings, an accordionist, tap and modern dancers, a yodeler and even a couple of small animal acts; but the show's dominant performers were the large groups of male and female vocalists, singing everything from country to opera to R&B; and lastly, were the groups and bands, which is where we fit in.

As for the black singers in the show's line-up, the Family Brown, who had actually won first place in this competition the prior year and by now were considered to be one of Western Michigan's hottest R&B acts. They were not competing in this year's competition but would make a special guest appearance after the competition was completed. So, of all of the performing/competing genres, our direct competition would be acts like The TMGs who were a self-contained band, but also backed up the Family Brown on this and other shows. There was

The Patterns Performance Poster

The Topics, who would later become The People's Choice and sign with Grandland Records, owned by Palmer James and Curtis Rogers, who were the writers, producers and record label of Al Green's first hit, "Back Up Train". And there were a couple more male and female singing acts, solo male and female vocalists, but not considered a threat or in direct competition with The Patterns.

For this talent show, all of the performers had to arrive and sign-in two hours early or be considered a "no-show" and dropped from the competition. This rule was strictly enforced, which was evident by a few acts coming in late and being told they could not perform. After we arrived, registered, put our uniforms in an area of a large-shared dressing room, we found seats in the back of this huge auditorium and nervously watched and waited for it to slowly fill up and for the show to begin.

This audience was a mixture of black and white, young and old local folks who came from various western Michigan regions and packed the entire house. Once the show got underway, we watched the first few acts and once again we anxiously awaited our turn to perform. Maybe forty-five minutes after the performances were underway, The Patterns were found and summoned backstage to prepare for our turn to perform. It was now about mid-show, and after the stage made sure our band members were in place with equipment on, our name was announced and from the wings, we walked out on stage.

As we had rehearsed so many times, we began our performance with "Born Free" and then went into "Cowboys to Girls" by the Intruders and we closed our set with "Ain't To Proud to Beg" by the Temptations, of which I sang lead. When we got to the line in the third verse, "If I have to sleep on your doorstep all night and day, just to keep you from walking away," the choreography called for me to take two steps backwards and fall into the bed-shaped arms of Nate, David and Sylvester. Well I took my two steps but when I fell back, they weren't there, and I landed flat on my ass. I patted one leg to the beat, so the audience could see me, still singing, then moved my other leg in time, sat up on my knees, still singing, never missing a line, then I stood and joined the group's movement.

I was hurting like hell and wanted to go tell my mama that these niggas just dropped me, but I had to keep on singing and dancing like it was all part of the act till the song faded out and the curtain came all the way down. The audience screamed, gave us a standing ovation and cheered for a long time after we finished.

As the next act brushed past us on his way to the stage, we left backstage through the first available doorway, doubting our performance and ultimate position among the top acts of the night. The four of us walked around the outer corridor of the auditorium until we found a door that would not lock on us and we went outside to talk amongst ourselves and critique our performance. We paced around laughing about me falling on my butt, while also sharing a little disappointment in believing that mistake in our performance had surely cost us the competition.

Without noticing, we had walked around the entire building discussing our performance and the performances of the more impressive acts that had gone on before us. Of those impressive vocalist acts and their backup band, The Topics hit the stage one or two acts after us. They busted out sounding and looking great in their white shirt, pants, shoes and even white cummerbunds, with black and white tuxedo jackets draped around them.

The audience, which was a mixture of black and white, young and old, local and regional folks, as was pretty much the entire house, was on its feet and in high gear as The Topics sang and danced like the world was on fire in Temptations' fashion. After their strong performance the talent continued, act after act, until the last participant, who I think was the yodeler and hog caller, made his exit from the stage and the show's host again took the stage.

He announced that the evening's competition had ended, and it was time for the judges to vote on who had won first, second and third place prizes. He further stated that while the judging would be done there would be a performance by The Brown family. Having set up while the MC talked, they made their way onstage to perform. Per usual they wowed the audience with their strong lead vocals, tight harmonies and precision dance routines. Fortunately, good or bad, almost every performing act was well- received, and the Browns received thunderous applause as they exited the stage.

After that, the MC announced there would be a brief intermission. So, the four of us continued to walk around outside, nervously laughing and talking; while making a conscious effort to not encounter members of the audience who were also milling around outside of the open doors to the auditorium, awaiting the word to return to their seats. Finally, after what seemed like a long time, we heard the announcer over the house speakers saying, "Ladies and Gentlemen, the judges have finished, and the votes are in. Please take your seats."

I don't really know how many minutes had passed, but I do remember the four of us rushing back towards the entrance at hearing the MC, followed by screams and applause from the audience. When we made our way back to the same door from which we had stepped out of, we stood backstage with the other talent show participants, anxiously clinging to every word. I would love to state the names of the second and third place winners, which was announced before ours; but honestly, everything else was a blur until the announcer said, "and the winner of the All City Talent Show is… The Patterns!"

In the midst of the screams and cheers from family, friends, judges and the entire audience, Sylvester, David, Nate and I hugged and slid each other five, proud, happy but in visible shock at the judging outcome. Yes, we had entered, worked towards, believed and put forth our best efforts to make magic happen and we succeeded. Yes, we had won the talent show. Most people there thought, and said, we'd out-sang and out-stepped everyone, including Family Brown. The Patterns had arrived; and I knew, from that point on, I was an entertainer.

As the post All City Talent Show days turned to weeks, we continued to bask in the personal confidence and public adoration of our victory and new-found fame throughout the Western Michigan music scene; but now we had to have our own band so that we weren't at anyone's mercy when a gig came through. So, we went right back to Sherman for help, which he was glad to give. In no time, the Patterns now had a backup band. From that point the Patterns rehearsed a few evenings out of the week as a full twelve to fourteen-piece unit, depending on which band member either left or was put out for one reason or another, but the nucleus and founding members remained loyal and strong.

Soon we were a preferred opening act for shows in the Grand Rapids area. Few would open for acts like Isaac Hayes,

Procal Harem, The Originals, among others. By word of mouth, The Patterns were gaining a reputation as strong performers and in no time, we were accepting offers to play in Jackson and Muskegon, Michigan and even as far as Fort Wayne and Gary, Indiana among other cities.

My world was becoming diverse at that time due to my life with The Patterns. By now, my infrequently playing in the clubs with the BarTees, school, home and my own musical world was well on its way, developing and taking form. During this period, my mom began to take an interest in what I was doing musically because Sylvester, David, Nate and I wanted to practice at our house, from time to time.

Although David and Nate were young and most times playful, she knew Sylvester was responsible, so she allowed us to rehearse there sometimes. She had known through the years that I was serious about the trumpet, but those rehearsals let her know I had that same passion for singing and she discovered that we were good. So good, that I would hear her proudly tell folks "my son, my brother, my cousin and their friend, Nate, have this group and they can really sing!"

I would drop by the restaurant where she'd sometimes work, and she would tell her friend, Ms. Della, and her friend, Mr. Champion, about the group. Ms. Della, who owned the restaurant, was mom's close friend; and Mr. Champion, affectionately known as Champ to us kids. Mr. Champ was the director of the Small Business League, which loans, grants and distributes funds to small inner-city business in Grand Rapids.

I met Mr. Champ through my mom's friend Della, who owned and ran the restaurant where my mom worked part-time and who also happened to be Mr. Champ's girlfriend. Della, through my mom, had told Mr. Champ about the Patterns and the type of talented, responsible young men we were. After meeting all of the Patterns at the restaurant one day he told us that he was in the midst of helping the TMG's set up a company so the Small Business League could give them a loan to buy new equipment.

Mr. Champ offered to help us in the same manner; so, at his urging, we formed a new company, held a few meetings to make plans and discussed what our start-up needs were. Sylvester, who I called the genius of the family, had written a proposal to the Small Business League, for a no-interest loan which would get new equipment for us and our band.

Once that part had been done, Mr. Champ told us to come up with an idea of a business we would like to have and run, so we decided a youth nightclub was really needed for inner-city teens, hence came our own venue, the Teenage Nightclub. Now of course we couldn't sell alcohol, nor keep wee hours like the established clubs and bars throughout Grand Rapids; but our club would provide the inner-city youth, ages thirteen through twenty, with a place to go.

Initially the live entertainment would be selected and performed by teen R&B acts from the inner-city streets; but later, after making profits enough to expand our business, we would branch out and bring named-acts like the Originals, and Jazz artists like Sonny Stitt and Ronny Foster, among others.

We found a two-story building that had formerly been a restaurant called Sayfee's, which had been a major steakhouse and eating establishment on Division street since 1947.

Our club seated about 350-450 people, surrounding a large bar in the front, Division Street side of the building. The youth only paid one dollar and fifty cents to get in. All of the proceeds went back into the kitty to cover operational expenses, pay off the loan and keep the club going.

Although, as things grew, there were quite a few inner-city teens now involved with the day-to-day business of running the club, initially this was predominately the Patterns' house. The Patterns performed there all the time, as did the TMG's and other local groups, The Teenage Nightclub broadened The Patterns' audience. We were now an established force in Western Michigan, and we incorporated our band with the vocal group.

Sylvester and I decided to pick up our horns to add to our existing horn section, so the Patterns became a self-contained act. In the beginning we had Butch Cook on Guitar, Searie Ross on rhythm guitar, Vicki Upton on keyboards, Bassie Cummings on Drums, Calvin Welch on Congas and Percussion, Jerry Wade on saxophone and Shelley Banister also on saxophone, which made us the only known R&B act in southern Michigan who boasted female members on saxophone and keyboards.

Something which stands out from that period was my singing "By the Time I Get to Phoenix", Isaac Hayes style, falling to the floor and hearing females scream. That's when it finally set in that females flocked to musicians. I could pick and choose as I saw fit. I loved moving the people, the adulation, the warmth the music created inside me, and the reinforcement from the audience. I was on the right track.

It was during this time The Patterns were supposed to have an audition with Motown, arranged by our friend and club manager Ken Patterson and his uncle, noted Detroit and Motown saxophonist Norris Patterson. After weeks of calls nd planning, Ken drove Della, my mom, Sylvester, Nate, David and me to Detroit in his car. We actually made it downstairs at Hitsville U.S.A., Motown's home and studios, and did the audition for Norris and a few folks there; but nothing ever came of it.

By the undercover way things happened, I always felt this was a scam on the part of Ken's uncle Norris. I remember sleeping in the car and feeling as if it were the first time I'd actually been somewhere. I was now sixteen years old, enjoying the music, the travel, and having so much fun; and for the first time in my life, I soon would learn about real love and affection.

Now the Patterns rehearsed in the evenings and almost every weekend at the Teenage Nightclub. Some of the other acts like the Soul Steppers, a female dance troupe which used to dance on shows before and with The Patterns, were allowed to practice at the club, as well; and that's how and where I met the first real love of my life, Tracie Babcock. Her older sister, Wendy, was also a member of the Soul Steppers; so, Tracie would come to most of the weekend rehearsals with her and we just started talking, while watching the girls practice.

Among so much else, I learned that Tracie was one of six siblings. The family lived in Kentwood, a suburb of Grand

Rapids, and at that time one could count the number of black families who lived there on one hand. To me, Tracie was different from most of the girls I was used to from my neighborhood. Though initially from the inner city, she was not a ghetto girl, but she was also not lame like most of the black "wanna be" white kids from the suburbs.

Although, at that time, Kentwood was middle class living in the metropolitan area, the Grand Rapids west side of town was the heart of the ghetto and the Babcock-Marshall kids' maternal grandmother lived in the middle of it; less than a block away from New Hope Baptist Church where the Williams, Jennings and Babcock-Marshall families were members, and or often attended.

Well, the Babcock sisters spent almost every weekend at their grandmother's house, giving them access to inner-city friends and family. They would most times walk to church from there and join their parents and the rest of the family on Sunday mornings. Our hook-up was encouraged by most of the folks in the Patterns-Soul Steppers clique; so, it was only a matter of time before we were an "item", sharing and spending long hours on the phone, when we couldn't get together.

I soon found out that Tracie was allowed to spend weekends with her cousin Karol, actually Tracie's stepdad's niece, who also lived in the inner-city not too far from where I lived. And I don't remember the timing, but Karol had become my cousin David's girlfriend, and with David and I being in the Patterns together and pretty much inseparable most of the time, this made it a lot easier for Tracie and me to spend time together.

It was 1970, we were teenagers and we talked about everything. Life, love, home, friends, family, school, hopes, dreams, etc. We laughed a lot about pretty much everything. Falling in love with Tracie was probably the easiest thing I had done thus far in my young life and before I knew it, besides the group, all my thoughts, my time, my dreams became about Tracie.

Although I had been sexually active for three to four years by now, Tracie was still a virgin, waiting for the right person and the right time to be deflowered. Well, it turns out that I was to be that right person, and together, we would create that right time and right place. As bad luck would have it, the very first time we had sex, she got pregnant, which would reveal itself within the next few months of our repeatedly creating the right time and right place to explore and love on each other.

With all things being new to us, as Tracie's body begin to change in preparation for pending motherhood, neither of us knew she was pregnant until Tracie's mother, having two older daughters, had no trouble spotting yet another pregnant daughter. And once she confirmed her suspicions, I would be the second person to whom she would loudly express her anger, disappointment and overall control with. I clearly remember, that day Mrs. Willie Mack Thurman to my utter shock, called me on the phone and began,

"Gregory Williams, my daughter Tracie is pregnant. What was you two thinking? No that's right, you weren't thinking, were you? Who gave you permission to do this to my daughter?" She stopped yelling as if waiting for me to speak with the wisdom of Solomon.

I stumbled through an answer and finally got out, …"Tracie did."

Her comeback was a lot quicker than my response to her question. "Well, Mr. Williams, I'm taking that permission back. From now on I'll tell you what you can and cannot do with my child. I'll take care of this myself and I forbid you to see Tracie and I forbid her to see you again!" She hung up the phone.

At first, I just sat there stunned. Getting sicker and sicker by the minute, I had to lay down, which soon made me so sick I would have bouts of stomach cramps, followed by my rolling around on the bed crying. For the first time in my life, I was devastated with a broken heart. After a couple of days of noticing that I was staying in my bedroom, my mom became concerned, asking me what was wrong. I told her about Tracie being pregnant and her mother's reaction. Mom tried to assure me that things would be ok. Caroline would call me to see how I was doing.

She told me that Tracie's mother had taken her to New York and forced her to have an abortion, adding to my pain, adding to my tears. Little did I know then that abortions would play a major role in my life for many years to come. I was one sad young man and every time I'd place my head on my pillow, tears would soak it. I dragged around like that for a while, my mom reassuring me every day my heart would heal. A couple of weeks had gone by and Tracie began to sneak and call me, which really made me happy, but we weren't able to see each other and wouldn't again till a couple of years later.

A month or so after Tracie had the abortion I learned from Bonita that Tracie had begun seeing this guy Hank Robinson. It seemed rather fast and it hurt like hell, but knowing she'd moved on, I slowly got it together, cut the string attached to my grief and I ran with arms open wide back to my true love, the music. I was still only sixteen years young.

Some time after Tracie and I were no more, I found that I had become over-cautious about letting my heart fly and with no real direction in affairs of the heart I continued to love various girls and women, but I don't think I ever fell in love again for many years thereafter. Besides, maybe having sex with different female friends, groupies and one night stands I'd meet while playing at the bars, out of reservation and fear, I blatantly refused to commit to anyone. And the band played on.

Now as with only a few select teen acts, The Patterns began seeking and accepting gigs at other local clubs, like the Golden Glow, The White Rabbit, The Riviera and even The Lime Light after the city made the owners close it and clean it up because it was an old west type saloon with gunfights, saloon girls and the whole shit. It was nicknamed the Bucket of Blood so that says how bad the joint once was. We would also venture out of the city to places like the Starlight in Muskegon, clubs in Jackson, Lansing, Kalamazoo, Ann Arbor, and others throughout western Michigan, so I was constantly meeting and experimenting with different young and sometimes older women.

One year or more after things ended with Tracie, I unintentionally hooked up with Debra Kantor, a female tenor sax player who had become a member of the Patterns for a short time. The reason I say unintentionally, I was initially not interested in Debra or anyone else, for that matter, but she pursued me to no end, until I finally said to her, "You don't really want to get involved with me. I can't give you my heart or love you like you want me to."

"But I love you and want you Greg" she interrupted, "and I know you'll want me too if you just give it a chance."

"Debra", I objected, "I like you as a friend and I like playing in the band with you and that's all, so don't be makin' no plans and don't keep buggin' me with that love me stuff and we'll be ok. OK?"

She agreed and started kissing my hand, then my neck and then my lips and, to my surprise, I resisted only a little. I didn't really try to stop her and that's how that short-lived relationship began. Debra was a beautiful dark chocolate girl who was half Mexican and half Black. She stood about five-feet-five or six, to my six feet; she had nice eyes, a pretty smile and gorgeous jet-black hair which hung down past her butt, and to me she was very attractive. I also came to know that, when it came to intellect and academics, this girl was absolutely brilliant, which is a quality I am so attracted to in all people, but especially women.

To use modern academic rating, Debra was a 4.0 student from kindergarten through her graduating high school at sixteen years old, and I'm confident throughout her entire educational years. To me, as brilliant as she was intellectually, she lacked a little in the common-sense area and was a little too outgoing/aggressive for my taste in the beginning. I knew this wasn't going anywhere, but I let it keep going, anyway.

In our talks about our lives and other personal stuff she told me that she had no parents but did have other siblings. She shared an apartment with her brother who was a few years older than she. He was really cool, so I could drop by any time and stay as long as I wanted, as long as I didn't wake him or keep him awake at night.

As things progressed between us, we talked more and more, after school, at rehearsals and often late into the evenings. She was bright and loved to laugh, so we hung. As we talked about dreams and plans for the future, I learned that immediately after school, she was headed to Michigan State University in Lansing, with the intent of becoming a Nuclear Engineer; and of course, I was to be this great musician and entertainer. In our talks, we understood and supported each other's dreams and that alone brought us closer. So close that we often wound up skipping school and spending days together in the bed or playing house at her and her brother's apartment. As we got to know each other more I saw and dealt with a few too many eccentricities for my taste; but between the sex and the laughter, I wasn't quite ready to move on, so I stayed to play another day. And another and another until something serious happened to wake up both of us.

Debra came up pregnant and upon our figuring that out, she decided that she wanted us to have the child. I didn't even blink to know that this would not be the right thing to do. My first (and then only) experience at pending fatherhood went so badly and I wasn't even allowed the time to consider what this could mean for my life or the life of the child's mother.

But this time, I was armed with experience, insight and a small voice in what should be the outcome here.

When I thought about it, I had been so in love with Tracie that I know if given the opportunity to be a father with her as the mother, I would have done just that, no matter the consequences. But with Debra, from the beginning all the parameters were different, being we went into this just for fun; so that's all I ever know and/or thought of what we had. We were barely alike enough to continue our sexcapades' but definitely not alike to build any real future together. In my knowing this, among other considerations, it was clear that we could not co-parent a child.

As my mind became adamant that this can't happen Debra was embracing that thought of having a little Greg lying in bed between us every night. With Debra having no mother or parental figure for help or guidance, I racked my brain trying to figure out how to get her to see things the right way, my way, on this issue. I discussed this with a couple of my family members, a couple of band members. I finally decided my best chance was to enlist the assistance of her brother and sister to help convince her it would be best to abort this pregnancy, which she ultimately did. Once she agreed to do this, I assured her that the pain of this would go away in time and she would see that this was definitely in her, my and the unborn child's best interest.

Even though she would verbally agree, I knew her heart was in total protest. Getting things set up, including finding the money to pay for this was not easy as legal abortions were fairly new at that time, but once Debra was on board, with the help of her brother who gave us the money, we made things happen. Over the next couple of weeks, Debra and I would talk about what had to be done, what life would be like if this didn't have to happen and even where our lives would go from this point. She would cry a lot and I would hold and console her, only leaving her side when I had to, but quickly returning.

And then the day for the procedure came. Not until it happened did I know that this would hurt like hell for me, too. This time I was actually a part of the decision to what some would even then call the murder of our unborn child. But then, like now, I honestly knew in my heart and my head, this was the right thing to do for the unborn child, then for Debra, then for me. She remained a member of the band and my girl till the time came for her to head to Michigan State University. We parted on good terms and I would not see or speak with here again, until she approached me back stage at a Switch concert some 10-12 years later.

In my opinion, my always having a keen sense of humor and a love for making folk laugh and feel good since I was a kid, during a weekend stint at the Starlight with The Patterns, I decided I'm just gonna see if I was actually good enough to do standup comedy. Well this night, I finally got up the nerve to take my comic relief to the stage. After our second set was over and the band had left the stage for our fifteen-minute break, I decided to walk right back up there, unannounced.

I began by loudly and rudely clearing my throat, interrupting most of the chatter that consumed the room and I began to test out my impromptu routine; which by the way was never committed to paper or rehearsed. In a free-flow style filled with deep south diction, expression and mimic of various people I had imitated throughout my life, I began by telling jokes I had heard and even some I had created over the years. I began talking about some of the funny people and things that happen to musicians i.e., hiding from groupies who follow U from place to place, handling drunk folk who get so involved with Ur performance that they think they can play your instruments. I also played with things like, getting past club owners' wives who keep hitting on band members, faulty equipment issues, etc.

My performance came across well with my bandmates, our guests and girlfriends and a half-drunk audience who helped my comic inhibitions dissipate. When I was done, I was surprised by the amount of laughter and applause I had received. I exited the stage heading for the dressing room, feeling like I had actually done something big.

In the dressing room, after a few handshakes and pats on the back from the fellas, it was back to the stage to finish our next two sets. When we finished for the night and were packing up, there were a few folks who stopped me to tell me how funny, how good my comedy routine had been. My knowing that it was well received by my bandmates and friends put me on a high for the rest of the night.

But on the ride back to Grand Rapids in the now wee hours of the morning, the more I thought about it, *I may be funny to family, friends and strangers and make people laugh, and I possibly could do comedy as a career*; but with my music, I could make folks laugh, cry, think, understand, see beauty where there was none. But most of all I could make them appreciate the parts of me that, for that time became completely theirs;

and with that conclusion, standup comedy was born and died that same night.

Actually, I too had tried my hand at criminal activity once and that was once too many! My first real time was when I was around fifteen years old. Although in my life it was never more than a step away, criminal activity was never an interest of mine and I would always steer myself in another direction when presented, but there was that time when I crossed the line.

I somehow started skipping school with brothers Mickey and Ricky who unknown to me liked to ditch school, break in houses and rob people, but their favorite game was snatching purses. One day while walking around with the brothers, Ricky said to Mickey and me, "Keep walking I'll catch up." Then he just disappeared. Well after we had continued walking about a block and a half we notice a commotion across the street, in front of the drugstore; and suddenly a lady hits the ground and there runs Ricky with something under his arm. "Let's go, he gots the muthafucka!" Mickey said. "Come on Greg!"

"He got what, Mickey?... and where are we going?" I asked.

"He gots that purse. Didn't you see that man? He gots the muthafuckin purse! We got to meet him at Friendly's." So off we ran.

Friendly's was the real skip-school hangout for most of the South Middle School students and was just a couple of blocks in the opposite direction from where we were then. Knowing this was wrong, I really felt bad about participating in this act. Even though I didn't know this was going to happen, once I was made aware, I felt bad, especially for that innocent lady.

Once Mickey and I got to our destination, there was Ricky, holding the lady's unopened purse under his arm, waiting for us to arrive. To my surprise he handed the unopened purse to Mickey who quickly opened it and dumped out the contents. After rambling through the contents, he found sixty dollars, of which he handed twenty to Ricky and twenty to me, keeping the other twenty for himself. Their rule was no one opens the purse till all involved were present and we share equally whatever was found. I mean, God, with that kind of honor, I knew these guys were cool! There was nothing else of value to us in the purse, so we threw it and the contents into the first trash can we found.

Having a few bucks in my pocket didn't completely rid me of my guilt and shame, but it did help since I wasn't the one who actually knocked that lady down. We went on with life, hanging and having fun and about a week later at Friendly's, when the waitress was busy away from the cash register, Mickey somehow leaned over the counter, opened the cash register, grabbed a handful of paper money and closed it back before the waitress returned. He then came over to the table where Ricky and I were seated, flashed a big wad of money and quickly put it deep into his pocket and signaled for us to get out of there. After walking a few blocks away, we stopped, and Mickey shared the loot.

Although, once again I was feeling the shame and guilt, I also was totally broke and had been for some time. So, once again I justified, then accepted the money, not even thinking that my time to follow suit would soon come. We hung out a little while longer, until they and I went our separate ways. A couple of days later, we caught up with each other at school and per usual, decided to skip class and head to Friendly's. After walking a few blocks Mickey asked who had hamburger money, but none of us did; so, of course, what came next was Ricky proclaiming "We gotta get a few bucks from somewhere." "Ain't it your turn to get a purse Greg?" he asked with a serious face. Yes, it was finally my turn to do the deed; to snatch a woman's purse.

Now, this thing here really went against everything in me; but I had become part of something, I accepted the rewards, so I had to put in the work also. Well my turn went like this. As we walked around and discussed just how I should do the deed, there was light rain. We came upon a high traffic intersection where there was a gas station on one corner, a drug store on another, a hardware store on another and a bank on the forth corner, with each business adjacent to other businesses, then single-family houses.

In talking we acknowledged that the bank was the best possible place for my maiden voyage into robbery, thievery, stealing, lying, cheating and all other forms of criminality and my new short-lived life of crime. As we stood a few houses down and across the street from the bank, discussing where we would meet once I was finished, we spotted my victim. There was a little old lady with a rain coat and plastic rain scarf on her head, carrying a small umbrella and a big purse.

I said 'later' to the fellas, crossed the street and stood semi-hiding next to a house. I now had a clear view of the bank doors in which my victim had entered. I'm nervous and anxious about what I was about to do, and after about 15 minutes I see the bank door open and out she steps. Just as she clears the bank entrance and is on the sidewalk I swoop down on this little old lady like a "bat outa hell", grabbed her purse and tried to run, only to be snatched back so hard I thought this old lady had dislocated my arm while hitting me upside the head, across the neck and all about the arm that I tried to use to protect myself from this umbrella-yielding athlete who was beating my brains out with what felt like the "bat outa hell"!

I was suspended for what seemed like a half-hour until I hit the ground and farted when my butt hit the pavement as she continued to swing. When she finally set me free so (I believe) she could change swinging arms, I jumped up and broke out running in a direction I didn't even know existed. I must have run about ten blocks at full speed before I slowed down enough in an effort to catch my breath, get my bearings and figure out what in hell had just happened to me!

I ended up making it to the backyard of my dad's house, where I hid for about an hour until I was comfortable that I hadn't been followed. As my head cleared I realized I had left the purse, left my partners, and left my dignity all in a matter of minutes.

Well, this time, shame and guilt didn't have to beat my ass because that little old lady had already done a damn good job of it! I kept thinking about going to jail and not being able to play my trumpet anymore. I hid in the backyard until it got dark and I went home. When I saw Ricky and Mickey the next day, they saw me first and were falling out laughing. They told me how crazy that whole thing looked and since I didn't meet them afterwards they thought the cops had got me. They claimed to have gone over to the old lady where a crowd and witnesses had gathered.

The old lady kept calling me a thieving bastard and said, "I didn't have nothin' in here but a letter anyway. I wish he would bring his black ass back here again!"

I Thank God I got away that day. Needless to say, I abruptly found out snatching purses could never become a part of my skills and claim to fame. Realizing the possible outcome of my actions, including how my act would affect myself and my victims, I then became so thankful that nothing had gone wrong and vowed never to do anything close to any criminal act again; and from that point I never did. If for no other reason, I needed to stay free of jail and imprisonment so that I could make music; and from what I could see, if I ever got caught up in the legal system, I could kiss my musical dreams goodbye.

Ottawa Hills Friends circa 1971

Since before I started kindergarten, I've always had an exceptional ear for harmonies and arrangements. I wanted to create and control what the musicians and vocalists would do. Besides singing and blowing my horn, playing the piano became another passion. Because we didn't have one at home, I'd play any piano I could find, and I'd learn every song I could. Coming out of South High School in the midst of the busing mandate, I entered Ottawa Hills High School and to my surprise, my friend and ex-social studies teacher from South High school, James Burress was soon to become principal of my new school.

We were close enough where I would call him James most of the time, immediately switching to Mr. Burress when faculty or other students who did not know about our long-standing friendship and family ties were around. He would help make my adjustment to Ottawa go even smoother because he, although slightly younger than both of them, was friends with my mom and dad; and he has watched me grow as his student at South, as well as often catching my performances at the various Grand Rapids clubs over the years.

James was well aware of and supported my talents. I was already an up-and-coming musician in Grand Rapids. So, through my then many experiences, I couldn't help feeling much older than most of the kids around me because I lived a life they'd never seen. Most of them knew little to nothing about street life, hadn't been exposed to the hilarious types I grew up with in the inner-city and were naïve, but curious about experiences, like sex and heartbreak, which had already become part of my life.

At Ottawa, most of the folks I would hang with, were like me, transplants from South High School and new folks who were in my homeroom and/or other classes with me. We were very aware and concerned about what was happening in the world and the mundane conversations about clothes, parties, who was going with whom and gossip, though touched on, we found boring. Many of us played chess, all played instruments or sang, danced, some wrote poetry and we were all accepting of each other's idiosyncrasies.

Some of us would skip school at our various homes, where we knew the parents weren't at home and didn't arrive until late. Therefore, we could clean up and air the house out from the weed we'd be smoking on the back porch before they got home. Most of the time some of us would couple off. Most often we met after homeroom, or during lunch time. I used everything I'd learned from the hood, my street smarts, and what I'd been exposed to in the clubs, to work the kids at Ottawa. Little did we know that we were all learning and developing much of who we'd become through our dealings with each other. I became known as an intelligent, funny, talented nice guy.

On the days I did go to school I would always get a Tonk game going in shop class where Rodney Trotter and I would always win the money because we were lucky. Little did I know then that a few years later Rodney and I would become self-proclaimed "Kings of Hollywood" for a short time in the late seventies. One year, my brothers, Art and Skip, who went to a different high school, my friend Rob Robinson and I set up a lottery, that covered Ottawa Hills, Union High, Central High and Grand Rapids Junior College. We'd create numbers and collected money from the students daily. It was better known as a numbers racket back then. We kept it on the up and up and paid if your number came out, but if it didn't, Oh Well!

Little did I know that this was my beginning in learning about business and how to accomplish legitimate goals. Lessons I would instinctively apply in addressing the needs and concerns of my bands and my recording, touring career. Between the numbers' rackets, skipping and hanging out with my school clique, I wasn't going to school a lot, though I somehow stayed abreast of all the class materials and lessons.

James Burress would often call my house and tell my mom, "Mattie, will you tell Greg he has a test tomorrow and to be sure and come to school and check in with me when he gets here."

My mom questioned me about not going and I'd tell her what I found out later Mr. Burress had said to her "because he's so intelligent, creative and could breeze through most classes, he's bored and uninspired by general education." Though there was a lot of money in the economy and a lot of programs, I needed to be in an environment with an emphasis on music, like the schools in New York, which were specialized but still had a liberal arts education.

High school was easy and most of my stimulation came from my group and the conversations we had about everything beyond being taught at school.

By now, I had earned a reputation for being a master musician, vocalist and arranger. This was the period I started toying with the thought of creating my own band. I knew I wanted people who could sing and harmonize like the Temps, but who could also play instruments like Sly and the Family Stone or many of the highly talented jazz musicians I would spend hours studying and learning in front of our stereo. I was practicing at home one day shortly after school had started, looking out the window from the living room, trilling like the birds outside, when I saw a black plain clothes police car pull in front of our house. Four white police officers got out and walked to our front door.

I immediately stopped practicing and thought of Art. Our lives had parted over the years in every way. I had been mentored in music by Mache and the older musicians and Art had been guided by Sam Banks, who owned the corner store in our neighborhood, ran numbers, had a gambling game in the back of his store at night and had a little-known secret. He was a long-time heroin addict. Art worked for and learned much of the street game from him and a few other older guys. Art dabbled in heroin, became a stick-up man and carried his pistol, even to school, whenever he went.

He constantly rebelled against the life's norm as a whole, in every way he could. At one point, he joined the Republic of New Africa, a black political group, changed his name to Sabu Aku Laheeb and was the only black man I knew, at that time, who tried to stop black people from calling each other niggers, which was something our grandfather disallowed in his family, anyway. Art and a few of his friends were arrested among the initiators of the 1968 Grand Rapids riots when Dr. Martin Luther King was killed.

I remember one day, while I was in my usual afternoon place, stuck in front of mom's stereo learning or practicing some new song, and once again the cops come-a-knocking at my door. I walked out on the porch, leaving my horn by the stereo because I didn't want, as Richard Prior would say, to

117

be no accident. I opened the door, they immediately flashed their badges and asked for Art; it was the FBI. I told them Art wasn't home and after interrogating me as to whether I was really Art, was he in there hiding, did I know where he was, which to all I answered 'no', they finally accepted my words as truth and left without saying another word.

I frantically called everywhere I thought Art would be, trying to warn him, to no avail. I sat in the living room, waiting for Art, and when I saw him coming up the street, I ran downstairs to warn him. Art had just turned and stepped into our yard when the FBI swooped in from out of the bushes, down the street and even around the corners. With guns pulled, they jumped out of the car, rushed Art, who instinctively raised his hands. They cuffed him, put him in the car and left.

When the trial finally came, Art waived his rights, copped a plea and was sentenced to five to ten years in prison. By the weekend he was moved from Kent County jail to Michigan State Penitentiary in Jackson. Later that day after he was sent up, I recall walking in the rain, crying and thinking about my brother's troubled life. He was a troubled, rebellious kid who had finally gotten himself caught up in the so-called criminal justice system for what would be years.

I thought about years earlier he had done a stick up and hid a long sock full of money in a hole in the basement wall. He shared some of the money with me but told me he'd kick my ass if I took too much.

The memories continued to come. Various people saw Art as a thug; a wanna-be criminal, even a drug-user; but not many of them had seen him hurt and cry out over life's injustices, like I had on many occasions. No one knew his pain in being fatherless, in being black and poor and in having no option but to play the fucked-up hand we had been dealt. I know him, I love him, he's my brother.

When I got home that evening, I went straight to my room, closed the door and continued to cry until I finally drifted off to sleep. Next day at school and for a long time thereafter, I felt as if a part of me was missing. With the exception of a few fucked up folks, my friends and associates who knew Art, how close he and I were and what had happened to him, rallied to be as supportive as they could be to me; but the pain of missing my brother was something that I would have to learn to live through.

A black choir had started at Ottawa Hills, and a couple of my teachers had encouraged me to be part of it. Due to my love of popular music as opposed to sacred, music, I wasn't interested in joining the choir, but since rehearsals were held in the music room where the piano that I would often sneak and play, I would stop in on their practice from time to time. Also, the choir consisted of mostly girls; and after the rehearsal I could have access to a piano for a short time without being disturbed, without being made to leave the music room. One day at the end of choir practice, per usual, I was playing the piano when I heard a voice over my shoulder.

"HI." Shortly followed by, "I can play the piano too."

I turned around and there was this very light skinned chubby guy with a thick head of curly hair hanging down to his shoulders like Priest from the movie Super Fly. I scooted over.

"Come on, sit on down."

119

I kept playing as he joined in on the bottom keys. I begin to slide on the seat to give him more room to sit as he started playing the chords from Stevie Wonder's "I Love Every Little Thing About You", to my funky arrangement, and I got up and stood next to see just what cords he was playing. He stretched out then and was using the entire key board and singing with so much ease and feeling that the hair on my arms rose. He finished, with his long, agile fingers resting on the keyboard and didn't look up. I raised my hand to slap him a five and my movement made him turn around and look at me. Seeing my hand in the air he smiled, and we slapped fives. His arms were so long he didn't have to stand, and I held his hand, shaking it.

"Damn man, you can really play. What's your name?"

"Bobby DeBarge, Bunny's my sister."

When he mentioned Bunny, I knew he had to be alright as she and I had become good friends over the past year. Besides being able to sing her ass off, to me Bunny was a skinny, pretty little freckle-faced thing and she was downright silly. She would keep everyone in stitches with her facial expressions, crazy words and physical antics. I was soon to learn that Bobby, though more subdued, shared similar traits. Once he let U in and you got to know him, he turned out to be a fool, just like Bunny. He and I came to find humor and make fun of most things and many people. It really didn't take long for me to know that he and I would become lifelong friends.

Often Bobby's sense of humor proved a little crude and more off the cuff than mine, depending on the subject-matter. For instance, if he was pissed off for any reason, he's been known to make a paper bag of dog poop (or even human poop if he felt like taking a dump) in a bag, placing it on someone's porch, setting it on fire and ringing the doorbell, then hiding nearby to watch what happens and other crazy things like that.

With effort, I could most times sway him to reel it in, but sometimes he would sway me to just go with the flow. So, whatever it was, in the newness of it all, he would accept me as I was, and I would accept him for him.

Chapter 4

Bobby and I

Greg, Laura Stone, Bobby

Bobby and I sang instrumental leads that day. We sang from the moment we got away from the school and out of ear shot from everyone. That's when I discovered that when he wanted to, his singing voice could go higher than Eddie Kendricks. Bobby had more range, and to me, his falsetto was clearer, more natural than The Delfonics and Stylistics and every other known falsetto singer.

We shared immediate magic that day which lasted till we split up in Franklin Park to take our different directions home. A day or two later I was a few feet from Ottawa Hills's front door when I heard that voice call my name "Greg" which he always pronounced "Grag." Turning around it was Bobby, walking towards me looking at the ground. I didn't even know he knew my name because the bell had rung just as we slapped fives, and he'd introduced himself the other day.

Bobby reached me and looking me in the face, cheesed wide and I thought he looked like a little kid, though he was only two years younger than me. We'd been walking a bit when Bobby opened up "Hey kids, shake it loose together, the spotlights shakin' loose something known to change the weather, we'll kill the fatted calf tonight, so stick around, you'll hear electric music, Solid walls of sound."

It was the first verse to Check Out Your Mind by the impressions and I joined him with the harmony I 'd been hearing in my head. We sang the first two verses, continued with the harmony through the bridge then bent over laughing at how we'd sounded. I think we must have sung every popular tune out at that time, "Psychedelic Shack", "I'll Be There", "Reach Out", "Make It with You"; even Crosby Stills, Nash and Young's, "Carry On" because they had four-part harmony. What really clicked and took us to another level was singing Herbie Hancock's "Red Baron". Bobby knew all the licks and the head, moving his fingers as if he were playing the piano and I moved my fingers to the trumpet, which I carried but didn't take out and play. We parted that day, walking backwards and smiling at each other, singing a riff from the Carpenters' "We've Only Just Begun".

As I continued my way home which was only a few blocks away now, I was in deep thought about my new friend. I was troubled by the way all the nails on his long, slender fingers were bitten down so far that the skin covered them, and they bled. I was alarmed by the way his hands constantly shook. I tripped on how he could smoke a cigarette down to the butt, put that out and soon light up another. Something was terribly wrong, but I didn't dare ask. From this, I knew God had sent Bobby to me to look out for and this I would do to my own detriment if necessary.

When I didn't go home early to practice my horn or hang with girlfriend/playmate Tammy, Bobby and I hooked up. He and I would meet up most days after school, in the same place and walked toward home singing together from then onward. I always found it peculiar how I never saw Bobby in school, though after our first meeting I would look for him some of the time when I was there. I also remember him coming to my house before I went over to his. We would go into my basement which I had decorated with a strobe light, a black light, black light posters, and my hand me down stereo system.

I played my trumpet along with every song that came on and I watched Bobby close his eyes and move his fingers to imaginary chords and licks. Eating together, something stood out to me. He was always hungry and devoured the food. When it was time for him to leave that first day he said we'd go to his house next because he had a piano and we could play together.

After hanging out after school a few more days the day came when without intent on for knowledge we kept talking and walked past our normal stop and finally stopped when he said to me, "Hey Grag. My house is a few blocks down the street. Let's go there."

"Ok man. Is it gonna be cool with your moms?" I asked

"Sure man. She probably ain't there no way." And we continued a couple of streets down till he turned, then we walked up a slight hill, which should have had grass but didn't and onto the porch and into the house.

The first time I walked into the DeBarge front door, I thought damn, to myself, because it was a bundle of activity with kids running around, throwing things at each other, people walking and music playing and a bunch of fun going on. The piano, which sat against the wall in the living room was a spinet, but well preserved. Amidst all the chaos coming from all directions, Bobby immediately took control and barked out a few orders which successfully quieted this lively place down some. As a couple of younger brothers, who I quickly learned were James and Chico started coming towards me Bobby proclaimed, "Hey y'all, this is my friend Grag Wilums."

I quickly heard hi's and hellos from what seemed like everywhere and I immediately felt warm and welcome. Bunny nor Tommy were in my sight initially, but I would meet them both at later times. Now El, Bobby's younger brother, was sitting off to himself, reading the Bible. Seeing me, with Bobby, he closed the Bible, walked over to me and extending his hand said" Hey Greg". Bobby sat down at the piano, played a chord on the piano and all activity stopped. It was music which quelled anything going on and everybody gathered around.

Tommy came from somewhere with his bass and I pulled out my trumpet. We sang the Carpenter's "We've Only Just Begun" and a few Jackson Five Hits. I was stunned when the whole family harmonized to "Oh Happy Day" and "My Sweet Lord". I realized this was a truly musical family and everybody could sing. There was always someone at the other end of the piano, playing that day. Excluding the DeBarge babies, Darrell and Carol, Bunny was the only one who didn't play. She stood, sang and looked after the little ones crawling around. I knew that's how they knew me; through Bunny.

Bobby and I had been friends for about two months when I felt comfortable enough to comment about his hands, which shook all the time and the nails which he'd bite to nubs till they would bleed. When we hung with a group of my friends he was stand-offish most of the time except when the subject music came up.

When we'd gone to a party, I would look up and find him in a corner by himself, not dancing and often chewing on his nails. He was withdrawn around people other than his family and a couple of his close friends and with them, he was sometimes hard and bossy. I'd witnessed one of his siblings having touched something of his and Bobby exploding into a rage, cursing, throwing anything within his reach and putting his hand through the wall. All his siblings would scatter, running for cover; even the little one's who'd be crawling on all fours were trying to hide. During the two months, I'd learned a lot about the DeBarge clan and their home. Popular music played when mother DeBarge wasn't home, and when she was there, which wasn't often because she spent most of her time at church, religious music played.

The DeBarge children went to church because they had to, and Bobby played in the church because it was expected of him. From what I would come to know, the one DeBarge who appeared devoted to God and the bible, the one who had a glow and special quality about him, was Eldra. Bobby told me that El spent a lot of time in the church's basement practicing the organ. He could recite Bible verses easier than most could recite their home addresses and even at that young age, their Uncle Bill, Momma, other folk he had witnessed his gifts; and more so, El knew that he was called to the ministry.

Don't get me wrong, even though he was a wealth of theological knowledge and could be a little preacher, El also was often witty, funny and wise beyond his years and most of all this kid could just kill on the keyboard. And as I would in short time come to know, any keyboard he touched seemed renewed from his awesome playing ability.

Over the coming months I found myself paying more attention to El after Bobby and Tommy and this was because I was overwhelmed by El's talent, diligence and commitment at such a young age. And it was even later than that I found out how superior his vocal abilities surpassed most of his siblings putting him right up there with Bobby and Bunny. Most of all I had much respect for his innate ability to stay focused in the midst of such family disorder. I knew I was gonna keep my eye on him. Now it would take just a little longer for me to get to know Randy, James, Chico and much later for the babies, the twins Darrell and Carol, but Marty and I had the trumpet in common, so we were immediately cool.

And of course, Tommy loved everybody, and everybody loved Tommy from the word go, so feeling comfortable with all of them came so easy as each of them showed me who they were, and quickly made me feel like one of the family.

Bobby was Mr. Fixit man in the family, and the man of the house when his father was absent. He could be tyrannical, but, he was useful and practical. I called him Mr. Rigor Mortis because he could rig anything electrical together with ease. I know he hadn't taken electronics classes in high school, but if he had wanted to, he could have had a career in electronics.

This was one of his many gifts. He could handle anything technical, without a manual. The dial on the washing machine had burned out so Bobby took it off and attached light switches that he had taken off various walls in the house and rigged them up to the machine. I watched in amazement as the machine came on when the light switch was flipped up and went off when the switch flipped down. The other cycles worked by flipping other light switches to a different position.

Sometimes, when someone in the house didn't follow Bobby's plan, his temper would explode and rock the house. However, it wasn't Bobby's temper which created another element in the DeBarge household, which I observed; fear. The children, and mother DeBarge moved with an air of apprehension whenever the door opened. It didn't take long for me to discover what they all feared; Bob DeBarge senior. His presence in the house caused everyone to move as if they didn't want to break or touch anything.

From what I would observe, his wife and the older children, except for James, were nervous and jumped whenever he looked at them and the signs of some form of abuse or fear showed on their faces. Mr. DeBarge demanded his space, through silence and a look whenever I was there. He'd sit at the piano, playing Hank Williams or country and western songs and sometimes one or more of the younger kids would sit at the piano with him. He was always friendly with me, calling me "My buddy".

A few times we'd sit and play spades together. After one of my early visits, Bobby told me "for some reason daddy seems to like you." Just a few weeks, after having come over to the DeBarge home when dad was there, Bobby later told me as soon as I walked out of the door his father had said to him, "Don't bring that 'black-mother-fucker' over this house anymore. He's fucking your sister." To which Bobby and I laughed our asses off.

"Your dad is a sick dude Bobby!" I blurted out. To his quick come back, "You don't know the half of it, man!" as we continued to walk and laugh all the way to my house. Whenever Bob Sr. would come home Bobby would always tell me funny, crazy and sometimes cruel things he would say about me and other people who would come around. But Bobby would keep inside the horrible things he had done.

Whenever Bob Sr. left for another of his long-distance hauls, I could hear the sigh of relief and I noticed the entire household seemed to relax. The fear he represented created a binding love the siblings shared, but it also made them constantly fidgety and nervous. I noticed the trepidation most in Bobby and as we walked one day, he was biting what little was left of his fingers.

"Bobby, man you need to stop biting your nails, they're always bleeding."

He moved each finger, observing the nails. "I know, but I can't. Let's get to your house out of this cold."

We quickly walked past Franklin park, our favorite stopping place on our way to my house, which was a few blocks straight on this street. He lit up another cigarette and started to smoke (which I was surprised he did at such a young age, but he always had a ready supply) as we walked, laughed, talked about music we'd recently heard. Finally making it to my house, we took off our coats and hung them up on the hooks in the hallway right next to the door.

One day, when Bobby and I were at my house eating and talking when out of nowhere the expression on his face grew sad and our conversation took a very serious turn. He began to shake a small bit as he started to talk. He started with, "Momma said that daddy would be home this weekend." He continued saying how his dad was gone most of the time driving a truck; but when he did come home on his infrequent visits, he would sometimes wake his older sons around one or two in the mornings, get them out of bed in their underwear and he would beat them with this thick leather belt, for no reason. Sometimes until they bled, then he would rub salt into their welts.

He would sometimes take them downstairs to the kitchen and make one or two of them clean the cabinets and walls, while the others had to get on their hands and knees and scrub the floors and baseboards with tooth brushes. All the while, he was telling them that what he was doing was for their own good. He'd sometimes call one of the older boys to come with him while the others knew not to stop working, only to molest him.

As his eyes welled up with tears he continued to share, "When I was five or six I had to go to the hospital one time because my father had put things up my butt. They told the doctors that I had done it, which they believed. And they took those things out, but what they didn't know that those things weren't all he was putting up there. Grag, since we were really little, he's did things to Me, Bunny, Tommy, Randy and sometimes even Marty." As heavy tears began to run down his face and onto his shirt, Bobby leaned forward and his head fell to the table like an over-ripe apple, shielding his face in his hands, as his body quivered. He stayed hunched over for a while, letting loose something, I felt, he'd been burdened with for a long time.

Stopping, then standing and wiping his eyes and nose with the back of his hands, I put my hand on his shoulder and squeezed it, not knowing what else to do. I was devastated by the things I was told that day. Although by now I had had a few girlfriends who had been raped by their father or uncles, but I had never known anyone who dealt with anything close to this. I wanted to console him but had no idea how except to, and I was truly at a total loss for words, but I heard myself say, "Don't worry about it, Bobby. It'll be ok. Let it go."

I said it, not really knowing at that time that he would never be able to let it go. I did not know then that this pain was so big and ran so deep that it had already destroyed any chance he may have to get around or over it. What this man had done to his own son, his own children ran beyond understanding. Beyond right and wrong, beyond logic and beyond forgivable. Once we got up from the table, we went down to my basement hideaway. Still in absence of the right thing to say, I just turned on my stereo, shut up and let the music play and play until it got late, and my mom called me, and Bobby decided he needed to go home.

What I learned that day haunted me throughout the night. I wanted to tell someone but didn't dare. Hell, I wouldn't know how to tell anyone the things he had told me. All I knew is that my new friend needed me. He needed my strength, my loyalty and my shoulder and I would be right there, keeping secrets, as long as he needed me to.

Of course, being Bobby's close friend meant being good friends to the DeBarge siblings and even another big brother to the younger DeBarge children. Now getting to know, becoming friends with Bunny, was familiar and easy. I understood her background, her call to and love of music. Her decency and her deep need to be accepted, understood and to belong and she understood me in the same way. We also shared the music, the dancing and a sense of decency. We loved to dance together.

I think there was another unspoken understanding Bunny and I had as we shared the gift of music. Even though she was raised and sang in the church, she knew a lot of popular songs, she had an ear and like most of these DeBarge children, she could sing anything after only hearing it once. With Bunny, being bi-racial, she was very light and very attractive, with the hair texture, most black girls wanted. These qualities elicited envy and jealousy, from both black people, due to her white blood and white people, who had funky attitudes because she had black blood. Bunny was small, but, as is said in the vernacular, she wasn't no punk and girls knew this about her.

Now, some people would call Bobby and me, salt and pepper, or cream and coffee, and we'd laugh; and I kind of remember the same things said when she and I were standing by each other or dancing. Bobby, like Bunny, knew a lot of gospel songs, some popular songs, but technically, he knew so little about music. I'd been playing trumpet for eight years when we met, and I'd been schooled technically in the classrooms, and by observing my uncles James and Sylvester, by playing with Mache and all the other older musicians who'd accepted me into their elite club of master musicians.

Over time I imparted everything I'd picked-up to Bobby; especially about learning tunes. The older musicians enforced the idea the more songs you learn, the broader your lyrical depth and the more you can say on your instrument because communicating musically, is actually about telling a story with each solo, or lyric. Playing snatches of different tunes, creates a context for the listener because they usually know the lyrics, and can hear what you're communicating by how you take the melody, which the lyrics are built from, and expand. However, you'd have to know a lot of songs, to play snatches of them and talk shit.

Bobby, I'd learned, knew some songs, but not a lot and being a member of all these record clubs, I had an unlimited amount of songs at my disposal. We developed a pattern; technical practice at school. Bobby would show me fingerings on the piano, I didn't know, and I'd teach him about chords, phrasing and how to resolve them. We also worked on licks, how to connect them to make melodic lines, different keys

133

and how Bobby could use his beautiful falsetto. Over time I noticed Bobby was often hesitant to sing most songs with soprano leads.

"Bobby, man, why won't you sing the Stylistics and Blue Magic and those kinds of tunes? I asked. They're in your range."

He leaned back from the piano and gave me that closed-mouthed grin, which, he knew, always cracked me up. "I don't like to sing them because I'm better than them." He stopped grinning and searched my face, his doe eyes seeking acknowledgement.

"You're right. You are better than them. However, you need to learn these tunes, man, because you'll be playing with other people and they'll call them."

He ran his hands over the keyboard. "Playing with who?"

"With other musicians, not just me. We'll be out there, man. You and I; and it starts right here in Grand Rapids at the jam sessions and getting together with other musicians. We should start our own band and gig."

He started biting his nails. "The jam sessions are on Saturday and you know how mama and uncle Bill are about serving God and not the devil."

I pulled his hand away from his mouth. "I'll ask mama."

Bobby played a chord with force, glaring at the piano. "You don't have to ask her. I'll be there."

"Bobby, man."

He started singing the Jackson Five's "I'll be There". So, I left it alone. I knew, though, Mama DeBarge was not a mother who anyone, except her husband, could just leave alone when it came to her children. I always thought she was one of the most complex people I'd ever met. She encouraged her children to sing for the Lord, yet loved the praise they earned from the world in which she didn't want them to participate.

However, there was another part of the world, to which she allowed her children to fall prey. The world of violence, psychological and sexual abuse to which she directly was no stranger. I witnessed several occasions when she was on her way to church, Bob Sr. had momentarily left and all the children, except Bobby, who was punching a wall, and Bunny, who quietly dealt with the wants and needs of the little ones. I have witnessed times when one child or the other would be holding onto Mama DeBarge, crying and begging her not to leave. I believe because they knew what their father was going to do to some of them.

I've seen her pull away from them, telling them she was going to pray about things, and she would leave. The young DeBarge kids would huddle together and only Bunny would try and comfort them. Bobby, having knocked holes in the wall, would ravage his nails, and I'd leave, trying not to cry most of the way to my house, feeling guilty, helpless and wanting to get Art's pistol, which he'd left in the house, and shoot Bob DeBarge Sr. I'd see Bobby the next day, depressed, distraught and sometime a little redder than other times and I could only imagine what had happened.

Back then, Mama DeBarge, also had a stellar voice, stronger than Bunny's and if given the opportunity, she'd musically cut them all to pieces. She and Bunny would give any of the contemporary gospel singers at that time, something to think about. Mama DeBarge, also had a deep spiritualism which, when Bob Sr. wasn't around, made her glow. She once walked up to me, her eyes misty, distant, and touching me with her finger, looked above my head. "Greg, God showed me this vision that my children were going to be known all over the world and you would be the vehicle they would come through."

A warm sensation trickled through my body. That's good to know," I said with a smile on my face, while not knowing the total ramifications of her now expectations.

She seemed to float away after that, humming as she walked upstairs. She allowed her children to sing, listen to and learn popular songs after that and she was even more welcoming to me in her home. When I was around, I too became one of her kids. I too had to get my butt up and help carry those sixteen to twenty bags of groceries into the house at 616 Giddings, which sat next to the alley, when that raggedy station wagon pulled up and she blew that horn. I too had to go look for Marty or Randy if they hadn't brought their butts home by the time they were supposed to. I too had to keep an eye out for Ginger, the family dog, who was affectionately called the neighborhood hoe by the DeBarge kids because days after she would drop one litter of puppies it seemed she'd be pregnant with another; even the dog stayed barefoot and pregnant.

I wonder where she got that from. I was now allowed to take Tommy, who always begged but couldn't get consent to leave, with me from time to time. Within no time, second only to Bobby, Tommy became my protégé and my little brother too. We'd go to Franklin Park, the Trotter family's (Rodney

Trotter's step dad) pool room down on Franklin and Eastern. He looked up to me, second only to Bobby. I had his back and he knew it. He would sometimes practice with Bobby and me and he learned all the songs we played. He refused to go to church, but now could go anywhere with me, because mama said so.

Mama DeBarge had another side I really enjoyed, and it emerged at different times. She too could be real silly and funny. Bobby and I had a friend, Jose Guyton, who was also a beast on the keyboard. People talked about him because he had bugged eyes, like a reptile. I always felt sorry for him when girls called him ugly and people had given him the nickname Hootenburger because that's what they said he looked like. He was the type of friend, if some trouble jumped off, he'd be there. We were in the DeBarge home and mama DeBarge came downstairs. She looked at Jose, stopped, sighed and walked past him muttering, "Lord, kill it fore it multiplies."

We all tried to stop, but once Tommy kicked it off, our laughter exploded and we fell to the floor, holding our stomachs.

I also admired the support system she had with the church, which was often feeding the DeBarge family and providing with them clothes and shoes. In the church there was a name for mothers like Mama DeBarge, rug-faced. We called them this because they spent many hours on their knees, praying. I often thought she spent so much time on her knees or at church that her children were doing things, like Bobby not going to school and she never noticed. I laughed at myself when I thought this because at this point, I mostly went to school only when I had a test or exam. The difference though, as my mother knew, I had Mr. Burress, who had my back. The DeBarges had no one.

I started taking Bobby to jam sessions with me and he was shaky at first, mostly from nerves, but, when they called a song, he played and everybody started shouting "yea", he was alright. He really cut loose when Mache, who didn't know Bobby, called The Red Baron and Bobby played a solo so bad that all the other pianists at the jam session gave him props and let Bobby play the rest of the night. Mache turned to me when we'd finished the tune.

"Who's that kid?"

"Bobby DeBarge,"

"The same DeBarge as that girl who sings at Abney's church every Sunday?"

"Yea, that's his sister."

"With talent like that and the right direction, he's going somewhere."

I looked at Bobby digging the response the older musicians were giving him.

Mache inhaled, contemplating his saxophone reed.

"There's only one thing I see though, and you haven't even noticed."

I watched Bobby more, trying to follow Mache. "What's that?"

"That little yellow nigger's been drinking ever since he's been here. He's got a bottle in his jacket pocket he keeps pouring into his coke and he was high when you two walked in. How old is he, thirteen?"

"Fifteen."

"You were maybe a couple years younger when you first came here and you hadn't drunk, nor got high yet and he's keeping it together, but he's tanked. Did you get him high before you got here?"

"No Mache, you know I don't do that before I play."

Mache elbowed me. "I know Greg. Your boy got issues at a young age and he's flying to carry them. You better watch him."

I couldn't tell Mache about Bobby's issues because Bobby was my friend and our secrets would be respected and stay between us. But still, I took note of what Mache said.

Tommy DeBarge couldn't wait to go to a jam session, and he'd pull me away from everyone whenever he could. "Greg, I'm ready. Ask my mother can I go to a jam with you." He was always outgoing, fun loving, adventurous and could thump that bass like he owned it.

I'd finally asked Mama DeBarge if I could take Tommy with me one Saturday. She agreed, and he was ecstatic. He was only fourteen and was jumping in the air as we drove away in my uncle's car.

"Thanks Greg. Man, I'm happy to get out of the house and get a break."

Glancing over I noticed his face had flushed red and his lip trembled.

"Dad's gone and Bobby sometimes treats us worse than Dad does. He's so mean, sometimes, it's scary. If you even look at anything of his he goes berserk and gets violent, just like Dad. Especially with James, because he's dad's favorite. I have to listen to the albums you lend him when he's there and learn the songs. If I touch them, he goes berserk." He gulped and wiped his eyes.

"Bobby does to us what Dad does when dad's not around Greg. He hates dad, but he's just like him in some ways. I'm glad to be away so I can get a break."

Turning away from me, he watched the city moving past and cradled his bass. Bobby was supposed to meet us at the session, but he didn't show. The DeBarge's cousin, Andre Abney, Elder Abney's son, a drummer, did show and he and Tommy, as a rhythm section, held musical court and funked out the house.

Mache stopped me as I was leaving. "Man, that's one talented family." He pointed to Tommy and Andre, still discussing music.

"Yea, Mache and they all come out of the church. Andre plays in his father's church too."

Mache raised his hands in the air. "Praise the Lord!"

I was driving Tommy home after the jam session and he was so amped at playing he rocked the car with his bopping and thumping his imaginary bass to every song. The radio played an oldie, "Our Day Will Come", which, along with Brenda Holloway's "Every Little Bit Hurts", always reminded me of Bunny singing in that range. Her voice was actually like Minnie Ripperton's and she could sing higher than the highest note on the piano with ease and clarity. Tommy must have picked up the vibe because he turned the radio down so I could hear him.

"You know, Greg, Bunny talks about you all the time. That's why we knew who you were before you came over to our house and we all liked you before we met you. But she's my big sister and I need to ask you something.'

I looked at him and he wasn't smiling. "Alright, hit me."

"You long-dicking my sister, ain't you?"

I knew his question wasn't only from Bunny talking about me. It was Bob DeBarge Sr.'s influence on his son, so I stayed serious to show him I was telling the truth. "No man, I'm not screwing her. Bunny and I are close as friends, and nothing else. Kevin's her boyfriend. You know your sister. She got a heart of gold."

"Thank You for Letting Me Be Myself" by Sly and the Family Stone came on and Tommy moved his fingers as if playing the bass line.

"He's her man, but you're her heart. You know it and so does she. It's cool, though. I just needed to hear it from you." Tommy then proceeds to pull out a joint and gesture like he's going to light it when I shouted, "What the hell are you doing?"

"Lighting a joint. You know what I'm doing."

"Not in here and not with me Tommy. You will not be getting high with me anytime."

"Aww come on Greg, man. This is some really pokenate shit. Come on…"

"What the hell is pokenate, Tommy?"

"Nigga you know; Some good weed man."

"Tommy, you don't mean potent shit?"

"That's what I said, ain't it? Aww you just trying to be funny Greg…"

We both laughed and didn't say another word once he put that weed back in his pocket. It was important to me that

Tommy knew I was serious. That I would not be one of his get-high buddies. We laughed all the way to the DeBarge home and Tommy got out of the car, embracing his bass.

"Nigga, I know you long-dicking my sister." He bent over still laughing and walked to the house, looking over his shoulder and pointing at me.

I waited until Tommy went inside and drove home thinking about the many faces of Bunny and how difficult it must be to be her.

In my reliving various parts of my years and experiences with the DeBarge family, I recall a time when my trumpet had gotten busted and had to go into the shop, so I was somewhat sad to be without my daily companion for a time. Feeling a need to help his close friend, seems from nowhere Bobby came up with a trumpet and gave it to me so that we wouldn't miss our days of playing together. After a few weeks, my trumpet was fixed and I had no need for two so, without thinking I pawned the one Bobby had given me. Sadly, it never dawned on me the real significance of Bobby's giving this trumpet to me or the possibility that he might want that one back.

The next time we got back together to make music, Bobby noticed that I had my own trumpet. After getting excited to see me playing my horn, we jammed for about an hour or so, playing mostly songs with trumpet lead and solos like "Red Clay" by Freddie Hubbard and "Pain" by the Ohio Players. After we stopped to take a break I noticed a serious mood change in Bobby and as I put my trumpet back in the case and he turned off the Fender Rhodes, he asked "Grag, I 'm happy U got Ur horn back so, what did you do with the one I gave you?"

"I pawned that thing man!" I said, sounding like it was no big deal. I then noticed how quiet Bobby had become. It then dawned on me that his feelings were hurt, hearing me say that I no longer had the gift he gave me. The one gift that sealed our friendship.

Now I'm beginning to feel strange, sorry and sad all at the same time because I can now, clearly see that I hurt my friend badly. I didn't think my getting rid of that trumpet mattered at all, once I got mine back. I didn't think that he might want it back to keep or even give to his little brother Marty (whom I later thought this horn may have been taken from in the first place) since he was taking trumpet lessons in school. I didn't think that Bobby's feelings, which were already fragile and over-worn would be hurt by my actions. I didn't think that maybe I should have shared the money I received from pawning that trumpet with Bobby. I guess I really didn't think at all!

And now, once again I must look, see and feel that all too frequent pain in his face. Only this time, I was the one who caused it and that hurt me more than I can say. Had I been thinking, everything I just mentioned would now be different and I certainly would have no reason for this painful guilt that was consuming me at that moment. Before I caught myself and began to apologize for what I had thoughtlessly done, I blurted out, "Bobby, I am so sorry for pawning the horn. I am so sorry for spending the money and not at least sharing it with you, but I really didn't think it mattered after mine came out of the shop. I am so sorry to know that this hurt you! I would never have done any of this had I thought it out."

Bobby interrupted me in saying, "Naw, it's alright Grag." But I could see it was too late. The damage had been done. It became clear to me that now, Bobby had one more person whom he loved and trusted, who had caused him pain. No matter the intent or lack thereof on my part, I now have fallen into that list of betrayals Bobby had experienced his whole young life and there was no taking it back once it was done. Although he forgave me, he would not forget and from that point, things were still good between us, but never the same. In no time, we continued on as if nothing happened, but in his heart and mine we both know a piece of our closeness had broken off, never to be repaired.

To this day when I remember that moment in time, I am still filled with guilt and I regret that in an instant of not thinking things through, I put a dent in what had become one of the most significant relationships of my life.

Chapter 5

My Nightclub Life

Young Greg (1970)

Growing into the music, and surviving as a musician, gave me the impetus for complete independence. Art was gone, mom had three other children at home, therefore another source of my revenue had dried up and my card games at Ottawa Hills were also no more; so, I took my winning ability at cards, into the after-hours clubs and anywhere I could find a game, I gambled. Looking for games exposed me to another type of people; hustlers, gamblers, pimps and whores; a few folks I had come to know through one side of Art's world.

Pete McFall was a family friend from the old Hall St. neighborhood, since childhood. My aunts and uncles who were not much older than me were the same ages as his older sisters and they were friends, as well. By now, although Pete and I shared a few of the same classes in high school, while I was becoming proficient and well known as a musician, he was up and coming in the street life.

Pete started pimping in Junior High School and had by now made a name for himself. He was a small built, slim, slick, handsome, light-skin brother, who slightly resembled Prince, with clear eyes, brown wavy hair and the gift of gab. He was the kind of young man who could sell a used car salesman a car. He too used to hang out at the local night clubs at a young age. He would sometimes make plans, gather up a few of his hoes, and meet me at whatever bar I might be playing in and flaunt them in my face. In all seriousness Pete would sometimes say to me;

"Nigga you better pimp dem hoes!" And we'd burst out laughing. "Greg, you've always got women around you and they'll do anything for you. You oughta pimp some of these hoes."

We were in high school and he already had about three steady hoes and some not so steady. I thought about the opportunity and slapped fives with him.

146

"Pete, I'm gonna pimp cities, not hoes. Man, me and this horn gonna have the world at my feet!"

He returned my five and we burst out laughing. Pimps loved to frequent the jam sessions. There were quite a few wanna be's, but a few were prominent at their business. That was my friend Pete McFall, who during that time had the school trade sewn up. These guys could relate to us musicians because, as I was told, "we're all in the entertainment business," and they ran the hoe stroll on Division Avenue in Grand Rapids, on which the Golden Glow was located. In the words of the great philosophers of Division Street, I first heard the expressions "pimp or die," or "pimpin' ain't dead, hoes is scared," and "bitch better have my money." These terms, which would years later become lyrics to Rap records, struck me.

An older guy Mike Sheldon, who had heard me play in the clubs and loved how I played befriended me because he used to play trumpet in high school. He came from an upstanding family, had a degree in something and his family was always trying to convince him to get an eight to five job, but he threw it all away to be a pimp.

Deciding to avoid the hustling world made me more committed to music and I began to feel a bit restless, wanting to do something on my own, musically and in life. Musically, the teenage nightclub was The Patterns' gig, but we were still doing cover tunes. The jam sessions were cool, but we jammed to other-people's music and not our own. I had jammed, for the first time with my dad and after we'd finished playing he'd put his arm around me.

"Boy, I didn't know you were that good. You got it going on."

Instead of thanking him, I moved away from his arm. "You should have been checking me out and then you'd have known."

Somewhere, inside me, I thought he should have known about me because he was also a musician; and my grandmother was the bartender where I played. I thanked him for the compliment, and I noticed how he beamed when the musicians in the club complimented him on having a kick ass trumpet playing son.

I was seventeen now and Sylvester, David and I had left The Patterns about a year ago. I joined a band that was once our rival group called The TMG's. That's also how I met my then main girlfriend May Montclair.

May was a little different from most of my earlier girlfriends. Although most of my earlier loves were short too, with the exception of Valerie, who stood five feet eight to my six feet frame, all including May were attractive. But May was lighter-skinned by comparison and although she played the good girl role, she turned out to be a bigger freak than I was. *The things we used to do* (well I'll save that for another life). She went crazy when she thought I was seeing or looking at another girl too much; even though I was always a gentleman and very loyal to my girlfriends.

My music came first, and they came second. May lived with her grandmother and younger brother, only four blocks from my house; so, she and I could see each other any time we wanted throughout the day, after school and after grandma went to sleep.

My life, educationally, was different because although I didn't go to school a lot, I kept abreast of the work. Mr. Burress, who was swiftly moving up the Grand Rapids political ladder through his position as principal and his community outreach projects, often asked me to speak to various groups, primarily white, as a representative on upwardly mobile black youth, throughout the city. They'd ask me questions about Grand Rapids black youth, and I'd discuss affirmative action programs and projects like the Teenage Nightclub, which had gained notoriety throughout the city. I always found it rather comical how James Burress selected me, though he knew about my attendance record. Remember it was he who told my dad about my skipping school back in my South High days.

Each time I'd finish speaking he'd give me a ride home, during which we'd talk about things. Not like principal to student but like older and younger friends.

"Greg, you're bright, intelligent, gifted and you need to do something with your future, other than an eight to five job and playing in those clubs."

What made me listen to James Burress was he never preached to me, nor scolded me and I knew he was correct. He'd known me since elementary school and had always believed in my abilities and supported me in ways that he could.

"James, I know. I'm just joining The TMG's but I'm always open for something new, I'm just not quite sure of what it is."

"I'll keep my eyes open and let you know if anything comes up. If it does, are you interested, Greg?"

"Interested and serious as a brain cancer," I quipped.

He dropped me at home and drove away, watching me in his mirror. I entered my home, changed and went to the club to play. Tonight would be my last Honeycutt gig for a while because The TMG's worked a lot, almost every weekend. I was excited about playing with them because they pursued me various times before I agreed to join and they played top-forty and original material, which would give me a chance to really test my skills. They were probably the best self-contained band in western Michigan, and they were also my age, younger than Honeycutt's cats, so after that night the BarTees would have to do it without me.

Returning early in the morning, mom caught me as I was coming in the door.

"Greg, I need to talk to you."

"Mom, I just got off work and I'm tired. Can we please talk later?"

"No, it gotta be right now!" We sat down at the kitchen table. "Greg, you have to get a job. You have to get a job or move out."

I thought she was joking, but the firm look around her mouth meant she was serious.

"You're grown now. You're coming and going at all hours, not going to school and I can't take care of you."

Even though for years now I was making enough money to take care of myself. Sometimes enough to give her some. At least enough money so I didn't have to have any of hers. I guess she and my stepfather, Frazier, wanted me to pay bills.

"You're acting like a man and now it's time you start living like one."

"But mom, I am a man! I'm also musician. Plus, I'm barely here and I am, taking care of myself."

She placed her hand on top of mine. "I know you're barely here and sometimes you do make enough money to take care of yourself. But you're still in my house, I have a husband and three other kids to consider and I can't take care of you too."

I moved my hand away from hers. I knew that she wasn't just speaking for herself.

"So, you're putting me out."

"No, I'm not putting you out. I just think it's time you get a job and start paying rent and you can't do that with that horn."

I rose from the table, angry. "Mom, you don't understand, and you don't want to understand. I'll die before I stop playing music. I believe in me and if you knew me you'd believe in me too! Okay, I'll move."

She looked straight ahead and not at me. "I think that's for the best." She said.

I walked outside, all my tiredness was gone; I sat on my mom's front porch and thought about what I wanted and what I had to do. I was angry with my mom because she didn't see me for who I was at that time. She had never really seen it and except for one time, she never really supported it. Here I was, one of the most sought-after trumpeters in Southwestern Michigan, and she couldn't see it. I had to turn down gigs because I was in demand and she couldn't see it. I was a talented, committed musician who frequently made money, but I guess not enough for her.

Although at that moment I felt like I was pushed to it, this was truly a coming of age moment for me. I thought, if anyone should have been able to see what I was and what I was bound to be, it should have been my own mom, but she couldn't see it and she wanted me to get a damn job.

It was while sitting there on the front porch, her porch, that it came to me that I had to start my own band, to call my own shots. I decided that I would model my band on the singing structure of the Temptations, with multiple vocalists and musicians who would be able to sing lead and background. Cats who knew how to harmonize but were also able to play the hell out of their instruments. I wanted my band to be clean, classy, and we'd play ballads, funk and whatever else came to us. I would do it and she'd see, one day soon, her son, Gregory Williams, movin' and shakin' the world.

I had hidden a few dollars from myself, money that I made gambling and playing with the Patterns and with Honeycutt's crew, so I left moms, looking for an apartment for rent. I remembered that I had just seen "for rent" signs on a few buildings on my way to and from playing at the American Legion with Mache. My favorite location was a few miles from where we lived before we moved to Alexander SE., right off the northeast corner of Paris and Wealthy Streets. So, I stopped, and the owner happened to be there putting finishing touches on the available apartment.

I really liked this huge converted home of now eight apartments, which turned out to be owned by Mr. Strickland, a friend of my family, who grew up with my uncles Thomas and Elvin. He invited me in to look around while he completed his work. It was a nice little brightly-lit one bedroom, with a medium size living room, a small well-decorated kitchenette and a private entrance in the back of this building. I fell in love with this apartment, so he and I began to discuss the application, the rent and the deposit. Although I had saved enough to pay the first months' rent I hadn't saved enough for the deposit.

Mr. Strickland was even kind enough to offer a lesser deposit, which could be spread out over my monthly rent, but still my moneys fell short. I was not about to commit to any deal that I wasn't sure I could live up to, so I thanked him for his consideration but told him that I'll have to pass for now. He kindly said "Sorry we can't make this work for you but check back when you're ready. Maybe this or one of the other seven apartments in this building will be waiting for you, so keep my number and just call me. And tell Tom and Elvin my pool cue is getting rusty waiting for them.

"We both laughed as I nodded my thanks and walked away. Now knowing that I needed to have more money to move out on my own, I headed back to moms. Once there, I knew what I had to do; so, I went in, packed and went to my grandmother's house, about 10 blocks from my mom's house on Alexander Street.

Mother met me at the door. "You can live here, Greg, and do what you have to do to make your music."

Being my mom's mom and instrumental in raising me, I knew she knew me better than anyone and her support bolstered my drive. She directed me to my room, formerly inhabited by my uncle James, now living back at the VA hospital in Battle Creek, Michigan; and I slept in my new surroundings until it was time for Darnell to pick me up for rehearsal.

The TMG's had recorded their first album a few months before I joined. They were just learning the business, didn't have copyrights on their songs, nor a distribution deal for their music; which unbeknown to any of us, meant they could easily get burned and ripped off for their rights and any income which may have followed. On our shows we played a few originals, some Sly and the Family Stone tunes, Donny Hathaway's music and our own arrangements of other top forty hits. We traveled all over the Midwest and a friend singer-songwriter Jackie Beaver, who wrote the hit, "Someday We'll Be Together" for Motown's Supremes, owned a small supper club in Georgia.

Jackie offered us an opportunity to play at his club over the summer when his band was on the road and he got us hooked-up with the then famous Helen Greer booking agency in Atlanta. Between the two of them, we managed to get a small Southern tour. It was the summer of 1971 and while many guys I knew, including one of my uncles, were being shipped off to fight in the Viet Nam war, I, having missed the minimum draft age by only two years, was buzzed to be really traveling as a musician and happy to be getting out of Michigan for a while.

Our entourage which consisted of band leader Tommy "McGee on keyboard, my dear friend and ex brother-in-law Darnell Wyrick on Tenor sax, Clyde Nelson on Alto sax, Randy Eason on bass guitar, Kenny Eason on lead guitar, Jeff Baxter on drums and our roadies Rock and Bobby Nelson who drove Rock's car with an attached U-Haul trailer filled to the top with our equipment, Kenny, and one prostitute, Lois Little. Darnell and Kenny drove their own cars and we hit the road.

The first performance was in Cartersville, Georgia at a club owned by our host Jackie Beaver. This club was in the downtown area and we took up temporary residence at a house owned by Jackie, also in Cartersville. It was midsummer, so you know it was hot and humid in Georgia. To me, what stuck out most was the way southerners partied. They came to dance, they were polite, very social and we didn't meet one young lady with an attitude. Playing from the bandstand we kept noticing all the women had big butts and the Eason brothers started a riff singing they weren't gone fall in love with no big butt woman, which later, after a slight title change, became a big hit for Joe Tex.

Second night at the club I met and hooked up with this girl Sandy who, unknown to her or I till later, lived three doors down from Jackie's house with her daughter, her mother and her younger sister. Sandy was twenty-two years old to my brand new eighteen years. She stood at five feet tall and had shoulder length jet black hair, which she wore straight with curls upward at the ends. Sandy had these gorgeous Asian eyes, silky-smooth skin, which was blacker than mine; and each time I saw her she was dressed sharp.

When we first met she wore this beautiful soft red summer dress, which was loose; but somehow still showed that she was built like a brick shit house, and to me, she was the sexiest woman in the club. From up on the stage she caught my eye as I watched her watch me till the set was over; so, from the minute she approached me when the band took a set break, it was on. Although I didn't have to, I asked her to stick around till the band finished for the night, which she did.

After the show, I informed Darnell of my intent and I rode with Sandy, who, along with a few other cars filled with women from the show, followed the TMG caravan back to the home where we were staying. Sandy and I talked so intensely, getting acquainted through the entire half-hour ride from the club to the house that upon our arrival, she turned off the engine and we spent the next three or four hours sitting in the car talking, till we noticed that the sun was up, and it was getting hot outside. From that point we went into the house where a few of the other visiting women were making breakfast for everyone in the house.

Without eating, Sandy and I slipped into the bedroom that I was sharing with Darnell, and she and I made love over and over till we fell asleep. When I woke up late in the afternoon, without a word, Sandy was gone but later that night she showed up at the club just before show time and it was on again, pretty much a repeat of the night before. My relationship with Sandy would only last over the weeks that I was there performing in the south but the impact and warm memories of my summer with her remains until this day. I guess that's because she was my first on the road relationship where I went into it knowing, .this can only be short term so enjoy it while it lasts.

Cartersville was also an eye opener in small town Southern life. Our crew, seven band members and two roadies, left Cartersville in route to open a date with Candi Staton in Laurel Mississippi. After driving for hours, it got dark and we were tired and hungry, so we drove on till we finally found this lone restaurant, more like a small diner. Upon entering, my eyes immediately went to the shotguns mounted on the walls, then to the few patrons who were all white folks and finally to the thin lipped, red-headed waitress, wearing a light blue dress, a white apron and a pencil in her hair; and was leaning on the end of the counter by the kitchen entrance, drinking a beer. Being from the north and totally unaware of the culture shock we were about to encounter, all nine of us walked into this restaurant.

Even though there were only about ten white folks in the joint who took note of our entrance into their world, they blatantly ignored our presence, as they ignored our obvious gestures for service. Kenny and Randy Eason, who had sat at the counter with Rock and Bobby, were getting antsy and about to act asses up in there till Darnell moved closer to them to keep them cool. After roughly ten minutes, the woman behind the counter cleared her throat and then asked in a nasty tone through her heavy southern drawl, what y'all boys want?"

"We want some food," Randy Eason blurts out, in a matter-of-fact tone.

The waitress takes out her pad from her pocket and the pencil from her hair, came and stood right in front of us, glancing over our shoulders at the other patrons. "I'll fix y'all sumpin' to go but cha can't eat it in here."

Kenny Eason leaned over the counter. "What you mean, we can't eat in here? This is 1970 and segregation is over."

The Eason brothers were half gangsters, originally from Newark, New Jersey and they, as all of us, weren't used to anyone talking to them like that without starting a fight. The waitress didn't flinch, and I heard movement, like shuffling behind us. Turning around, I saw about three white men, stroll out of the front door and head for their trucks. The others, in the restaurant, moved towards the rifles on the walls.

The waitress again leaned towards the Eason brothers. "I told you I'll fix y'all boys sumpin to go, but cha can't eat it in here and that's what I mean. And if y'all know what's good for ya. Y'all take what I fix ya and leave."

The men who'd left had returned and were sitting in booths with their shotguns. Unaware of what was taking place around us, Randy stood up next to his brother. Darnell, Clyde, Rock and I grabbed the Easons. "Man, let's get the hell out of here while we can."

"Hell naw!" said Kenny as he turned around and spotted those men with the shoguns, then quickly said, "Yeah, let's get the hell out of here!" which is what we did.

That night we ate out of a little Stop-N-Go market and made our way to our hotel in Laurel Mississippi, talking about our experience at that restaurant the whole way. Things weren't gonna get any better that night either. After confirming the motel information and checking the map, we soon found the Mississippi state line Best Western Lodge and pulled into its huge, almost empty parking lot right outside of the registration desk. It was close to midnight so "McGee, Darnell, Rock and I went in to register the band while the others rested and/or slept in the cars.

We all looked back and forth at each other upon noticing that the guy at the desk wasn't really friendly, as he told us that the rooms had to be paid for up front. This was new to us, but it was late at night and we were too tired to argue about anything. He told us that our rooms were around the side of the hotel, so we took our room keys, got back into our cars and drove around the parking lot to find our room numbers. While riding, someone commented on how far we were driving to get to these rooms. Upon arriving we discovered that we had been put in the back of the motel on the first level. This pissed us off because it had to be the farthest point from the front where the office was located.

Again, too tired to complain we begin to unload our personal bags and head for the rooms. Once the first room was opened Kenny shouted "Fuck this shit. I ain't sleeping in this muthafucka. Look at this shit!" Kenny was pointing at the room's window. As dark as it was outside, you couldn't help but see that the window was void of any outside light and this room and all of our rooms were built on the side of a mountain. Upon further examination of all five rooms, it became clear that none of us had any kind of view of the outside or to an alternative exit, if by chance we needed one. McGee blurted out, "You can stick your hand half way out of the window and touch the mountainside." Also, three of the rooms were half cleaned with un-vacuumed carpets, open plastic drinking cups, two half-made beds and even cigarette butts left in ashtrays.

We hadn't been in Mississippi a full twenty-four hours and we were already being treated like niggers at every turn. Darnell, McGee and I immediately got into the car and made our way back to the front desk to complain about the rooms. When we confronted the desk clerk with our concerns, he started out saying that the rooms were fine, and all of the other rooms were full or reserved so he couldn't change them. We knew he was lying because the parking lot of this two hundred room motel was almost empty, but there was no sense in trying to fight with him.

We were outraged, but still tried to keep cool heads, telling him that this wasn't going to do and demanding he change all of our rooms, till he shouted in an accent, "Look! I done told y'all that I ain't gonna change no gotdamn rooms. And you boys better be glad you got those! Now get on fo I call the police." Left with no option, we went back to the rooms and let everyone know what had taken place and suggested we deal with it since we had no choice.

The following morning, we got up, packed up and quickly left the hotel after trashing most of the rooms in protest of the treatment we had received and sped towards the Alabama state line. Frightening thoughts of how our racial encounters could have turned out burned in my mind as we made our way to our next gig. Although Grand Rapids was and I'm sure still is one of America's most racist cities, we were not used to such blatant prejudice. Arriving at the Mardi Gras in Mobile, Alabama was like stepping into yet another world. We did not know the Mardi Gras was a legendary night club on the southern "chitterling circuit" hosting big-named and up-and-coming artists for decades.

As we pulled up, I abruptly shouted to get everyone's attention as I pointed to the marquee sitting on top of the building. It boasted upcoming two-day performances by Al Green, followed by two days of Johnny Taylor two weeks after we finished our dates there. Darnell and "McGee got out of the car and went to a payphone to call the club owner, Mr. Earls to let him know that we had arrived. He must live close by because it seemed he showed up in less than ten minutes. Mr. Earls was a short very dark-skinned, funny-looking black man, about four-feet-nine or ten, with long hair around the sides of his head which was goose shit slick on top, with long sideburns. Looking like a cross between George Jefferson and black Bozo.

When he opened up the door to the club, we exited our vehicles and entered the club for the once-over. It was a fairly large place, which could seat five-hundred or more people comfortably. This place had a festive, colorful décor and appeared to be a somewhat upscale place. It also had a small hotel upstairs, which too was owned and run by the club owner. We were booked to perform here six nights, Tuesday through Sunday. The contract called for two forty-five-minute sets per night and provided our fee, hotel accommodations throughout our stay and full payment at the end of the six nights. After meeting Mr. Earls, the owner of the Mardi Gras, going over the performance contract and checking out the stage he escorted our entourage upstairs to the hotel and were checked into our rooms.

From first glance we could all see that we were this hotel's only guests.

While unpacking I heard a frightening sound coming from down the halls, so I stuck my head out of my room, as most of our group did, and found the sound was coming from McGee's room. Clyde and I rushed down the hall towards the room followed by the others. Once inside we saw McGee pointing. Clyde and I ducked as we saw something flying towards us. Once it landed on the door behind us we could see that it was a roach. A flying roach! About one to two inches long and it could fly! Alarmed, a few of us rushed back to our own rooms for close inspection and as expected, those damn roaches were found in every room so again everyone converged on McGee's room where we quickly decided we had to get the hell out of this sorry excuse for a hotel.

Grabbing our luggage and meeting in the parking lot, someone tried to find Mr. Earls to let him know that we couldn't stay in his hotel, but he was now nowhere to be found, so we took off in search of acceptable lodging. Our quest didn't take long as we found a Holiday Inn with enough available rooms a few miles from the Mardi Gras. After check-in we all went to find a restaurant to have dinner. After that, some hung out while others returned to the hotel and rested till sound check the next day. Upon our return to the club Mr. Earls greets us by saying, "Helen tells me you guys are really good. She said y'all be tearin' up these dates she booked for you here in the south." All of us nodded in thanks and looked at each other smiling, knowing that we were kickin' ass everywhere we hit.

McGee told Mr. Earls he needed to speak with him about the hotel upstairs, to which Mr. Earls agreed, but said he needed a few minutes to finish re-stocking the bar and he would come to the stage once finished, "So, y'all go on up on that thar stage and let me hear what I done bought." We were good and we knew it. We left our audiences knowing it; calling for more. We made our way to the stage where our equipment had already been set up early that morning by our roadies, took our personal axes and were all set to warm-up and get in sync with the house sound man.

We started by playing "Thank You" by Sly and the Family Stone, then half of "Rainy Night in Georgia" (Rainy Night in Grand Rapids) by Brook Benton, intro through the first chorus of "We're Still Friends" by Donny Hathaway, which was one of the few songs I sang solo lead on, "Deeper" and "XYZ", both TMG's original releases and ended with James Browns "I'm Black and I'm Proud". As we stopped the last song, folks looking in the open door and sitting at the bar yelled and applauded and Mr. Earls came over said, "Now see, that's what I'm talkin' bout. Hee, hee. Ain't nobody lied on y'all! That was quality shit y'all just played, Hee, hee, hee!"

We finished packing up and left for the hotel to rest up to get ready for show time which was at 10pm. There were a few women waiting outside for us; so of course, they went to the hotel too. Later, back at the club it was on and poppin' when we stepped in through the employee entrance. This place was packed on a Tuesday night. The juke box was blastin,' folks were dancin,' the liquor was flowin' and fine women seemed to fill every table in sight. Yeah, it was on and poppin'! We went straight to the dressing room, changed into our costumes, said our usual prayer and hit the stage after the jukebox was turned off and the house lights were dimmed.

Everybody in the band was geeked-up as Mr. Earls stepped onstage and introduced us. To a fair amount of applause, we quickly broke into Sam and Dave's "Hold on, I'm Coming." Folks started clapping and moving their heads, a few couples started dancing in the isles and by the time we got to the chorus, sounded like the whole house was singing

"Hold on, I'm coming, Hold on, I'm coming." That was all she wrote! The Mardi Gras was completely under the control of the TMG's. And that's the way it remained during the second show that night and both shows the next night.

We were now having big fun and our pick of almost every dress that walked through the club's door. But by the end of that second night things abruptly went downhill. Kenny Eason, who was heavily addicted to heroin, got seriously sick and had to be taken to the hospital emergency room where it was discovered that he had contracted hepatitis some time ago. That night he was treated and released with strict instructions to return to Michigan and seek immediate hospitalization for proper treatment or he could die. As if being without our brother and guitarist wasn't enough, our music was always guitar-driven, and the void left by Kenny's absence would certainly grind our train to a halt.

So, in considering who we could possibly get to fill in for Kenny while Rock and Bobby drove him to the airport for his journey home, it was decided we'd call on the only logical choice, Bunny's ex, Kevin Murphy who was the original guitarist for the TMG's. Kevin had left the group a year or so prior to my becoming a member, during his tenure, Kevin played lead guitar and Kenny played bass guitar but switched to lead and brought in his younger brother to play lead upon Kevin's departure.

After Darnell and "McGee contacted Kevin and his agreeing to join us in Alabama to finish out the dates of our southern tour, the transition of getting Kenny home in Grand Rapids safely and Kevin to Mobile with us took a little over thirty-six hours so, needless to say the TMG's were the guitarless TMG's for that Thursday night's shows. Let's just say as tight as this band was, we knew something was missing and it showed.

After making it through both sets, we quickly headed back to the hotel, critiquing our night's performance all the way. After a brief band meeting in McGee's room, each of us went to our own rooms, sad about Kenny's illness and absence and anxiously awaiting Kevin's arrival and possible rescue of the band, I went to sleep. Next morning, I was awakened by pounding on my door. It was Darnell and Kevin, who had just arrived from the airport. Of course, this was a welcomed wake-up because now we could see if we could salvage this date and the remaining dates on our summer tour.

I quickly got showered and dressed to join everyone else for breakfast, only to find that once again, I was the only one ready to go, with the exception of Darnell, Kevin, McGee and Rock, who were all waiting in the hotel lobby. Once the band members assembled we hopped in our cars and drove to a nearby restaurant. During breakfast we all welcomed Kevin, thanked him for coming on such short notice and began to get him up to speed on our set list of songs and who did what in the performance thereof. We even replaced a few songs that Kenny sang lead on with songs Kevin sang or played lead on when he was a TMG. "McGee called Mr. Earls and made arrangements for someone to meet us at the club to unlock the doors so that we could start rehearsing as soon as we were finished eating.

Once at the club, the rehearsal went well. We rehearsed from early that morning until around three pm, making sure Kevin knew that show from top to bottom. From that point, the day passed by quickly and before I knew it we were ending the second show. Other than a few kinks that no one noticed but the band, all went well, and Kevin had made it through his first night. He really proved to be a trooper, playing the hell out of his guitar, holding down his vocal parts and being the entertainer, we knew and needed him to be.

Well, the music got better but conditions didn't. By Friday, we were running out of money for per diems and incidentals like the cleaning of our stage costumes, and those daily long-distance calls to Jackie, Mrs. Greer and Grand Rapids to check on Kenny. At Saturday afternoon sound check, all hell broke loose! "McGee and Darnell approached Mr. Earls to ask for an advance on the weeks' pay so that we could get through the next two days.

Mr. Earls started yelling so loud at them we could hear him from the other side of the club as his two employees did. "What the fuck do y'all want now?"

Both "McGee and Darnell were a little stunned by Mr. Earl's comeback to their question, as all of us looked at each other wondering has this nigga gone crazy. All of us stopped what we were doing and rushed to where they were standing. Mr. Earls continued talkin' smack saying, "Look! I been puttin' up with y'alls prima donna shit since y'all got here. First my hotel ain't good enough for yo black asses, then yo junkie-assed guitar player done fucked up and got sick, you bring this new guitar playing muthafucka in here and he ain't shit. And now you gonna ask me for money? Tell you what,

I'll pay y'all what you're due when y'all finish up tomorrow night; that's what I can do."

Clearly outdone and angry at all this man had the nerve to say to us, Darnell, trying to keep his composure, continues to explain our position about the clubs' hotel problems and the fact that we need money because we had to spend our petty cash on food, flying Kenny back home and mostly on accommodations, which were clearly supposed to be covered by our performance contract, and now we were broke... but Mr. Earls wasn't hearing it.

"Y'all northern niggas must think y'all shit don't stank, don't cha?" He said with a smirk on his face. "Who y'all think you are, the Temptations? Y'all finish up for the week, I'll pay y'all and y'all can go on wherever the hell yo next show is." Angrily, McGee began to shout demands at Mr. Earls to "pay us what you owe us for the days we had already performed, and we'll leave."

Mr. Earls shouted back, I don't owe y'all shit and y'aa ain't getting shit from me!" At that point, we had all heard enough and the entire band surrounded Mr. Earls to prevent something crazy from happening. Out of nowhere, Clyde, then Jeff, and even Kevin began to shout at Mr. Earls, but he stupidly stood his ground.

Randy shouted, "This short, sawed-off, black bozo-looking muthafucka ain't getting away with this shit," as he began to lunge at this man. We grabbed him and held him back because we knew it was over if he had gotten Mr. Earls.

Almost in unison everyone yelled, "You gonna give us our money!", as we backed Mr. Earl up against a wall. Now, in fear for his life, Mr. Earl pleaded "alright, alright. Ain't nothing but a misunderstanding. That's all it is. I'll give y'all the money and you's can get the hell out of my place; just back up and let me get the money out of my safe." Although Rock and Bobby followed him to his office door, once inside Mr. Earls quickly let us know we had made a life-altering mistake. Next minute we saw Rock and Bobby backing away from that office door as Mr. Earl emerged pointing a double-barreled shot gun at us. We all leaned back. I raised my hands.

"Since y'all young muthafuckas gone come up here in my house and demand that I give yous something I'm gone give yous this. These last couple of nights y'all didn't play worth shit and" pointing at Kevin, "y'all could've left his good guitar playin' ass at home for my money. Tell yous what, I'm gone give yous young niggers some lead in y'all asses if y'all don't get yo raggedy shit off of my stage and get the hell out of my place."

Enough said! We all packed up and loaded our instrument trailer faster than we ever had before and left Mobile, not looking back till we pulled over at a truck stop at the Alabama/Mississippi state line. Since we didn't get paid for that whole week at the Mardi Gras and had to spend what we had to survive our week there, we couldn't pool together enough money to get back to Georgia or to buy food for everybody. Some of the guys had to call home and have money wired through Western Union for food and gas. It was really hot and humid, and we were hungry, tired and sweaty; as we waited for hours at that truck stop until the fellas called home again and were told money had been sent.

First, we ate; then we drove straight to Cartersville. Fortunately, Jackie and his band were on tour, based in

Memphis and playing dates in the surrounding areas for that whole month, so we could fill for his house band.

Playing at Jackie's for that next week was fun, especially since we didn't have to run from any more shot guns. Again, we stayed and rehearsed at the house in Cartersville by day and played at the club at night. And then again, there was Sandy, living three doors down and waiting for me to call her again. This summer was one I was never going to forget or ever really get over because life had finally opened up all of its doors and windows for me to see everything it had to offer, good, bad and ugly; and still I vowed to give my life to music.

Throughout that week of playing at Jackie's club, there were a few music legends like saxophonist King Curtis, bassist Willie Weeks, singer Millie Jackson, and even Junior Walker, among others who passed through and sat in with us for a song or two.

I have this wonderful, profound memory of meeting this go-go dancer named Phyllis who sometimes danced at the club. She came up to me, introduced herself and struck up a conversation in her thick southern accent with "where y'all from?" What stood out most to me about Phyllis after her genuine compassion for people, was her attitude overall and that perfect little butt. We talked through her and my every break and continued well into the wee hours of the morning at the band house. She even wound up staying with me for a few nights before the TMG's had to leave for our next performance date. Phyllis was about four-feet-eight inches tall, light-skinned, with flaming red shoulder-length straight hair, the cutest smile and the body of life, once I got her out of those clothes.

I remember one-day Phyllis brought her sister Carla to the band house with her. She too was, friendly, beautiful and also spoke with a heavy southern accent. I introduced her to everybody in the house and she joined in a conversation between Jeff, Clyde, Bobby and Darnell, as Phyllis and I eased on into my bedroom where we stayed for the next few hours. When she and I finally submerged, we found that Carla had hooked up with Darnell and they were talking and laughing on the front porch. They signaled for Phyllis and me to join them. Carla starts joking in her country slang, "Phyllis just got some, Phyllis just got some," to which we all burst out laughing.

The four of us sat, laughed and talked on that pouch for a while till we all decided to go and get something to eat before taking the sisters home. They lived in Rome Georgia, which is roughly thirty miles from Cartersville, so it was a quick after dinner trip, with the girls directing and narrating every turn and landmark. The funniest part of the trip was when we drove past the police station. At that time, it was a small refurbished gas station with a two-car parking stall with one car in it, like something out of Mayberry RFD. When Darnell or I asked about the one lone car, Carla quickly blurted in that thick accent, "That's Parker's car. He de only police we gat!"

I don't know who started first, but Darnell or I were laughing loudly when Phyllis input, "That car don't move much 'cause it be right there every time we go by; and it don't even have no radio in it." Through my laughter, I happened to say, "He don't have no radio? Why?" The sisters yelled out in their own country chorus "Cause he ain't gat nobady to caul!"

By this time, we were all laughing uncontrollably, as the sisters motioned that we were approaching their front door. When we finally regained our composure, Darnell and I walked the sisters to the house, stood on their front porch, coupled off and talked a short while longer till it was time to hit the road. As Darnell and I started on our journey home, we began to discuss our surroundings and how far from Grand Rapids we were. We realized that, although our directions were easy enough to follow, we had been so consumed, chatting with our dates that neither of us paid much attention to the lone backwoods country roads that we had traveled to get Phyllis and Carla home.

After riding past a few blocks of small homes, we soon found the road which had brought us into Rome. As soon as we made our turn, everything was suddenly pitch black, as there were no street lights, no homes, no business, no anything but randomly lit sparse farmland and the headlights of Darnell's car on this road to the state highway, which would take us back to Cartersville.

As we drove on we were talking about the two sisters we'd just left and about this adventure we were enjoying here in the south. As we continued driving we saw a light in the distance. We initially thought the fields had lights, then we thought they were on fire but the farther we drove, the larger the light got till we could finally recognize what it was. The sky was lit up around this large field, little more than a half mile away from the road.

Darnell pulled the car over and stopped as we could make out that this field was full of hooded men with torches burning. We weren't sure if our lights had been seen, so Darnell turned them off as we focused our eyes in disbelief. We were shocked to hear each other say simultaneously "It's the Klu Klux Klan!" We had run up on a hood and sheet-wearing, crosses and torch-burning Klu Klux Klan Rally.

"Greg, that's the Klan and if they see us, we some dead men." Needless to say, once we really realized what was happening, Darnell sped into the darkness without turning the cars headlights back on, traveling for what seemed like forever, until we were surrounded once again by stark blackness. We finally arrived at state highway 411, turned onto it without slowing down and made our way back to the safety of Jackie's house in Cartersville.

The next day, as Darnell and I shared our adventure, our plight with the rest of our crew, everyone listened in disbelief. I know my nerves were still messed up when I saw Phyllis that next night and told her what had happened. When I finished telling her, she commented, "Oh Yeah." Like this shit was an every week occurrence for black folks down there.

As the band's last week in Cartersville was coming to a close, Phyllis and I didn't know how, when, or even if we would see each other again; so, the last couple of nights after leaving the club, we would stay in bed, without getting up for food or drink; bathroom breaks only until we both had to get to the club for work. "Greg, I want y'all to know that y'all make me happy. What I like about y'all is y'all ain't lied to me and told me y'all in love and y'all gone come back and marry me. Women really hates that, and that's why they end up getting snappy with men, especially y'all musicians. I know what this is about and so do y'all, so let's not play games. Never lie to women because it makes them hate y'all. They may not like the truth, but when y'all tell them the truth, they learn to deal with that. I like y'all and if y'all want me to come sees y'all while you down here call me. I'll be there."

Phyllis cried when we left and I knew, if I ever came through Cartersville again, I'd find her. It was time for the TMG's to move on. Our next date was a one-nighter in a predominately jazz club called Dante's, down in Atlanta's Underground, then another one-nighter with Clarence Carter in Nashville Tennessee. After that, we moved around the South doing a few more shows, playing covers and our original songs around Tennessee, and finally heading back to Michigan.

Chapter 6

1971/TMG's/Grand Valley

rriving back in Grand Rapids, I temporarily moved back
to my mom's house, preparing for my last year of high
school. I was in limbo, just hanging loose, close to home for a
week or so. The TMG's had scheduled rehearsals, but no
immediate gigs so I had only limited responsibilities. Once
school started I ran into April. She was small, about five feet
two without shoes, brown- skinned, thick and fine to me. I
had met and hung out with her in a group setting a few times
before the TMG's summer tour but now we began dating and
seeing each other on a more consistent, exclusive level.

April lived a few blocks from my mom with her
grandmother and younger brother Todd who was my
younger brother Eddie's best friend. She and I would skip
school and wind up in bed at her house till close to time for
her grandmother to get home. After sex we would laugh and
talk about everything but mostly our dreams with me always
telling her, "I'm gonna be a big star and you can be right there
with me if you're good."

A couple of times we got busted in bed by her cousin
Ester, but she never told on us, and still somehow April's

grandmother seemed to know something was going on as she would give us this look and say things like, "Alright now. Y'all be careful. Don't you two forget that I was young once."

When she was gone, we'd look at each other, puzzled by what she might really know. Like most young couples in the dating stage, we did everything we could together and when we couldn't see each other, we were on the phone as much as possible as the weeks speed by.

Fortunately, after this little tour, I had finally saved enough money to move into my own apartment, so the first place I went was back to Mr. Strickland's on Paris and Wealthy. He wasn't there when I arrived, so I went to the back of the building to see if my apartment was gone. To my surprise it was vacant, so I left my phone number with a note explaining that I had come by and if the apartment or any other was available I still wanted it and was financially ready. He didn't call me back by the second day, but to my surprise he had stopped by for a visit with my mom. He told her he was giving me the apartment and left the keys with her. He told her to tell me he'd come by the apartment sometime over the next week so that we could finish the business. Finally, I had my first apartment.

Although we remain lifelong friends, I don't remember ever quitting the TMG's but when I finally looked up, they were no longer a part of my world, with the exception of Darnell and I hooking up and hitting the jam session from time to time. I felt good because I had my apartment, I had my girl and mostly I had my music and I knew it was going to take me where I wanted to go. I was also happy because while I was on tour my grandfather had moved in with my mom; so, I would get to see more of him; and my brother Art had been paroled from prison and was getting his life together.

The clubs I'd been playing most of my life were still flourishing and I enjoyed going to them to check out the bands, many of them passing through Grand Rapids. I helped Art move into an apartment with our friends, James Dumas and Duane Parnell. The four of us had hung out from time to time before Art had gotten locked up. Once again, the four of us got together and hung out like old times. One night we went down to the White Rabbit and a band from Akron, Ohio came through called Just Us.

I liked their sound and approached them after the first set, only to find that they had heard of me and my trumpet playing before they came to Grand Rapids. I had made it a habit of always carrying my mouthpiece, with my horn nearby, and after talking with them for a while, they asked if I wanted to sit in with them, to which I said "Yes." I played on stage with them most of the night. I knew most of the top forty songs they performed and punted well on those songs which were new to me, so I fit right in. When this second set ended they huddled together as I cleaned and put away my horn.

"Greg."

I turned to face them. The leader, Greg Stocks, who was also a trumpeter and one of the bands lead vocalists asked, "You want to join our band?"

I'd just got off the road with the TMG's and I was free, so I said, "Sure. When?"

"Right now."

They were all smiling and nudging each other. I informed them that I had a few loose ends to close, but I could join them in Akron in a few days; so, "Let me do this and I'll join you all in less than a week."

They wrote down and gave me all of their contact information, we shook hands and I split. I was so hyped up when I got to my apartment that night, I wanted to call April, but it was too late, so I'd have to wait till morning. I drifted off to sleep thinking about how great it was going to be playing with Just Us. The next day I was awakened by my phone. It was April calling to see what I had to do that day. She said that she had stayed at home from school hoping that I would come by, so I told her, "I have to take a shower and I'm on my way. You're not gonna believe what I've got to tell you."

I cleaned myself up and made my way to April's house. When I told her my news she wasn't as happy for me as I wanted her to be, but she did understand and finally accepted that I had to go. We spent the rest of that day making love and talking about her visiting me if I had not come back in a few weeks.

We reluctantly got dressed and I got out of there and headed to my mom's just before her grandmother came home from work but not before promising I'd call when I got to Akron. When I got to my mom's, I told her that I was going back on the road to play. I gave her the details, she gave me her blessings and two days later I arrived in Akron by Greyhound. Once there, I went straight to the band's rehearsal, reacquainted myself to all of the guys, got a rundown of what to expect about my living and working conditions and finally I called April as I said I would. Being the new guy, I immediately befriended the other outsider, bass player, David Holmes, from Brooklyn, New York.

I stayed with Just Us in Akron for about a month. It was a gig full of promises, but little work, little money. I stayed in Greg's parent's home initially but had to leave after a week or so. Through the band I met this chick, with whom I 'd spent a night in her apartment, but it was full of roaches, so I left there and stayed at the band house until I couldn't take living like that anymore. One day I checked in with my mom and spoke with my uncle Albert who was there at the time. In our catching up, he asked me how things were going, and I told him, "Thing are alright here, just looking forward to this show we have in Canton this weekend and'...."

But, with him knowing me, he obviously heard something in my voice and cut me off saying, "Hey, I just bought a brand-new Delta Eighty-Eight and I need to put it on the road, so why don't I come down and check your show out?"

"You know that would be great, Albert. I'd love to see you." I responded,

"Done deal then; why don't you give me the info on where you're playing and me and Della will see you at your show."

"Cool. We're playing at The Baby Grand." As I was reading the show flyer to him I was thinking how much I love him, as even though he's my uncle he's always been a big brother to me, as well. He felt I needed him then, and he's coming.

After speaking to him, the rest of that week my heart was a little lighter and my head became a whole lot clearer. As he said, Albert was at the club to see Just Us perform the following Friday night in Canton, Ohio. He had brought his soon to be wife Idella, already my aunt because she was my stepfather's sister, and another carload of his friends. I heard him asking for me outside of the dressing room after the first set, so I quickly went out to find him, invited him in and I introduced him to my band mates.

When the show was over I rode with my folks from the club to the band house and by the time we reached there I had decided it was time to put this band behind me and roll back to Grand Rapids. So, we picked up my clothes, I said my goodbyes to David and whomever else was there and hit the road with my uncle and his party with Akron and Just Us, now a part of my past. I hadn't been home from Akron but a few weeks when James Burress contacted me.

'Greg, I have something for you if you're interested."

"I'm interested in anything, right now James."

"I can help get you into Grand Valley College because even though you have poor attendance, when you finally decide to go to school, your grades are good, so we should be able to work with them to get you in."

I heard the catch in his voice. "Okay, what do I have to do?"

"All you have to do is get your GED and you can start in February; and since Grand Valley is only about twenty miles away, you can still do your gigs here every weekend."

My high school class would be graduating in June, it was now only January; and second to playing my music, getting an education, a degree was always something I planned to do, just how I didn't know, until now.

"I'll do it. This is just what I need."

"There's something else I need you to do."

"Anything."

"The people who are funding this program need to see a face and hear a candidate speak. I want you to address them."

"What do I talk about?"

"Talk about your experiences in high school and how going to Grand Valley will set you on your path."

"That'll be easy."

I'd spoken to James Burress on a Monday and I addressed the civic group on that following Thursday. It was the easiest speech I'd ever given because I spoke about myself, my love of words, music and how the school system hadn't provided a place for students like myself. I made my refrain, just like a refrain in a song, how college, was the key for different students to develop their skills and gifts.

Mr. Burress hugged me when the evening ended. "That was a home run Greg. I knew I could count on you."

I was pleased, because he was pleased, and it was another step in my life. I had to spend a few days in the Grand Rapids Public Library, studying, in order to get my GED, but like always, I applied myself and retained enough information. Studying there was kind of boring and the lessons were easy, so I easily passed the test and was soon on my way to college. The weekend before packing up and heading off to Grand Valley, among other things, Bobby came to mind.

I had missed my boy, my partner in musical crime all that time I'd been gone, so I just dropped what I was doing and went to look for him. First, I sought out his close friend, Wilbert Haines, knowing that's who Bobby would be hanging with after I left, but Wilbert had not seen him lately and had no idea where he could be found. I drove around to Franklin Park, the Trotter's pool hall on Franklin and Eastern, among other places he and I could be found prior to my leaving for Akron.

With my horn in hand, I headed down to the jam session at the Golden Glow, where I quickly found out that there was no jam session today, so I turned to leave when I heard someone yell, "You finally made it back from Africa didn't you?" as he began to laugh really loud. As soon as I heard that laugh, I instantly knew it was Ed Honeycutt, so I turned around. When we got close enough we hugged, and he waived for the waitress as we sat down for a drink and a chat.

First thing Ed said as we sat down was, "I knew that was you as soon as I saw that horn in your hand. Hey Greg, come on and do this gig with me tonight?" Once he told me the when, the where, and how much, I gladly nodded my head in agreement as we continued to catch-up. After spending nearly half an hour with Ed, I asked him if he had seen Bobby lately; but he too told me that he hadn't seen him in a while.

Once we finished our drinks and said our goodbyes until tonight, I spoke with a few other folks I knew in the bar and left heading to the Track Two to see if I would find Bobby there. When I arrived, parked, grabbed my trumpet and headed for the door I ran into a few people coming out. I asked about a jam session but was told there was no jam session there anymore; so, I went in to find out what had happened and why.

There were less than a dozen folks in the place with a few at the bar and three folks around the pool table, but I recognized no one, so I exited as quickly as I had come in. With no jam session at either place that day and no one had seen Bobby around, I finally went to the DeBarge house; and although neither Bunny nor Tommy were nowhere to be found I spent time catching up with Randy, Marty and James about what had been going on since I left. I was told that Bobby was with his cousin Andre, who he'd been hanging with most of the time since I left. Finding them was easy because I had hung out at Andre's apartment before leaving with the TMG's and I knew they'd be in the basement on the instruments.

When I arrived at Andre's place, I rang the bell, knocked on the door and waited patiently till Andre came and opened it. There was a difference though in Bobby. His speech was a little slurred. He and Andre were glassy eyed. I found out they'd been drinking cough syrup, along with smoking weed. My older musician friends had taught me syrup was the appeasement for junkies, or heroin addicts, when they couldn't get a fix. Bobby and Andre drank it to augment alcohol or anything else. What I didn't like was its effect on Bobby's singing voice. He was "pitchy" and had trouble hitting his high notes. I told him what I was hearing and being Mr. Fix it, he played it off by saying he wouldn't drink it when he sang.

Playing together though, despite that syrup slur, was vibrant and as the three of us jammed, a light blinked in my head.

"Bobby and Andre, let's form a band."

Andre asked, "Where are we going to play?"

"Let me worry about that. Besides Tommy, who are we gonna get to play with us?"

Bobby's wide grin let me know he had something in mind. "Wilbert Haynes on guitar and our cousin Stanley Hood," Bobby said.

Stanley, a saxophonist, who had recently moved to Grand Rapids from Lansing Michigan, was available and always ready to play. "Let's get everybody together and we got a band."

Andre played a roll on his drums and said, "It's a family band except for you and Wilbert."

I looked at Bobby who'd heard what I'd heard from Andre. We were always like that, tuned in to something happening, at the same time. I said it before he did.

"Two and the Family. That's the name of our band. Two and the Family. A moment of clarity passed between us. This time in my life was very full and I had so much going on; starting a new band, a new job and soon to start college. I got a full-time job at Keebler bakery and played gigs with The Bar-Tee's, what I called the pick-up band with Mache and Honeycutt, at nights.

Two and The Family rehearsed as much as possible and we had a special sound because we were young, everyone could sing, harmonize and play instruments. I discovered James Burress had bought into a club, along with my longtime family friend, Raphael Gooch. Raphael, though a few years older than me, I knew well, as his momma, Miss Lilly Mae, was one of the few neighborhood moms where my extended family lived on Hall Street when I was nine or ten. Miss Lilly Mae would protect us, pamper us, discipline us and made all of the neighborhood kids feel loved. Raphael and his younger brother, Brock, grew up close with my uncles Oscar, Albert and Sylvester, with Art and me as tag-alongs, so we were like family.

They called this nightclub the Track Two. Well-known and unknown artists like Sonny Stitt, Nancy Wilson, Junior. Walker, and other headliners came through there. One day I went to the club and found James in the office. He stood, as usual, and extended his hand.

"How's school?"

"Easy and a bit boring; however, I know it has a purpose though, so I'll handle it."

"I know you will. Is everything okay?"

"Yes, I just wanted to discuss some business with you."

He leaned forward. "I'm all ears."

"I have a new band, called Two and The Family. Most of the musicians are from the Abney's and the DeBarge family."

"You must have Andre and your boy, Bobby."

"Them and Bobby's brother Tommy on bass, and another cousin on sax. Then there's, me on trumpet and Wilbert Haynes on guitar."

James held up two fingers.

"That's the Two and The Family."

We laughed together.

"That's it."

"Everybody in that band can play, Greg."

"And most can sing too. " He opened his calendar. "And you want to play here?"

"Yes sir. I spoke with Raphael and he said whenever you guys had an opening we'd be called, so I'm already on your books I just wanted your support."

He studied his calendar. "Okay, you know the booking is Raphael's thing, but I'll check with him and maybe we can do this. Mondays, as you know, are dark nights for musicians, so you can play then. We'll call you if someone doesn't show and if you want, you can be the opening band for whoever doesn't have one. I know Raphael told you that the money's not going to be long, Greg."

"He did. But I also know you two will be fair to us."

Standing, we shook hands and I nearly jumped for joy knowing I'd just booked my first gig for the band. Telling Bobby and the family about the gigs at the Track Two motivated all of us and we practiced hard. Having the DeBarge's and their cousins made the singing part easy because everyone in the band could sing and we harmonized easily. Bobby was true to his word and was never high on syrup during rehearsals. At our first gig we set the house on fire and every time we played after that was like a house party.

I was a couple of months shy of my eighteenth birthday. Getting my GED, during January and playing with BarTee's and Two and The Family. Fact is, I was supposed to graduate high school the coming June but instead I entered Grand Valley College, as an English major in February of 1972.

Grand Valley was what I needed at the time. I moved into a campus dorm room with an old friend, Bradley Moore. I've always been faced with forks in the road and being a college student didn't stop that tendency. Once I settled in at Grand Valley I found that I had many friends there who I'd grown up with, including the first true love of my life, Tracie Babcock, her best friend Lynn Wilson, and Marvin Johnson, who was a jokester from my family's church, Peanut Walker and many others, whose names elude me at the moment.

I met and befriended a lot of folks from other cities in Michigan, as well as folks from across the US. Going to Grand Valley was initially difficult, because, per always, school was too easy for me and I had to force myself to attend the classes; not because of all of the fine women I'd encountered there, but all in all, I was having the time of my life!

After classes were paid for and books were bought from my financial aid checks, I bought my first car from my mother. It was a 1969 Buick Lesabre that my step-father had given her when he bought a new car. She sold me the car because it needed some work and she hadn't gotten her driver's license yet anyway. Little did I know that the car was really a piece of shit that smoked so much, one friend, Irving Junior laughed saying that he "knew it was me coming up the street from three or four miles away." The damn thing needed a valve job which, of course was not in a college student's budget; and I didn't know about it till after I bought it. Anyway, I drove it to get to and from the city for rehearsals, gigs, shopping and when Marvin, Peanut and I had no other ride to get away from campus.

Besides my studies, once again I returned to gambling in order to supplement my lack of income. When almost broke, I quickly pulled together enough folks on campus to start a Tonk game. Marvin, Peanut, Hook, and a heavy brother from Detroit would strike up a game in the cafeteria, in the commons, in the dorm hallway and even in the laundry room. Didn't matter; game's on!

Even though I had a music theory class where we only talked about instruments, I still kept my trumpet at hand and would whip it out of my case and play whenever I found the right moment. Going to Grand Valley soon became fun because Marvin and I made it fun for ourselves and anybody, male or female, who wanted to hang with us. So, you gots to know there were always more females.

Most time in my life, I've worn caps or hats. I even wore hippie attire and carried a shoulder bag, from my early teens into my twenties. I remember I had this leather hat with a wide flat brim that I was wearing from the start of my days at Grand Valley. I was also wearing a small beard during those days. Well Marvin, being his normal funny/crazy self, messed around and looked at my hat, my glasses and my beard and blurted out "Billy Paul" in front of everyone within earshot and we all fell out laughing; so, from that day on my on-campus nickname was Billy Paul. That's what my new friends called me, and many new people came to know me by that name, which was after the singer of the hit song "Me and Mrs. Jones". My first year at Grand Valley really went by fast. In, or better yet, at school during the week and playing with Two and the Family or the BarTees over the weekend my life was great, and still moving fast.

During my second semester I get a call from Darnell Wyrick. He had stayed with the TMG's until their recent break up, then played with a few different acts, but was now frustrated with the lack of bands there were in our area for him to play with; so, he decides that he too should go back to school. I hooked him up with Mag Dolly, the counselor James Burress put me with to get into Grand Valley. She immediately helped Darnell get the grants and financial support he needed to get into Grand Valley. At that same time, Brad, my then roommate, told me that he was moving off campus at the end of the current semester, so without any issue I set it up so that Darnell could become my new roomie. That was really great because not only did Darnell and I have a long positive friendship, but we could now practice new songs and horn techniques after classes, and also drive in to the city on weekends for the jam session at the Golden Glow to sit in with different bands who came through the Track Two.

Sadly, this only lasted for one semester because one night close to the end of that school term, while I was playing a gig with Two and the Family, Darnell had sat in with a well-known Ohio band, whom had a reputation for killin' on stage, called TNT Flashers. This was a seven-man self-contained show band who already had two trumpets, but after hearing Darnell they wanted him bad and asked him to go on the road with them. Darnell jumped at the opportunity to play and left school to join the band.

Though feeling a little sad to see him go, I was really happy for him because I knew, like me, playing music is all we were really about. As I knew he would, before Darnell left, he assured me that if anything opened up or he ran across an opportunity that fit me, he'd be calling; and off he went. My next few weeks were full with tests and exams and weekend dates with Two and the Family.

Sometimes Bobby would find a ride out to Grand Valley, but mostly I drove my old raggedy car to town at least a couple times a week so that we could rehearse, hit the clubs for a bit, or just hang out.

Before I noticed, I was enjoying my second year at Grand Valley when one night the phone rang.

"Hey college boy. Are you still a musician?"

I recognized the voice immediately. It was Darnell Wyrick.

"What's happening, Darnell? You know me, I'm a musician first and everything else second."

"That's just what I want to hear. Something's up and I need to know if you're interested."

"Shoot."

Darnell was always a solid, serious cat and I knew if he was calling me, it was something good.

"I'm in Phoenix, Arizona, with the TNT Flashers. A spot just opened in the horn section and I immediately thought of bad Greg. You interested?"

"Yes. Of course, but it depends on a couple of things. Are we going to be touring, playing around Phoenix, or what?"

Darnell started chuckling.

"Greg, it's better than that. We're connected to Barry White and we're waiting for him to bring us to L.A. to sign us on his new production company. You ready for that?"

The name Barry White made my ears ring. Looking around my dorm room, I focused on Darnell. Although he was now on the other side of the country, before he left Grand Rapids we had come to be tight, living and playing together; and we supported each other in every way. Grand Valley, and a degree, represented a stable future, but music was my one and only love.

"Yea, I'm ready but…"

"Okay, I'll call you and tell you when the ticket will be there."

"Okay, what happened to the other horn player? People don't walk out on opportunities like this."

"He and the keyboard player got tired of waiting and lost faith. You know, the whole stability thing. It'll get us every time."

I heard but didn't really hear the last part of his sentence because my mind locked on the words, the keyboard player.

"So, you need a keyboard player too?"

"Yea."

"Good because I got somebody, and you already know what he can do."

"Who's that?"

"Bobby"

He inhaled and held his breath. "Bobby DeBarge?"

"Yea man. Bobby DeBarge. He's better now than he was before, and you know how he can sing."

The dead silence sound coming through the phone indicated he was thinking about Bobby.

"Darnell. You know I've been waiting for this call and I'm excited about the opportunity, but I can't leave Bobby here in this Grand Rapids shit."

"I don't know Greg" He said with a big sigh. "But I will see if the other guys in the band are game and I'll get back to you."

"Cool."

Hanging up the phone, I thought about Bobby, and how it had come to me, that God had placed Bobby in my life for a reason. I knew the reason was for me to take care of him and our destinies were also linked. He was a younger brother to me. I had to look out for him and walk with him through doors that he would not be able to open on his own, but doors that would also benefit him. I could clearly see Bobby had overcome more, at his age, than anyone I knew; and because of the years of psychological damage, he didn't have the personality to promote himself.

Next day after class I got that call from Darnell.

"Your ticket will be there tomorrow, so you have two days to get here.

We don't have a ticket for Bobby because the guys had somebody from here, but I told them you didn't want to come without Bobby. Can you guys come up with some money? Are you even sure about him Greg? You know I saw some stuff."

I stopped him. "Have I ever done anything that that wasn't reliable or straight up?"

"No."

"Then trust me with Bobby, and hopefully we'll both see you in two days."

191

"Hey Greg, why don't you go and see if Mr. Champ can help?"

"Yeah, I already checked and got a number on him and if I can't figure out another way, I'll go see him tomorrow."

We hung up and after packing my things, I left the dorm room, the dorm, the campus and Allendale… never to return as a student. Leaving Grand Valley, bags packed, horn in hand and the decision in my pocket, I sought those who meant the most to me to share my news.

The first place I went was directly to the DeBarge house, at Six Sixteen Giddings, to talk with Bobby. I was speeding on the freeways, then on the streets with so much smoke coming out of the back of my raggedy ass car that I know folks thought my hoopty was on fire.

Fortunately, Bobby was at home in nowhere near a good mood, as I heard him yelling and cussin' from across the street, as soon as I turned my car engine off. I don't know what was wrong, but it was bad, because I as I got closer I heard more yelling, something breaking; and when I knocked on the door I saw the curtains open and close quickly, as if someone was checking to see if I was the police.

Whoever was in there took their time to respond to my knocking and when Bobby finally opened the door, his eyes were red; his hands were trembling frantically, and he had this mean look on his face, which took a while for him to break; even though it was me. He gestured for me to come on in, but I quickly said, "No man you need to come out here. I've got some important talk for you."

He blurted back, "I know it's gotta be better than this shit I'm dealing with here; give me a second, let me get a jacket on." I stepped back out of the doorway and waited on the porch for a few minutes till he came out. I hit him quick with, "You say you wanted to play music, right?"

"You know that. Let me have a cigawreck, Greg."

As I pulled my hand from my pocket and passed him my pack I continued... "Well, we've got a chance. We got a gig with Darnell Wyrick and this band called TNT Flasher. They want us to join them in Phoenix, Arizona in a couple of days to get tight before we sign with Barry White's new production company."

"Greg, stop bullshittin." He looked straight into my eyes as I just stood there. "You ain't kidding, are you? How'd they know about us?"

"Darnell's in the band, he called me, asked me to join cause their trumpet player quit and I told him about you."

Bobby leaped from the porch, past all of the stairs, onto the sidewalk and we laughed loudly.

"There's one catch, we've still got to get you there."

"They didn't send me a ticket, Greg?"

"They didn't know anything about you until I proposed you to Darnell, then he proposed it to them, only to be told that they couldn't afford to pay for both of us. They were gonna hire this guy from Phoenix who had played a few gigs with them since their keyboard player left with the trumpet player, but I convinced Darnell that I'd find the money and we'd get you there; so, he convinced the band to hold off on the other guy. You know how that is. So, we have one day to get that money, get ready and be on that flight together."

"But Greg, you know I ain't got no money."

"Neither do I, Bobby; but somehow, I'll get the money, you just get ready."

"Shit, I'm ready now. Let's go."

We both laughed a big, hearty laugh and hung out in front of his house for a little while longer, talking about what we were getting ready to do. Then, I realized since I've talked my way up on this, by hook or by crook, I'd better get that money; so, I decided to get going and I told him I'd pick him up early in the morning.

I left there and while driving away it dawned on me; all this talk about flying and I had never flown in my life, but I wasn't about to be afraid, I was getting my ass on that plane, or whatever else it took to get me and Bobby to Phoenix, Arizona. By now it was late, so I decided to use the rest of the evening to make a few stops to say goodbye to my uncles Sylvester, Albert and Oscar. I ran by Art's to let him know that he could use my car while I was gone, as long as he took care of it.

I ran by an after-hours house to see if I could run into a couple of folks who owed me money and if I could win a little shooting craps to get that plane ticket tomorrow. I was dead tired once I made it back to mom's house in the wee hours of the morning, so I sat down and that was all I remember. I woke up just before noon the next day still in my clothes, so I hurried to my car, grabbed my packed bag, carried it inside and up to the bathroom to bathe, shave and get ready for my last full day in Grand Rapids.

When I was done, I looked for mom, but she was nowhere to be found. My grandfather, who now also lived there was sitting at the kitchen table.

"Boy what's got you all lit up? What is it?"

Sitting next to him at the table, I placed my hand on his and said, "granddad, I've got this opportunity to go play with a band in Phoenix, Arizona, who's waiting to be signed by Barry White. They've already sent me a ticket."

He grasped my hand. "and what about school? You're doing so well, and Mr. Burress and that girl Magnolia worked hard to get you in there."

"I'm leaving school, granddad."

Letting go of my hand, he touched my face, then replaced his hand on mine. "I don't agree with this Greg, because an education is something no one can ever take from you and you can build your life from having it. I think you should finish school and get a good job. But if that's what you want to do, go ahead. I hope you don't live to regret this."

"Granddad, it's what I've got to do; so I won't regret it." I left the kitchen, and looking back at him, I saw him bury his face in his hands as he had often done when he was in deep thought.

I too was in deep thought, as my grandfather was a good, strong man sacrificed his childhood dream of becoming a singer, who overcame the obstacles of growing up poor and black in the south, to finding and holding stable employment and taking care of and raising his eleven children. I always respected him and wanted his respect and sub-consciously his approval.

After granddad, telling the others should have been easy, but it wasn't. Neither was it easy finding money for Bobby's plane ticket out of Grand Rapids. One day didn't leave much time for either. Putting one foot before the other, I headed to mother's house to tell her my plans.

Forever encouraging, she told me to go on and follow my dreams and "Just pray every day and ask the lord to guide you, and you'll be just fine. To those who much is given, much is expected, and you've been blessed and given in abundance by the lord, Greg."

I so loved this woman. Her approval and acceptance of me meant the world to me throughout my whole life. Most times in the darkest of dark, she was my light and her words were my constant companions. Of course, her support filled up more than half of what I was to carry with me on this journey. With time running short, I decided telling my mom and getting Bobby's plane fare would be my priority before catching that flight in the morning, so my next stop was the Small Business League to see Mr. Champ.

When I arrived he was there, but in a meeting, so I patiently waited. While sitting there I am imagining how life would be in Phoenix, then in Los Angeles. I thought about what these 7 new guys would be like as musicians, friends, co-workers and fellow dreamers. I imagined how Bobby and I would fit in and about our having never been that far away from Grand Rapids.

Even though it took close to an hour, it seemed like less than a minute had passed before Mr. Champ emerged from his office with his usual broad smile and a big cigar nestled between his large fingers.

"Sorry for the delay but come on in! You know you're looking for a bout to be rich man," he chuckled. Now tell me what I can do for you Greg. I know a big-time music man like

196

yourself don't have much time for social calls anymore!" We both laughed as he escorted me in. With him I learned it's always best to get down to business, so without hesitation I asked, "Mr. Champ, can I ask for your help again?"

"If I can do it, you know I will."

"It's not for me. It's for Bobby DeBarge. The band Darnell is with asked us to join them in Phoenix, and they're sending me a ticket, but we have to get Bobby's. Is there any way you can help me with that?"

Mr. Champ puzzled his chin.

"I walked back in from lunch to a message that Darnell had called, so I guess this is what his call was about too, huh? Well give me a minute."

I waited inside his office, cradling my horn and thinking about how thankful I was to have someone that I could go to in a pinch and about how much I appreciated Darnell, because he was forever on top of things that were important.

"Greg," as he walked back into his office with that broad smile, "So, you three Grand Rapids men will be joining up with Barry White?"

"Yes sir, Mr. Champ."

"Now you know you have to show the world what Grand Rapids men are made of, don't you?"

"We'll do that."

"Son, give Della your flight information and you and Bobby come by here tomorrow and I'll have something worked out so you two can fly together."

"But Mr. Champ, the flight is leaving in the morning."

197

"Well that just means we've got to move a little faster, don't it? What do you say we meet here around six pm, that should be enough time to work this out?"

"Thank you, Mr. Champ."

"No, thank you Greg. You know it's my privilege to help my boys, anytime I can."

Leaving the building, I jumped in the air. I knew Mr. Champ was watching me and I wanted him to see how happy he'd just made me.

When I walked into mom's house, this time she was home watching her soaps. I came in and sat down, catching the last few minutes of *All My Children* before talking. As the closing theme played and the credits rolled, I asked if we could turn the television down, because I had something to tell her.

She immediately cut me off saying, "Daddy told me you are planning to go to Los Angeles with Barry White? What's that all about?"

I laughed at the fact that the simplest information gets confused from one person to the next. "No, no mom. Bobby and I leaving for Arizona in the morning to become members of a band Barry White manages." I could see the bewilderment on her face, so I quickly continued.

"See, Darnell called me yesterday and asked did I want to join the band that he left school to join last year, remember? This band, TNT Flashers are in Phoenix, preparing to be signed by Barry White, who is going to be their manager and send for them to come to L.A., sigh a record deal and make a record."

Mom settled back on the couch with a concerned look on her face but before she could say anything I interjected, "Mom, I know this is my shot and like I told you before, I'll die to do my music."

"So, school don't matter anymore huh? And what happens if this band turns out like the last, how many bands you been with now? Six? Seven?"

"I gotta see. This is what my life is made of, but this time there is a real record deal with a big star attached. I just gotta see mom."

"I know YOU GOTTA SEE!" she said in intense tone. So, when are you leaving?"

"I'm out in the morning with Bobby at my side, if all works out today."

"I hope it works this time, Greg."

"It will mom. I'll make it work!"

"I know you're going to see mother before you leave?"

"I've already done that; but if I have the time, I'll stop by again on my way to the airport and please tell everybody else I don't get to before I'm gone. Now I gotta make sure Bobby's together and I'll get back later."

I left mom's house and took my time absorbing the sights of my neighborhood, my complete surroundings, all the way to Bobby's house. Once in, I found him at the piano, as usual.

"Man, Greg, you look happy."

"Aren't you? You should be too."

"You know I am, man."

"That means that everything here is Ok and you're ready to go, right?"

"You got that shit right.

Making my way back out of the front door I said, "Well were on our way to Phoenix, partner. I picked up your ticket around five pm. Our flight leaves at ten-fifteen tomorrow morning so I'm at your door at eight am, ok?"

"OK. See you in the morning, Greg."

With hell-bound determination to make that flight to Phoenix, Arizona tomorrow morning, I'm now getting a little nervous because I had never flown on an airplane before. Not scared, just a little nervous. I drove through the city, checking out the sights, while stopping to visit a few more relatives, mostly my elders, to say goodbye before I made my way to Mr. Champ, promptly at five pm.

True to his word, he had both tickets in hand. He gave me a big long hug; then grabbed me by both forearms and held me there for a second. I could see the pride beaming from his smile as he said, "I know you're gonna make it this time. Even if it don't do all that you want it to now, it's gonna set you, especially you, up for that big win Greg. All of y'all think about old Champ out there in Phoenix, while you're doing big things with big people, ok?"

I promised him that I would as I thanked him over and over trying to pull myself away for this emotional departure.

"Love you, Mr. Champ," I heard myself say, as I closed the door and started my car. He had been good to and good for all of us inner-city kids. He projected a positive self-image and self-importance and he instilled in those of us who were open and mature enough to receive it, a sense of pride and value in every aspect of who we were then and who we are today.

That night, after making a few final rounds to sign out with my folks, I dropped by the Track Two to have a drink and get with Raphael and James to let them know I was on the way out again. I caught Raphael at the bar, talking with this fine sister. I wasn't about to interrupt but he hailed me over, introduced me as his little brother Greg as he poured me a shot of Royal Salute, a less expensive version of Chivas Regal made by Chivas Brothers, which he knew was my favorite scotch at that time. Surprising to me, the woman knew who I was, got off of her stool and extended her hand and said, "Hi I'm Mae, and you're that bad-assed singing and trumpet playing young brother I heard and seen down here and at the Golden Glow aren't you?"

I smiled, and before I could speak, Raphael put my drink in my face and cut me off saying, "Yeah that's him and he'd love to sit and chat for a while, but I'm tired of him stealing all the women in here so he' got to go! Right Greg?" As all three of us burst out in laughter, I saw James Burress on the other side of the club locking the office door. I quickly told Raphael, "Bobby and I are out of here heading for Arizona in the morning to sign a contract with Barry White."

Raphael, with this puzzled look on his face, started to speak; but I cut him short saying, "I'll be right back."

As I was approaching James, he saw me coming, gestured me over and before I could say a word, he spoke. "You don't have to tell me what you're getting ready to do. I heard about it from your uncle. Life's about pursuing your dreams and you don't want to grow old, stuck in Grand Rapids thinking *what if*. I want you to do this for me though,

SWITCH, DEBARGE, MOTOWN & ME

Greg. Don't drop out of school. Take a leave of absence and that way, if it doesn't work out, you can always return. O.K?"

"Okay James. Thank you for everything and I promise you, I won't let you down."

"Greg, you can never let me down because I believe in you. The only person you can ever let down is yourself."

"Well, I'm not going to do that."

"Greg, you know I know that. You take care of yourself out there..." We hugged, I made my way back to the bar and shared my news with Raphael while I finished the new drink he had poured for me and left it at that.

I hopped in my car and drove back to my mom's and parked in front of the garage. Unbeknown to me then, that was for the last time I'd drive it because I left it for Art to drive; but one day the car stalled on him and instead of him getting it towed and fixed, he just left it on that street. After collecting tickets for illegal parking, the car wound up being towed and sold by the city; and I would wind up coming home two years later, only to get detained and hauled to the police station for excessive unpaid parking tickets, which I didn't know existed. I had to pay to get out of that holding cell and avoid full arrest and being thrown into the jail's population.

Chapter 7

Barry White's L.A.

242 North Forge

Bobby and I made that ten fifteen United Airlines flight and arrived in Phoenix, Arizona, ready to play, or so we thought. Getting to Phoenix and joining a new band was like eating a fresh bowl of unfamiliar fruit. Darnell and David D picked us up at the airport and took us to the motel where the band had been living for the previous four months. Bear in mind, this was February 1973 and even though it was ninety-nine degrees in the shade when we exited the plane in Arizona, it was still bitter cold in Michigan when Bobby and I hopped on that plane with our winter gear in tow. Before all individual introductions were made Jody and Mutley quickly pounced on Bobby and me, cracking jokes about our long, heavy wool coats, fur lined leather gloves and my ear muffs, like that was our initiation into the band.

On the verge of taking offense at the intensity of their taunting, I abruptly and matter of "factly" woke their ass up with "and you two don't have long-assed coats and gloves packed up somewhere, do you? Don't real men get cold in cold weather or are you two so hot-blooded that it doesn't matter to you?" Everybody, with the exception of Jody and his kiss-ass sidekick Mutley who tried to play it off unsuccessfully, burst into laughter. I, of course, went up to each new face and introduced myself and Bobby before we were shown where we would room. While unpacking, it came to me, with Bobby and me becoming roomies, I would now come to know faces of him I hadn't known before.

As of this day TNT Flashers consist of Jessie "TC" Brown on lead vocal and percussion, his brother Stanley Brown on lead guitar, Joseph "Joey" Sims on drums and Tony "Mutley" Jordon, the other trumpeter, who were all from Steubenville, Ohio. Vincent "Vince" Jefferson on bass came from Pittsburg, Pennsylvania, leaving the Grand Rapids boys, Darnell Wyrick on saxophones and flute, Robert Louis "Bobby" DeBarge Jr. on keyboard and vocals with me on trumpet, keyboard and vocals. I realized I'd seen the band in Grand Rapids a year or so earlier and I'd heard, they were the baddest band in Ohio, next to the Ohio Players, who were already famous. This group consisted of eight attractive guys with so much talent. They were known throughout the Midwest as a tight show band.

Although I wasn't yet sure it would translate into record sales, they proved to be the best band I'd ever played with. As the days moved on, Bobby and I became friends with everybody, including Pie and David D, two guys who were TNT Flashers roadies and assistants. Earlier on, we got closer to some more than others but, we were all a band of brothers in no time. TNT Flasher had left their Ohio homebase with their van, an attached U-Haul trailer full of musical equipment six months earlier, working their way across country with a paying date here and there until they arrived at their destination in Arizona.

Art Barrett, who the band had met and accepted as their manager a few years earlier, lived in the suburbs of Phoenix and Arizona which was one state away from California. The band was connected to Barry White through Art, who was Barry's friend. Somehow Barry owed Art a favor and signing the Flashers would be the pay back after closing a deal for his company, Soul Unlimited Productions with RCA Records. Art was financing our food, gas, motel and our rehearsal studio, where White Heat practiced for six hours a day. Fortunately, Darnell, the Brown brothers and even Vince were totally open to new ideas, where Jody and Mutley came around slowly to accepting Bobby's and my musical contributions.

Although Darnell, Jody and even Vince sang along on most songs, TC and Stanley were the Flashers sole lead vocals before Bobby and I were allowed to lend our voices in lead and background vocals. TC had a gruff, strong baritone voice similar to Marvin Junior of the Dells or Teddy Pendergrass; while Stanley, who sang in a first tenor-alto voice had his own unique sound and was excellent at slaying songs originally sung by females like Aretha Franklin, Chaka Kahn, and he even included a Neil Sedaka song to our set while playing a mean guitar.

After putting Bobby and me through the ropes, teaching us their complete repertoire, we only did one or two gigs while preparing to meet, sign and record with Barry White. While waiting in Phoenix for the call, money was tight, we had barely enough to eat, especially since there was no real work for us in the Phoenix area, but we hung in there. Bobby and I had met a few people through other band members and then a few of our own, folks who passed through the motel where we stayed. It was during this time Bobby began to flourish as a person. He became more engaging with people and not so withdrawn. I watched his confidence grow with each practice because his contributions were thoughtful, instructive and always added to the group sound. When we weren't rehearsing or practicing individually we all hung, getting to know each other.

When Bobby and I first arrived in Phoenix, among other things, we were told that Barry was to soon send one of his staff producers to work with and prepare us for the recording sessions that were slated to begin immediately after we made it to L.A. to sign the contracts. After about two months in Phoenix, Barry's friend, singer, songwriter and producer Bob Relf arrived. Bob had also been a hit recording artist himself, known for being half of the early 1960's R&B music duo Bob & Earl whose song, Harlem Shuffle hit the charts in 1963. Now Bob would drive or fly to Phoenix and spend about ten days working out song arrangements, go back to L.A. for a few days and return for another week or so to create and tighten up the music we were going to record.

Now Bob was all of five feet, two inches tall and looked like a Native American with thick wavy black hair and keen features, but he was mixed with black and Indian and had a serious speech impediment. Actually, he and Bobby looked like they could have been closely related. Bob would stutter and try to communicate while pointing his right index finger in your face. Like the drunks I'd seen so often as a child, down on Division Street and at Campau Park, Bob kept a pint, a/k/a "short dog" of Cutty Sark in his back pocket and each hour, the more he drank, the redder his face got and the more he cursed. By the end of every day, he'd be sloppy drunk and calling us all kinds of mmmm ma ma muthafuckas and telling Jody to "wa wa wa watch yyyo yo tempo baby."

Most of the time we'd laugh off what he'd say, and when we became closer we'd sometimes tell him if he weren't drunk we'd kick his ass. He'd be so drunk he wouldn't remember a word of what was said and the next day and it would start all over again. Nice when the day began, then pissy drunk and nasty as the day ended. A few of us, Bobby included, tried to get close to Bob. We were excited about having a real record producer work with us and get us ready to cut professional records. Most of us found that when he was not drinking, which was almost never as Bob would begin hitting that short dog when we saw him in the morning till the bottle was empty, he was a nice guy. And he knew music, how to arrange and produce a song like nobody any of us had ever met; but catching him anywhere near sober was rare. When we were lucky enough to catch him halfway straight was mostly between liquor store runs.

I'd always make time to talk to Bob, sober or drunk until he started slobbering, stuttering and cursing, then I'd have to get away. As we got to know him, Bob actually turned out to be an extremely intelligent, talented, kindhearted man. He was very sensitive, and the closer I got I could feel his deep-rooted sadness, a sadness he tried day after day to drown in a short dog of Cutty Sark. As Bob got to know those of us who were open enough to see and accept him for who he was, he would share more about his own musical career and a little of what Barry White was like and what we could expect from him. But when annoyed by a question or statement, Bob would shut you out in a heartbeat, saying "Wha,wha, whaa ever ba,ba,ba, ba, baby."

I fondly recall the time, drunk-assed Bob Relf fell on the bottle in his back pocket and it broke. What cracked us up was he quickly jumped up, touched back there, felt the fluid running down his leg and said," lord, please let it be blood."

One particular incident between Bobby and me still stands out in my mind. We'd been writing and practicing new songs for the record. The band was working on material that some of them had written for this album project, as well as trying new songs they had just come up with. Bob also presented two songs, one he had written and another that Barry had written for us. Although Bobby and I individually and collectively had some incomplete ideas which could have been presented, there wasn't one song finished enough to present. Besides, neither one of us had written a song that had been recorded before.

Often after rehearsal, we would stay at the studio and practice more or kick around some ideas for new songs. Finally, we completed one called "I've Been So Lonely." Bobby came up with it and sang the melody on the verse and I came up with the B section and the hook and fed him my words and melody until we had structured a complete song. It was a good song and we knew it. As we kept going over the song until we both agreed that it was finished, Bobby says, "I think Stanley will do a great job on this."

"The hell he will," I quickly blurted out. "Man, we wrote this, and you just sang the hell out of it and you're thinking we gonna let anybody sing this but you?"

"Greg, this song is not made for my register. It's made for a high voice."

"...and you've got the best one I've ever heard man."

"But I don't sing up there."

"I've been hearing you go up there on almost every song since I met you, and now, when it counts most you gone tell me you don't sing up there?"

His lips narrowed into a stubborn line. "Naw"

"What do you mean naw, Bobby? Man, your voice is better than anyone out there and it's unique. Plus, it adds to what we're doing."

"Naw, Greg, if I sing up there, people will think I'm a sissy and I hate sissies."

"Is that why you won't sing in your tenor voice? Bobby people won't think that. They'll be too busy loving the way you sound. You've seen how they girls act when you sing. Come on man, you know I wouldn't have you doing something to make you look bad. You need to sing more songs in your false. It sounds natural and it's beautiful."

He leaned forward, focusing only his eyes on me. I didn't blink. It was he and I and nobody else existed.

" You think so Greg?'

" Look at me. You know me. Shit, I'm sure."

"OK, Mappy. I'm gonna think about it so you'll leave me the hell alone for now, right?"

He laughed, I laughed, and we kept on playing.

The next day he still wouldn't sing our new song during rehearsal, but like always, we stayed after and rehearsed the song over and over until we knew it in our sleep and the following day we showed it to Bob Relf and the band. They loved it and that was the beginning of Bobby's falsetto career. It gave the band another element which couldn't be touched because in my opinion, no falsetto, then, or now, has ever been able to come near Bobby DeBarge's.

Bob Relf had prepared us and our songs for recording and he returned to L.A. We'd been there about four months when Art got the call and we loaded the U-Haul trailer with the band's equipment and our clothes, ten guys filled the van, with Stanley driving. Yes, we finally headed for L.A. with Art leading the way in his big Cadillac. We left early, drove all day and got to L.A. in the wee hours of the morning. I remember watching the signs, getting off the 101 at Sunset, passing Hollywood High School and turning onto LaBrea. We stopped and parked a few buildings down from where Barry had his offices. We were tired, funky and anxious to meet Mr. Barry White. Once into the dimly lit office, Barry, who was surrounded by three other men, seemed to fill up the entire room. We sat and he ignored us, not even looking our way while talking back and forth to Art and the other men. This made us even more intimidated and everybody was fidgeting.

When Barry White finally looked up he said, "So y'all this bad-assed band Art been talking bout for such a long time, huh? He say Y'all's a muthafucka. Right, Art?"

Art began to nod his head in agreement as Barry continued "We gone do this deal see, but I'll tell you this right now, if you fuck with me, I'll fuck you for life!! You got that? I'll fuck you for life!!" As Barry looked away, Art comes from the back into view with these big contracts, thirty-six pages of writing each. With the exception of our roadies, Pie and Davie Dee, he passed the contracts out to each of us with one pen to sign the stack of agreements. Barry resumed eating, smacking on a large box of what I later found out was Tacos.

Having heard somewhere that you don't sign record company contracts without your attorney, and seeing that no one else was going to say anything, I mustered up the strength and blurted out, "Mr. White, don't we get a lawyer to help us read these contracts?"

That whale of a man abruptly turned and roared at me in that deep, resounding voice, "Sign the muthafucka!"

Stunned as all hell, I looked up as the others dove in with that one pen in hand to quickly sign all of those papers. Not knowing what to do then and not about to get left behind, just like all of the other TNT flasher members, I signed it; after which, I felt very uncomfortable because I had no idea what I was committing myself to. I was never one for monkey see, monkey do; but I really didn't know enough to be afraid, so yes, I signed them too.

Right then, I made up my mind that I would never again sign anything I hadn't read and understood first or had an attorney to help and advise me. For years to follow, whenever I could, I went to libraries and even borrowed books from anyone who had them so I could learn everything about contracts. But here, I knew if I stood alone and didn't sign it I wouldn't be a part of this deal. I would no longer be a member of this band. When I later got my hands on and looked over the contracts, I noticed but did not understand what it meant when it stated "the name of the group will be White Heat and Barry White shall be the owner of the name. In time, not only would I come to understand it but all of us would regret it.

White Heat promo shot

Once the signing was over we were introduced to the folks in the room as someone opened a few bottles of bottom-shelf Champagne and we all toasted our record deal. The men, who we later learned was Barry's crew, was this Jewish guy Larry Nunes, Barry's close friend and spiritual advisor, Tony Sepe, Barry's manager was an older Italian man with salt and peppered hair, who looked like every movie mobster I had ever seen. Blanchard Montgomery, Barry's close friend and business associate, was a big black man with a perm similar but longer than Barry's. Blanchard was huge like Barry but taller, towering around six foot five inches. We quickly learned that instead of Art, Blanchard would be our new co-manager with Barry White. There were a couple of other men whose names and functions I don't remember to this day.

After the toast, Barry had us get our clothes and park our locked U-Haul trailer directly behind the building in their parking lot. Once back in the van we followed Blanchard a couple of miles and arrived at Howard's Weekly Apartments, about half a block north of Hollywood Boulevard, where we lived for the next eighteen or so months. Howard's Weekly was a semi-converted apartment hotel, with oversized-sized single, double and triple occupancy rooms which included twin beds, two dressers, two closets, a small eating area, a hot plate, a small refrigerator and extra cabinet space for food storage. Just inside the hotel's entrance was a huge enclosed lobby area complete with a wet bar, a color TV, two round tables with chairs, various couches and seating areas, which you had to be a key holding resident to get into.

Soon after moving in, we commandeered this whole area and made it our conference center. This was the place where we could visit with our guests most nights until ten pm, as guests were not allowed in the rooms after office closing hours. Also, I don't know if it was Blanchard's or Betty's rules, but girls could spend no more than one half hour in our rooms per visit. Again, each of us had roommates and though Bobby and I roomed together in Phoenix, here in Cali, Bobby roomed with Stanley because he always had the weed and other drugs and I roomed with Darnell, placing TC with Vince, Jody with Mutley and David D with Pie; as it was in Phoenix.

Howard's Weekly was run by this overweight, gravel-voiced Irish lady named Betty, who had Strawberry blond hair and arm fat that flapped every time she would raise or lower her arms; and her assistant, Wayne, a little guy who was built like Barney Fife from TV's Andy Griffith Show, but was a serious Elvis Presley fan who would often try to dress like him while going about his hotel duties trying to keep the tenants in line. These two people we would come to like, and they came to like us; and as mean as Betty could be to most of her tenants, she kind of mothered over the TNT Flashers, eventually referring to us as her boys.

Throughout our residence, the entire cast of characters who moved in and out of Howard's Weekly were colorful and would most certainly remind you of something out of a sitcom. Kind of like Good Times meets All in the Family.

As we settled into our new life, we were given our signing advance, which included in part an eighteen dollar a week food and incidentals allowance per man; nine dollars on Tuesday and nine dollars on Friday. After a few days of getting settled in our new surroundings, we were informed that leaving all of our stage equipment in the U-Haul trailer in back of the Soul Unlimited Productions offices as instructed, the trailer and all of its contents was stolen. This meant everything had to be replaced, so Soul Unlimited advanced us money to buy new equipment, which till this day Darnell and I believe that Barry's folk stole and sold or even gave away our equipment in effort to render TNT Flasher's indebted and controlled.

One day all of us piled into the van and followed Blanchard down to West L.A. Music store to pick out and purchase all new equipment, from a whole drum set down to my Selmer Paris trumpet. Bobby got a new Fender Rhodes piano and a Clavinet while Darnell picked out new Tenor and Alto saxophones and a new flute. Like I said, everybody got new equipment, even David D and Pie got new hard cases to carry our stage gear in. Soul Unlimited Productions set up and paid for our daily rehearsals at Lou West Studio on Santa Monica and Western.

When finished with rehearsal us younger guys - Bobby, Pie, David D and I - would often walk along the streets of Hollywood coming to well know our surroundings. Although playing chess and spades were all of our favorite pastimes back then, pinball was my specific game and my hustle, when I could afford it and I rarely lost when one of the Hollywood folks was fool enough to bet me. My guys would stand around and talk the unsuspecting victims into playing me because they knew that once I won we would all eat or play off of my winnings.

Grand Rapids isn't a small town, it's a city, but it was nothing compared to L.A. and Hollywood Boulevard was full of left-over hippies, wanna-be actors, singers, musicians and all other kinds of life-like hustlers, male and female prostitutes, head shops, and people mentally out there all the time. The band owned a van but individually, we didn't have cars, we didn't have money to go to movies, clubs or other events but we did have each other, Hollywood Boulevard and Howard's Weekly and that was more than enough entertainment for all of us.

After getting past our initial culture shock we did begin to meet and socialize with Hollywood's regular cast of characters. I remember this was also the period that Joey changed his name to Jody saying that "this name fits my personality better." Remembering Johnny Taylor's hit record "ain't no sense in going home, Jody's got your girl and gone;" A lyric that he would certainly live up to in our future together. A few of us even had friends and relatives who lived in L.A. prior to our arrival who we sometimes reconnected with.

For me and subsequently Bobby there was Steve Jones who used to be my brother Art's best friend when we lived on Paris St. Steve, who had moved to L.A. from Grand Rapids a few years earlier and his fine wife Sheri would come and get Bobby and me from time to time and take us to family cookouts, to drive-in movies and sometimes just driving around L.A., exposing us to some of what southern California had to offer.

There was also Mickey Rooks, Richard Brown and a few others, most of whom I had known since I was a youngster as our families grew up around and respected each other. Although Bobby had relatives living in L.A. he really didn't hook up with any of them until his cousin Andre Abney came out. The Abney family was big and well-known in various Pentecostal churches throughout the whole country. Pastor Abney's older sister Clara, who Andre moved in with, lived in L.A. and owned a soul food restaurant about a half hour away from the Weekly; so, Andre would come up and hang with us often. I had known Andre for quite a few years. We were friends and had played at jam sessions and in Two and the Family together; so, he, Bobby and I used to hang a lot.

These relationships, which some I still hold dear to this day, were really appreciated at that time because all of us were so far from home, living our dream but gaining nothing tangible.

Of the memorable events and functions TNT Flashers were allowed to attend or participate in while signed to Barry White, RCA had a large signing party for Barry White's Soul Unlimited Productions, whereby TNT Flashers, Tom Brock, Gloria Scott, Bob Relf and newcomer Danny Pearson were included. Of the acts managed by Barry and Soul Unlimited Productions, White Heat was the only self-contained act on the roster, so we did play at Barry and Glodene's wedding reception but did no other gigs for the entire time we lived in L.A. Mostly we practiced and recorded. We'd been in Hollywood for a short time, but quickly came to know our way around our immediate vicinity.

White Heat – Barry's Wedding (1974)

White Heat – Barry's Wedding (1974)

One afternoon while Bobby, Pie, David D and I were heading back home, we came upon a crowd of people on Hollywood Blvd. surrounding some activity about two blocks before out turn. They were blocking our route home so as we came closer we heard this voice with a German accent.

"No baby. Don't hit me babee. Vy you hit me baby? Please baby. Don't hit me babee".

As we tried to walk around this group I could see this tall, medium build, very dark-skinned sister with a wild-ass Jimmy Hendricks hairdo, knocking this blond haired, blue eyed white guy around on the ground against a building. He tried to get up and she'd knocked him back down, as he kept pleading, "No baby. Don't hit me babee."

"Shut up you bitch muthafucka!" she shouted in this high pitched, squeaky, Evilene from the Wiz's voice as she slapped him again.

The more he said that, the more she hit him across his face and upside his head. He was trying to crawl away, and she'd pull him back, flip him over and continue tagging him upside the head. She beat him until she could hardly breathe, while yelling, "You Nazi muthafucka!" She finally stopped hitting him and walked away leaving him lying on the ground.

"I luff you babee." he yelled to her back.

As the crowd thinned, Pie and I went over and picked him up.

"Sank you my bruthaz's." His nose and mouth bled and bruises all over his face and he was shaking like Don Knotts in a crack house.

As he was dusting himself off, Pie suggested that he come back to the Weekly with us so that he could use the bathroom and clean up a bit, so off we all went.

"My name is Bernd; Bernd Lichters. I'm come from Hamburg, Germany."

Here was this tall, lanky, scraggly looking blond haired blue-eyed white guy, with this very thick German accent and a noticeably large, protruding Adams apple. He was trying to pull himself together, after just getting himself beat half to death by this crazed black woman from hell. Burns, as most folk call him till this day, wore this light brown cotton stay pressed suit, light blue cotton shirt and he carried this brown briefcase. I mention the suit because from the day we met him and all of the time the Flashers were in L.A. he wore the suit every day. It was always clean and pressed with not a wrinkle showing. After he cleaned up in Pie and David D's room, they gave him something to eat, then joined the rest of us back in the conference center where we normally spent our evenings.

Bernd talked with everyone, as I soon came to understand that he really didn't know how or when to shut up. But as others began to move away from his never-ending mouth, not wanting to be rude, I listened to him as he tried to explain what we had witnessed him enduring earlier. He told me that the woman's name was Cynthia and she was his girlfriend and that she had gotten mad because he hadn't found a job yet and had run out of money.

"But why did you let her beat you like that? On the street in front of everyone?" I asked.

"Oh Grrek." Which is how he pronounced my name. "She don't mean no harm mon."

"You can't tell me that from what I saw man," I insisted.

"She luffs me mon. Her little boy Karroni, he luffs me too, Grrek"

Bernd became a regular, coming around us often for refuge, friendship and sometimes food. We didn't have much but most of us had no problem sharing what we had with our friends. From what we learned, Bernd was an accountant who aspired to be in the music business. He hung around various musicians in Hollywood and boasted about his friendship with Little Richard who he had met at the Star Club back in Hamburg, Germany. He'd sometimes come and hang at our band rehearsals a Lou West Studios or we'd hang out on Hollywood Blvd. But mostly he would meet us in Howard's Weekly lobby, we'd go "shmoke za veed" and come back to play spades, chess and talk. Or in Bernd's case, listen, until we couldn't take no more; then, walk away leaving him there talking to whomever he could find.

When I felt like listening, I'd learn more about him, his life in Germany, a few of his friends and even the fact that his father was dead and mother, who's name Muttie was the German translation for my mother's name Mattie, had remarried a Nazi officer when Bernd was in his teens.

Hollywood in the early seventies was a melting pot for dreamers and crazies of all shapes and sizes, from all walks of life with all kinds of schemes, plans and ideas of how they were going to make it and we were dropped right in the middle of all of the animated characters. Of course, with TNT Flashers being a band of dreamers we were magnets for all kinds of folk. Each of us made friends, struck up relationships and pulled women, most of whom were more than happy to help us on our journey to success. Unlike many of the Hollywood wannabees, we had a real record deal; so that automatically put us at the top of the list for pimps, drug dealers, actors, athletes and intern groupies seeking a name to use and an arm to be seen on.

Although not all of us were up for it, not one of us had a problem with the ladies. Many times, we would meet groups of them and invite them over to the Weekly; or one of us might meet and date one and she would end up bringing a friend or three on her next visit. When one of us would meet and hook-up with a chick, it was a band rule that the roomie would volunteer to leave and or stay away from the room so his roomie and the girl of the evening could get some time alone; as long as Betty or Wayne didn't bust him slipping her back to his room. Over the year and a half White Heat wound up living in Hollywood, in Howard's Weekly Apartments, other than TC and Darnell establishing meaningful, long-term relationships that would last far beyond the band's California adventure, the rest of us had girls we would hit, quit and ease on down the road.

Although none of us were addicted to anything, we were exposed to and experimented with various drugs. I recall during this time, it seemed like everybody in our extended clan (with the exception of Darnell and Vince) smoked weed and it was readily available at every turn; my drug of choice became speed, uppers, amphetamines and they were often available. Till this day, I never liked or took barbiturates, pills, syrup, and definitely not heroin; but when I was high on either, White Crosses, Black Beauties, Cicos, Stats or other available amphetamines and uppers, I wound up being my most creative and most animated.

From time to time, most of us would get away on individual outings, and most week days during the week, before and after rehearsal, a few of us could be found at the corner of Whitney and Hollywood Blvd. in Johnny's Steak or The House of Pies, where we would befriend and hang out with some of Hollywood's then lessor known talents, like Comedians Whitman Mayo and Don Bubba Bexley of Sanford and Son, Comedian Dap Sugar Willie, best known as Lenny on Good Times. This unique collective was also Motown hit record producer Bobby Bell, up and coming actor Reggie Dorsey, and a host of new friends, new girlfriends and new situations.

By now, even relatives from home or out of state start popping up. This begins as a good thing because, although we had good times with new friends and new lives, all of us still got a little homesick, from time to time. While going through my already arduous financial period, Art, my brother appeared out of the blue, on the run from the Grand Rapids police and the state of Michigan justice system, with nothing and no one here in California but me. This made things even more difficult because, after discussing it with Darnell, my roommate, I had to, I chose to let Art stay in my room and share my weekly eighteen dollars. Although he meant no harm, his presence did harm as I was trying to live my life and build a life through chasing my dreams.

For the two months that Art was with me I had no idea he was running, hiding from the law; and it obviously did not occur or didn't matter to him that my putting him up was putting my freedom in danger; even though, other than my childhood incident with the Smith brothers and that ladies purse, I was not one to break the law and was never accused or arrested for anything. One day, a policeman appeared at my hotel, with a warrant for Art while we were at rehearsal.

When we finally finished and made it home, Betty called me into the office to inform me about the officers and their warrant. Art and an accomplice had robbed someone back in Grand Rapids. The accomplice got busted and snitched on Art, who upon hearing that the police were looking for him, he ran and made his way to me in California for shelter. The Grand Rapids detective division traced him to L.A., to Howard's Weekly Apartments and with the assistance of L.A.P.D came looking for him but did not find him.

The detectives came back the next day, talked with Art and gave him the option to go with them and be arrested in L.A. and await extradition or fly back to Grand Rapids by the end of that week and turn himself in. Art opted for and made arrangements with our family to go back to Grand Rapids for arrest, the trial and sentencing. I again was sad for him, but truthfully relieved as his criminal life did not fit into my dreams. I loved my brother, but I did not like his choices. Once he was gone, I jumped back into the swing of things and began to play cards more with some of the Weekly's cast of characters like Shawnaday aka Shawn the black porn star, Machine gun the "wanna be" black rock star and Revvi, a white guy who ran the head shop around the corner on Hollywood Blvd.

From my memory, Barry never set foot in Howard's Weekly, but he did have Blanchard, or others from his staff check on us and sometimes collect us and bring us to his office or someplace else so that we would be around him. To everyone around, he would look at us and say in his heavy, resounding voice "White Heat. Bad muthafuckas! That's my group. Bad muthafuckas!"

The day we got the word we were going to start recording we partied that whole evening away. We told all of our friends that we were finally going to get into the studio. Recording our album was exciting. Although Bob Relf drank every day, during our recording sessions, he tried to tone it down now, back here in L.A.; because he never knew when someone from the company, even Barry himself might pop in, which did happen from time to time. We recorded most of our album at Whitney Recording Studios, the place where Barry recorded the majority of his hit albums.

White Heat album cover

I remember one day, we had just exited our van and were in front of a different recording studio in Hollywood standing with Barry. Earlier, he had pulled up in his Rolls Royce Silver Shadow, jumped out with these humongous Bermuda shorts and had ashy legs. You know we couldn't laugh, but we all wanted to. Of course, me and Bobby clowned this big ashy ass man with this coiffed perm in these Bermuda shorts. Just as Barry made his way across the street where we were, a big new Mercedes pulls up and stops in the middle of the street. The driver sticks his head out of the window and yells, "Is that Barry White?"

Before Barry could look up good, the man yells, "Hey, I've got a towel and a beach ball in here if you want." Now you know we burst out laughing, even Barry. We could not hold back the laughter any longer, then Barry yells, "Aw shit. It's Sonny Bono."

As he and the driver of the Mercedes wave to and point at each other while laughing louder than any of us. We finally got a good look at that driver and sure enough it was Sonny Bono. He stayed there for another minute or so, as he and Barry yelled back and forth to each other.

After that, we all hung outside with Barry for about a half hour, getting to know him better, talking and joking about various things. Soon we went into the studio and prepared to track a few of the songs we had been practicing since Bob Relf showed up in Phoenix. The first song up was If That's the Way You Feel, a song that Barry and Bob co-wrote. Then Barry began production on the one song that he wrote for our album, "Take a Look at Yourself." He took his throne. Barry sat behind the console while we, the rhythm section was in the studio ready to start tracking and waiting for Barry to start the tape; when all of a sudden, the phone rang and over the house speaker Barry says, "Hold up for a second White Heat."

While we waited for him to finish his call, Stanley was tuning up, Jody was playing to check out the headphone sound of his drums and Bobby was playing Stevie Wonders "I love Every Little Thing About You" on the rented Fender Rhodes piano. All of a sudden, in this intimidating voice Barry yells over the speaker, "Stop the session! Stop the session." Startled, we looked at each other befuddled, and Barry yells, "Stanley, put down that guitar and Bobby, stop playing those got-damned blues. Bitch done burnt the greens."

Again, most of the band fought like hell to hold back the laughter, with little success. As funny as that moment was and as much as all of us wanted it to be a joke, it wasn't. Bob Relf came into the big room and without further explanation told us to pack up our equipment. While we were breaking down our equipment, Barry exited the booth, made his way to his car and was off. Whatever really happened ruined Barry's mood, Barry's attitude, and the whole damn session for us. By the time we tore down and made it out of the studio and into the booth, Barry was gone. The Flashers wound up going back to the Weekly and were informed the session would be rescheduled in a couple of days. We were later told that Barry's wife, was cooking soul food and left the greens unattended a little too long and they were ruined.

This moment clearly defined to me how important food was to Barry White. After buying all kinds of pizzas for the whole band during an afternoon in the studio recording on the White Heat album, I've actually witnessed the man eat a large pizza with what looked like everything including jumbo fried shrimp on it by himself. I remember Barry's appetite was as big as he was.

Anyway, my being new to professional recording studios, I observed and learned everything that I could while working back at Whitney Recording Studio around Bob and Frank Kegmer, Barry's personal recording engineer. I watched everything everyone did in the studio and even learned the roles that each member of the studio personnel played. I learned that tracking meant to record the session/performance to tape. I picked up that 24-track machines had different uses than a two-track machines, among other recording needs, techniques and responsibility.

From time to time, White Heat would go to the studio to record and Barry would be working on his own albums in another room. I recall standing outside of Barry's session listening, as he was mixing this song called "Can't Get Enough of Your Love Baby." As we were a little more than halfway through the recording of our album, Barry had all three rooms in Whitney Studios tied up, completing his album in one, cutting new tracks for Danny Pearson in another, and overseeing Bob Relf produce our sessions in another room.

Never wanting to impose, I stayed my distance till invited; but when possible, I would try and ease up to Barry, who often appeared intimidating and unapproachable while working. He'd be in the studio laying a track or just listening. Catching him alone one day, I approached him. "Barry, how do you know when to stop a take? When you've got the track, you can build on?"

"Greg I knew you'd be asking me questions soon enough. Come with me."

I followed him into the office he had commandeered and made his own, which smelled like a Mexican restaurant. We sat at a table. He opened a bag, took out twelve tacos and gave me two of them and we ate as he talked.

"Try to get it done in two. You can cut a track as many times as it takes to feel good, but on two or three usually does it for me. At this level, a good musician should be able to read it and play it in one take. Some jazz musicians never do more than one take because they don't want to lose the spontaneity. But this is R&B, pop and soul and you do it till it feels good to you," he said.

"Thanks for the input." I said asking, "How'd you get started in the business?"

"Other than TC and Darnell, you the only one out of White Heat that's not afraid of me and would ask me some shit like that. I've been seeing you, checking me, checking you out, so don't think you slick." His laughter filled the room.

"I was a session drummer and I could sing. I learned to write my own songs and was determined to learn how to record them. It was straight ahead after that. The music saved me from being in the streets and penitentiary. I'd be dead or locked up if I hadn't got into the music game. Most of my boys from back in the day are either dead or locked up somewhere. It's a muthafucka out there boy. You know, I like you Greg because I was just like you. I kept my eyes open, learned as much shit as I could, asked questions when I could and kept my mouth shut otherwise. But you also gotta know when to speak up and when to shut up though Greg,"

He stood and we'd finished eating. "Come on man. Back to work," he said.

I watched him go into the booth, put on his headphones and hit the playback button. He smiled, watching me, watching him and I returned to my own session.

One of the things that I was somewhat disturbed by, but could never get answered, was how Barry and a few of his immediate employees could drive big cars and live in luxury homes while White Heat had to live in a hotel with no transportation and try to survive off of eighteen dollars a week. It seemed to me that Soul Unlimited productions, Blanchard Montgomery, Barry White or somebody could and should have found or put us in the position to seek out work and we should be getting paid for the sessions we were doing, but nothing came up and our struggle continued.

We continued our daily routine of meeting in the lobby to hang or play cards. We would pile into the van on most weekdays for band rehearsal, then head back to the weekly for more meeting and hanging in the lobby. After cooking most of our meals on the hotplates in our rooms we would meet and entertain new friends or head out to explore Hollywood Blvd. and play pinball machines. One day while out on the Blvd., Bernd appeared out of nowhere, as usual, with bruises all over his face, and suit all dusty.

"Man, what the hell happened to you this time?" David D asked.

"Nussing mon," he replied.

"What do you mean nothing, Bernd?" I asked. "Here you come again, suit all wrinkled, face all fucked up and you talking 'bout nothin'? Come on man."

"No mon. Cyncia and I just have disagreement at home, mon. Nussing serious, bruzza," he said. "Cyncia and I get married last veek Grrek. Karroni in now my son too now, mon. I go beck to Hamburg for a vile. In couple dase I go beck."

"Why are you going back to Germany, Bernd "

"It is my muzza Grrek. She not do zo vell, mon. I go zee about hur, plus it is time I redo vizza, but I come beck soon. You zig, mon?"

"Yeah, I dig. You gotta give me your address just in case the band leaves L.A. before you get back, so that we can stay in touch."

"Zat be a good cing Grrek. Maybe ve'll make record together. I come beck with manee mon and ve make record."

"Cool Bernd." As I thought, White Heat would move back east for more than a year before we saw Bernd again. Per our word, Bernd and I did stay in touch and among everything else we continued to discuss making a record together. It was now late 1974 and the weeks passed quickly as White Heat worked on the album, until our participation was finished. From there, it took another month or so for us to finish recording our parts of the album before Barry White, Bob Relf and Frank Kegmer, Barry's recording engineer, stepped in to complete it. We were called in to Barry's office for a meeting and told that we were done in the studio, so we could head back east, put a live show together, prepare to tour and promote our album once it was mixed, mastered and released.

Then, each of the ten of us were given three hundred dollars, a one-way plane ticket to our individual hometowns and instructed that we would be brought to our new home base in Akron, Ohio in one month to get ready for the road. After that we had a few days to pack up and say our goodbyes to everyone.

Finally, at Los Angeles airport, Darnell, Bobby and I signed out with the other fellas, boarded our plane Grand Rapids bound. After settling in for the long flight to Chicago, then home to Michigan, I sat quietly thinking and remembering my past year plus in L.A. Good times with the few yet special relationships with friends from home, including Jay and Laura Stone, Steve and Sherri Jones, Richard Brown, Micky Rooks, and new friends like actors Don "Bubba" Bexley, Dap Sugar Willie and a few other of our Hollywood Blvd. family. Even more so I thought about missing Bob Relf, Blanchard Montgomery and especially the times spent with and around Barry White.

Now that was all over, and with what I thought to be a brief pit stop in GR, my life was about to step into high gear.

For a short while, it was a little different being back in Grand Rapids after being gone for little over two years;, even a little more for Darnell who left Michigan to play with the Flashers before I started at Grand Valley in 1972. Although happy to see and spend time with my family again, Grand Rapids appeared to not have changed and/or grown at all for black folk. In the inner-city I would find the same guys hanging on the corner of Franklin and Eastern that I left there. My heart was happy to be there for that short time, but my dreams couldn't wait to get out of there. While in GR, on hold till a departure date to reunite, White Heat was confirmed.

I remember receiving one copy of the completed and newly unreleased White Heat album in the mail from Soul Unlimited Productions and RCA Records. Bobby, Darnell and I hung out with our individual family and friends during the brief hiatus, but we would keep in touch with each other. Excited to see the finished product, we immediately contacted each other upon receiving the album, acknowledging our mutual excitement but also our disgust at the fact of only receiving one album each. Yes, the cheap bastards only sent out one copy to each band member, leaving friends and family, even our mommas, to trek down to some record store to buy a copy, if they wanted one.

Well the three of us took this too in stride, while waiting on the call saying things were set for the band to come together in Akron. It would soon be time to work out our show, prepare to hit the road and promote our new album. After a couple more weeks, that day finally came. Yes Darnell, Bobby and I got the call and were on the greyhound a few days later in route to Akron, Ohio. Once there, the reunion was special and joyous, as not only were TC, Stanley, Darnell, Jody, Muttley, Vince, Bobby, David D, Pie and I back together; we were now RCA/Soul Unlimited Productions artists who were about to take the world by storm!

Yes, we're now back in Akron Ohio. I had lived there for a short time in 1970 when I joined the band Just Us, but I had not been back since. Strangely enough, I did remember Akron to be as similar to Grand Rapids in size, population, weather, visual surroundings, even the look and mannerisms of people as it turned out to be, so other than the geographical newness, I was at home again. I even had family there, blood relatives

233

on my father's side; but I had not really gotten to know or even be exposed to but a few of dad's folks in Grand Rapids while growing up. So, I really didn't know these people; but I was welcomed by the few that I did meet and spend time with during this time in Akron.

The band quickly settled into the home owned by Tommy Upshaw's parents, which was being rented for us by Soul Unlimited Productions. Initially, Soul Unlimited also provided a small monthly stipend for food and basic amenities until we could start performing again. This house was an older, large, two-story, three-bedroom home, which we turned into a four story six-bedroom home by making additional bedrooms in the attic and basement. After little over a one-month break, the ten of us were back together again.

This time there was no weekly allowance because we were there to get our show together so we could perform and promote our soon-to-be released record. Instead Soul Unlimited sent monthly checks to cover rent, utilities, groceries and petty cash for group incidentals. David and Pie cleared the living and dining rooms of all furnishings and set up all of our equipment; which is where it remained set up for our rehearsal and was only taken down when we had a gig. During our settle-in period, we met new people and made new friends quickly.

Tommy Upshaw began to play a more active role in the White Heat entourage, working with TC, Darnell and the rest of us in various ways and going out with us to every show. Again, we were living in a house owned by his parents, which he had set up for us while in L.A. and he had returned to

Akron just before we moved. Tommy also proved resourceful in helping us get set up with services and relationships with various folk, including the weed and the speed men. If we needed anything, Tommy knew where it could be found. Little did I know, when meeting him in L.A. that he and I would become lifelong brothers and remain close till this day. Among others who would become part of our Akron family, Tommy introduced us to his cousin Carol, who was a few years older than any of us but fine as they come; and with her came her friend Ellie, also fine. Both of them were good folks who would shop and cook for us, they would make sure we didn't need anything and would even come, pick us up and show us around Akron once in a while. Mostly, they were more like big sisters or relatives. We grew to be close and stayed that way the entire time I lived in Akron.

White Heat had been living in Akron for about four months and gigging most of that time. One day, out of nowhere, I received a postcard from Bernd. He was still back in Germany, doing CPA work. He told me that Cynthia and Karroni had moved over there with him for a short time but had moved back to L.A. and he was saving money and making plans to join them in the coming months. I took the time to write him back and after that we kept in touch. Every month or so when I could afford the postcards and stamps I would write him, and he would write back. Most of the time he would tell me how he was going to get a budget, come back to the states and make a new album with White Heat and I would be the one to produce it. I listened to him, but the more he mentioned it, the less I believed; but still it was nice to stay in touch with my foreign friend. When the band wasn't working, Bobby, Darnell and I would sometimes get someone to drive us back to Grand Rapids for a visit. Even Mutley began to roll with us, so he could spend time with Bunny and after a couple of times, he would strike out on his own whenever we got a few rehearsal/gig-free days.

Although, like most bands, most artists, we sought out fame and fortune through a hit record deal, but what TNT Flashers, now White Heat, had and knew we could count on, was a great show and a reputation for burning up the stage. Our only job was making music and performing; so, when the work dried up, so did the money. It was those times that I was thankful that I really did it for the love of the game and thankful that the women in our lives believed in us and financially helped us get over the humps. Other than Stanley and Vince, none of us ran short in the girlfriend department. Darnell, TC, Joey and Mutley always had a girlfriend somewhere.

White Heat performance (1975)

I remember Joey having this big colossus of a girl, who was at least six feet three, weighing about two thirty, who, to him, was so unappealing that he had to drink Mad Dog 20/20 to be with her. I'd hear him talking to her on the phone before she visited, " Sure, you can come up and bring the money. But don't come here without the Mad Dog."

And now even Bobby had hooked up with this girl we met at a show in Sewickley, Pennsylvania. It was funny because, from the time I met him, girls would always talk about how fine he was and sometimes they would hit on him; but I never saw or knew about him being with a girl and he and I never discussed him ever having a girlfriend, except maybe when joking; but this time he was really seeing somebody. Whether it started out of necessity or not, Bobby chose this little girl named Flossy, who fell in love with him the minute she saw him on stage. Over the months after getting together with Bobby, Flossy would drive up to Akron once or twice a month if we were not working, get a hotel room where she and Bobby would hold up for two, sometimes three nights, but not days because he could only take so much and had to be with us. And when she'd leave, Bobby would have enough money to last till the next time she came up.

Of the different girls Jody was juggling then, Cathy Biggums lived in Canton, Ohio, which was one town over from Akron, so she would make her way to see him no less than twice a week all of the time we lived there. Cathy had a younger sister named Chris, whom I met and quickly became involved with for a few months. I liked her more than the few others I had dealt with while living in Akron, but our relationship was short-lived too because my life was all about the music and nothing or no one would change that. Besides allowing these women to come around for sex, for laughs, a few dollars and sometimes to provide temporary distractions, nobody got to stay. We had the music and each other and that's the way we liked it.

For each of us, gearing up to perform was a big deal, especially since we could now include our own original songs to the show; although Darnell and I were performing our own records with the TMG's back when we toured the south that summer. For White Heat, TC booked the gigs, he and Darnell took care of the business, and the band worked around Ohio, doing a few dates in other parts of the Midwest. TC was the principal showman of the group. From one performance to the next, TC was unpredictable; but was a hell of an entertainer from the word go. On the other hand, Stanley would sing his songs and ease back in with the rest of the band on stage. Although initially, Bobby had reservations about stepping out front, but the issue was almost forced because, since our records had yet to become known, we had to play identifiable songs which were top-forty radio hits. So, we picked our favorite songs, then designated from TC, Bobby, Stanley and me, depending on whose lead voice fit the particular song.

At this time our set list included popular R&B songs of the day like "Disco Lady", "Hope That We Can Be Together Soon", "Reasons", "Sweet Thing", "Inseparable", "Love Won't Let Me Wait" and "Fight the Power," to Name a few.

TC was the consummate entertainer and a very outgoing person over all. He was also pretty persuasive while booking a show for us. He used his charm to get us gigs, with a few major artists, including a Midwest tour with Graham Central Station led by Larry Graham. We opened for them once and afterwards Larry asked his promoter to book us on all of the remaining Ohio dates. Working with Graham Central Station was big fun as every member of the band, including Larry's wife Tina and his mother Dell, proved to be great people and big fun to hang with. Larry and I clicked as I came to find that he too was kind, considerate, funny and had a way of making everyone feel welcome. I learned that side of him, along with his early live performing experiences came from Dell, who was Mama Dell to us all.

Here and there, when there was a minute to chat, I recall her sharing stories with a few of us about herself, Larry, and her lounge act the, Dell Graham Trio, which Larry joined as a teenager.

While performing with Graham Central Station at the Akron Civic Center, the opening was an act named Raw Soul, from which Tommy Upshaw pointed out the sixteen-year old percussionist, singer by the name of Phillip Ingram. Upshaw explained that Phillip was the younger brother of one of Akron's premier musicians James Ingram, who had left Akron for L.A. a couple of years earlier with the band Revelation Funk. Revelation Funk was also a well-known and respected funk band from the Ohio valley. During the intermission between White Heat and Graham Central Station's performance, Phillip and another Raw Soul member wound up in the dressing room and we struck up a conversation. We actually talked through the entire break till we heard the announcer readying the crowd, as Larry and the group made their way onstage.

Both of us wanted to catch Graham Central Station, so I told Phillip where the band lived and invited him over as the room emptied, to catch the show. Within a week or so Phillip called me and shortly thereafter he came by the house. With the instruments always set up, I started to play one of the keyboards and invited him to join in with me. I had the opportunity to hear him play and sing and was blown away by this talented youngster. He had a voice like a bell, played percussion and had no vices, as in he didn't drink, or smoke anything. Phillip was a great talent, and, in my opinion, he could master anything he touched; but what I appreciated about him most was his grounding. I had never met a more solid, dedicated person at such a young age. In most ways, he reminded me of me and my unspoken commitment to be better at everything I chose with each day that passed. From our first meeting, I knew that I had to work with him, to share with him, and to teach him the few things that I knew that he didn't know about how to win at this game called the music business. We quickly became friends.

Throughout my life, I have remained outgoing, personable and open for new friends, new challenges and new adventures; so, Phillip was a welcome addition to my ever-growing circle, as was another new friend, Rod Mosley.

Rod was a poet turned lyricist who lived directly across the street from where we lived. This guy was about twenty-five years old, tall and black; maybe a shade lighter than me, with thinning hair on top and very feminine. He wore glasses with thin black frames and most times he was in jeans and colorful lumberjack shirts. He wasn't flamboyant or overt; but if you looked and listened to him long enough, you'd know that he was gay. I came across a few sissies while growing up; but, except for the one time a guy hit on me in Hollywood, I really didn't know anything about gay men. This guy Rod would hear us rehearsing from his apartment. From time to time he would pass by our front porch and he would always speak to whoever was out there.

One day after rehearsal, I was sitting on the porch swing by myself and Rod was passing. We again spoke; but this time he began to strike up a conversation to which I listened, then responded.

"Hi I'm Rod Mosley. I live right there, across the street. And you are?"

"Hi Rod. I'm Greg Williams."

"I've been hearing you guys play since you moved here. What's the band name and do you play, sing or both?"

"The band is White Heat." I wasn't about to tell him that we had just gotten dropped and Barry took his name back… "and I play trumpet, sing, and play some keyboards."

"Yeah. I hear different voices all of the times, songs that I've never heard before, and those horns,.. man, you guys a great."

"Thank you," I said.

"Do you write songs too?" Rod asked.

"Yes sir. I'm still developing there but one of the songs written by Bobby and me made our first album."

"Man, that's great!"

From that point, Rod and I became friends. He told me that he wrote poems and he had this stack that he wanted to turn into songs. He then asked if I would read a few of them and if I liked any, would I write some music and help him turn them into songs?

"Greg, if you like any of my poems and decide to work with them, how much will you charge to put music to them?" he asked.

"Let's first see what you've got and if I can help you do what you want to do. If so, maybe twenty, twenty-five bucks apiece?" We shook on the deal then he asked me to come over to his place and see what he had. I shook my head yes and started getting up from the swing to follow him.

He quickly gestured for me to stop then said, "By the way, I'm gay. Do you have a problem with that?"

I was kinda glad he brought up what I'd already suspected before I did, I responded jokingly. "No. Not if you don't. By the way Rod, I'm not gay, do you have a problem with that? " to which we both laughed and proceeded to go across the street.

I didn't care that he was gay, as long as he didn't try to push up on me. I found that he wrote good lyrics and he'd pay me twenty-five bucks a song to put music to his words, this was going to be easy. Hanging with each other was what most of White Heat did after rehearsal with the exception of Vince who mostly kept to himself. I always assumed him to be sexually straight, as I had seen him with one girl during all of that time we were in L.A. and before that I had heard him mention a girlfriend in Pittsburg; but most times, other than rehearsals and onstage, Vince was alone. He would leave the house a few days out of the week, but no one knew where he went or what time he'd be back, with the exception of rehearsal for which he never missed, nor was he ever late.

Now with Bobby, that was a different story. He had become the social butterfly in California, and here in Akron he would hang with everyone and had limited alone time, as the majority of us did. There were occasions when I'd catch him in solitude, either angry at someone or something. I could quickly tell when he was approachable, or not. I remember one day, while I was coming in from the porch I heard him yelling inside of the house, at the top of his lungs; so, concerned, I jumped to my feet, running towards the sound of his cursing and screaming. As I approached the front door I heard him say, "God dammit mama,…"

Once I heard him say mama, I stopped dead in my tracks because I knew it was time for me to head in another direction. Just as I turned my back to head back outside I heard this crash. Bobby had slammed down the phone so hard he broke it into what sounded like a million pieces. I just kept on walking till I was out of range. I had experienced him unleash his wrath on his mom before on more than one occasion and when he finally went there, it wasn't nothing nice.

On one occasion while we were growing up in Grand Rapids, I remember rushing to the DeBarge house to pick Bobby up to go to another band's rehearsal. Maybe three or four houses before I would reach the DeBarge home I heard Bobby yelling and cursing at the top of his lungs at someone. I could not make out what he was saying; but I knew by the tone and by past exposure to his attacks on his siblings, this one was a little over the top and there was sure to be a few new holes in one of the undemolished walls before this was over. I slowed my stroll, hoping I would hear this stop before I reached my destination, but it didn't.

As I walked up the first stairs I heard another voice cut him off, yelling in direct response to Bobby's attack. Once I could make out who it was, I was shocked that Bobby could speak in such a way to his own mama. In my house, as in most black households, that kinda shit could get you killed. You don't disrespect your mama for nothing and live to tell it and here Bobby was saying things to her like she had a tail or something. Things that I knew he would never dare to say to anyone in the street. At that very moment I knew that he was living and dealing with some problems that I, his best friend, would never understand and never be able to help him get past. I also knew, now I had come across a side of my brother, Bobby DeBarge that once unleashed upon the world at large would destroy him, everyone and everything in its path.

I stopped on the stoop in front of the house and did not dare move until I heard Mama DeBarge's voice, still yelling back at Bobby, trail off as she made her way down to the basement. Bobby's yelling died down too as sure enough, his fist went through the wall in the dining room. To this day I don't know what that argument was about, and I was not about to ask ever. I sat there for a few minutes longer and Bobby must have passed a window and saw me sitting there because then he yelled to me in a much calmer, but tense voice.

"Mappy, I see your ass out there. You still wanna go?"

"That's why I'm here man, if you're still game." I quickly responded.

Give me a minute, I'll be right out. I got to get the fuck out of here anyway. Wait just a minute." He said, stepping away from the doorway. After that I knew things would start out tense with us but if nothing else, hearing the music we were going to make would bring him out of whatever mood fighting with his mom had just created. I wanted so badly to help him forget and be free of the demons that so blatantly plagued his life and mostly his every waking moment. This was my brother; a younger brother whom was placed in my heart and hands to love, support and help him grow for a shorter time than I could have imagined. Remembering those moments in time were abruptly halted by Bobby's voice saying, "I see you like playing with the gay guy from across the street, don't you?"

He was looking over at the poet's house.

"Yeah I do," I said, "He's a nice guy with a good sense of music and he's one hell of a poet. I think something might come from his work and I'm definitely happy to make those few dollars for working with him."

Bobby turned to me. " Greg, I want to tell you something about me."

"What are you going to tell me I don't already know? We've been boys a long time."

"I'm like your boy Rod from across the street."

"What do you mean Bobby?" I asked actually unaware of where this conversation was coming from or going.

"Greg, I'm gay. I like some dick and ass too."

"Bobby, I kinda wondered, but was never sure. I remember fine-ass Andrea all over you in Phoenix and you screwing Maria in Hollywood."

To which we both burst out laughing, falling all over ourselves. After a minute or so of joking about the Maria situation, we calmed down and got serious again,

"Yeah man." Bobby input. "I never did fuck Andrea; and Maria, I fucked for you."

"Yeah right nigga." I laughed and threw a fake punch at his shoulder.

"Really man. I can do a girl once in a while, but I mostly I like boys," Bobby said.

"Well that's too bad for you nigga, and more women for me. Really, I don't care what you like, as long as you don't try and do none of that shit to me."

He faked a punch back at me.

"You ain't my type, and you too old anyway."

More laughter and conversation followed. He and I decided to walk towards Akron University which was roughly three to four miles from where we lived. We talked with each other like we used to when we first met. We talked about everyone from my brother Art and Bunny to Barry White and Bob Relf, and everything in between. Fortunately, during this moment in time our laughter would turn to tears and back, and yet I knew in each of us, this was for different reasons.

Bonding between Bobby and me seemed to have gotten subdued in our later days of Hollywood; as he and I assimilated with our band and our surroundings, so this moment was a very special, unforgettable moment for me and hopefully for him. After the laughter, Bobby stared at me with this serious look on his face, as if there was much more that he wanted, needed to say but he held himself back and we soon found ourselves back at home.

A few weeks later, we received that letter from Soul Unlimited Productions. The letter was informing us that they were not going to pick up the option on our contract, which meant we were dropped from the production company and the label. This was a crushing blow to all of us. To add insult to injury, the letter said that we were to no longer use the name White Heat in any form, as Barry White and Soul Unlimited Productions was the sole owner. This too had been part of that contract we weren't allowed to read. And to make matters worse, a week or so later, our bass player Vince, stole off like a thief in the night to join Barry White who'd hired him right under our nose. Vince was always the kind of guy who had very little street swag, but he practiced and honed his craft incessantly. You only had to tell or show him what to play once, then he'd play it perfectly. From the time I met Vince, I only knew him to have written one song called "People Get Funky", which he spent all of his free time practicing and rewriting to no end. That too became a joke to the rest of us because we'd be downstairs or outside in a group or with our female guests and he would be up in his room playin' and singing his heart out, "People Get Funky, Right On." And we'd fall out laughing.

He was the kind of musician Barry White liked and he played with Barry until Barry died on July 4, 2003. Vince too died in 2008. I could understand Vince leaving to go with Barry, but what hurt was his keeping that horrible secret and not telling anyone. Vince knew we were getting dropped by Barry before we did. Vince, Barry and Blanchard had intentionally deceived us. The week before we got that letter, Vince claimed he needed to go home to Pittsburg to check on his family, knowing full well that not only was he lying about his family, but he was never coming back because he was on his way back to California to become Barry White's bass player.

I was angry that he could be that damn deceitful. Unknown to me at the time, that action was my introduction to how callous and underhanded the entertainment industry, the same music industry that I had long since committed my life to, could be. Although everybody took it hard being dropped by Barry and even more so how Vince was stolen away from us, in defiance thereof we vowed to keep pushing. From my view, although everyone was taken aback, Bobby and Mutley were visually affected more than everyone else by our losing our contract. Mutley, who had been swept off of his feet by Bunny, had wanted to quit the band for some time now; so, our being dropped from the contract gave him the perfect excuse to make his exit, which he did. Bunny and Mutley, who had talked themselves into a serious relationship on the phone while we were still in L.A., hooked up as they had discussed, after White Heat completed the album.

Instead of flying back to Steubenville with TC, Stanley, Jody and Vince, Mutley flew to Grand Rapids with Bobby, Darnell and me to be with Bunny. Once White Heat reunited in Akron, Bunny and Mutley were frequently back and forth between Akron and Grand Rapids to be together while the band rehearsed and gigged, before getting the letter from Soul Unlimited Productions. Once that letter arrived, I believe it took all of two weeks thereafter for Mutley to tell us he was finished playing music and he moved to Grand Rapids to start his life as Bunny's husband.

Bobby, on the other hand, contemplated leaving and going back to Grand Rapids when Bunny came for Mutley; but took time to acknowledge the piece of shit life he would be going back to and opted to stick it out. But even then, his shoulders sagged, and he withdrew again, not wanting to play or do anything beyond our mandatory rehearsals for a while. Like the ghost of Christmas past, Bobby's ugly behavioral patterns, like frequent loud outbursts at minor disagreements over the bands lack of money, what there was to eat, where we could or could not go, etc. were revisited upon us.

On one occasion, he got mad about the fact that Darnell's girlfriend, Linda was allowed to live in the house with us for a while. Of course, other members of the band had no problem with it, but Bobby harped on it till he became so angry that he put his fist through his bedroom door, which in turn made some of the other band members upset and angry with him, but after a few words he was left alone. For a short time, everyone and everything was somehow wrong to Bobby, but he eventually did pull it together and put the frequency of his ranting in check.

It was times like this that I dreaded because I understood his pain, but I also knew that the pain he would unjustly cause others might one day be his undoing and once he came back to the planet it was business and/or playtime as usual. Well, now we needed a bass player to continue to gig while we pondered our next move and recording rebound, so I suggested Tommy DeBarge. Initially Bobby protested and tried to discourage the idea but at my and Darnell's consistent urging he soon came around there too, so we called Tommy. Tommy was playing in a band in Lansing most of the time, but their work and membership wasn't solid, so Tommy happily agreed to come and join Bobby, me and the rest in Akron.

Knowing that Mutley had quit too, Tommy asked if we needed another horn player because their cousin Stanley Hood, who played with us in Two and the Family was in the current band with Tommy and he wanted to come and join White Heat if we wanted him. Having played with Stanley, I really liked and respected him as a person and as a musician. I quickly vouched for him with the band and everyone agreed that he could join us, as well.

With it being settled that Tommy and Stanley would join the band, there was one more problem to solve. The Flasher's didn't have enough money to send for them, nor did they have money to come to Akron; so, Stanley's brother Elmer, agreed to drive them to Akron and we agreed to scrape up enough gas money for him to get back home. That turned out to be a beginning and an end because Tommy and Stanley were welcomed into the band; and with the exception of a brief moment in California a few years later, I never saw or spoke with Mutley again.

Having Tommy and Stanley join the group was a shot in the arm. They were talented, young and good-looking guys. And Tommy was silly as all get out, so he consistently provided comic relief and by now he was an incredible bass player. Creatively he was better than Vince because Tommy, though not the technician Vince was, had a feel and finesse compared to few. On the other hand, Stanley, who came to the table ready with his alto and tenor saxes and his flute, was a much more serious musician than Mutley and could therefore play, dance and contribute better than Mutley ever had. They were just what the White Heat needed.

Although the dates with Graham Central Station were gone, TC was still able to come up with club dates for us, so the revised TNT Flashers moved on. Still haunted and hurting by being dropped by Barry White and RCA Records we continued. About a month had passed and TC booked our first post-Vince, post-record contract gig, but we would continue to use the name a while longer. During this time, I truly became an Akronite; meeting new folks, going to the parks, hanging at a few house parties and bars and even visiting Philip and a few other new friends up at Akron University. I even stepped up visiting cousins from my dad's side, which I had never known or even known about until later months of living in Akron.

Through my folks and various others, I came to know the local black bars like the Hi-Di-Ho and lounges, the Silver Leaf and Helean's Heaven, which had live entertainment. I later found out the Silver Leaf also had a Saturday afternoon jam session. Of course, I couldn't wait to tell the fellas but most of them weren't interested in going; but coming from Grand Rapids, Jam sessions were my and Darnell's thing. I cut my teeth at jam sessions and I was not about to miss making my way down there to add to my wonderful jam session memories. One Saturday, Carolyn picked up Darnell and me and took us down to the Silver Leaf so we could sit in. From that point I was hooked again. Recording artist or not, I needed to play different music other than the White Heat repertoire. And I again needed to fellowship with musicians other than my immediate brothers. This quickly became my thing. Every weekend that White Heat wasn't working Darnell, I and sometimes one or more of the others made sure to be front and center when the first note rang out at the Jam session.

In a short time, I became a sought out regular. I made friends with the house musicians like Laddie Fair, Milton Tabler and Reggie Evans among other Akron musicians and was quickly asked to play gigs at other nightclubs. So, if I was in town and had no White Heat commitments, I quickly took all offers to come and blow my horn in Akron and surrounding towns, like Youngstown, Canton and even Cleveland. I had quickly made a name for myself on the Akron night-time music scene with folks sending me drinks and requesting I play Red Clay by Freddie Hubbard, before I could get my horn out of its case. I also became popular with the women, many who claimed they only came down there to hear and see me. I would hang out and even went home with a couple of them over my year or so of living there; but I wouldn't let myself get too serious about any one woman because I had tried a serious relationship before and learned that I loved too hard; so for the time, I refused to let anyone come between me and my music again.

I recall one day as the end of White Heat unknowingly drew near. Bobby was sitting on the porch of the band house and watched me coming from across the street where I'd go and write music with Rod.

"Greg, I'm getting sick of this just playing and it not going anywhere."

"Bobby, you don't know where this is going. Give it time."

"I gave it time with White Heat and now we don't even have the name anymore. We can't even use the record to get gigs. I don't want to go back to Grand Rapids and all that shit at home and I feel like I'm stuck here. That girl is basically feeding me, and it turns my stomach to touch her, but I need her help."

"It's going to happen for us Bobby, just hold on."

"Greg, I thought this was my way of getting away from everything and now it's gone down the drain. I hate this fuckin' life."

It became totally clear to me then, that Bobby genuinely loved music but was also using it as an escape to run away from his pain, while for me, it was a vehicle to my dreams. I wished I could tell him what I was now seeing in him, but I couldn't because everything was too sensitive for him now and I didn't want him to blow up on the one ally he'd had for what seemed to be forever, me. To everyone's surprise but mine, Bobby quit the band and left for Grand Rapids a few days later.

Through a referral from my friend Laddie fair, we met Arnett "Arnie" Hayes, an incredible organist, singer from Mansfield Ohio, who had a high first tenor voice in the range of Bobby's but actually sounded more like Ted Mills, of Blue Magic (Russell Thompkins, Jr of the Stylistics and William Hart of the Delfonics). Arnie was heavyset, brown-skinned with a short afro and he stood about five-six, five-seven and was always dressed to the nines. He was intelligent, friendly and engaging; even through his speech impediment often frustrated him, he would always work through it and complete his point.

Although the White Heat sound was full, tight and contemporary, from day one Arnie proved a welcome musical and vocal inclusion. After only a few rehearsals he, Tommy and Stanley Hood fit like a glove and White Heat was ready to hit the stage again. Although work was sporadic, we continued performing around Ohio, Pennsylvania and Kentucky, at least once a month. After a few months, Bobby would return for a few months and we would have the great sound of Bobby and Arnie on Fender Rhodes and Clavinet and Hammond Organ respectively, but after a few months Bobby quit, once again leaving the band in the lurch.

Carrying a total of thirteen people, eight men in the band, Pie and David Dee - our two roadies, Doc, who ran our lights and special effects, his assistant Alice, and Tommy Upshaw who assisted Darnell and TC with the groups business, was now becoming difficult without the limited financial support of Soul Unlimited Productions.

I recall how hard things got for us financially. Although most of us had girlfriends and/or family members who would give small amounts of money to help us stay afloat, that money was used for personal needs and was not meant to or was not enough to support the band and company; so, we did see some lean days. There was one period, roughly a week where we didn't have money for food; so those of us there ate on this huge block of cheese that Stanley brought home one day and pasta that TC somehow got from the "Stop-N-Go Hoe".

The band slowly dissolved, which took some months after Bobby and Vince left. Even though both of them had been replaced, it became very obvious that this band was doomed; and within a year, White Heat, now TNT Flashers again, might be over soon. At the onset of the White Heat break up I remember saying to Arnie, "Hey man, if White Heat don't stick together, I'm gonna put my own band together and I want you to consider being one of the lead vocalists and the main keyboard player. Would you be open to that if I make that move?" I asked.

"Yeee yeeea yeeah mamama man. I'd la lovvve to plplaplplay with you man. You gagagot my information just let me knnnnow." Arnie finally got the words out.

Happy with his response, I kinda tucked that idea away until the end of White Heat's days was blatantly clear. In a matter of a few short weeks, as gigs and finances continued on a downward slope, one by one the members left the band until there was no one left in that big Akron band house but me.

I had no idea what was next for me, but I refused to throw in the towel and move back to Grand Rapids, which at the time was my only option besides staying put; so yes, I stayed.

Fortunately, various musicians around Akron whom I had met and jammed with had asked me to play gigs with them, and I could make a few dollars while doing it; so, I made it known that White Heat had split, but I was staying and looking for work. Living alone after years of living with up to sixteen others took a while to adjust to. I would spend much of my alone time practicing my horn, writing lyrics and making plans about my future. I had, some time ago, envisioned my own band of young good-looking guys, on similar levels of talent and vision as me, so that we would, on one accord, go out and conquer the music world together.

In my thinking, with the exception of Tommy DeBarge, Arnie and Darnell, who would also be my business partner, most of the White Heat guys were older than I felt anyone in this band should be. Bobby too was young enough but his psychological issues and now drug use made me know, *don't even go there!* While alone in that big house in Akron, I would plan my work and work my plan. When the opportunities came, I would practice and workout with the few Akron musicians I had befriended during my time there, which after a while turned into live gigs at the various urban bars and clubs that had live entertainment.

Having learned with Bobby that I could pretend to be a student at Akron University and slip into one of its piano rooms in the music building to practice, I would spend hours there almost every day, practicing, listening to and even joining a few other piano players who could also play by ear and were open to share ideas and techniques with me. When not hanging and or practicing by myself or with the a few Akron musicians, I would spend my time hanging with Vicky or with my close friend from home Pam Howard who happens to be the sister of my brother Art's ex-girlfriend Marion and the aunt to my nephews Tony, Nate and Sean and my niece Tianna. I would also spend time with Carol and Ellie who would sometimes just drop by the house to check on and hang with me and my friends, Judge and Jackie Moore, and a few others.

For close to a year, after Stanley, TC, Joey, David D, and Pie went back to Stuebenville, Darnell headed back to Cali and Tommy and Stanley headed back to Michigan, I lived alone in that house until even my local gigs at the bars dried up.

As my food and funds repeatedly began to run seriously short, I realized if I didn't find a new way to make enough survival money soon, I'd have to go, even if it meant back to Michigan, as at the time I had no one and there was nowhere else for me to go. Although I was filling in the holes of my life here in Akron, I also missed the camaraderie of being in and living with a band, as I had most of my life. I would speak a few times with Darnell, but I didn't speak to any of the guys after they left Akron. Some of the women they left behind would stop by the house and see and even hang with me from time to time; but by now, I had made a few close friends, so I was rarely lonely.

Of my friends, I continued to receive postcards from Bernd who was still in Hamburg Germany. He would repeatedly tell me he'd be back in the states to have me produce an artist he was then trying to manage, and he would be getting the money from the Pall Mall cigarette company to make a record. His postcards became humorous because even though I held out hope against hope, I never really believed he'd come through on anything; because over time and seeing the plight of his life in Hollywood, to all who knew him, Bernd had become more of a character than a person one would think could really deliver on anything. He seemed to always try too hard to fit in; but on the other hand, he was a decent guy, and he was my friend; so, he had my respect, my loyalty and I would always hear him out and encourage him to bring it.

Sometime after White Heat was gone, I was able to call Bernd in Hamburg. In catching up on what was happening with each other, including discussing White Heat's breakup, I let Bernd know that I had plans and it was time I put my own band together and would possibly need his help to work with me in selecting business folk, record companies and other possible industry associations. We even discussed at length the possibility of him acquiring / funding out if I would let him be manager for my band, to which I told him we'll have to see.

Actually, during and after the White Heat performance dates with Graham Central Station, Larry Graham and I had repeatedly discussed him managing my new band, but ultimately, that wasn't to be. At the same time White Heat broke up, Larry was in negotiations for his solo deal/career, also on Warner Brothers Records, as well as his having newly become one of Jehovah's Witnesses, both which drastically consumed his time.

I had learned from working with Barry White, from making plans to work with Larry Graham and soon to learn from Jermaine Jackson, what they wanted to do for my bands and what they wound up doing turned out to be two different things. I later confirmed all that I had learned about this when I too became a manager, while still trying to be an artist. An artist is an artist and a manager is a manager. An artist who manages an act may have the best of intentions from the start, but their schedules are so busy, they can't handle another band because they're usually tied up trying to keep themselves and their own act together. And let's not throw in their own egos. People are either managers, or artists and the two never really mix well.

As the days wore on with no work, no income and no support in my immediate realm, I knew the time had come for me to move on, so I contacted my mom, informed her of my current plight and I made plans to head to Grand Rapids. Within a few short days, with my then girlfriend Vicki's offer to drive me back home, I said my goodbyes to as many of my friends that I could find, packed all of my belongings and got ready to move on. Before hitting the road, I found Phillip and told him I'd be back and we'd form a group, then we left for Grand Rapids. Laughing, talking and singing all the way made this journey seem to go by fast for Vicki and me, as in no time we pulled up in my mom's driveway. As initially planned, after a short rest, Vicki hit the highway headed back to Ohio, leaving me to deal with my new reality.

Once again, it appeared that Grand Rapids was something I just couldn't leave alone, as I was back there again. The faces of all those I loved never gave off any "I told you so" attitudes and no one said a negative word but only expressed happiness over seeing me healthy and happy. My mom welcomed me, asked briefly what happened and never asked what I was going to do next. I told mother, my grandmother, I wasn't giving up; another opportunity had arisen, and she encouraged me to stay with it. When I saw Reverend Snell, I talked around the subject of the music business; and with my grandfather, I explained that I was putting together my own band and that I would only be in Grand Rapids for a short time. I found Grand Rapids pretty much as I had left it. Art was still serving his time in Jackson Michigan Prison. What bothered me though, was the news about Bobby. He wasn't living at home, and his family was being tight-lipped about his whereabouts; but, Tommy and others told me, he'd become a heroin addict, or what we called at that time, a junkie.

I was so disappointed I didn't want to see him, and he didn't look for me. Subconsciously, though, and retrospectively, I did go looking for him. I went to a church service at Bethel Pentecostal, telling myself I wanted to hear some good music, but truthfully, I was hoping to see my boy, Bobby. I encountered Mama DeBarge outside.

"Greg, I see you've come to get the spirit and change your life."

I nodded, looking around for Bobby. She ushered me inside. Bobby wasn't there. The service was jumping, full of great music and the congregation was in high spirits. People were speaking in tongues and shouting. Mama DeBarge was sitting behind me.

"Speak Greg, let the spirit speak through you."

I said nothing. With her whole hand, she slapped the back of my head.

"Speak!"

I opened my mouth, but nothing came out and she hit me again. I began to wonder; *did I do something wrong. Was I taking a beating for something?*

Again, she yelled, "Speak!"

260

A high-pitched sound came out of my throat. She hit me three times and I made more sounds. What she didn't know was I was making those sounds, trying to stop her from hitting me in my head because it hurt. She hit me really hard and I gave a high squeal.

Mama DeBarge stood, raising her hands in the air and the congregation stood and exploded with people jumping, writhing and shouting. I raised my hands in the air, stood and walked out of the church, shaking my hands. Outside, I walked home rubbing my head and swearing I'd never go through that again. Making it to my mom's, again, I sat on her front porch, my thinking place, and thought about what I was now going to do with me. I wanted to be a producer, I wanted to write songs to fill a void and create a sound of my own. I could see and hear the music within. I walked around Grand Rapids, concentrating on this sound that I heard and envisioned. What stood out to me, for the first time in years, was Bobby wasn't in the picture; which was strange because I hadn't thought about doing things without him until his problems made him walk out on White Heat for the second time; but where and how Tommy fit in, I could see clearly.

Starting in October when I arrived, most of the time I spent in Grand Rapids preparing for my new life was spent doing what musicians call wood-shedding. The idea is you go into the woodshed and get your skills and music tight, then return to the world, ready and blowing. After confirming that Bernd would soon be headed to the states, I contacted Darnell and told him what I had been up to and with Bernd's help it would move forward quickly. I let him know that if he wanted I'd keep a place for him in this new band I was putting together. I informed him that once the new ideas were recorded with the money Bernd would be bringing with him, Bernd would come to L.A. to shop the tape and I and the rest of the band would shortly follow, once a deal was secured. While in Grand Rapids, I woodshed with my uncle Sylvester on bass, Melvin "MC" Clark, a GR guitarist I'd known for years, and Andrew "Drew" Brown a longtime family friend who'd built a studio in his house.

We worked music almost every day and after Sylvester and Drew would get home from work, we'd lay down tracks, most of the evening. Among other ideas, Sylvester and I wrote Pall Mall Groove, which was eventually part of the Hot Ice and Smash albums; and I musically conceptualized the band by putting all the parts I heard on tape so my new musicians could hear and learn the sound that was growing in my head. Sylvester was my ideal bassist, but he had a new son, a steady job and I knew he wouldn't leave his new family, so I had to let the dream of us working together sit for now. Andrew was also locked into Grand Rapids, his family, his job, his life; and therefore, I knew I'd have to stick to my initial plan and lock in another drummer. So, with MC being a definite part of my plan and Phillip Ingram, who was my first choice on vocals and percussion some time ago, I began to envision who else would become part of this new unit.

Through Phillip I had met and selected Eddie Fluellen, a trombonist and classical pianist, and saxophonist Reggie Manley - both of whom played with Phillip in Raw Soul. Arnie was to be the co-lead vocalist and keyboardist, Tommy would be on bass, with me on Trumpet to round out the horn section.

Within my last few days before leaving Akron in route back to G.R., Phillip introduced me to Bruce Gillespie who had also been a member of the band Raw Soul. Bruce had a great look and easy-going personality. Upon hearing him play for a quick few minutes, I decided he had to, and he immediately agreed to be a member of my new band because his timing was steady as a clock; he clearly had finesse and total command of his impressive drum set, and he was extremely talented and funky as could be. He definitely fit my vision of this new young unit I was pulling together; so, all was set with the Akron members before my return to GR, and now my three months here was about to end.

Before I left Grand Rapids this time, I sought out specific relatives to let them know that I was leaving again in a couple of days. Something in my spirit made me know this would be for the last time I'd live here.

I had already filled mom in on my plans, so my next stop was granddad. I knew he'd be sitting in his chair on the porch listening to his Detroit Tigers play ball.

His wide-toothed grin welcomed me.

"Granddad, tomorrow I'm leaving town again. I have this opportunity to go. I'm putting my own band together and I'll become a record producer."

"Boy you just cain't get that out of your head, can you?"

"No, granddad. I'll die to do my music"

"And what about takin' care of yourself Greg? How you gonna do that?"

"I'm gonna do it through my music. I'll make a good living."

"Boy, I thought I raised you better than that. A man learns something useful in life, gets a good job and takes care of his family. You started to get your education out at that college and just quit that to run up and down the road with some band, and how far did that get you? You wound up right back here, didn't you? Now here you go again chasing that music. Greg, a man needs to have something so he can stand on his own two feet. That music ain't secure boy. You're a Williams, and I expect you to act like one. I 'spect you gone learn one way or the other."

He stopped talking and focused his attention on the game. The conversation was over, so I walked over and hugged him and slipped away. Walking, my head whirling with Granddad's words, because I know he felt; he was telling me what was right. And maybe it was right for his youngest son, Sylvester, or even Art… but not for me. I was cut from a different cloth. I had dreams to chase and nothing was gonna get in the way of that! I walked away with positive strength because no matter what, I knew my granddad loved me and I loved him; and in spite of what was said, I knew he only wanted what was best for me. I also knew that one day, I would make him proud. I would make all of them proud, and most of all, I would make myself proud!

Without knowing it, I suddenly realized I had walked all the way to Reverend Snell, Art's dad's house. I knocked and he opened the door. He had been sitting in his living room reading a dream book for determining numbers, when I entered.

Without saying hi he opened up with…"what's wrong with you?"

I laughed at how those who knew me, could read me.

"Daddy, I'm putting a band together so I'm on my way back to Akron Ohio."

"On your way where?"

He'd placed the book on the table but picked it up again.

"On my way to Akron."

"And Greg, what cha gonna be doing there?"

"Daddy, I'm putting my own band together and becoming a star."

"Become a what? Boy you ain't gone be no star! You ain't gone be shit."

The book, in front of his face, separated us.

Opening my mouth, then closing it and stopping myself from snatching that book and hitting him with it, I picked my pride from off the floor, wiped his words right out of my head, and told him I loved him as I waved good bye.

"Oh. So, you don't want to tell me more about you going away?" he asked.

"No. I think I said enough. Take care of yourself," I said as I damn near ran through his front door. As I made it to the sidewalk I had to shake all of him off as quickly as I could. I knew he didn't mean that as it came out, even though it had conviction. I knew that was just his normal crazy ass being somewhere else when I wanted him to be there with me. I wanted his blessing as he had always given. Thank God I didn't need it. I began to jog, and for the first time in my life, I heard horns beeping, cars passing by, snatches of people's voices, music being played, my breathing, birds and everything moving in life, all in time.

It was a melody of life and I was in tune with all its workings. In spite of my last goodbye, I knew, from that moment, I was doing what was right for me. My choice had opened a door connecting me with everything, and tingly bubbles floated in through my blood. Carrying these sensations, I went to mother's, my grandmother's house. She met me at the door, opened-armed for an embrace.

"I heard you're bout to leave us again. Come inside and get something to eat."

"Thanks mother, but I'm too wired up to eat." I stood by the kitchen table and she hummed, while preparing a plate for herself; a good sign. Sitting down, she pointed to a glass of water and said, "get yourself some out of the refrigerator and have a seat and talk with me Greg." Her voice was trembling a little as I pulled up a chair and sat down.

"You are getting ready to go away from home again and I hope I'm here when you get back if the good lord lets me live, but I want you to remember that I love you. You got to always put God first in everything you do and go on out there and you show them what you're made of. You hear me? You let them know that you're there."

"Yes mother. I will." I began to get misty-eyed but remained in control.

"And I want you to remember something and don't you ever forget it. Just do the best you can, and you won't go wrong. And Greg…"

"Yes mother?"

"Don't never bring home no white woman." Stunned, I almost expected a laugh, but as I caught my breath, I realized who I was talking to. Mother was serious. She didn't crack a smile as she kissed me on my cheek. Then, per always, we sat and started discussing religion, politics, other current events and the plight of black folk in America, until it was time for me to leave.

"Now you make sure and call me, ok?"

"I will mother."

"I love you, son."

"I love you too mother," I said, as I made my way out of the door in route to Kent County Airport.

Chapter 8

Bye Bye Grand Raggedy; For Good!

Hot Ice

Bernd flew into Grand Rapids the afternoon of December 12, 1976. I had borrowed Sylvester's car earlier that morning, so I picked Bernd up from the airport. I was expecting him to show up in that light brown cotton stay pressed suit, of course cleaned and pressed per usual, but I quickly saw among other things that changed in the almost two years since I had last seen Bernd, he was now wearing jeans and sporting a "Natural Doo" (a hairstyle which straight, thin hair was treated with chemicals, which made it course, and curly, then shaped into an afro).

And here comes my friend Bernd, stepping off the plane, all bundled up for that Michigan and Ohio cold, sportin' a "Nacha Doo"! So, the laughter I anticipated at the sight I would initially see, easily gave way to my joy in actually seeing him and acknowledging the dreams of my new band was now under way. And this enhanced my enthusiastic reunion. After getting him and his bags in the car we headed to find him a hotel room for the night. He got checked in and I accompanied him to his room to drop his bags off before we went to dinner.

"U zee I make it here Grrek," he said loudly as I close the door and he begins to unpack his bags and pulls out a thick brown envelope. "and zig zhis mon, I brink zee maanny just like I tell you I vood."

"Yes, you are and yes you did, and I'm happy you were able to keep your word."

"You zee mon, zhis it vat I do! I keeps my vord Grrek!" he added. Then he pours the contents of the envelope on the bed, I see a stack of traveler's checks, which he quickly tells me totals Eight Thousand Dollars minus his transportation cost to the states. We shared a joyous laugh, as he meticulously hung his clothes, put three over-starched and labeled shirts in the drawer, placed two pairs of shoes neatly under his nightstand, and he assembled his toiletries. In a flash we left his room, hit the road and soon after found a place for a meal and a drink. We sat and ate, while catching each other up on what had been happening individually, since we had last seen each other. We also discussed the band, the new music; and reviewed our pending course of action. Hearing Bernd's tone and his overall attitude at that moment was the beginning of many red flags, but I chose to give him the benefit of the doubt and assume he was just excited to be here; so, after dinner, I took him back to his hotel and I left so he could get some rest.

I spent the rest of that evening finishing my goodbyes to my folks as Bernd and I would leave the next morning for Akron. I made the rounds to Andrew's and MC's to say my goodbyes. MC wanted to hang with me on my last runs, so he went with me to Sylvester's and there the three of us hung laughing, talking and drinking, till the wee hours of the next morning till I had to leave. Before I dropped MC off at home, I told him that Bernd and I would set things up and I would call him in a few days. I went home and finished my own packing and without any sleep, around seven am, Bernd and I made our way to the Greyhound station and were soon Akron Ohio bound on a bus.

Forgetting how Bernd can and will talk you to death, I caught hell most of the early part of the trip while desperately trying not to fall asleep on him. The trip took about seven hours and once in Akron we rented a car for the first week, checked into a hotel room; and I immediately called Phillip to let him know I was back, like I said I'd be. At that time Phillip was fresh out of high school, and only seventeen, so I had to go to his home and talk to his parents, who were religious and very family-oriented. The next morning, after having breakfast with Bernd, he stayed at the hotel while I took the rental car and drove to Phillip's home to meet his folks.

Talking to them was like talking to my own family because I sensed in them, morals, values and teachings similar to those the Williams' family maintained and lived by. When speaking to Phillip's Dad and mom, while brother David listened intently, with my brand of confidence and self-assuredness, I explained my plan, my intent, the work and finances I had already put in and most importantly, I assured them I'd look after Phillip. I may have even come off a little cocky in insisting my plan was definitely going to work! I then asked for their blessings, which after hearing me out and discussing me and my plans among themselves, with the exception of Phillip's next older brother, David, who at that time was an outspoken cynic, I had their consent and support.

Before Phillip and I left to go to Eddie's, when the opportunity presented itself, David hit me with his two cents about folks talking but never delivering on things like this. Among other things, I tactfully said, "I'm not other folks and my plan was going to work!" as Phillip and I made our way to the door. We ended the conversation with him saying, "Uh huh, we'll see!"

Although I was confident he and I would come to like each other, David's blatant skepticism kinda pissed me off a little, since he really didn't know me "from Adam", but I didn't let on and kept it moving. Sometime during the recording of Switch's first album David came out to California for a visit. After he and I shared a warm greeting, he pulled me to the side and said, "Greg I'm proud of you man. You did it."

"You know me, man. I give everybody a hard time but you, you made me back up and shut up because you said

271

what you were going to do, then you did just what you said. I know my little brother is in good hands with you and for that I thank you."

"No David, I thank you for sharing what you just said." I chimed in. "You weren't the only non-believer in the beginning, so I caught hell, but I knew what I wanted and was gonna die trying to get it! I'm just happy I was able to make believers out of Phillip and the others." We hugged and walked back into the studio where everyone was waiting. I recall this like it was yesterday as with most of my Akron Ohio memories.

After meeting with his family, Phillip and I continued to catch up with what life's been like for each other as we headed to see Eddie. Shortly after, we picked up Eddie and the three of us to talked and got caught up on the way to the hospital to see Reggie, then to try to see Bruce. I shared with them my game plan for pulling the band together. Bernd and I were going to head to Mansfield the next day to set up shop and have each member join us down there as soon as transportation and living arrangements for the band were set up, which should only take a few days.

At the hospital it took us a while to find and get to see Reggie because if I remember correctly, he was in the middle of a test or treatment when we arrived and we'd have to wait, so we spent the time discussing our dreams for this band, for our lives and really getting to know each other. Once Reggie had been returned to his room, we were informed and shown where to go. The three of us walked into this larger than normal hospital room, where Reggie's bed lay in the center, surrounded by various hanging metal fixtures which appeared to support his arms and legs. As we drew closer to him, Reggie's male nurse moved away from his bedside. Reggie heard us approaching but could not move a muscle to see or greet us until the three of us had surrounded his head and he could look directly up and speak to us.

I don't know if it showed, as I tried to keep my composure, because I was devastated to see this man like this, which I fought to keep those emotions under control. I really didn't know Reggie then, as I had only met and been around him once. This was the day I heard him play a little something on his saxophone and asked him to be a member of this new band I was forming and yet he was my brother and bandmate from that day. My compassion for human life stood front and center. While still in Michigan Eddie had told me the extent of his own injuries and the fact that Reggie's paralysis was from the neck down; but from what I was witnessing and had to come to grips with, was the fact that this man would clearly never walk or use his arms again.

I recall being startled at seeing four thick metal prongs, which actually looked like a larger version of those claws in an arcade vending machine that contains small toys and stuffed animals, inserted in the front, back and both sides of Reggie's head. I was later told by his nurse this was placed there to hold his head still and in place. This is when I understood and accepted the extent of his paralysis. Although lying there flat on his back, hooked up to various machines, with tubes and wires attached to him and all of the metal fixtures invading his body, Reggie tried to show optimism while expressing his joy in seeing us and knowing the band was about to begin.

Although none of us spoke on the accident itself, we did discuss the fact that I was finally back to move forward with plans for the band to cut this record and head for Hollywood where we would become famous. We all laughed and talked about the band's pending start day. Moving to Mansfield, rehearsing, going into the studio, cutting the demos and even things we wanted to do in our future live performance.

Reggie's efforts to assure me, Eddie and Phillip that he was going to beat this temporary paralysis sentence and join the rest of us in Hollywood did not fall on deaf ears and was followed by our sincere encouragement, in the midst of our individual thoughts and my unspoken doubt that this would ever be. I genuinely liked this guy and really wanted him to be well and possibly join us in California.

The move to California came to be much later but the quadriplegia remained and left our brother Reggie with a fragmented life until he died years later, but still much too soon. Reggie tired in what seemed like no time because we were enjoying our visit; so, Eddie, Phillip and I left him, after assuring Reggie that I'd get back to see him before I left for Mansfield. The three of us left his room and did what we could to pull our emotions together as we walked out of the hospital.

From there, we would continue to discuss Reggie, among other things on the way to Bruce's house. Now, in my being kept abreast of things while in GR, I had also learned that Bruce's mom had died somewhere around the same time as Eddie's and Reggie's accident, so I also wanted to make sure I expressed my sorrow for him and his family's loss, first thing. When we arrived at the house, it took Bruce a minute to come to the door and as soon as he welcomed us in he offered us a seat, asked us to excuse him for a minute and abruptly exited into another room.

Of course, Eddie, Phillip and I were cool with that as we heard him yelling to various young folks, whom we found out were his brothers and sister, telling them what they better do now. After a couple of minutes, when things quieted down throughout the house he returned, clearly exacerbated; but with a smile and a happy greeting for all. The four of us began to catch up as I quickly shared my condolences at the loss of his mother. The tone in the room became subdued as Bruce shared details of his mother's unexpected passing, how her sudden death caught everyone in the family off guard and left them devastated.

Due to the fact that there was no dad or anyone else to step up, he was the oldest. This meant, now Bruce had to become head of household to support, raise and take care of his siblings. This also meant that he was no longer able to join the band. From that sharing, the whole tone of our conversation changed as this news surprised the three of us. Of course, we understood and gave Bruce nothing but our support and encouragement with his new path in life.

He continued to express his own sadness and disappointment in no longer being able to be a part of this exciting opportunity; but what was also made clear was, he understood and accepted that taking care of his family was exactly what he had to and would do. To ease things up in the room I began to make light jokes, so all of us laughed and chatted for a short while until it was time to go. Again, Eddie, Phillip and I wished him the best, and we all said we'd be in contact from time to time.. As we began driving, I was consumed in thought as to how I would fill this new void in my band, in my plans. The three of us began to name and discuss drummers we individually knew in the Akron area who might possibly work with and for the new unit; but nothing real would come of it that night, so we resumed discussing Reggie and Bruce's situations.

By now, it was evening and each of us was hungry, so I dropped Eddie at home, then Phillip and I joined Bernd back at the hotel and we went to dinner. While he and I began to discuss our individual progress of the day, I spoke on my new dilemma in losing Bruce, the band's drummer. I informed him that Phillip and I were going to make calls locally to find a replacement, but no one had immediately come to mind for either of us. In my having lived and played in Akron over the past couple of years, I knew other drummers. Even a few very good drummers, but none of them fit the image I had in mind. Before I could say more Bernd interjected, "Vhat about Jhody mon?"

I quickly snapped back, "Bernd, my plan is to have all young, handsome, talented cats with fresh minds and fresh outlooks. That's the look, the sound and overall image I want and that's what I plan to stick with." I said this while considering my current situation, knowing I had to quickly find and lock in a solution. "Besides, since all of White Heat's members had left Akron, I'm not sure where any of them are other than Darnell, Bobby and Mutley."

Although I did have ideas of who I could call and possibly find out where each one of them were, my mind was stuck on new, young musicians, new music, new look, new name and everything new; so, this time I knew we would make it! So, I simply changed the subject by saying, "between Phillip and I, we should find someone locally by tomorrow, before you and I leave here for Mansfield". We then began to review and discuss what we had planned upon our arrival in Mansfield, what had to be done first, second, third and so forth to be set up for the band to arrive in just a few days.

We talked while we finished eating. I was quite tired after this long day, so I went to my room and went straight to sleep while Bernd stopped at the front desk. Unlike the day before, the night went by in what seemed like minutes and I was still tired when my alarm went off; but there was too much to be done, so I wasted no time taking my shower and getting dressed to meet Bernd in the hotel lobby.

We found each other, hopped in the rental car and drove away to find a place for breakfast and begin our planned day. Bernd wasted no time to inform me that he had found a hooker and took her back to his room after diner last night. I listened but didn't comment or show any interest, so the subject just melted into the air. We found a breakfast restaurant and grabbed a newspaper on the way in. Once seated, we ordered our food and started making a list of the various things we would need to get the band off the ground.

As he and I were putting our thoughts to paper I couldn't help but constantly focus on the fact that I was still without a drummer and I nor anyone else had thus far come up with an alternative, till again Bernd brought up Jody. This was at a time my heart and mind were open to change, but Jody and I were brothers who had never had any real problems with each other since the day we met. Yes, I wanted fresh new blood in this band but with Bruce now unable to fill the shoes that were once exclusively his, I would have to do something and do it now.

So, after breakfast we went back to our hotel, where I immediately began to make futile calls to see if one other drummer could possible work and to find out where White Heat members had gone since the breakup, and more specifically where Jody could be found. Fortunately, TC and Stanley's sister June gave me a phone number where she believed Jody could be reached. In my finally accepting that Jody would be a good choice as the drummer for my new band and not wanting to waste any more time, I called the number June gave me and to my surprise Jody answered the phone.

He too was very surprised and excited to hear from me. He welcomed my call saying, "Geez man it's great to hear from you. How are you? Where are you? What's going on?" he asked with all the wonder and enthusiasm of a five-year-old.

"I'm great man and I'm here in Akron," I said.

"How long have you been there in Youngstown?"

Between the mutual excitement with so much to ask and say, our words began to stumble over each other a little. We questioned how each other was, how things were since the band broke up, where and what our other brothers were up to and so on. As that talk moved on I said, "Jody, I'm here in Akron because I 've started a new band and I'm calling U to see if you are interested in joining us?"

He listened quietly as I began to discuss my plan, then interrupted me saying,

"Greg, I'm living with Jackie now."

Jackie was Jody's main girlfriend for years and the mother of his toddler son, which I learned when she popped up with child in her arms in Phoenix during Bobby's and my first few months as members of TNT Flashers.

"Man, we got married after the breakup of White Heat."

"Congratulations man!" I slipped in as he continued to speak.

"Since we got married and moved to Youngstown, I had thrown in the towel about doing music anymore and I gave her my word I was done, because after all the times we (TNT Flashers) tried and never made it, I had to make some changes for my life. And you know that Jackie hung in there with me through all of the different bands and the ups and downs. Now I've got a wife and a son and I gotta think of what's best for them too.

"I understand Jody; remember I was on that dream train too, but we can't let that setback stop us. Tell you what, how about I come up and we go get a meal and talk?" I said, knowing if he took a minute to hear me out face to face he too would see where my head was at.

Then he threw in, "Greg I'd like to see you, but I don't want you to think you gonna come up here and change my mind."

"I accept that Jody, but I just want you to know my plan is gonna work! This time it's gonna work. And I know you, like me, can't stop playing music for too long."

I paused just long enough for that to register, then trying to not sound too anxious I said, "Tell you what, what are you up to tomorrow?"

Jody explained that he wasn't working yet and had no major plans, so he and his son would be home all day. I took a breath to think out the things Bernd and I had to get done before heading to Mansfield and asked, "How about I call and come see you tomorrow evening?"

"That would be great Greg. Jackie will be home and can watch Dink (Jody's son's nickname) while you and I talk."

"It's a deal. I'll call tomorrow before I head your way," I said, and we hung up the phone. I began to feel a little better having spoken with Jody, even though nothing was definite as yet; but maybe, just maybe he would be the solution to my dilemma. In my knowing I wanted to discuss things with Jody without Bernd convoluting the conversation with redundant shit, which would in no way be a valuable contribution I decided not to mention Jody and the fact that I was going to see him.

Bernd and I spent much of the following day shopping for the things we would need to set up shop. With the band needing its own transportation, first we followed up on an ad we found in the newspaper for a 1970 Ford Econo-line van.

When we reached the home and owner of the van, we saw that it was somewhat beat up and rusted out a little, but Bernd test drove it and it ran very well and the guy only wanted Three Hundred Dollars for it, so we bought it. With Bernd driving the van, as I hadn't learned to drive a stick at that time, and me driving the rental car, we made our way to the Ohio DMV to register the vehicle and get new plates and tags. After that, we dropped the rental car back at our hotel then our real quest began, to find and buy other needed things.

Throughout that day, Bernd and I ran from place to place knocking things off of our list. As we filled up the van, made restroom and restaurant pit-stops, the day went by quickly. By evening, we had found and purchased items like home furnishings, including: cookware, bean bag chairs, beds and air mattresses, among other thing, enough to accommodate nine men. What was left to buy was a few instruments, including amps and a PA system; and we would look for a house large enough to accommodate living and rehearsing, once we made our way to Mansfield the next day.

Once back at the hotel, I opted out of having dinner with Bernd and instead I called Jody, made sure he was available and we were still on, told him I was on my way and I drove to and met him at his apartment in Youngstown. After I parked and found his apartment, I knocked. Jody opened the door and invited me in. He and I hugged like we hadn't seen each other in many years, as Jackie and lil Jody came into view from another part of the apartment. I spoke to her only to hear a mumbled response, which let me know I wasn't a welcome sight to her, and Jody saved the awkwardness of the moment by saying, "Hey Greg, let's go out on the balcony where we can catch up."

Under the circumstances this was music to my ears. Per usual, it was cold outside in the middle of this Ohio winter, but Jody and I were both bundled up and with what we had to share, the cold didn't really matter.

Once on the balcony, our reunion was definitely a happy one. We fell right in, laughing and talking about everything and everybody, sharing mostly fun and happy memories of our years together, as well as catching each other up on what happened since the White Heat break to date. Once I began to discuss my current plans, my new band and where I knew it was going, between my jokes to keep things light, the conversation turned serious for both of us; as I knew going in, this could be an uphill challenge. But I also knew what was in Jody's heart as was in mine; the music!

I listened intensely as Jody began to share where he was at that point in life and why he'd come to certain conclusions and decisions. "Greg, when White Heat broke up I was lost and angry. Signing with Barry wasn't our first deal, it was our third and they all fell apart. After coming that close to making it for like my third time, I felt betrayed again. By Barry, by the business and my music; and once again, the rug was pulled right from under us. I don't wanna go through that again. I can't go through that again Greg. Now I've got a wife and a kid looking at me, counting on me to do the right thing for all of us!"

Finally pausing and taking a breath, I spoke. "I understand, Jody, and I really don't want to sway you if that's what you honestly feel, but…" I knowingly told Jody a lie because I did want to sway him. In my own desperation I had to sway him with whatever words or tactics I had within, because I had everything I needed for my super band except a good drummer; and despite my earlier position, I was happy to change the makeup of my vision to include Jody. With my and Bernd's schedule in my mind and knowing that Bernd would have to exit this picture very soon, now Jody had to be the one to fill the shoes of my right arm and it was my job to convince him and convince him now.

"Man, you gotta know that this shot, this band is different than White Heat, than TNT Flashers, even than Charmin and the Tissue!" we both laughed at the first name for the Flashers. I continued, "And Jody, this band will be totally different than any of the bands I've been with because this one is my dream! This is going to be the band that I envisioned, man, years ago. The band who's so talented that each man can and will sing and play all instruments and the band who is so spit and polished they light up the stage before they set foot on it. A band that is young, energetic, personable and fine enough to grace any album cover and yes, that band which nobody can deny! Jody, this time were gonna make it!" I said it with such confidence and conviction that I felt it throughout my entire body, and he'd have no choice but want to be a part of this.

I proceeded to explain my overall vision for this new band, about the songs I had already recorded while I was in Michigan, about my plans to cut new music. I told him that Bernd was also with me in Akron to manage the band and he brought money with him that he had gotten from the Pall Mall cigarette company to finance the recording and Get this band off the ground.

"I hear U man and I really like what I'm hearing, but I've still got a lot to think about."

"Jody, I know I come out of nowhere with this plan, but I also know that music is what you were born to do and making it is what we're gonna do!"

"I'm with you Greg, I see this so clearly and if these guys you have are as strong as you say, let's do this man!"

I hadn't seen Jody this happy since we signed the contract with Barry White. In the White Heat days, Jody and Muttley were tight, Bobby and I were tight; even though I admired, respected and had a longer history with Darnell more than anyone else in the band, due to being the business heads for the band he and TC were tight. Stanly was a free spirit, so he would hang with friends inside and outside of the band; while Vince, being the eccentric of the family, mostly stayed to himself when the band wasn't rehearsing or hanging together.

But throughout all of that time Jody and I were brothers. We did share and live the dream together. We had positive impact on each other's life and mutual respect throughout our years together, so working side-by-side again will be great. It was clear to see his joy and excitement as we talked.

Then, with a sudden serious change of face, as if someone had just punched a hole in his pretty, big red balloon Jody flipped the script with, "Now here comes the hard part Greg. I've gotta go tell Jackie what we're about to do and boy she really ain't gonna wanna hear this! See, before we got married and moved here, I told her and told myself that I was done with the music business, and I've even been looking for a regular job too. But I've gotta do this with you man. I am a musician and I cain't be nothing else," he said with a strained look on his face, as if he needed to convince himself.

"Tell U what, let's go someplace and get some coffee and talk some more. Hang on, I'll let her know we're gone, and I'll come right back." Jody then stepped into the door of his apartment. I had a minute to look around the complex while thinking about what else he and I would and should discuss before I had to head back to Akron. Just as memories of the White Heat days began to drift back in my mind, out of nowhere all hell broke loose in Jody's apartment. There was shouting and yelling, as Jackie was verbally beating Jody down; but he was able to get a word in here and there.

As they began to turn up the volume I heard Jackie yell to Jody, "There you go again, joining another damn nonprofit organization! Just what do you expect me and Dink to do while you're God knows where playing with your friends?"

Jody quickly came back at her, but I couldn't make out his response. At that point I had moved to the far side of the balcony in effort to not listen, so I really couldn't understand anything else that was being said by either. I just hoped it didn't get violent or go on much longer. As Jody was getting the last word in, he stepped out on the balcony and said, "Come on Greg, let's get out of here..." to which I quickly complied."

Once out of the door and on the way to the car, I asked, "Are U ok man? Better yet are you gonna be ok?"

"Yeah man, I'm fine and she'll be alright too. She better," Jody said while trying to shake off the negative energy.

He and I hopped in that cold car, turned the heat on full blast and he directed me to a coffee shop not too far from his apartment. By the time we got there, all of the negative energy had dissipated. We both ordered coffee and a snack, and we began to talk business. Jody again asked who each of the committed musicians were, where they were currently and how quickly would we assemble.

As he and I bantered back and forth over the existing set-up and personnel, including Bernd's role Jody inputs, "Greg,

I don't want to just be one of the fellas, I want to be involved in the business also. I haven't just been sitting on the sidelines all of these years without learning anything and I've definitely got to have a voice in my future."

To which I said, "Of course, man. Me, you and Darnell can run this thing and make it happen. Your experience and talent are invaluable. As soon as we all get together in Mansfield we can get started.'

"Thanks Greg. I'm sure you understand how I feel, we're gonna make it this time, partner!" He said with a broad smile on his face.

Jody and I sat there laughing, talking, planning, remembering and enjoying sharing musical dreams again for another hour or so. In both of us, realizing the lateness of the hour and the fact that I had to drive back to Akron that night, we decided to call it a night. Before dropping him back at his apartment I assured him that Bernd and I would have the house and be ready to go over the next couple of days; and I would give him a call with the info.

Just as he was getting out of the car he said, "Thank you for thinking about me Greg. We're gonna make it this time and don't worry about me, I'll be there as soon as you give me the word."

"See you in a few days Jody." He closed the car door and I hit the highway, headed back to Akron. Once on the road, having accomplished my mission, I was too excited to be tired; so, I must have driven over the speed limit because I made it back to Akron, to the hotel and to my bed in no time.

The next morning, after I had seen or communicated with my new band members, including a call to Arnie to let him know that Bernd and I had made it to Akron and would be in Mansfield later that day to get things rolling. Finished with breakfast, Bernd and I re-packed the car and headed to Mansfield, Ohio, to set up shop. At the onset of this journey, it was understood that Bernd was to be our manager and I would be the leader of the band and the producer of the music.

While in Michigan I had written and arranged a few songs for the new band and project. On the way Bernd and I talked some and listened to the radio whenever we could find a decent black radio station here and there. During the ride, I slipped into the conversation that I had talked to and met with Jody last night and that he agreed to be the drummer for the new group. Bernd abruptly interrupted me asking

"Vhy didn't you tell me that you were gonna see Jhody Grrek? I vould like to zee him too mon."

"You will see him in a couple of days Bernd," I said to calm him down.

"He's joining us in Mansfield, once we've got the house set up. He'll be here with the rest of the band, so you and I really have to get this done quickly."

"I know zis Grrek. Zee, I got it under control. I have everysing under control, mon." Bernd replied with such arrogance; and I again saw more of those red flags and knew they would get worse over the coming days. As Bernd and I prepared for the band to join us in Mansfield, various things he did and said quickly let me know we would not be able to work together long. But as with most first negative signs, in the thrill of what was finally happening, I overlooked it.

Upon our arrival in Mansfield, we checked into a hotel. I first got to my room, caught my breath and called Arnie to let him know that per my word, I had arrived. Early the next day Bernd and I went to what would be the band's temporary home to empty the van and familiarize ourselves with our new home and surroundings. Upon dropping the things that we had purchased for the band's new band house, Bernd and I got back in our new used van and headed first to Greyhound to purchase bus tickets for Tommy and MC and then on to Akron, picked up Phillip, on to Youngstown, picked up Jody and headed back to Mansfield.

As soon as the house phone came on, I made a call to Tommy and MC to let them know that their tickets were paid for and waiting for them. Since no one answered at MC's I called the DeBarge home and spoke to El who told me that Tommy was nowhere to be found and he didn't know where to look for him. But, having overheard the explanation, Momma DeBarge took the phone from El and said, "Hi. I know you're looking for Tommy and he hasn't been around here for a couple of days, but he'll get back here soon."

"Ok. But as soon as he gets there will you please tell him that his ticket is at Greyhound waiting for him and I'm waiting for him here in Mansfield."

"You know I'll tell him as soon as his big head walks in here, because this is the call he's been waiting for. It is all he talks about; Greg and the new band."

"Ok Thank you. I'm gonna call MC to let him know what's …"

She quickly cut me off before I was done, saying, "Greg, I know you're going to look after Tommy, so I'm not worried about him. It's Bobby I'm worried about. I think he's going to kill himself with those drugs. Can you send for him too?"

I could hear the worry in her voice, but besides the problems I knew would come along with Bobby, I had already asked Arnie and he agreed to complete the sound I sought for this new band, so I was moving forward with what I had.

"Etterlene, you know how much I love Bobby, but I can't do it. The drugs he's on are serious and he'd only ruin what I'm trying to do. I can't do it now, but I'll try to hook him up once I get this off the ground. I promise."

Her voice broke. I heard her sigh. "I understand and I'm thankful you're taking Tommy. I know all of you are gonna be just fine, cause we're all in Jesus' hands." I hung up with Etterlene and fought back the sadness that wanted to consume me. I had told her, as I had told myself and the few others that had asked, that it was Bobby's drug addiction which kept me from adding him to my new group, while conveniently omitting the fact that he was also too difficult to deal with ninety-five percent of the time; complaining about everything, everyone, not being able to trust, believe or act on faith as this dream of making it in music requires.

Having often been frustrated in working with irresponsible, difficult musicians, I handpicked each member of this band for their musical and vocal talents, for their looks but most importantly their ability to get along with me and each other. Bobby was the handful of issues and psychological problems that I could not take on just yet, as I had since the day we met. I did not want to destroy this band's chance of survival before it was able to get off the ground. My instincts and insight repeatedly told me that my new unit would not survive his poison in the long run, successful or not. I also knew that once my new band was off the ground Bobby would be the first person I would go back and get because I loved him. God sent me to him to protect and support for the rest of my life and because he was one of the most talented people I had ever met in my life. So yes, as bad as this sounds it was convenient for me that heroin had control of his life to the point that he was unavailable for me to deal with him at that time.

Now, Tommy was another story. Besides his talent and good looks, I knew he didn't carry nearly as much negative psychological baggage as his older brother and I also knew Tommy's love and respect for me, made him loyal to me as long as I could help him get out of his own way. Like now, even though he promised me he would be ready when I called on him, I didn't know if he would come back to the planet long enough to get my message, pick up the bus ticket I had waiting for him and get his ass on the bus. I knew I would continue on, but I would wait and keep Tommy's spot in this band open until I had no other choice but move on without him.

Tommy had earned a track-record for getting caught up in things and getting lost along the way, so his tardiness here was no real surprise; but just the same, I needed his ass here; and how dare he leave me hanging like this! I wasn't mad, but I was and would be concerned until he got here. I just hoped he realized that this was his chance at a new and much better life and I really didn't want him to fuck this up. With everyone and everything moving right along, I continued to call Etterlene for Tommy, but she could only repeat that he was nowhere to be found. But she would have the brothers keep looking and let him know I'd been calling constantly; so, Jody suggested we call a guy named Jerry Williams, a bassist friend who's' brother Tyrone was an original member of the Flashers.

Although he did not necessarily fit my initial vision for this band, Jerry was a guy and a good bassist who was close by in Steubenville and was looking for a band to join, so Jody suggested that we at least meet and talk with Jerry about filling in until Tommy DeBarge arrived, which we did. Jerry agreed and was with us in Mansfield the next day.

As it stands, I've got Jody, Phillip, Arnie and MC here in Mansfield, Jerry whose filling in until Tommy arrives, and Eddie who is a firm member but will join us in Cali. I have Darnell who's already on the west coast, Reggie whose place is on hold should he ever get physically able to join us and lastly Bernd, the "mis-manager" who's really beginning to drive me and everyone else crazy by trying to ride shotgun over my band, over my dream like some deranged slave master; Unbeknown to he or I, not for much longer!

Once everyone understood what the goal was, understood what was expected of them and had settled into our temporary life, we began to rehearse. Getting the core of the new songs together, vibe-ing with each other musically, laughing, talking and getting to know each other was our complete agenda at this time.

Fortunately, after a few days in I called Tommy one last time before throwing in the towel and he answers the phone. He begins apologizing all over the place for being MIA. I let

291

him know the band wasn't waiting, but his ticket still was waiting for him at the Greyhound bus station if he was ready to use it. Then I said, "Tommy, everybody is here getting things done, so if you're serious this time, get your ass on the bus and get here."

Thank God Tommy arrived three days later. When he called, Bernd, Jody and I picked him up and all was on from that moment forth.

With the exception of Bernd, the ages and personalities of the individuals in the house worked well. Once again, Tommy was the jokester of the band and kept everyone laughing. I was amazed at how much he'd grown as a person in the year I was gone, but not surprised at how he'd developed as a bassist. Tommy practices relentlessly and his timing was impeccable. He stayed real close to Jody, who was a good entertainer and showman, but had problems maintaining a steady tempo. Tommy actually helped keep him steady.

Tommy's favorite targets, for his pranks and jokes, were Arnie, who had a ferocious stutter, and Bernd, with his German accent. Bernd used the word muzafucka like he wrote it; and his favorite line was, "I gots da veed, mon." Meaning weed. Tommy really laid into him when Bernd went out one day and returned with his re-done perm, like an afro, and proclaimed, "I am broza now Grrek."

"You've always been a brother Bernd," I said, trying not to laugh.

Tommy mimicked him so much and so accurately that we begged him to stop because our stomach's hurt from laughing. Bernd's antics were very comical but often

292

annoying because he didn't know when to give things a rest. Basically, he was a good dude who meant well, but he would talk you to death and have the audacity to get upset when you couldn't listen to his many unfounded, illogical hypothesis any longer. He was one person, who could talk his way into a great deal then talk himself right out of it before the conversation ended. His and my initial understanding was, by him getting the money for me to start and record my band, he would be the manager; but after being around him under these circumstances, I quickly learned that I could not allow him to represent me, my dreams in no way, shape or fashion because he would ruin everything he touched out of sheer ignorance.

Underneath his arrogance and total lack of understanding of how to deal with most folks, Bernd really was a nice guy who had no malice in his heart; so now, with our arrangement underway, I decided to deal with his personality as much as possible and try to teach him who I was and how to deal with me. As Bernd paid the bills and bought additional necessary things for the house, the band and I created a rehearsal schedule. Besides being the founder/organizer, I was also the cook of the house on the few days we ate home-cooked meals, a skill I had developed and become pretty good at since my preteen years. Beyond using my kitchen skills, this meant there was a lot of cheap fast food being eaten in that house also.

We kept the house as clean as a band of young musicians could but didn't really have much time to socialize with folks other than band mates. We were on a mission that called for complete dedication and focus. We had an eight-song demo to get completed so we pretty much ate, slept and drank the music. I came to know that Tommy, Phillip and MC hooked up with a few girls from the neighborhood who were attracted by the music like moths to flame, after Jody and I took those fateful flights to L.A.

All of the band members set up the equipment in the living room, just as White Heat did in the house in Akron and the new band jammed and began to know each other musically. With Jody and Tommy already having a serious work regimen from the White Heat days, they were tight from the start. Now with Arnie on keyboards, MC on guitar, Phillip on percussion and me on the Fender Rhodes, the new unit became a reality. Our rehearsals were serious and tight. Under my direction, everyone learned the songs I had written or arranged, Jody's songs, and an idea Tommy had come up with.

Our days were filled with music and vocal rehearsals. Because we didn't really know anyone in Mansfield but Arnie and each other, in the evening we spent our time playing spades, laughing, talking and watching television, while a couple of us at a time would play chess. Now and then over that short period, a few of us would get out of the house and explore the neighborhood. A couple of times after rehearsal, Arnie who was home in Mansfield, would fill his car up and take as many of us that would fit out for a burger or to the pool hall or arcade; while Jody, Bernd and I would hang behind and strategize what Bernd would do with the masters in L.A.

Initially we had decided to put the shopping and other business in his hands. Yes, with each day we grew tighter as a band, as friends and as housemates in a short time. Jerry had become such a part of the overall; even after Tommy arrived, Jerry stayed on as one of the fellas, through rehearsals and even the studio sessions, returning home to Steubenville only after Jody and I left for California.

After a couple of weeks, we had a solid compilation of about eight songs. As the band got closer and the music got tighter, the more outrageous Bernd became. Besides being bossy, and his dictatorial attitude towards the band, the music and me, it became clear that he was using money which should have gone for the band, to buy large quantities of weed and ugly ghetto prostitutes. I thought, since he had gotten the money, he was entitled to a few personal pleasantries, as long as it didn't interfere with the music. However due to normal bills and Bernd's excesses, the money was dwindling fast; so, with Arnie's help, we found a local photographer and had a few pictures taken of most of the new band members which included, Phillip, MC, Tommy, Arnie, Jody, Jerry and me. This took some doing but Jody and I also convinced Bernd to pay an extra month on the house bills and expenses before the money simply ran out.

On top of everything else, the prostitutes were causing trouble because they'd be kicking Bernd's ass and coming to the house at all hours, disturbing everyone. Well, Bernd's antics, excuses and attitude all came to a head one day in the studio. We were recording overdubs on a track and Bernd kept pushing the talk back button, stopping us to tell us what he liked and did not like about what we had just played. His persistence had long past irritated everyone, including MC who was trying to complete a guitar solo. After a few more times of this shit and seeing MC's frustration on top of my own, I stopped the band and went inside the booth to talk with Bernd.

"Bernd, you don't play an instrument, you're not a producer and you don't know shit about this music, so stop interrupting us," I said.

Suddenly he began to yell. "I do know vhat I say mon. I'm in chage Grrek."

"Say what Bernd? You don't have a voice when it comes to my music, understand?" I started, but was cut short by Bernd saying...

"I'm in charge of za buchet, Grrek."

"I know you're in charge of the budget Bernd, but what the fuck does that have to do with this music? The budget gives you no authority when it comes to creating and recording this music. You're stifling folks' creativity, irritating and pissing everybody off. Plus, I'm getting sick of watching you waste the money. Money which you got to make our record, but you're spending it buying weed and trickin' with them ugly hoes. Now you touch that button one more time and you and I have got a real problem."

He turned red and puffed out his chest. "Fuck you, you muzafucka."

I looked out at the band, who were watching us. They couldn't hear us, but they see our mouths moving, our body language and how we were becoming more agitated. I know Bernd and I had to be an alarming sight, because when I finally get angry I move around and use my hands a lot, while Bernd flinches constantly and looks and acts like a sodomized goose when he's flustered. By now Jody had left his drums and was coming through the doors.

"No, fuck you, Bernd. Fuck you and this whole shit!" I yelled.

"I can't take no more of you. You've got to go."

Coming out of the booth and returning to the studio, I read the concern in everyone's faces.

"This muthafucka done lost his rabbit ass mind, y'all, and he's got to go, right now. I know y'all sick of him too, so don't worry guys, I made him pay all of the bills upfront, when he was buying all of that weed and paying them ugly hoes. But, we still have to make every moment count to get this demo done. We have a few more days, then Jody and I can try to get to California."

Fortunately, we'd recorded the bulk of all the songs and were just adding voices, embellishments and the final touches. I knew, after we finished recording that day Bernd would have to be dealt with promptly and I had already planned with Jody. I also knew Bernd had to give the Pall Mall people something for their money and he needed some music, so I had Tom, the studio owner and engineer pull up the songs White Heat had written and recorded just before we broke up.

We didn't have the money to pay for the studio time, so the tapes were left there till the bill could be paid. Using some of the money Bernd had for the band, we paid White Heat's past due bill thereby getting ownership of the abandoned tapes.

I left the booth, got my notebook and wrote this release agreement claiming ownership of the recorded master reels, firing Bernd and describing all the reasons for his firing. I also specified he was to have nothing more to do with the band or me from that day forward. Coming back into the booth, I thought Bernd and I might go to blows because he was still red-faced, and his hands were balled up into fists. I put the paper in front of him. "Sign this Bernd."

He read the paper and tried to negotiate it; but realizing that I wasn't about to budge from my position, he bowed his head, signed it and walked out the studio, speaking in German. I knew he was hurt which made me a little sad because I did not want or anticipate this outcome, but he really had himself to blame. I told Bernd before this whole thing got started that I was very serious about making it in the music business and I would let nothing, or no one stop me, but that in itself is hard for most folk to understand. Since he couldn't play an instrument and join in, Bernd wanted to control something that not only could he not control; but no matter what he'll never really understand. Well, the true Bernd showed up and showed out. bringing with him such a negative impact; and he had to go before he destroyed the moral, the music, the business and the whole damn thing.

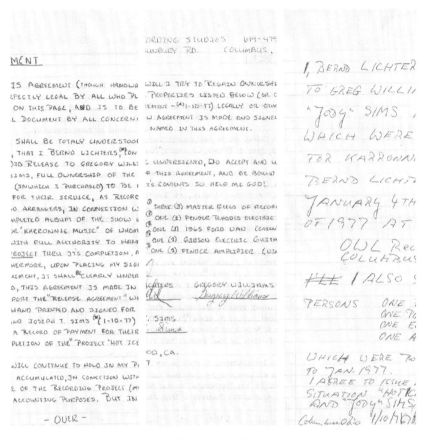

Bernd Contract Release

According to what I'll call Bernd's exit contract, his compensation would include publishing and licensing rights to the remaining White Heat song masters, which we had to pay for from the monies Bernd was able to get from the Pall Mall Company at the onset of recording any new songs. Being mostly green to the ways of music industry contracts, I did not include how the rights and entitlements of master ownership would go, as I also failed to secure songwriter agreements.

On top of this, even though Bernd was incapable of making any musical contribution whatsoever and his limited misguided business decisions, Bernd would be listed among the producers of the masters and have complete control thereof; but, it was also agreed that should he get the project released, he was supposed to compensate each of us as artists, writers, arrangers, musicians and Darnell, Jody and me as producers by paying royalties, once the album came out.

None of us have seen a royalty from this project to date. While saying his goodbyes to the rest of the band, Bernd had the studio personnel gather up and pack the White Heat song master reels for him; and without another word to me, he left the building. He apparently went to the house, packed his belongings and left for L.A. that same day; and Jody and I didn't see him again until back in L.A., after we had met Jermaine and Hazel, but before we signed with Motown.

He had left us with the van, left us with the few instruments purchased with the budget, and most importantly, he left us alone. After the session ended that day, with the exception of Arnie who had family waiting at home, we all went back to the house, trying not to show the serious concern building up about what we were gonna do now.

Not wanting the younger band members to worry, Jody and I went up and down, back and forth discussing, first with the band and later by ourselves, what and how things must happen from this point. We had to reassure everyone that Bernd's absence was a positive move and things would definitely continue moving forward. Once away from everyone else, Jody and I did some serious talking about our next move. We knew that the studio was mostly paid for, up to mixing and mastering; we knew that the household and utilities could stand at least another six weeks, since we had Bernd pay up and over what was needed, so no immediate worries there. The fellas would stay put and we would send for them shortly.

Jody and I decided with Bernd gone, we would have to go to L.A. to shop our own tape, but the real question was how? How would we get there, where would we live there, how and where would we get enough money for the two weeks we were working on a deal?

We based on our own confidence, arrogance and downright musician's ignorance; and the answers came almost as quickly as the questions. First thing Jody and I did was call Darnell, fill him in on how everything had gone thus far and about the split with Bernd; and we asked if we could crash with him and Linda for a few weeks while we got situated. Throwing his total support behind the plan, Darnell instantly opened his heart, his mind and his home to us, as soon as we could get there. Next thing was how in the hell were we gonna get to L.A.?

Knowing I had no money and no real way to get any, Jody suggested he'd get money from Jackie and possibly one other girlfriend for the plane tickets, so with that, it was on me to call home for a few bucks that Jody and I could eat on; and per always, my uncle Albert came through without hesitation. Now the next concern was getting the music mixed and mastered by the studio on credit; and lastly, when would we leave for L.A.?

With one serious conversation with Tom the studio owner, it was decided that, since the White Heat masters were finally paid for, we could repeat that same deal, whereby they would complete the mixing and mastering of all of our songs and they would provide us two cassette masters to shop with and we would pay the balance owed once our deal with any record company was made; which actually happened some three months later.

After making sure everything else was worked out, Jody and I decided to lock in our flight for February Eighth, Nineteen Seventy-Seven. All problems solved!

Over the next few days Jody, Phillip, Tommy, Arnie, MC, Jerry and I put on our "open for business" and "no bullshit allowed" attitudes and hustled till the creative part of the project was complete.

The tracks, vocals, arrangement and production of our new demo recordings were, mixed, mastered and compiled down to two, two-inch master reels for making additional copies and two cassette tapes. One to be left with the band and one for Jody and me to take to L.A. to shop. At the end of those last few days, we were all exhausted yet satisfied with what we had accomplished. Now ready to go out and conquer the world, once back at the house Jody and I planned what was next to be done and called a meeting with the fellas to tell them what the plan was from here.

"Hey fellas," I started. "Now that we're done with a picture, bio and the masters, Jody and I are going to L.A. to get a record deal and I'm sure we'll have one in two weeks," I proclaimed!

I knew Arnie would be the first to speak up, saying, "Two weeks? Come on man."

My instant comeback was, "I'm serious man. With everything we've got going, this is gonna happen, Arnie."

"You know, if anybody can do that, Greg can do it," Tommy threw in proudly.

I knew, he said, what everyone else, even Jody, was thinking. "Have I ever lied to any of you?" I asked.

From around the room, verbal and nonverbal acknowledgment came with Tommy summing the response up with, "No, Greg, you've never lied to me."

"Then y'all trust me on this one." All of us spent the next hour or so discussing and planning what would happen with the band as a whole while Jody and I went off to make things happen.

During the next twenty-four hours, things moved really fast. When morning came, the entire band had breakfast together and we continued talking about getting everyone to Hollywood once a deal was locked in. Jody and I packed all of our personal belongings, then we went to the studio to conclude all band business and pick up the two cassettes, one to take and one to leave with the band.

While there, we received messages that Jackie had called, stating airline tickets had been purchased and were waiting for pick-up at the airport. What Jody and I had yet to discover till we arrived at the airport ticket counter that Jackie had purchased two first-class tickets in Jody's and my name. Upon completing our business at the studio, all of the fellas jumped in the van and we headed to Port Columbus International Airport for Jody's and my long flight to Los Angeles.

Chapter 9

SWITCH, MOTOWN and ME

Rick James, Jermaine Jackson & me

Well, Jody and I made that fateful journey to Los Angeles. We hit Hollywood armed with one tape and blind confidence we were gonna get our record deal.

While on our quest this day and after being rejected in our impromptu, chance meeting with then RCA Records President Don Berkheimer, we stepped back out on Sunset Blvd., headed east and wound up stopping two blocks from RCA at this tall office building, just off of the North-East

304

corner of Sunset and Vine. In front of the building was a large emblem of the letter "M" resting on top of a few short stairs and another one, front and side on the top right corner of this 22-story building.

Unknown to either of us at the time, this big "M" represented, of all places, Motown Records! Not knowing where we were and what was about to take place, Jody and I made our way inside the building and stopped at the big business directory, which was mounted dead center of this lobby. We began to scour this directory for an attorney to represent us in a newly decided claim/suit against Barry White. When we came upon the name "Kirk Lawson, Attorney at Law" on the directory, it was clear that both of us somehow felt he was the one who could help us slay this dragon named Barry White for the rape and robbery of our band White Heat, in having used our talents while treating us like "red-headed" stepchildren.

Upon giving us the boot, since the band's name "White Heat," was created and owned by Barry, he took ownership of that name when he dropped us from his roster and from RCA Records; leaving us nameless, homeless and stuck in the mid-west. To add insult to injury, Barry White even stole our bass player Vince, who initially allowed the band to think he was going home to Pittsburg for the weekend, when in actuality, Vince and Barry had been plotting behind our backs that Vince would join his band once White Heat was dropped. Anyway, Jody and I had took note of Mr. Lawsons suite number, hopped on an elevator and headed to the twentieth floor to Mr. Lawson's office suite. Once in the lobby, Jody and I waited our turn to speak with her as she was engaged in conversation with this small thin black man, who we took to be an attorney, working in the suite. As he was given his mail and began to walk away, the receptionist looked towards us and asked, "may I help you?"

"Yes, we're here to see attorney Kirk Lawson," Jody said. Upon hearing his name, he quickly stopped in his tracks and said, "I'm Kirk Lawson. What can I do for you gentlemen?"

To our surprise, Mr. Lawson stood about five-feet six to Jody's and my six feet tall, and he spoke with this thick southern accent.

"Hello, I'm Greg Williams and this is Jody Sims. We were in a band called White Heat, produced and managed by Barry White and signed to RCA Records a couple years ago."

He reached out to shake our hands, welcoming us and he invited Jody and me to follow him to his office. Once in and seated, he listened to our tale of woe, asked a few questions and quickly shot our dream down because we did not have any contracts or documents from the Barry White deal to show him. So, in this case he had no choice but to let us know there was nothing he or anyone could do without contracts.

So, no dragon would be slain here today, and Jody and I would have to keep it moving, emptier than we were when we first walked into this building. I can't recall how or when; but in sharing our life story and then current condition and circumstance with Mr. Lawson, we discovered that not only did he sound like a knowledgeable and bright attorney, he was a kind, compassionate man; because Jody and I exited his office downhearted, but twenty dollars richer because, upon having heard our story, he clearly took pity on us and reached in his pocket and loaned us twenty dollars to eat off of for the next few days.

Again, we thanked him for his time, advice and his money, promised to pay him back when we returned with the record and management contracts, and made our way from his office suite onto the elevator to begin our journey back to Darnell and Linda's couch and floor.

The irony of our leaving Kirk Lawson at the precise moment and selecting this particular elevator, we had no idea nor could anyone have guessed what fate had in store for us, our bandmates, and indirectly our families lives forever.

While it seemed to me, to us, that time was standing still, suddenly three elevator bells rang simultaneously announcing their arrival. Of these three possible chariots to the ground floor and out of this tower of doom, together we picked the elevator and got on, not knowing that this elevator would bring us face to face with our dreams, our destiny because two floors down, Jermaine Jackson of the Jackson Five, wife Hazel Gordy Jackson and Motown Records were waiting to join us on our ride down and pick our lives up forever.

As the elevator bell rang announcing its stop on the eighteenth floor, Jody, me and a couple of others moved back to make room for whomever was to join us. As this black couple entered these doors, Jody and I looked at each other, immediately knowing who our new arrivals were. Because this particular elevator was partially full of people between them and us, all four of us simply smiled, nodded in acknowledgement of each other and continued on in silence.

After traveling from the eighteenth floor with a few additional stops and travelers joining our journey, the elevator finally stopped on the 5th floor and the Jacksons got off and were gone as quickly as they had appeared. Jody, me and other elevator occupants continued downwards, stopping floor after floor until we finally arrived at the lobby, the elevator doors opened, and everyone exited.

At that moment, Jody and I were suddenly face to face with a rude awakening and a more than probable lost opportunity, but without a second thought we recovered and prepared to make up for our temporary "duh" moment by repeatedly pushing every button in sight hoping for an up elevator, without one word between us. We knew we had to try to catch the Jackson couple to follow through with what we came to Hollywood to do and watched the magic happen from that point.

We stepped into that elevator praying we would catch them and like in a fairy tale we stepped out into a whole new world. Now our trip back up was no easy effort either. Back on with a few new occupants, this same elevator finally began to rise. Jody and I feverishly pushed the button for the fifth floor until we finally reached our destination.

We jumped out and ran down this long corridor, seeing signs on the wall pointing to the parking structure exit. Upon arriving to the exit door, just outside we saw Jermaine and Hazel stopped, sitting in their car as if waiting on Jody and me to come running through the door with cassette in hand. Jermaine was in the driver's seat initially looking down inside the car for something.

When they saw us running towards them, instead of showing fear, he lowered his window as he and Hazel smiled to welcome us. I've always been sure of myself and never recall myself stuttering before; however, after a brief "Hi, I'm Greg" and "and I'm Jody", I tried to talk, but stutter is all that would come out.

"We, we, we, don't want to ta-ta-take up too much t-tt-time but we go-ga-got, this tape and we, want, we want you to listen to it," I said.

To my surprise Jermaine stuttered back. "Yu you ah you're right on time. Ah I, ju ju jus just stopped here toooo to lo-loo-look for a ta-ta-tape to play."

Totally caught by surprise to hear Jermaine Jackson stuttering for the first time, I somehow spoke clearly this time.

"Well, will you give this a listen?" I said, giving Jermaine the tape. "We know you're gonna like it!" Jody chimed in, as I came back with, "Its' new music by our new band. Here's a number where we can be reached."

Oh, oh, okay. I'll, I'll, I'll, listen tooooo, it," Jermaine said. He took the tape, shook both of our hands, he and Hazel still warm and smiling so all of us said our goodbyes as they began listening to the tape brown drove off in their new brown Rolls Royce.

As Jody and I watched them drive away, he blurted, "Hey Greg, you know we just gave him our only tape."

It then dawned on me too that we had given up our one tape without a second thought! "Yeah man but you know we had to do that. We couldn't miss that moment."

"Yeah. I agree. This is so exciting ain't it?" said Jody."

Yes, we were floating, hoping, praying, thanking God and believing something wonderful had happened to our lives this day, and we were right! Man, what started out so crazy turned out so right. After we made it back to the first floor and out onto the street, we headed west on Sunset towards home with a stop on the way to get something to eat with the twenty dollars Mr. Lawson had loaned us. By now, we had forgotten all about our visit at RCA Records.

Still full of adrenaline, excitement and serious hunger, we found a little, cheap coffee shop down on Vine street and went in. This place was small but clean, with a few customers inside; so, Jody and I went in, ordered our food and talked about this insane day we had been living. We must have spent hours there talking and reordering coffee because when we finally looked up, it was now dark outside; so, we paid our check and continued to dream about what might be next as we headed back to Darnell and Linda's.

When we got there, without taking time to catch our breath, we immediately filled Darnell in on our crazy day. We talked about the possibility of Jermaine and Hazel calling us back, till bedtime. After pink rolling up our hair, it was Jody's turn to sleep on the couch, so I took the floor, but tonight it was really cool because I somehow knew it won't be long now.

Upon waking up the next morning I sensed a promising day ahead. With Darnell and Linda off to work, I, then Jody awoke to get cleaned up and start our new, normal Hollywood day. From yesterday's thoughts, we began discussing who we should try to see today until it hit us like a ton of bricks, hell! We don't have a tape!

310

"I guess that whole thing with meeting Jermaine Jackson of the Jackson Five and his real pregnant wife Hazel Gordy Jackson, Berry Gordy's daughter really happened yesterday, huh Greg?" Jody asked. The two of us shared a giant, hopeful laugh and as in disbelief, we began a total playback of the events of our yesterday.

As the sunlight had left for the day, another Cali winter night was upon us so, with the few dollars we had bummed off of Kirk Lawson, we decided we'd walk down on Santa Monica Boulevard and grab a bite. As we were ready and about to leave, the phone rang so I answered it.

"Ha-ha-hello, ca-ca-can I s-s-speak to Greg and Jody?"

"Yes, this is Greg," I said, hoping this call was from who I thought it was... and sure enough.

"Hi. It's Jermaine. Ha-a how are you guys?" Before I could respond he continued with "Ha-hay-hazel and I, liiiiike, you ga-guys tape. "That song called "Can This Be" is a smash." As Jody was yelling hi to him through the phone I was thanking him for liking out tape. Jermaine then asked, "Wa-Wa-What you gagaguyzz u-up to?"

"We're not up to anything, Jermaine. About to go out for something to eat," said Jody.

"Ma-ma-my wife Ha-Hazel's in labor and I'm here waiting at the hospital. Do you, do-do you guys wanna come ddadown here? Can you guys come-come down here so we can-can ta-ta-talk?"

I wanted to scream Hell Yeah! But since he didn't know me, I decided to contain myself and ask, "Where are U at? Jody and I will be there as soon as we can, just tell us where it is."

311

He told us Cedars-Sinai Hospital in West Hollywood and that was all I needed to hear, so I told him that we would get there soon. After hanging up, Jody and I got the address of the hospital from Linda, called to get the correct bus route and directions and hurried over there.

From Darnell and Linda's front door to the Cedar's maternity lobby took us just short of an hour. Jermaine was sitting in the waiting room alone, watching the television. As soon as he saw us walk in he stood up to shake our hands, looking very happy to see us.

"Hi-hi guys. Thanks for coming down here." He said. Hazel's in there having the baby so the doctor sent me out here. We-wa-wa-we- listened to your tape all the way home last night an-an and we-e l-l-like it. While we were still shaking his hand, Jody and I thanked him for liking the tape, for calling us back and for asking us to come and hang with him here at the hospital.

Jermaine had this broad smile on his face and asked "What-what do y'all want me-me to do-o?"

"If you can help us, we want a deal" Jody quickly blurted out.

"Ha-Ha-Hazel and I ar-re, starting a-a company in Motown called Ya-Ya-Young Folks. You guys ca can be, our fi-i-i-rst act, ok? Wha-wa-wa- what do you-uo you guys call yourself?"

"First Class," Jody proudly stated to which I nodded in agreement.

From there we talked for at least two hours. As we got acquainted, we talked about birthdays, our ages, our zodiac sign, about the band, how we got to L.A. and he told us a lot about Hazel and himself, his family and more about Hazel's and his new venture.

We'd been talking for a good while when, Jackie, Tito and Marlon arrived. Jermaine introduced us and told them we were part of a band he and Hazel might be working with. The brothers shook our hands and encouraged our working with their brother and his wife as our conversation grew branches. I remember how elated I was because these were the coolest people I'd ever met. Not that I've ever been star struck but here I was, spending time with four-fifths of the world-famous Jackson Five, and true to their public image they were nice and down to earth folks.

After a while, Jody and I tried to leave, feeling this was a family moment, but they engaged us even more. Within an hour of their arrival Michael and Randy arrived and they too joined in the conversation. Soon after that Jody and I excused ourselves, and we all shook hands and said goodbye. Once back on the street, Jody and I jumped in the air screaming, and danced all the way to Darnell and Linda's home where we were staying.

I had taken for granted that Darnell would be with us in the new band, but I soon learned otherwise. Darnell and Linda both worked days, so he didn't really have the time to hang out with Jody and me; so, when we finally made the time to discuss things further, we sat down and put him up on where things were at and going. After everything had been said, Darnell shared his concerns about Motown's negative reputation and said how he wouldn't want to put his musical career in their hands should they offer a deal.

I immediately understood and accepted what he was saying because all of us had heard the negative stories about Motown throughout the years; but personally, I never bought into rumor in any walk of life and didn't seek out Motown for a deal. But the way this chance meeting occurred, I knew it was an act of God and a possibility that I wasn't about to walk away from. My faith and optimism were in control and I could only see the win in signing with this company.

Before now I had never considered Motown in my dreams of having a record deal. I can't say I had not considered it because of the negative things I had heard or because I considered it out of reach. Anyway, Darnell then told us that Bernd had contacted him and asked him to be the leader of a band, Hot Ice and under that name he would sign a deal with Polygram Records Germany and release the White Heat/TNT Flasher recordings that I had suggested he pay for and take from the studio shelf in Ohio.

Hot Ice (1977)

I then agreed to go back into the studio with Jody, Darnell and Bernd to finish production on that material. Even though I accepted Darnell's pass on Motown, and subsequently Switch, I was somewhat hurt and disappointed because after basically growing up together, being in local bands, being college roommates and his getting me into TNT Flashers/White Heat, I always knew Darnell and I would make it in music together.

Although not in Mansfield from the start of this new band, I knew once I had gotten things off the ground he would be a part of it. See, from what I knew, he and I were like-minds when it came to diligence, responsibility and over leadership, I knew that we would be at each other's side. But I would soon come to learn that even the best laid plans are subject to change, especially when there are elements beyond your control. Having not spoken to the guys since the day we arrived nearly two weeks ago, Jody and I placed a call to them back in Ohio, but the phone had been disconnected.

We tried to reach Arnie but there was no answer at his home either, so I made a call to the Ingram home to find that Phillip was there. Once he came to the phone, I told him about our meeting Jermaine and how we had given him our tape and again I assured Phillip that we were gonna get a deal. I was surprised when Phillip told me that after they had run out of food and the heat in the house was about to be shut off, M.C. had gone back to Grand Rapids while he and Tommy had come to Akron a couple of days earlier and would be living with his family while I worked things out in L.A.

Although Bunny and Mutley volunteered to come to Mansfield and take Tommy back to Grand Rapids, he told them no. He had told Phillip much about his home life, including about the physical, sexual and emotional abuse he suffered for years, and how he really didn't want to go back there, so Phillip asked his parents if Tommy could stay with them for a little while, till I called for both of them; and they kindly agreed after telling Tommy that he would have to be responsible and work for his keep, just like Phillip would. Once again, I was appreciative for the Ingrams. Phillip yelled for Tommy to pick up the downstairs phone, so Jody and I could talk with both of them.

While waiting for Tommy to pick up, Phillip added, "Hey Greg, Eddie is out of the hospital and ready to come, but there is no change in Reggie's condition."

I chimed in, "That's good news about Eddie. Let me have his number and the Hospital number for Reggie if he's allowed to accept calls and I'll call both of them." To which he did, as Tommy happily picked up the phone and joined in the chat.

Tommy immediately started stuttering like Arnie, to which all of us burst out in laughter. I jokingly scolded Tommy for doing that and Jody got in asking how Tommy was holding up and repeating what we had just told Phillip. We then told them that they could get ready to come soon, said our last, and hung up the phone.

We then called M.C. who had been back in Grand Rapids for a week or so and had gotten back into his old routine awaiting my call. Once he answered the phone, not knowing who was calling, I asked laughing, "You ready to roll Baba??"

"Hey Baby. I been waiting for this call, ha, ha, ha! I don't care what you got just get me outta this muthafucka." He laughed.

"Help is on the way, M.C. Jody and I met with Jermaine Jackson today and I know something's bout to happen, so hold on a little longer."

After M.C. proceeded to tell me what was happening on the Grand Rapids music scene and complain about being buried in waist-high snow, we confirmed again that he and the others would soon be joining us in Hollywood, and we got off of the phone.

Jody and I couldn't sit still from excitement and happiness. We went back out and walked around Hollywood, elated over the fact that this shit is real, and we were about to close a record deal that I told the fellas I'd get in two weeks. After a while we decided to return home for the night.

After couple of weeks back in L.A. Jody and I connected with Bernd when he came by Darnell and Linda's apartment. Unknown to Jody and me, the two had reconnected soon after he left us in Mansfield. Initially, I was a little apprehensive after our last scene, but Bernd quickly made excuses for how he acted; but they carried no truth whatsoever.

After seeing Jody and I weren't having it, he apologized for how he dealt with us and tried to laugh off his poor handling of our business. After a minute or so of watching him squirm, we forgave him anyway, knowing that we would never work together as artist and manager, or any other business capacity again. After that, he acted as if everything was OK and asked Jody and me to work with him, Darnell and then noted studio engineer Roger Dollarhide to complete overdubs and mixing of the White Heat throwaways for release in Germany and all of Europe, under the name Hot Ice.

In our wanting to help make Darnell's and Bernd's project successful, Jody, Tommy, Phillip, MC and I would dive-in to help, cleaning up, adding and producing this music also. Jody and I shocked Bernd by telling him about our then pending deal with Motown. I recall his, Roger's and even Darnell's thoughts and input was so negative, both Jody and I asked them to shut the fuck up because they didn't know what they were talking about when it came to our relationship with Jermaine and Hazel and our level of communication with Motown.

From that point on, although we would never do any business with Bernd and intentionally kept hanging with him down to a minimum, we forgave him and went back to our friendship; and together we completed the project. Bernd had the songs mastered and including a couple of deals for the same masters, he now, some thirty years later has them on the internet as Smash and he has a website full of lies, misplaced ego and misinformation about how HE started it all. What a fucking joke!

Although the new band, which we were by now calling First Class, was totally excited and committed to our pending deal with Motown, Jermaine and Hazel, all members would put their heart and soul into completing the Hot Ice project since we knew that it too would represent us should it ever see the light of day as an American release, as well as what Bernd planned to do in Germany; but again, Motown and whatever they asked of us came first.

Jody and I were given permission by Motown to use the phones anytime and get free albums from the mailroom and other miscellaneous minor privileges. We began to tactfully take advantage of them all by placing our first call to the guys in Ohio. Phillip answered the phone and we told him about our meeting Jermaine, how we had given him our tape and that we met with him again the next day. Again, I assured Phillip that we were getting a deal with Motown and he, Tommy, Arnie and MC would be coming to California soon.

Phillip then added, "Greg, Eddie's been cleared by his doctors and is ready to come, but there is no change in Reggie's condition."

I then let him know, per our conversations with Jermaine and Hazel that things should begin to move fast from here and bus tickets would be sent soon. To get things rolling, Jermaine and Hazel informed Jody and me that their next move would be to introduce us to representatives of Motown's business and creative department.

The following day, we got a call from Lee Young Jr., Motown's head of legal, who invited Jody and me to have lunch with him and Skip Miller. It was clear that Lee and Skip wanted us to be impressed and a little psyched out because the extended invitation was for us to meet them at the world-famous Brown Derby restaurant on Vine off of Hollywood Blvd at 1 pm the next day. This would be our first-time meeting Lee and Skip, and little did any of us know at the time, they would both be directly involved with our career in one way, shape or form from our beginning to our end at Motown. And I'm proud to say, despite the ups and downs of my years at Motown, I consider both to be my good friends.

This lunch meeting was to begin shortly, after beverages were ordered, so Jody and I again ordered our new favorite drink, Chivas Regal with Coca Cola back, which Lee and Skip found funny, while both discretely tried to hold back their individual laughter. Once they ordered their drinks, they informed the waiter we would need a few minutes, so he disappeared.

Feeling a little apprehensive, not wanting to look stupid or be the butt of a joke, before anything else could be said I sincerely asked, "Is there something wrong? Did we order a bad drink or something?"

"No not at all!" Lee quickly interjected with a chuckle.

"It's just that real Scotch drinkers' usually have their drink either neat, on the rocks, with a Perrier, Club Soda or water back, but usually never with Coke." Then Skip also laughed followed by me and Jody.

From that point I knew that I and believe that Jody never ordered and or drank Chivas and Coke back again. After that ice breaker, the conversation moved right along with a lot of questions and answers by everyone at the table. The feeling of coming off unsophisticated hung with me throughout that meeting, mostly because it's the truth; but the mutual exchange continued, and a lot was learned by Jody and me that afternoon.

As with most new things we'd pick up, we would spend hours discussing and analyzing all, once we got to ourselves. Of the various important issues and concerns discussed, it turned out that as part of our deal, Motown would want to have ownership of our master, which our demo songs were on. We learned that this was a common practice with most new artist signings with most record companies. This is done to make sure that the artist or no one other than the record company has possession and/or rights to legally manufacture and release product on the newly signed artist. Product that could compete with, interfere or disrupt the record company's control of the artist and subsequent releases.

It was also questioned and suggested that Jody and I be given artist, songwriter and producer contracts, then create our own production company where we could sign the rest of the group to us and if we chose we could give them money from the advance we received. Not totally understanding all of the ramifications of making this type of deal; but hell-bent on not alienating or becoming superior to any of the fellows I had pulled together to make this unit.

I quickly stated for the record, "No! I pass on that suggestion. All of our band members were in this together. From where I stand, that's how it will be from beginning till end."

To which Jody stood in agreement stating, "That's how it's gotta be with us."

So, with that, the four of us at the table moved on and began to discuss the various steps that need be taken so the band can get to L.A. and prepare to do a showcase presentation for various Motown executives and some staff before they would decide to sign First Class to Motown. Once it was decided to move things forward, at the urging of Jermaine and Hazel, at Motown's urging and expense, they moved Jody and me into the Holiday Inn on Highland Ave in Hollywood, allocated us weekly per diems and sent bus tickets to all of the other band members to journey to L.A.

With things beginning to pick up for us, Jody decided he should take time to return to Youngstown, relocate his wife and young son to California, while plans were being made for the other band members to join us out here. While waiting for the guys to finally arrive and the showcase to happen, Jermaine, and I started hanging more frequently. His main protégé, at that time, was Michael McGloiry and they were together much of the time working on music for Jermaine's forthcoming solo album, so he would sometimes pick me up or I would meet them at the studio since it was also located in Hollywood not too far from my hotel, or up at his and Hazel's office in the Motown building where the three of us would laugh, talk, get to know each other and most importantly, write songs together.

Even though Jermaine was busy and more often than not playful, I sensed certain loneliness in Jermaine. His brothers had left Motown in 1976 and although he had contact and even got to see them, from time to time during that period, the close bond was obviously broken due to the different paths they were now on. I picked up he missed the comradery of his brothers and McGloiry and I, and later Switch somewhat filled the void. At that time, Jermaine had no idea what fun and craziness he was in for once he started hanging with the fellas who would soon become known as Switch.

A week or so after checking into the Holiday Inn, I met Lenny Williams, ex-lead singer for Tower of Power. Lenny was also at the Holiday Inn as a guest of Motown, while negotiating, and about to sign his deal with the label. Lenny and I became instant friends and later introduced him to my bandmates upon their arrival to L.A. Between Motown making the travel and lodging arrangements and the fellas being notified and preparing, it was about two weeks before they all arrived.

While on hold, I repeatedly called Arnie, to fill him in and get him on the next bus, I hadn't caught up with him yet, but I didn't think he was avoiding my calls, I just thought he was busy; and I didn't have a way to leave a number for him to call me back, so I kept calling Ohio again and again. After more than a week of calling, I finally did reach Arnie real late one night, waking him up.

"Arnie, what's happening, man I've been calling you all week. Like I promised, we got a deal man!" Arnie was quiet so I continued. "Man, we're gonna have a deal with Motown. They're sending bus tickets for all of you to come out here so we can do a showcase and get signed."

I heard Arnie breath heavily into the phone, but still saying nothing. I thought he was trying to get his thoughts together to keep from stuttering.

"Th-that's goo goo good news Gr Gr ahh Greg. I'mmm ha ha happy for you guys, but Sue and I talked about it an an an an and I'm not coming."

"But Arnie, we got the deal man. I've been hangin with Jermaine Jackson from the Jackson Five, man; and Motown wouldn't be sending you tickets if they weren't serious."

"I ca ca cain't coco come. I'm sorry Greg bu bu bu bu but I' I I'm not coming."

"Ok. Ok Arnie. I got it, but you're really losing out. You take care man."

I hung up the phone. I didn't understand what I was hearing. What I had to accept. Here I had basically built this group around Arnie's life. Moving to Mansfield because it was Arnie's hometown and so he wouldn't have to leave his family or drive up and down the Ohio freeways in all of that snow, ice and bitter cold; writing songs that would fit his voice and style of keyboard playing; catering to his schedule for band and vocal rehearsals.

This dirty muthafucka! I thought to myself once it set in that he really wasn't coming. He could have told me this shit before I left Ohio, chasing this dream and saved me the grief that was now staring me in the face. In my mind, Arnie's refusal to come put me in the worst dilemma I'd ever faced. We now had a pending contract with Motown and no lead vocalist. I'd written songs and molded the band for multiple vocalists, with someone who could sing in a high falsetto, and do duos with Phillip and now I had no one. The one option I had, presented something I didn't want to deal with; pain, chaos and destruction, so Jody and I pondered over what could be done if Arnie didn't change his mind, which actually, he never did.

Well, just as Bernd tried to sway me to get Jody when we found out that Bruce could no longer be with the band, Jody tried to sway me to get Bobby to fill Arnie's void. I resisted, but the fact remained that something had to be done now. I was totally confident that no matter what, we could get a deal elsewhere; but I wasn't about to let this opportunity, this bird in the hand just slip through our hands because Arnie wouldn't come. Although he had been very important in the beginning, I could not allow him to fuck this up for the rest of us. A serious decision had to be made because Motown would want to hear the band soon after they arrived, so there was little time to try to figure something out.

This dilemma rarely left my mind. The more I considered calling Bobby, the more I thought, more than likely he would fuck things up;, but maybe, just maybe not before the band was strong enough to stand on its own name and I had become a record producer. Well, Bobby was my brother and he too deserved this shot; but again, and most important, the thought of losing this deal with Motown was too much; so, it outweighed the fact that I wanted life free of Bobby DeBarge's fucked up issues.

Then and there I decided to bite the bullet and let it do what it does! After sharing my thoughts with Jody, understanding there might be major problems, he was excited about the thought of Bobby joining us. Even though he knew Bobby could be and had been a handful, to my knowledge, he had no idea of the extent of psychological damage that had festered inside of him. He had no real idea, as I had, that Bobby's drug use was way beyond an escape or cry for help, but more another few miles down his inevitable road to self-destruction.

With the exception of Jody's return, now the fellas were here in L.A. and settling into the Holiday Inn where Motown had put us up. I waited a few days till everyone was situated and getting past the awestruck maze of actually being in Hollywood. One afternoon, I called all the guys in the room, except Tommy, who was talking on the phone to his family in Michigan because I'd told him my decision first.

Once Jody, MC. Eddie, and Phillip were in my room, I began with, "Guys, Arnie's not coming. I called him when I called you guys and various times since, only to be told that he can't come; and I'm left with no choice, so I'm gonna call Bobby DeBarge and see if he can come. They did not know the extent of my reluctance and concerns, but they did know that I had some kind of problem with what I had decided to do. Eddie did not even know Bobby at that time, but Phillip and MC certainly did. Since MC came to L.A. from Grand Rapids, I asked had he seen Bobby before he left. He said he hadn't, but he knew from mutual friends that Bobby was strung out on heroin.

I loved Bobby and I wanted to help him, share this dream with him once again and to laugh and talk and even cry like we used to. But the thing that I didn't want, which I knew had to come with him were the demons that haunted him. Those that were imposed on him during infancy and would dwell inside till the day he died. I was also worried what influence he was going to have on Tommy, who didn't have enough sense or concern to be scarred. In my knowing much more than I wanted to about the sexual deviance which existed in the family and largely perpetrated on the brothers by Bobby, I was definitely concerned; and yet due to the reality of all the circumstances, I was helpless to deny him his role in this dream, knowing left to his own devices he and he alone would turn this into a nightmare.

Other than the weed that, with the exception of Phillip, all of us smoked everyone else in the group was solid and had no real bad habits. I was bringing someone with bad habits into the band because, in the front of my mind, I had no choice. No other option. While waiting on the last member of our newly formed band to arrive, bond and move forward with us, I showed the guys around our Hollywood surroundings, my favorite haunts and where the good, cheap food was. A few of the fellas had friends and/or relatives here in California but we waited a while to make contact and invite folks up to the hotel; so, when we weren't with Jermaine and Hazel, or helping Bernd with the Hot Ice project, we would just hang together.

We would walk around Hollywood, make new friends and meet girls who would frequently end up in our hotel rooms and beds. Of the earliest visitors, I remember when I met James Ingram for the first time when he drove up to see his baby brother Phillip. James had been living here in L.A. for a few years, now having packed up his wife and child and moved from Akron with his then band, Revelation Funk. In talking with James, I was informed that, at that time, the band members had since gone their separate ways and that he was currently playing keyboards in sessions and was the MD for Ray Charles.

Five days later Bobby arrived on the Greyhound, so MC, Tommy and I trekked down to the Hollywood station to pick him up. The second he stepped off of the bus I said to myself, *Damn, looks like he's still trying to shake that shit."* With one look, I surmised he'd probably been using for most of the trip and had probably run out of heroin on the last leg of his five-day trip to Los Angeles, because he was white as a sheet, he looked weak and he was stinking of stale sweat and vomit. Once we got Bobby to the hotel, Jody, MC, Tommy and I had to get him to the room, which he was to share with Tommy. It was clear he was still going through withdrawals because one minute he was cold, the next minute he was burning up.

He also couldn't control his bowels and frequently vomited as nothing, including water, would stay on his stomach.

Bobby's first forty-eight hours in California were mostly spent in bed. As he got stronger, Jody, Tommy, MC and I took care of him. Over much of these four-five days, the only thing that would settle Bobby's stomach was coca cola and bread, until finally he was able to walk around and go outside. As he healed, the only real difficulty with Bobby's situation was we had to keep Jermaine, from coming by the hotel to meet Bobby, until he was through kicking this Heroin addiction.

Although Hazel was preoccupied with being a new mom, among other things, per the past few months, Jermaine wanted to hang with us and he would call and ask questions like, "Wha wha what are you gu gu guys doing? "When will ya ya y'all be bebe ready to begin rehearsals fa fa fo for the showcase for Motown?" and "Ddddon't you guys wa wa wanna go do do do something?"

After giving him excuses for a week, we told Jermaine we were ready to get to work and the next day someone from S.I.R aka Studio Instrument Rental's rehearsal and showcase studios called me at the hotel. This person and I talked for a short while, until we had locked in a rehearsal schedule for the band to prepare for the forthcoming showcase with Motown.

Starting that next afternoon, we rehearsed daily for two weeks, primarily teaching Bobby the new songs from the demo which got us in with Jermaine, Hazel and Motown. We also finished and added two of Bobby's original ideas, since Bobby, Jody and I had already recorded and performed this song with White Heat. We also included Stevie Wonder's "I Love Everything About You" to showcase Bobby's full range.

Since everyone, including Jermain and Hazel, was totally comfortable working at S.I.R., it was decided that our showcase would also take place there in a much bigger room, for the following week. Now since we were also getting per diems, Jody and I suggested that all of us run out and pick-up new clothes for this maiden performance, and on the day before, the seven band members got a late start, but walked up and down Hollywood Blvd from one end to the other, Vine to Highland and back-again to shop for cheap clothes to wear in our performance.

After a bit of walking and shopping, Tommy yelled out, "I'm hungry. Can we stop and get something to eat?" As if in practiced unison, everyone chimed in; so, we walked a little longer and found a little, cheap coffee shop down on Vine street and we all went in. This place was small, but clean, with a few customers inside; so, we figured it should be cool and we wouldn't have to wait long to be served.

Once inside, the only waitress met us at the door with menus in hand and showed us to seating which would accommodate all of us. She proceeded to pass out menus and asked, "Do you fella want coffee?" This lady, who was dressed in a wrinkled black and white waitress uniform was short with stringy black hair and had possibly a Korean/Japanese accent and spoke severely broken English; so badly we barely understood her when asked "you want orda now?" I'm sure most of us had a puzzled look on our face because she moved in a little closer to us, raised her voice as if we had a hearing problem and continued to ask "Orda! You want orda now?"

Finally catching on to what she was saying, we signaled for her to give us a minute as we began looking through the menus. Again, she headed towards the kitchen and continued her conversation in a foreign language with whomever she had been speaking with when we walked in. Being hungry for real, it didn't take any of us long to decided what we wanted, so Jody attempted to hail the waitress to come back. She was looking in our direction but continued here conversation. Finally, after our hailing for her to come to our table a few more times, she arrives and again asked, "you want orda now?" Had she not asked this question before, none of us would have understood what the hell she had just said; and trust me, ordering our food became a united nations summit as her broken English, her funky attitude on top of her limited understanding to our repeated explanation as to what and how we wanted our food cooked, this took more time than expected, before she finally said okay and headed to the kitchen.

After feeling that our orders were finally understood and provided to the cook, we began to share and discuss some of the things we had found while on this shopping exploration. After a few minutes, our waitress returned with our food. As soon as it hit the table, I tore into my cheeseburger and onion rings and everyone began eating what was delivered. Before letting the waitress walk away, Jody looked up from his food. "This fish sandwich is burned!" he declared to the waitress. Although she was in sight, standing by the kitchen door talking to someone, she could clearly see Jody trying to get her, but took her time anyway.

When she finally made her way to our table, Jody repeatedly tried to explain that his food was burned as she kept asking "Wha? Wha" as if she didn't understand. He finally said in a stern voice, "My sandwich is burned, can U take it back and bring me one that isn't burned." Again, she asked "wha, wha?" Seriously hungry and frustrated Jody said "look lady. I can't eat this! I want another sandwich." She then looked at the sandwich, looked towards the kitchen, looked at Jody and said something in her language and again to Jody with a serious attitude.

"Dis U awdud." In turn he stated angrily, "I didn't order no burned fish sandwich, lady!" In a really loud, nasty tone she yells at Jody "Dis U awdud, dis U awdud!" Jody looked at me and said, "Man, this is really fucked up!" The waitress then gets frantic and starts pacing and waiving her arms in the air, yelling at Jody in that horribly broken language. "Fuk me??, Fuk you! Fuk you mother!" Jody gets real mad and I break out laughing at what she said. As Jody puts both hands firmly on the table and attempts to rise, she continues to yell at the kitchen, then back at Jody in her native tongue for a few times.

While all of this was going on, out of the corner of his eye, MC sees this huge Asian guy in a nasty looking apron and a dirty chef's cap, coming out of the kitchen, waving a big meat clever! As it appears he's coming our way, MC stands and all but screams at all of us. "We gotta go y'all, we gotta go! Look at this muthafucka! Look!" All of our heads turn in time to see this big, dirty, four-hundred-pound cook coming out of the kitchen heading our way, with this big-assed meat cleaver raised high over his head like he's about to chop the head off of a chicken.

Everybody in the place stands as we damn-near trample over one another and that little bad English-speaking waitress, as we try to get to the door and get the hell out of there. Needless to say, we didn't get to finish eating in that place, but we didn't have to pay for the food we didn't get to eat either. Once outside the restaurant and totally clear of that situation we made our way back to the hotel restaurant. Over the next couple of days, we were seriously worked and did our thing preparing for what would be for Bobby, Jody, Phillip, Tommy, Eddie, MC and myself the most important performance of our lives.

Meanwhile, Jermaine and Hazel had done their due diligence by researching the name First Class, so collectively, we, along with Jermaine and Hazel had put a lot of work in preparation for our new, soon to be unreal life!

Finally, "It's Showtime!" and as the fella's and I take the stage, we looked out in the audience to see too many of the Motown stars and dignitaries including Berry Gordy; Smokey Robinson; Berry's sisters, Gwen Gordy Fuqua and Anna Gordy Gaye; his brothers, Robert and Fuller Gordy; and his niece, Iris Gordy; along with producers, Jeffery Bowen and Hal Davis; Billy Davis; Greg Wright; and a lot of others, whose names and faces I knew well from album covers, liner notes, magazines, television shows and other press outlets I had devoured over my years of studying the who, what, when and where of my destined profession.

As I glanced around, I saw that also in attendance was then Motown president, Barney Ales; executives Suzanne de Passe, Suzanne Coston and Tony Jones whom I had already met with Jermaine head of marketing, Skip Miller; head of sales division, Miller London; and others unknown to us. I knew I must be in record business heaven; as, with the exception of the specific names and faces I now found myself surrounded by, I had dreamed this dream many times throughout my life.

Well it was time to get this party started and once we hit that first song, I forgot about all of the folks and concentrated on the music. We heard applause and shouts of "yeah", as we played, sang, performed and transitioned from one song, one lead vocalist, one instrument and one place on stage to another. My band was the shit and I knew it! We kicked ass and we knew it. When the complete performance was finished, they gave us a standing ovation. Mr. Gordy was the first to approach us and the room got quiet as soon as he opened his mouth.

"Hazel and Jermaine said, "You guys were good, but I never imagined you were this good! Your show was really exciting. We've got some work to do but you guys make it look easy, so I'm sure we'll make things happen. Welcome to Motown."

Suzanne de Passe, chiming in right after Mr. Gordy, "You guys are great. I've never seen so much switching in my life." Referring to how each of us changed from one instrument to another to vocals effortlessly.

"You guys are amazing. Beautiful songs and great lyrics." Were among the various compliments and comments we received from many of the guest who were introduced or introduced themselves to us after Mr. Gordy spoke to all of us. We had finally the moment we waited and worked for since Jody and I spent that afternoon, evening with Jermaine pacing the halls of the hospital, while Hazel lay in labor. The moment that I was totally confident would come, from since the day I sat on my mom's front steps and created the group that would become known as Switch.

Yes, we had successfully made that big step and were finally moving forward in a big way. Meeting, greeting and shaking the hands of Motown's founder, creative family and other dignitaries had each band member on a high; yet I could not wait to get back to just the seven of us to revel in and savor our victory. Later, back in our hotel everyone gathered in my room and we were reliving our awesome showcase. Among many other things, we also discussed the fact that we still did not have a name for the group and just as Suzanne de Passe's words resurfaced in my mind, I was not alone because suddenly I hear "Did you all hear what Susan de Passe said about us switching?" Jody asked.

"Sure did." I jumped in…"and that's our new name."

"What's our new name?" Tommy asked.

"Switch." I proclaimed.

Yeah, sounds good to me, everyone chimed in agreement, so that was that. We had a new name, a new opportunity and we were all floating ten feet off the ground.

Over the next week or so, the band or at least Phillip, Tommy, Bobby, MC, Eddie and I had time to just hang out and explore our surroundings, while waiting on the contracts. When they came, I, having learned to understand some contract language after the Barry White fiasco, took a deep breath and started trying to read one of the three thick artist, songwriter and producer agreements, which all were between nineteen and twenty-four pages long. Somewhat overwhelmed, I remember discussing with Jody the fact that we needed to find an attorney, as soon as we could. While glancing over these documents and having little to no understanding of what they said, Jody and I made a plan to hit the streets the next day and take them to the only attorney we knew, Kirk Lawson.

When we walked up to Mr. Lawson's office and asked his receptionist was he in, she called him and he actually came to the lobby, saw Jody and me and made time to see us that day without an appointment. We chatted and updated him on what had occurred with us since our last encounter. After scanning through the pages of the artist agreement without really reading it, he pushed his chair back from his desk and proclaimed, "Gentlemen, I don't see where I get my money."

Jody and I looked at each other stunned. We were both taken aback by attorney Lawson's reaction. We had brought the contracts to him because we wanted to employ him and all he could see was how he was supposed to get paid. He then tried to speak a little longer, explaining his position; but Jody and I were in sync and were thrown by his first thought. So, we thanked him, told him we'd find out if Motown would advance us his fees and left.

Needless to say, Kirk Lawson and an attorney whose sole priority was not so blatantly "my money" was the subject of the rest of the day. In my having come to know and befriend Kirk in the following years, I can see a possibly misunderstanding of his intent; but then "my money" was the last thing Jody and I wanted to hear, knowing that it should have been understood that our attorney would be paid for their services from the contractual advance.

For some reason we returned to the Motown offices the next day and we ran into Joy Santos who was a Jobete executive at the time and also girlfriend of my friend, Funkadelic member Billy "Bass" Nelson. Joy and I had met through Billy, so we struck up a conversation about my band being offered a deal with Motown.

While sharing with her our encounter yesterday with Mr. Lawson, seeing our consternation, she waited until there was no one around and had us follow her to her office. We talked a little more and she discretely advised Jody and I on how ruthless and underhanded the record business, and more specifically Motown, could be. She hammered the importance of our finding a strong attorney to get the very best for ourselves up front. Before we concluded, she handed me a piece of paper and said "There is a good law firm called Cooper, Epstein and Horowitz in Beverly Hills, who specializes in entertainment law. I know Jay Cooper the head of the firm. He'll help you. Give him a call right away."

Thanking her, we called the office the next day, which was a Friday and after saying Joy referred us, we were able to speak directly to Jay right away. After hearing us out he said he'd be happy to meet with us and possibly take us on as clients, then he requested that we bring the contracts with us and he set an appointment for Jody and me to come in the following Monday. Jody and I made our way down to the prestigious offices of Cooper, Epstein and Horowitz that following Monday morning.

After the receptionist confirmed our meeting with attorney Jay Cooper, she offered us refreshments as she showed us to a client waiting area away from the main reception area. This was seriously a plush office suite. After a few minutes, Mr. Cooper emerged with a young protégé. He introduced himself and the young man beside him as Michael Bourne. He invited us to walk with them to his office.

I remember, after Joy's build up, Jay came off as expected. After an exchange of proper greetings and my thorough explanation of why we were there Jay got right down to business. He reintroduced Michael, explaining, "He is the firm's newest and brightest attorney and if you guys have no objections I want Michael to work with us since he actually cut his legal teeth on Motown contracts." He and Michael shared a light laugh.

Jody and I, shaking our heads in agreement, "Yes. We're with it."

Jay then said, "then gentlemen I leave you in very capable hands; of course, I'm here whenever you call." We all thanked Jay and he exited the room.

Michael again extended his hand and asked, "Shall we get to this?"

"Definitely," Jody said, as I pushed the agreements towards Michael.

He first picked through the stack and stopped to glance over the artist agreement, which was a thick thirty-six-page document. As he read, Jody and I sat, quietly sizing him up. I was pleasantly thrown off by his initial appearance. Michael was a young blond-haired, blue-eyed, pale-skinned white guy with an eastern European look. He stood about 6'3" tall, a little taller than Jody and me. He was wearing a plaid shirt, jeans with a thick brown leather belt and very expensive, stunning pointed-toe alligator cowboy boots.

When he spoke, his voice was basically soft- spoken, but his tone was firm and matter-of-fact, as he began to explain to Jody and me the paragraphs and terms of the artist agreement. Of course, most of the contractual language was unclear to Jody's and my untrained ears; but I found, after having had a little study of contracts, the more I heard the clearer things became.

As Michael read on, he stopped to explain the reason there were three contracts. One was for our exclusive services as artist, another for songwriter and the last for producer, and all members were to sign individually and collectively. Allowing a minute for Jody and me to ask questions and understand, he continued reading until he got to the paragraph which stated Motown shall have sole ownership of the group's name and I abruptly interrupted him with, "Michael, that's the one issue I'd dreaded would be in here."

"Is this such a problem for you, Greg?" He asked

"It most definitely is, Michael," I stressed.

"Please explain your concerns," he said.

"We have to own the name, no matter what has to be done. It's just that simple," I said, not leaving room for anyone else to speak. "We went through this with Barry White and White Heat and I refuse to let it happen to me again." I explained, seeing an expression of concern come over his face.

"Greg, with Motown, I know this is going to be a tough one, as in most industry contracts, record company ownership of an act's name is pretty standard, but let's see what we do with that. Let me be frank with you, though. As I look at these agreements, they are created totally in favor of the record company, with little benefit to you, until you get a hit record. Among my other concerns, Motown also wanted to cross-collateralize your artist, songwriter and producer contracts," he said.

I know I looked puzzled because before I could ask, Michael continued to explain, "Cross collateralization means the artist, songwriter and producer contracts are inner connected to the other and with reference to royalties are treated as one agreement. In other words, none of you will be paid one dime in royalties, if any are earned, until every cost incurred by you and on behalf of each group member as contracted artist, writers or producers is paid back. Now once you have a hit record we can renegotiate this contract, but right now they have you by the balls. I'll do what I can with things including the name, you'll decide what you want to accept and what's left we'll handle later."

In today's record negotiations, to cross-collateralize, which is currently offered by most major label deals, is called a 360 deal, whereby the record company signs the artist, then invests in the artist's musical and visual image or brand-merchandizing and live performances. This way the company will recoup and earn income from all applicable artist, songwriter, producer, performance and merchandizing revenue.

When Michael got back to us after a couple of days of dealing with Motown's legal department, among discussing all aspects of the contracts he told me, "Greg, they balked and flatly refused to negotiate ownership of the name."

I abruptly responded, "Michael, after what White Heat went through with the Barry White deal, I will not just give my group's name to Motown or anyone else, so please tell them that I will go back to Grand Rapids and work in a factory before I give them ownership of this name!"

While Michael passed on my final response to Motown and waited for their comeback, Jermaine, Hazel and Motown's legal department heads shut off all communication with me and the group for the next two weeks, clearly waiting for me to break and change my mind, but that day did not come.

When they finally got back to Michael they'd agreed to let me keep the name, but I had to relinquish some of my other rights. Each member of Switch signed five-year contracts as artists, writers and producers which included royalty advances enough to afford us bi-weekly salaries and pay all attorney fees.

Some six or so months later, Michael Bourne went on a skiing vacation with his dad in the sierras. They were caught in an avalanche and killed; leaving Switch without legal representation. I was sad for a time to come because, although I hadn't known Michael long, in the short time we worked together, he gained my trust and convinced me he had Switch and more so my best interest at heart, which I've come to know, is not a typical trait for a lawyer. Michael listened and understood my every concern and later translated them into legal language with which we could confront the stack of contracts and ultimately Motown.

By this meeting's end, I still hadn't quite grasped the full extent of cross collateralization, but I did not let that get in the way because we would soon be Motown recording artists. Something that eluded me during the courting and signing period was the awe of my band actually being offered and ultimately signing with the great Motown Records; the current home of R&B/Pop legends, Smokey Robinson, The Miracles, The Temptations, Diana Ross, The Supremes, Stevie Wonder, Marvin Gaye, among other great singers, bands and performers. And let's not forget the hit producers like, Jeffery Bowen, Hal Davis, James Carmichael, Pam Sawyer and others.

Once Switch was signed, we also became part of an elite group of new recording artists, which I called Motown's babies. This group of youngsters included, Jermaine Jackson, Rick James, High Inergy, Tina Marie, while also on the label were acts like The Commodores, The Dynamic Superiors and a host of other acts, actually too many to mention, whom Motown signed and recorded, but for one reason or another they never surfaced.

For Switch, signing the contracts included an advance, which in our case was a sum of money allocated for each group member individually to cover personal and living expenses. Most record company signing advances are usually paid to the Production Company and/or artist in a lump sum, but we were offered and accepted ours in the form of bi-weekly salary checks, paid out on the same schedule along with Motown employees and a few other signed artists. This process was really great for us and many artists who did not have accountants or someone with experience handling large sums of money to cover a lengthy period of time.

Little did we know that this bi-weekly payment was as good as it would get for us during our stay at Motown because then and even after, we did not receive any royalties. To this day we're still waiting for a royalty check.

With me, there was also the looming fact of management and how we were coerced into signing a contract, which at the onset was a blatant conflict of interest. Yes, Jermaine and Hazel did bring Switch to Motown, so it's clear that without them the Motown contract that we now know would not have existed. They also believed in and nurtured us in the beginning and for that alone they should have been and were well-compensated.

But starting from the time they were contracted and paid, the work was mostly absorbed by Motown as the company took over, making decisions as to what happened with and for the group which ultimately stripped Switch of its rights to have management ,which protected and stood up on our behalf and definitely stripped the group of the vast majority of the income which should have come from record sales and concert performances.

Fortunately, we endured and survived that injustice, also in effort to get to the next place. I began to see a pattern of compromise, which troubled me deeply; but my then rationale was, for my talent, for my dreams this is not too big a price to pay.

Chapter 10

Contracts Signed & Moving to Montague

Switch at Montague Home

After living in the Holiday Inn on Highland at Hollywood Boulevard in Hollywood for a few months, once the deal was signed and our bi-weekly checks began, Hazel and Jermaine helped us look for a house. After a few days of learning potential good areas, on our own, we found a house with three bedrooms and a den in the San Fernando Valley, suburbs of Los Angeles.

Bobby, Tommy, Phillip, MC and I moved in, while Eddie and Jody found individual apartments with their families. In this house, Phillip had his room, I took the room across from him, Bobby took the room in the back of the house which had its own private entrance, while Tommy and MC converted the den, which was in the very front of the house, into a shared bedroom. The joined living room and dining area was where we initially set up our equipment. The house sat on a small grassy lot and had a fenced-in backyard where we and a few friends would hang out occasionally.

The surrounding neighborhood at that time was a predominately white, middle class, family-oriented scene, where kids rode their bikes and skateboards throughout the day and well into dusk. There were often backyard Bar BQ's and birthday parties, and most folks were friendly. Of course, we made friends with as many of our new neighbors who would open their hearts and minds and accept our friendliness. Once the word got out about this new band living in the neighborhood and the sight of Jermaine and Hazel's light-chocolate Rolls Royce frequently parked in our driveway, other neighbors quickly began to wave and speak to us, as we would walk around.

We were made to feel like a welcome addition to the neighborhood in no time, with Tommy often making the rounds and visiting and meeting families in our block around dinnertime. As with most houses where musicians rehearse and congregate, the young and teen neighbors tend to walk, ride and stop by frequently, once the music cranks up, as would various friends whom we had reconnected with from home or met since coming to California. We decided to make the living and dining area our practice room just as White Heat had done back in Akron. In our being a new group of poor musicians, never having performed together or earned money working, we needed musical equipment.

Hazel and Jermaine had us create a list and Motown advanced us money to buy the equipment we wanted, except for the Hammond organ I asked for because they decided it cost too much money. At that time, I did not know it was my money that was being spent, money that I would have to pay back. Instead they chose and bought me an Arp Odyssey synthesizer that initially, I was embarrassed to have because I didn't know how to use it until a female friend was over to the house while we were just jammin'.

In her having never seen a synthesizer before, she asked me what it does. But I couldn't tell her because in all honesty, I didn't have a damn clue how to run it and make music with it. The next day I drove to every music store in Hollywood till I found a book about my Odyssey. I bought it, took it home and would woodshed in my room, reading the owner's manual till I couldn't read any more. I waited till the wee hours of the morning when the fellas were either asleep or in bed anyway, I plugged headphones into that Odyssey and played with every knob, button and slider until I could hear, control, manipulate and create any and every sound that thing was capable of putting out.

Switch adapted a routine of practicing about six hours a day which really got the band tight. We developed an intuition about each other, being able to hear where the other was going musically and vocally, and our harmonies became clearer every day. Jermaine would often get his bass out of his car trunk and join us, we'd write songs, and we constantly bounced ideas off each other. We would often have after-practice jam sessions in the living room.

Of the many friends who used to hang with and jam with us, Rodney Trotter and MC were tight back in Grand Rapids, so they just picked up where they left off. Andrew "Drew" Brown, who had actually help me start this whole thing with my uncle Sylvester and MC, Alonzo "Piggy" White, a longtime friend and bass player, Bobby and Tommy's cousin Andre Abney, Phillip's longtime friend Kevin Dorsey, David "Dr. B" Bradford, one of the bands new friends and a host of others, especially new female friends, would converge on our house daily until I restricted the gang visits till evenings so that group members and residents of the house could have some private time, as well as uninterrupted rehearsals.

In those early Motown days, other than Jody, who had the family car he drove out from Ohio with his wife, I was the first Switch member to get a car. With a few dollars left over from the master purchase deal with Motown, I bought Drew's used 1975 Oldsmobile Ninety-Eight, which he had driven from Michigan in his move to California. From time to time the group would have to go to Motown's offices in Hollywood for meetings or other minor outings. A few times Hazel and Jermaine, or Jody would pick some of the band members, but most of the time Bobby, Tommy, Phillip and MC would ride in with me.

All in all, most of the time you could not have found a happier group of musicians than us. We had signed a major record deal and we were sitting on top of the world. Besides the fact that we were finally able to live our dreams making music all day and having to do little else than be musicians, we now had money coming in twice a month to take care of ourselves. Money to do and buy things; to go out for movies and entertainment, money to take others out and pick up the check if we chose instead of asking and/or waiting for someone to give or send us money to buy food and necessities.

Now that the legalities were done and put to bed, we would practice at our house daily. Sometimes we would trek down to Hollywood to have creative meetings with Suzanne de Passe and her assistants Suzanne Coston and Tony Jones who was also de Passe's cousin. We would also meet with Jermaine and Hazel in the Young Folks offices in the same building.

I recall a meeting with the two of them where they told us that we were to meet and possibly work with Motown staff producer, Greg Wright, who also happened to be Dianna Ross's live band's musical director. We were to also meet with husband and wife writer/producer team Mike and Brenda Sutton in a few days to hear and discuss possible songs for our first album. We talked about, as Hazel put it "daddy's big plans for you all."

Our trips to Hollywood and, better yet, Motown were exciting, informative and often fun as we learned about the company and the people we were now signed to make music with. This time Hollywood was a very different place with an

347

altogether different significance than with my, Bobby's and Jody's first time there as Barry White, Soul Unlimited Productions and RCA Records artists. We could live in decent place with windows, versus the shabby hotel Barry White's company herded us into for nearly eighteen months. We would be able to drive our own cars, live in our own homes, have relations with folks outside of the White Heat circle because we would soon be on a salary and be able to afford more than a cup of coffee.

Yes, based on the way this particular contract and deal was structured, to some degrees we could feel more like people, versus merely a disposal product. Most times, while in the Motown building we would talk to the receptionist and other employees that we'd meet. We would, most times, hit the mail room when we first arrived to holla at our friend Tom DePierro, to pick up the new singles, album releases and promotional items by Motown superstar artists, such as: Stevie Wonder, Dianna Ross, Smokey Robinson, Thelma Houston, The Commodores, Undisputed Truth, The Dynamic Superiors, Jermaine, and even music from up and coming artist Rick James, High Inergy, Syreeta Wright & Billy Preston, Flavor, The Dynamic Superiors, and various newly-released records. I guess word had spread quickly around the company about Jermaine's and Hazel's new act because, from the beginning, we were welcomed and made to feel like members of the Motown family.

As signed up-and-coming songwriters and producers to Motown, Jobete and Young Folks, which was the name of Jermaine and Hazel's in-house management company, among other things we were now allowed to do, Bobby, Jody and I were given access to the budget and studio time to explore our creativity. Even though Phillip and Eddie tried their hand at writing, of the music that came from the then six of us, Bobby's and my songwriting and production skills proved to be the most commercial and only grew throughout our years at Motown.

During this time Tommy and Eddie did very little writing, or even co-writing for the group; but Tommy would spend hours on end practicing with Jody, perfecting the bass and drum lines to our songs, while being horn players. Eddie and I would write and arrange horn parts to my songs and Eddie would sometimes write out the charts, break them down and even co-conduct recording sessions of our musical arrangements for the huge horn sections.

With the exception of Jody who also had a finished ear, the others backed up and brought their songs to Bobby and me for acceptance and possible help in completion. Most of Switch's own meetings, rehearsal, arranging and even the songwriting took place in the band house on Montague.

One afternoon while we were rehearsing, Hazel and Jermaine called and said they needed to come by later that evening and meet with us during practice. All of us who lived there dove in to tidy up where needed, as our rule was to keep the house clean and everyone did their best to honor that rule. We would often make our guests help us clean up behind themselves before leaving. When the Jacksons arrived, they were their usual warm selves; but in no time, they became serious as we all sat down looking back and forth at each other.

"We've got a lot to tell you guys about some things that are taking place now on your behalf and about things set to happen with and for you, but right now we need to know from you guys' mouths who's the leader of the group." Hazel stated.

I was so surprised, I couldn't speak. What the hell was this question and what were they up to now. This totally caught me, hell, all of us off guard because they knew I put this band together. From handpicking each member to getting the money to cut the demo, which I and Jody had given them that got this whole thing started. They also knew from the word go that I was also the spokesman on all issues. I had authority in every meeting we had thus far, and I was the one who fought for the group. Without a doubt, I was this band's founder/leader. The group members didn't hesitate.

"Greg!" Everyone but Jody confirmed.

As if the fellas might say something other than what they did, Jody's face twitched upon hearing the band members' abrupt and loud confirmation. Hazel thanked the group and without a breath she began to tell things that had been put in motion on our behalf to get our first album moving forward. Jermaine quickly started laughing and playing with Tommy about his bass and asking us about what music we had been working on. Hazel followed him with how soon would we be ready to present new album possibilities.

MC quickly turned his amp back on, started to play around, Jermaine grabbed Tommy's bass to play with MC and from that point, it was on. We jammed close to an hour until Hazel reminded Jermaine that they had to get going because someone was waiting for them, so soon after that, the music stopped as they began making their way to the door. After all of the hugs and goodbyes between the Jacksons and the band, I walked outside with them to their car. Although I was still pretty shaken by what they had done, I held my tongue till they were in and about to start the engine.

"You know, that was not cool how that was handled," I said.

"Greg, we needed to know who to talk to," Hazel responded.

"You knew and everyone else knew who the band's leader was before all of that. You and everyone else have directed all questions, problems and business to me since we got here, so why do this now? Was that about Jody? You do know the way you two approached that will cause problems and hurt feelings."

"We're sorry, but that had to be done. Yes, we all knew but we just needed things clarified so when things come up, everyone knows where they are to come."

All of us grew quiet, as Jermaine turned the key to start their car. Then Hazel said, "We're sorry, Greg. We'll call you later, Greg." I returned to the house, and once inside, I saw everyone but Jody who was waiting for me in my room. I knew he had something to say to me, so I went to look for him.

"Why didn't you stand up for me Greg?" he said, as soon as he saw me at my bedroom door.

"Stand up for what, Jody? I did put this group together, planned it, got the funding for us to record and I've done almost everything else since, while you go and take care of your family, which was fine with me. I consulted with you about some things, but ultimately the decisions and actions are mine, along with the responsibility when things go wrong."

"If it weren't for me getting those tickets we couldn't have gotten here, Greg."

"I know that man, but that has little to do with who started this band and who's the leader by that fact alone."

He stepped back from me, his jaws tight and eyes narrow.

"Okay Greg, that's cool," he said angrily and turned to walk away, and I touched his arm.

"Everybody in the band has a say and you know it, Jody; and you more than anyone else. Don't let this come between us."

He removed my hand. "I said it's cool Greg."

Shoulders slumping and sulking as I had seen him do before, he walked out of my room straight through the front door, without saying a word to anyone. I followed, trying to talk and make him feel better; but when he got in his car, slammed the door and drove away, I turned and headed back inside.

When I walked back in, MC and Phillip were waiting for me to discuss what had taken place; while Bobby and Tommy had gone into their respective bedrooms, but Bobby quickly came back to join in the conversation. We started discussing how Jody reacted to Jermaine and Hazel's inquisition and all acknowledged that their approach, though actually necessary, was tacky, with Bobby adding, "Greg, you let him feel like he was running things too, but we all know who the group leader is."

352

"I agree, this is largely my doing, Bobby, but you all know that is just my way. I don't feel the need to throw things up in anyone's face about who I am and what I do. I let my actions speak for me. We are a group. Everyone here should have a voice in the things that affect their lives, so I've always welcomed all input."

I thought to myself, *yes Jody was right by my side, making decisions and making things happen with me, once he came aboard in Mansfield, but truth is, I conceived and put this band together and got things off the ground. I got Bernd to finance the demo and I'm the one who everyone brings the problem to and am definitely that guy the fellas, Motown and all else accepted and respected as the leader of this band. There was no question as to who, but I was saddened that my brother was hurt and blamed me as the cause of his pain.*

"Greg you've been this nice muthafucka since I met you, but some folks misunderstand that is just you and you make them think they're more than they really are," Bobby added.

"Yeah mon." MC interjected in his imitation Bernd accent. "You allvayz be za nice muzza fucka Grrek. Allvayz mon!"

All of us burst into laughter.

Phillip began to grab and start playing Tommy's bass as he reiterated parts of Jermaine's conversation about our working with the Suttons and Greg Wright.

Bobby, who was now at his keyboard, abruptly cuts in saying, "As long as we get to cut our stuff first, I guess it's alright," as he turned on the Fender Rhodes.

I immediately thought to myself, *Aw shit. Here we go.* Knowing the possibilities that statement could hold and hoping Bobby would stay humble and thankful for the opportunity we were blessed with long enough for us to at least get off of the ground.

MC, who had been holding his guitar when I came in from outside, turned on his amp and began to play a slow and funky groove. Eddie at the piano, played around MC's grooving. In short order, out comes Tommy, Phillip handed him his bass and he moved to the drums as each of us joined MC, with me being last, playing the melody after pulling out my trumpet. Jam Session! Conversation's over.

Living together, though financially and work-wise was practical and much fun, it further exposed everyone's personal habits. Although Switch was a family, while Jody had a life with his wife Jackie and their son Jody "Jr. aka Dink, Eddie had his life with Sally and their dog Shuggie, while the fellas of Montague St had each other and all that came with that. Among other things, if you have any secrets they no longer belong to just you, as everyone living under your roof ultimately knows what and who you do.

Bobby, who everyone knew was picking up boys and bringing them into his room for sex, was usually a hot topic among the guys in the house. Once outside in the backyard, anyone could look into Bobby's room. It was house knowledge that from time to time he was seen putting things into young boys, the same he had told me was done to him by his dad. MC, Tommy and I just shook it off. Phillip was the most outraged by Bobby's behavior; but he never challenged Bobby, either out of respect for Bobby's rights to his own preferences or because he knew, as I did, the futility in what would certainly become a volatile confrontation. Nonetheless, this was something none of us condoned and definitely did not want around us or for any of our guests to be exposed to Bobby's sexual proclivities for various reasons.

But again, for most of Switch, the real conflict was this is our brother Bobby, take him or leave him. And most of us stood by that and protected that side of him, until he made it no longer possible. Due to our closeness in dreams and circumstance, Switch had its own family and for that time we were supposedly part of the Motown family. Prior to signing with Motown, I was often warned "Motown will chew you up and spit you out," or "They'll steal your money" which I always ignored, but I don't remember once hearing "They'll steal your heart and soul," which was something I would come to learn the hard way over the next few years.

Being part of the Motown family also exposed us to the various Motown politics, philosophies and class levels. We were initially exposed to major differences when certain Motown execs became aware of Jody and my friendship with Tom DePiero. There was subtle discouragement by Jermaine and Hazel, among others, of our fraternizing with him because "he was not on our level" and artists didn't hang with the "others", meaning those who were merely company employees or not handpicked by the Gordy clan. This, of course, was an effort to exert some level of control over us, as they would attempt to do again and again over the years.

With us this time, understanding that Jermaine and Hazel knew things that we didn't know about Motown's plans for our future and also accepting the fact at that time the two of them sincerely had our best interest at heart, we still ignored their advice and tried to maintain our friendship with

Tom, as no one had the right to tell any of us who we could befriend. However, something was obviously said to him because he became distant during our mailroom drop-ins and he stopped coming over to the house and would completely shy away from us anytime Motown brass was around, so outwardly our friendship took a nosedive.

Tom eventually left Motown to start his own dance/disco label, Airwave Records. We remained in touch and would even get together for a drink from time to time; but the relation never really survived the Motown execution. A few years later, I remember the day I stopped by the Airwave offices to see Tom, only to find that he was in the hospital very sick. I was told that he was sick from some disease called GRID. At that time, even though the disease was new we were led to believe that Tom had a possibility of getting better, but he never did. Little did any of us know that we were staring a new killer disease in the face;, this disease would become known as AIDS, and a world epidemic would soon follow.

Shortly after Switch signed our contracts, our brothers, Drew Brown and Rodney Trotter, were included in a large ensemble of musicians and recording artists who were scheduled to perform for some sort of benefit concert at the Shrine Auditorium in Los Angeles. This concert was to include some of our new friends like, known entertainers: Billy "Bass" Nelson, Tiki Fullwood, Eddie Hazel and Glen Goins of the Funkadelics. Like back in Grand Rapids, when one of us found an open gig or jam session, we called on each other to get involved, so MC, Bobby, Tommy, Phillip and I were invited to come and play.

Thinking this was not a big deal we agreed to play and had even gone to an impromptu rehearsal with a few of the musicians who were committed to perform at this event. As with the vast majority of our individual and collective lives, this opportunity to play alongside these well-known, well respected musicians was new and exciting; so of course, we innocently shared this info with Jermaine who in turn discussed it with Hazel. Before nightfall, I received a call from Hazel informing me that "Switch cannot participate in that gig. "You guys are under exclusive contract to Motown and therefore you can't just do things as you used to."

Well, to my understanding we were signed to Motown as recording artists, having little direct effect on us as performing musicians; but I also had to acknowledge the fact that with all of this being new to me and Switch, we needed to follow closely what Jermaine, Hazel and Motown would tell us because I wanted to learn and I didn't want to mess up any relationships and/or plans for the group. So, I agreed with Hazel, explained the conversation to the fellas and canceled our participation the next day. From that point, even though I acknowledged that Motown's need to be in control would take some getting used to, I would do all that I could to avoid rocking the boat.

I later realized that was a defining moment in my career as a trumpet player. Due to their justification in pulling the rug on this date, this also included most public jam session sit-ins were off limits and that ultimately caused me to lose outlets to keep my chops and skills sharp. Yes, the one love, the one bridge that had taken me through most things, good or bad in my life, was now being put down and cast aside because, other than in my home and in random recording sessions, I had nowhere to play. This alternative turned out to be the biggest regret of my life till this day. Although I could sing, dance, arrange and perform over the years, it was mostly my trumpet that brought me this far in life and the decision to put it down would change my identity, my life forever!

There was now so much to experience and learn about our new record company, our new managers and our new lives. I also came to know that in the music business, trust and loyalty comes in short supplies, when all I wanted to do was build and maintain a successful musical career, a successful life for me and my brothers; and Motown often made that hard by their efforts to separate, manipulate and control me and various members of my group. I learned even more about Motown's demand for control when MC had become an issue because he had fallen asleep and snored in a few meetings, among other things.

I recall being approached by Jermaine and Hazel informing me, "Greg, Motown feels that Melvin needs to be let go. He's becoming dead weight and the group can do much better without him." Hazel stated. Although I sensed that they had other motives in wanting him gone, I had to deal with the situation and inform the fellas and then Melvin about this new occurrence. All of us loved and respected MC as a person, as a musician and as our brother, so this insistence was not an easy pill for any of us to swallow. Although a strong individual, MC had his own mind and way about him, which sometimes left him misunderstood by some, Hazel and Jermaine included. He was also a non-conformist which gave the impression that he was aloof and defied authority. I know firsthand this is not the case, but merely one of the ways his personality came across.

Now to add to his issues with Motown, prior to joining me, when Sylvester and Drew were back in Grand Rapids to work on the demos for my new band, MC had some family altercations that had been under review by Kent County Child Protective Service and ended up in Michigan courts. This was unknown to any of us during the early stages of Switch and the recording of our first album, but this problem began to rear its ugly head when the Grand Rapids District Attorney's Office and Child Protective Services pressed the issue and built a criminal case against MC. Through his social security number, they found he was an employee of Motown Records which was in Los Angeles, California, and that's where he was.

Motown was contacted and informed of his warrant, they in turn call me into the office for a meeting. After this came out, MC had to go back to Grand Rapids to stand trial, thus, the problem was solved for Motown and sadly for Switch also, as the band's decision to fight for MC became a moot point altogether. Ultimately, MC was convicted and sent to prison. Before leaving, he sat down with all members of Switch and openly and honestly shared with us what had happened and what he may have to do to resolve it. His candid explanation of the occurrence and his subsequent actions was accepted and appreciated by all Switch members, yet his abrupt departure left Switch without its guitarist. Now, besides missing our friend, our brother and band member, we would have to use studio musicians to fill that void left by MC.

Fortunately, all of Switch really liked Michael McGloiry and Ronnie Vann as musicians and as people, so the recordings moved forward without a hitch. By the way things went down starting with Motown telling us we had to just dump MC, I knew then we would be in for more rough rides in certain areas of our journey with them. Although things moved forward from there, it didn't take long for more underhanded shit to rear its ugly head. One evening after rehearsal, Bobby and Tommy pulled me to the side. I could see that they were both upset.

Bobby spoke first saying, "Greg, you won't believe what they did, man."

"Who are *they*?"

"Hazel, and Jermaine, and we know they were speaking for Daddy."

We stepped outside.

"Greg, they offered me and Tommy a new contract and band of our own."

In shock at hearing this, my mouth would not close.

"They did what?"

Bobby said, "Yea man. They said we could leave Switch and form our own band if we chose. I couldn't believe they'd try and do that to you man. We told them no right away. When we asked about what would happen with Switch, they said Switch would have their deal and U two would have yours. I told them no! We're not leaving you." Bobby insisted.

"See Greg, this kinda shit is why we can't trust any of these muthafuckas."

"That's right, man." Tommy added. They could see the hurt and bewilderment in my face.

"We're sorry Greg, but you need to know what these muthafuckas will try behind your back and how they really are."

My mind immediately flashed back to my first meeting with Motown's legal department. *Jody and I were taken out to lunch at the world-famous Brown Derby restaurant, right off of the corner of Hollywood and Vine by Lee Young, Jr. head of Motown's legal department and Skip Miller, Vice President of Sales. After discussing our need to quickly hire an attorney and other aspects of our signing with Motown, it was suggested to Jody and me that he and I make our deal as a production company; then we sign everyone else under our production deal, and then put each man on a salary as employees to our company. At that point in time, I didn't totally understand how a production deal worked, but I wasn't really interested if that meant that members of my band would not be equal partners. We eat, sleep, work as one unit and I wanted us paid as one unit.*

Well, understanding that the offer was primarily made to Bobby more than Tommy, I thanked them both for their honesty and loyalty. Sadly enough, it was a short-term loyalty, due to their ongoing psychosis from injury past; A loyalty that I would not see again from Tommy and only from Bobby during the last year of his life; more so the last weeks of his life as he stayed in my home. We all hugged and went back into the house.

My antennae never went down about Motown after that and I realized I had to be very vigilant with them because since Michael died, I had no one to help fight the powers that be, other than Jody who knew no more about the business than I did. In the beginning, we were side by side; but he too would soon slip away due to misunderstandings about his role in Switch.

I also began to see Jermaine and Hazel differently as they could so easily smile in your face, knowing that evil and deceit lurked in their hearts and minds. Now initially, I didn't know if Berry Gordy was behind everything that happened at Motown because there were so many different folks in so many different departments, players and games and always too much going on to keep track; but it was crystal clear to me that, although Hazel and Jermaine were our managers on paper, daddy Berry was calling the real shots.

I remembered in a one on one conversation with Mr. Gordy, he used the adjective principled when describing his daughter Hazel and here I sat wondering how much principal went into this underhanded act. And, if Bobby had bitten on their hook, how much principle would be applied in conveying the outcome to me, Jody, Phillip, Eddie MC; or how in the hell would principal even matter? Again, I'm so thankful that, per always, God was in control.

This was the beginning of change in Bobby after his encounter with Hazel and Jermaine. The other band members noticed it but didn't understand what was behind it. Some of his old agitations and patterns from before and during the White Heat days began to resurface. He started to curse at the sound of Hazel and Jermaine's names, becoming agitated when I'd discuss Motown's plans for us and a couple of times he had even tried to tip the piano over, Eddie's heavy Yamaha Electric Grand, when something hadn't gone his way. He would curse people out at random, storm out of a rehearsal if someone disagreed with his idea of what to rehearse first.

Fortunately, none of us were too quick to fight, so unless Bobby physically attacked any of us, which he was definitely too light to fight, we would just walk away and ignore his craziness until next time. As our transition from infant band to signed recording artists began to take shape Bobby also became more open with his gay lifestyle, bringing his male sexual partners to the house and subjecting the rest of the band to the wild, noisy goings-on. He would sometimes do his thing when one or more of us, his housemates had guests, causing us to abruptly gather our folk and leave the house before everyone became completely aware of what was happening. When I'd mention to him the effect his actions were having on everyone, before I could ask him to tone it down he shouted, "Fuck them. They shouldn't be coming near my room anyway."

"But Bobby, we all live in this house and people have to go in and out. You could at least close the blinds and tone it down."

He wouldn't budge.

"Tell them muthafuckas not to look or be listening at my shit, Greg."

I'd just walk away from him knowing that this was just the beginning. I also knew that I, or no one else, would be able to live with this shit much longer. In an effort to protect the group's reputation and avoid subjecting others to his lifestyle and preferences, I refused to expose new friends and business acquaintances to this kind of shit and within a few months I moved.

While practicing at the band house, among the many songs that were written by all of us individually and collectively, I wrote "Come on With the Come On", which I later renamed "We Like to Party" while Bobby came up with the song "The Best Beat in Town", which he originally called "The Best Beef in Town" but was changed because of the sexual connotations.

The latter started off as a joke because Bobby would walk around the house holding his crotch claiming, "I've got the best beef in town," to which most of us would have a big laugh. I personally found it disgusting, but knew if the song went anywhere, we would change that name. One day during jam time he starts playing the keyboard riff and singing, "Best beef in town, best beef all around," again and again.

Immediately, Tommy grabbed his bass and joined in. Phillip quickly jumped on the drums; but when MC and Drew came in from the front porch, Phillip gave Drew the drums and jumped on the Congas as I hopped on my keyboards and MC plugged his guitar into his amp and it was on. We must have had fun jamming that hook for a good half hour before Bobby stopped us and included his first line, and Tommy added a change.

After that, the rest of the arrangement came easy. Over the days to come, once the song was taught to Jody and Eddie during a Band rehearsal, Jody added more lyrics and a bridge and "Best Beef in Town" became a fun song to play. Once we had laid the song down in the studio and decided that it should definitely go on our album, the name was changed to Best Beat because the former was too suggestive.

Jermaine and I co-wrote "I Wanna Be Closer". This song was a little challenging because of the harmonies; so, Phillip, who'd sang in chorus at school and had vocal training, finally suggested that Eddie, who was a classically-trained pianist, sit down at the piano with us and work with each part. It took us three tries to get the harmony right, and when we did, that was it. Jermaine heard us and raised both hands in the air.

"Man, y'all, sssound, like soooooome damn, angels."

Tommy mimicked Jermaine's stutter, which cracked us all up and Jermaine laughed but didn't stutter. Noticing his reaction, the rest of us tried to get our composure until Jermaine said, "That's not funny Tommy. Ya ya yall niggas."

And that's all it took. All of us just lost it, falling on the floor laughing; even Jermaine. In the beginning he was good for us and we were good for him. Because of the purity and innocence in each of us. We jelled personally and musically, and we had fun at work and play and especially with the ladies.

After that, I wrote songs with Jermaine and Switch worked with him on his album, *Frontiers*. However, the album was released, and I was given credit for only one of the songs I had co-written. (which would again happen with one of Switch's biggest Hits "I Wanna Be Closer") I walked right up to Jermaine. 'I'm letting you know this shit ain't cool Jermaine. I co-wrote these songs with you and there's no mention of me anywhere."

Jermaine tried to reassure me with a touch on the shoulder. "I nununukkknow Ggggreg. The th they mmmade a mmistake man. Iiii'll get it fixed."

"Yeah please do that, Jermaine, cause this ain't right. If you don't want my help no more that's ok, but don't rob me of work I already did. You need to know that I won't play that shit."

I left the office fuming and went to the studio. Jermaine's, Hazel's and Motown's workings were becoming clearer to me every day and one fact stood out, if you didn't know, you will be taken advantage of. I didn't know at that time the Motown machine operated in such a way that if no one questioned how they could do some of the overt violations of others' rights, they would continue as if nothing happened. I was determined to stop being victimized. Once you became aware of their slights, which was really stealing, you were treated differently and not always in a good or respectful way.

Shit was seriously cutthroat! I came to realize that this was the way papa bear, or better yet papa Berry ran his ship. From my first-hand experiences I came to know that Motown Records was far more business and less family than the image portrayed. Berry Gordy's own lyrics "your love gives me such a thrill, but your love won't pay my bills, I need money!" spoke volumes about how he ran his ship.

Switch, like most of the Motown artists, had to bring hits, money to the table or be treated like bastard stepchildren. Soon enough we would endure that cold, heartless stepchild treatment at the hands of Berry, Hazel and even Jermaine, who I know was only following the leaders; but in the meantime, we showed promise as hit makers, so Motown's best was made available to us, including Berry Gordy himself.

We learned Berry Gordy had no set working hours and sometimes he'd go into the studio late at night or in the wee hours of the morning and have the engineers put up and play what we were doing. Mr. Gordy's listening to our music prompted him to call me one night to say, "Greg, I called over to the studio earlier and told Georgia to make room and time for you, Bobby and Switch to come in whenever you want, so don't wait to hear from Jermaine and Hazel, just call down there, they'll be expecting you."

Georgia Ward was then Hitsville's head of traffic/booking. Being told this, I thought this meant that Bobby, Jody and I had proven ourselves as producers and although I didn't like or understand some of Motown's underhanded ways, I felt somewhat secure.

After that, Mr. Gordy went on to say, "I just listened to a few of your songs and you know you're writing good music, but your boy Bobby is also kicking ass in the studio. You might want to step it up Greg."

Later, Bobby told me he'd received the same calls from Berry Gordy, claiming that I was kicking Bobby's ass in the studio. Bobby and I got a good laugh at that, realizing Mr. Gordy was trying to inspire us by making us compete. Throughout my years as a singer/musician, I never saw myself as a competitor to anyone. I liked to learn from everyone that I thought was good and had something to teach me, but most of all, I had to be the best that I could be. And when it came to Bobby and other members of Switch, in my mind it was all about bringing what you have to the table because we're in this together and were all gonna eat anyway, but as Berry pointed out, a little healthy competition could be a good thing.

At that time, it hadn't become clear to me that no matter how good my or Jody's songs and productions were, no matter how strong Phillip's vocals would get, while at Motown, as with most Motown acts before Switch, Berry had selected his solo star from the unit and my and the other member's efforts would always take a back seat to Bobby's work, as long as we were signed to the label.

In the middle of that first year, I had moved out of the house into an apartment with my friend Carla, a tall, blond-haired white girl that I had befriended back in the White Heat days of Hollywood. Though never intimately involved with Carla, she and I had become friends when we met in 1973. By chance she and I reconnected while I was living at the Holiday Inn awaiting the arrival of the fellas and picked up where we'd left off prior to White Heat moving back east. After Switch moved away from Hollywood into the house in the valley, she came by a few times and I would go to her place. We talked a lot about our now personal lives, hopes and dreams, so it was no secret to Carla that the band house had gotten a little too full and hectic for my changing life.

She and I would get together and hang out. We'd go to arcades or to the movies or just hang out by the pool in her complex, so when she had to evict her roommate for nonpayment of rent she offered me the room before trying to find another tenant. Knowing we had a bonus check coming on top of our bi-weekly salaries, I accepted and moved in within a few days. Little did I know at the time that Carla would soon have to move out and I would soon move Bobby in. Although I had moved into my shared apartment, I was still with the fellas at the band house every day, all day because with the exception of Jody and Eddie, everyone else in the band still lived there, and we would rehearse, have jam sessions, group meetings, congregate and party with friends almost every day.

Jermaine and Hazel would often come out to our daily rehearsals and in short time we began to have production meetings with them and a few Motown producers. Now that they had turned the Motown machine on for the forthcoming Switch project, besides Jermaine, Bobby, Jody and me, we narrowed down other possible Motown in-house producers to include, such as: Michael and Brenda Sutton, Greg Wright and Michael Lovesmith.

As our first album project began moving forward, Berry Gordy would call us up to his home to review and discuss the musical ideas we had recorded on cassette tape and he also made it a point to explain various other aspects of the record business and the over-all project that would come into play as we worked on our first album.

A short time after the recording process was underway Berry Gordy was provided tapes from every session, often popping up while we were in session, claiming just to pick up his tapes for the day. In his liking what he was hearing from those tapes, he decided that since this was Bobby's, Jody's and my first shot at professional record production he would get hands on with Switch's first album, show us the ropes and assist us in making better records. He also brought in his close friend and a partner in musical crime songwriter, record producer and once Motown staff member Jeffery Bowen to work with him in showing Switch how it's done.

Mr. Gordy had introduced Jeffery to Switch at a production meeting at the Gordy mansion. Now Jeffery was a tall, stringy, wooly-headed man mixed with Indian and Black. From liner notes I had read over the years, Jeffery was notable for his work at both Motown Records and Holland-

Dozier-Holland's Invictus and Hot Wax labels, through which he had worked with The Temptations (producing on albums *The Temptations in a Mellow Mood*, *A Song for You*, and *Wings of Love*) and others. He had also worked with Marvin Gaye, Funkadelic, Parliament, and Chairmen of the Board for *Invictus* among various others.

To Switch, Jeffery was kind but direct, animated and funny and to this day I have nothing but fond memories of him and our time together. Jeffery would later meet and marry Bonnie Pointer of the Pointer Sisters, and he would become her producer. Once he was onboard with our album project, things quickly moved forward from that initial meeting; and exclusively for the Switch project, Berry and Jeffery Bowen formed a duo/team, calling themselves the Bewley Brothers.

They worked closely with Bobby, Jody and me in the production of our individual songs chosen for this first album project. From the initial meeting with our newly formed production group, I immediately knew this was a serious opportunity for us to learn and grow from the best. This experience made it very clear to me, where the creative magic of Motown began. Collectively we spent time going over every aspect of each song, with the Bewley Brothers, allowing Switch to have control over our individual creations; but patiently pointing the strengths and weaknesses in each song from beginning to end, then showing us how to make each song and production stronger.

I remember often comparing these moments to those I had spent under the auspices of Barry White, noting that, although each of these three men - Barry White, Berry Gordy

370

and Jeffery Bowen - had their own unique way of making music, all three were genius in their creation of hit records. Besides being taught how to make good records, we were also about to be taught how to become stars and the real work I referred began like this. A song written by Bobby, titled "I Wanna Be With You", had already been selected to be our first single release.

We had recorded around 10 songs and were beginning to add finishing touches or what was called sweetening the songs. Sweetening was the process of adding string, horns, more percussion and even sound effects after tracks and vocals were completed. We were mastering the album, adding touches, and I was a little overwhelmed handling the responsibilities of the band, recording, arranging for studio time and my limited personal life.

I was piddling around the house one day, thinking about adding the finishing touches to the album, when Bobby, sitting at the piano called me over.

"Check this out." He played a beautiful, mid-tempo song idea for me and hearing a hit, plus loving it, I walked towards the phone to make sure our studio time was set.

"That's cool Bobby, I like it." I went to the phone and picked it up.

"What's the matter nigga, you don't like my song?" Bobby, red faced, his eyes narrowed, stood up from the piano.

I realized, thinking about the studio, I hadn't given my boy the attention he felt his song deserved and our friendship warranted. I put the phone down. "I'm sorry Bobby. It's beautiful, funky and its bad. Let's call Mr. Gordy and see what we can do with it."

We called Mr. Gordy at home and he came to the phone.

"Mr. Gordy, this is Greg Williams and Bobby DeBarge. Bobby's written this phenomenal song and we want you to hear it."

"Okay guys, I'd like to hear it. Can you send it to me?"

Bobby was on the other line. "I don't have a track, just me singing and playing the piano, do you have a minute to hear it?

Mr. Gordy immediately sayin go ahead, Bobby began to play and sing as I came in to the living room and held the phone close to his mouth.

After playing the intro, singing the first verse and chorus, Bobby stopped as Mr. Gordy excitedly yelled through the phone, "I think that can be a smash guys!

"Tell you what, I'll set up the studio and you guys record the song and get it to me."

He hung up and the next morning, after getting a call from Georgia Ward letting me know it had been cleared by Mr. Gordy, we went straight to Motown's recording studio. It took us four days to get the recording done and we left a cassette of the song for him with the studio's front desk. Later that night, he called us at some ridiculous hour, as usual.

"It's a smash. It's a smash. I'm thinking this might beat "I Wanna Be With You" as the first single from your album. We'll have to see."

He hung up and Bobby and I both were too excited. The song was "There'll Never Be", and it became our first single, which kicked our career to an auspicious beginning.

Next was compiling the whole album and creating our album cover and press photos and information. Our first photo shoot was fun, and we were grooving to our own songs playing throughout the shoot. In this shoot the photographer took pictures of us with our favorite interests. I was in my then favorite sweater and dress slacks with a pad in my hands; Eddie with his tennis racket and his dogs; Jody with sports balls; Bobby with a cat; and Phillip and Tommy with books.

There was an album cover and publicity photos created from these shots, but they were rejected. Upon seeing the cover, to put it mildly, Mr. Gordy was so outraged, that he called a meeting with Switch, Jermaine and Hazel, Suzanne de Passe, then president of A&R, Tony Jones, Suzanne Coston, Nancy Leiviska, Suzy Ikeda and the other department heads involved with the art direction for these early photos.

Once everyone was present, he went off! He stood at the head of the long conference table and began to bang his fist on it yelling, "Who authorized these mediocre pictures? This is a cheesy album cover. Don't you people ever treat my band like this, I won't have it! Now do this shit over. Set up another shoot again and do it right this time." He pointed his finger at the responsible staff members and left the table as they dropped their heads and wouldn't look at us.

The following Monday I received a call from Hazel informing me that Suzanne and her team would be taking Switch shopping for clothing for the upcoming album cover and publicity photo shoot in a couple of days. Suzanne had hired Ciri, a noted stylist to work with us and find clothing for the shoot. Over the next couple of days, we took L.A. shopping by storm. Going to high end expensive clothing stores, designer clothing and footwear stores, small boutiques and even thrift shops looking for clothing and accessories that would create exceptional individual looks for each band member. With the help of Ciri we picked our own clothing and accessories to create a look that would represent our individual personalities as well as a group look.

Though the overall image created from our collective ideas went from casual to dressy, Bobby, Jody and I selected sport jackets and scarves, which the later was an in accessory at that time; Phillip, Tommy and Eddie selected more comfortable and playful looks, which really worked well for each of us and this time we were more than prepared.

SWITCH

Switch Promo #1

Switch Promo #2

This next shoot took an additional three days and the end result featured hundreds of pictures and images to be used for press and publicity photos, promotional items, city bus and free-standing billboards among other uses which made our faces and our look identifiable, worldwide. With this photoshoot, Switch set a new trend in dress codes for R&B group/bands, which many acts still follow today. During this photo session, each band member would play different instruments and sing live, just as we did in the showcase we did for Motown to get the contract. This became a classic album cover, which has since been displayed in many record stores and on the walls of many a young girl across the country and around the world.

"There'll Never Be" was our very first release in December of 1978 and Switch had arrived and as Jermaine would say about the record, "It went straight to the top."

The second hit from the Switch album was "I Wanna Be Closer". Although it was a well-kept secret for far too long, the song was written by Jermaine and myself and my name and credits were omitted from the second version of our first album cover and label and the signed song agreement was never submitted for credits.

Again, I confronted Jermaine about the absence of my credits, only to be told it would be straightened out on paper and with the next printing of the album cover. Of course, this too never happened. What did happen was, I was beginning to subtly become ostracized and labeled difficult for standing up for the injustices Jermaine, Hazel and Motown were beginning to impose on Switch, and more so, me.

Through most of my life, in difficult situations I could at least turn to my trumpet and find inner peace; but, due to Motown's imposed contractual artist limitations and in my desire to become a better keyboardist and producer, I stupidly stopped practicing and playing my trumpet around this time. This mistake was also lessened because I was getting noise complaints from management of my then apartment complex. Yes, I had put the majority of my life, heart and existing into this trumpet and subsequent abilities and uniqueness, only to abandon what had not and would never abandon me. I sacrificed the ship that brought me across from nowhere to somewhere, and slowly my desire to play dissipated and slowly but surely came to haunt me, from that day till this.

During those first couple of years too many negative or unsavory things would have happened to Switch at the hands of Motown, which was either forgiven and/or forgotten because we were living the dream in grand style and refused to let what was then a little rain spoil the day or our happiness. One reason we were happy was, after completing the first album, per the artist contract, each of us were due to receive a bonus per project. Because none of us had ever had much and definitely hadn't made any real money playing music, we had individually and collectively put in a lot of time discussing and planning what we were going to do with that money.

Our New Cars

Immediately after the first bonus check was handed out we all bought vehicles. Bobby and Tommy went out and bought brand new Alfa Romeos which were high end very expensive sports cars. The rest of us tried to get cars which were reasonable to our new-found riches. Now, Phillip being the most practical of us, bought himself a used four-door wine colored Fiat. Eddie bought a new Blue Cougar with Orange trimmings. Now, Jody and I traded our current cars in for newer ones. Unknowingly, Jody and I bought Lincolns the same day. He bought a Mark IV and I got a 1976 Town Car. Both Jody's and mine were silver; his with red interior and mine was grey inside.

While most of the band made good use of their cars, the DeBarge brothers had problem after problem until both cars were wrecked and finally repossessed by the finance company to never be returned. Besides too many traffic citations and infractions, in a fit of familiar anger, rage and insanity, Bobby used his car to actually run a man down, opening what could have ended with a vehicular assault or manslaughter charge; or at the very least, an attempted murder charge due to the seriousness of the man's injuries.

Eddie and Upshaw lived in the same apartment building on Tamarind Avenue in Hollywood. While leaving the building after visiting Eddie, Bobby had a negative encounter with another tenant who resided in that building and just happened to be a small drug dealer, which was no secret to every tenant in the building. Their disagreement turned into an argument and things escalated. Infuriated by Bobby's insults and threats the guy came towards Bobby; but before he could get close enough to get physical, Bobby ran from the building with the guy in hot pursuit.

Fortunately, Bobby made it to the street and into his parked car, getting in and locking the door just as the man had caught up with him. As Bobby started up the car, the man turned and began to walk back towards the apartment building, yelling, cursing and throwing his hands in the air, gesturing what he would do to Bobby. Now safely in his car but insanely angry at this man, Bobby put his car in reverse, backs up out of the parking space, throws the car in drive, then, with tires screeching, he turns and runs up on the curb, onto a hill of grass and onto the sidewalk and hits the man, running him over.

On impact the man flew up in the air and was tossed into tall busses, which separated the adjacent building. As the man was rolling off of the bushes Bobby backed up, put the car in drive again and hit the man again. Due to the extreme loudness of the entire incident, by now various tenants and neighbors were witnessing the entire event in disbelief. Someone had called the police when the fight began and unknown to Bobby or the man the police were on the way. After Bobby had hit the man for the second time, he backed the car down to the street while yelling out of the window, "Now Muthafucka, how you like that?"

As he drove away in one direction the police were coming up from the other.

Witnesses ran to Clarence's rescue, helping him out of the bushes and to his feet. He was clearly hurt but was able to stand with the help of bystanders; but once the police arrived he refused to discuss what had transpired or press charges on

Bobby, out of fear that his own drug dealing would be discovered and he would be arrested, so the whole matter was dropped.

Years later Bobby and Clarence ran into each other just outside of my apartment and Bobby's apology to Clarence was accepted. And on another occasion when leaving Bunny's Hollywood apartment, Tommy crashed his new forest green convertible 1978 Alpha Romeo into her building. He forgot to put the car in drive from reverse, so he stepped down hard on the gas and the car plunged through the wall of the apartment complex into a bedroom. A couple who had been sleeping in their bed in the building he plowed into ran outside naked, after being frightened by the crash. They immediately rushed to rescue Tommy who sat in his car knocked out on impact and covered with plaster. When he came to, he was physically unharmed but totally disoriented.

When it was all over, fortunately his insurance company paid out a lot of money to cover the car and building damages, but they canceled his policy thereafter. For the rest of Switch, things went a lot smoother with the purchase and upkeep of their cars. All of us bought new wardrobes and other personal items with the bonus checks and we were flying high. More than a year had passed since signing with Motown; and after we finally finished recording the first album each of us was elated for various reasons, not knowing the real work was about to begin.

Chapter 11

Lankershim--Bobby & Latoya

Kathy's – Baltimore (1979)

At this time, Bobby and I lived together in the Lankershim Blvd. apartment. While living there, we shared the same house phone, but had separate phones in our bedrooms. Among the various group members, family and friends who would call the house throughout the day and night, I'd sometimes get calls from Berry Gordy in the wee hours, just to check up on the group and see how things were going over all. This happened to become a very important time in

Switch's development as a unit, in our career, and in our relationship with Hazel, Jermaine and Motown Records as a whole.

On one of our infrequent off-days at home, Bobby was playing this rhythm at the piano, which sounded so good, it pulled me from my bedroom.

"What's That?'

Bobby, again, had that gleam in his eyes and that wide smile he gave me when he'd hit on something he really liked.

"I don't know, it's this thing I keep hearing and the words *I call your name* keep coming. I need your help."

We sat down at the opposite ends of the piano, like we did back at Ottawa Hills when we first met, and we started working with the melody. I wrote the lyrics and we arranged the bridge to "I Call Your Name", which Bobby had been playing. It took us all night to finish the song and we took it into the studio, taught it to the fellas and we laid down the rhythm track the same day. Bobby sang the lead verse and we left the song unfinished.

Then unknown to us, per usual, Mr. Gordy was provided cassette copies of the days we worked in the studio and after hearing our latest work, he called us about one in the morning raving about the song and told us he'd informed Hitsville studio to give Bobby, Jody and me carte blanche and total studio access from that point onward. With that now being accessible to us, we continued to record, feeling excited about what we were doing and really grew closer together as a band during the recording of this first Switch album.

I recall Switch having a two-week break, prior to beginning the recording of our first album, I was informed that my mom was recovering from a brief illness. Nothing too serious, but I just wanted to see her face and know for myself that she was alright and since this was over the Thanksgiving holiday it would be a good time for me to spend a few weeks with her and the rest of my family. Since I last went there two years ago, I decided to go home to Grand Rapids for a short time.

After a few days there I got a call from Hazel Jackson, which began as what I thought was an innocent check in, "how are you and your family doing" call. But after the initial banter, Hazel begins to tell me that Jermaine was to perform in a big holiday show at the Los Angeles Forum over the Thanksgiving weekend. She proceeded to say that "Daddy, Jermaine and I thought it would be a good idea if Switch were to be Jermaine's backup band for this performance," to which I immediately said "yes!" with excitement, because we would finally hit the stage again, which I so missed; and in my mind, we would be introduced to a big audience. Hazel continued, "and when you come back to L.A. you'll be working on your album for a while; so, if you want to finish spending time with your family it's ok and we'll just use the rest of the guys."

What Hazel omitted from this conversation was she had already scheduled rehearsal and informed the other Switch members this would be taking place. Being new to Motown, management and record company dealings on this level, I didn't know if this was how business was normally conducted, whereby the company could use the act in whatever capacity or musical setting that they saw fit, but what I did know right then was what she was saying to me did not feel right.

Not having ever been an insecure person, I did feel upset at the thought of my band performing at any time without me, or at least without my direction; so, I quickly said, "Hey, I'll cut this visit short and get back to rehearsal. When do they start?"

"Greg, you don't have to, it's not that big a deal. Rehearsals have to start tomorrow, and the guys will just be back up musicians anyway. Don't you want to spend more time with you mom?" she insisted.

"Yes, I did Hazel, but this is a big deal to me. Switch is my band and I don't want them performing without me, so when is the first rehearsal?" I asked, adding

"I'm on my way home." Feeling the tension in my reaction, I heard the sound of shuffling paper as Hazel said, "Greg, I understand… if that's what you want to do."

And she proceeded to read off the rehearsal particulars, after which we said our goodbyes. I remember hanging up the phone. Hazel's thoughts and actions could have been perfectly innocent and sincere; but from certain things I had witnessed, experienced and had to accept from Motown, this gesture was suspect, so I immediately questioned, "What the fuck are these folks up to?" *Whatever it is I'll be there to deal with it,*" I thought.

I had never dealt with being part of a band which someone tried to divide like this. I would have thought that in every situation the band was more valuable to a record company and especially a manager, as a whole. But this was the beginning of many lessons I would come to know about Motown and its vision for Switch and about the recording industry, as a whole. Needless to say, I explained to my mom and family that I was cutting my trip short, and why. I got on the phone and changed my flight, packed my bags, said my goodbyes to everyone that I could that night and caught the morning flight heading back to L.A.

Throughout this period of Bobby's and my living together in the Lankershim Blvd apartment, cemented everything from our past. The friendship, the kinship, the silly moments and hours of laughter was only a small part of what he and I shared after living with bands and interruptions for years now. The Fender Rhodes sat in the living room and we'd play together almost every day and all hours of the night.

Bobby never brought any boys to the apartment when we lived together. LaToya Jackson though, was a frequent visitor. Bobby had been introduced to the Jackson family by Jermaine, who'd taken us all to meet his family at the Encino estate. From where I sat, they were always a very hospitable, kind and warm family. The DeBarges and the Jacksons shared large musical families, a religious background... and I knew this.

After meeting Bobby, various Jacksons had spoken to various DeBarges, by phone, a couple times when I'd been there; and it was during one of those conversations that James DeBarge and Janet Jackson had met. Little did any of us know then, that those two would wind up becoming what they ultimately became to each other. Bobby met and became friends with LaToya at the Jackson home. I watched their relationship develop, as we were recording our first album. In no time she and Bobby were together a lot, at my and Bobby's apartment, at the recording studio and other places. She would pick him up in her mom's red Mercedes and take him to movies, to the beach or just to hang out.

She and I too grew to be friends and would talk a lot on the phone and when we'd see each other. She was well-rounded and stayed abreast of everything like politics, music, history, science, fashion and whatever was current in the world. Sometimes Bobby would come home, and he'd find her and me sitting there talking away, oblivious to his entering the room. Fortunately, when it came to women, the trust appeared to exist between Bobby and me, that there was never a moment of insecurity about his lady carrying on a conversation with me first, when she'd call or pop by when he wasn't home. A few months into their relationship, I noticed some strains between them because LaToya seemed to be impatient with Bobby a lot.

I knew this because I'd hear her say to him, "You don't understand what I'm talking about, do you?"

I'd be in my room and peek out, seeing her sitting on the couch with her arms crossed and Bobby frowning or biting his nails. I recall one time she came and knocked on the door immediately after Bobby had left, as if she had been waiting for him to leave. I had been tinkling on the Fender Rhodes but heard a knock, stopped playing and went to the door. Before I could explain that Bobby had just left, headed to the store, LaToya, walked right in and plopped down on the couch, turning to me.

"Hi Greg. Before you say anything, I saw him just leave. I hope you don't mind but I need to talk with you."

"Of course, I don't mind. Come on in."

"He doesn't get it."

"You mean Bobby?"

"You know who I'm talking about, Greg. Don't play that."

"Okay, what doesn't Bobby get?"

"He doesn't get the fact that a couple needs to have a lot in common to maintain a relationship. I really can't talk to him about a lot of things and he never regurgitates anything I try to teach him."

"First, what does regurgitate mean?"

She hit me on the arm. "Why are you playing with me. I'm serious. I know you know that word, but he doesn't, along with so many others and that's a big part of the problem for me. He's handsome, very talented and he's sweet Greg; but he lacks education and is unsophisticated and there are only a few places we can go because of his manners and home training. Believe me."

She didn't know I really had never heard and didn't know the meaning of regurgitate yet.

"He loves you, Toya. I've known him for a long time and I've never seen him like this with anyone."

"I know he loves me, and I love him, Greg; but, it takes more than love though to make a relationship work. We're from two different places and I just can't get over that."

She dabbed at her mascara and got up to leave.

"You don't have to leave. Bobby will be back soon, and you know he'll want to see you."

"I know. Greg, and I'm sorry, but I have to go. Thanks for letting me vent."

Emotionally shaken, she left our apartment. That was the last time she visited Bobby there, and soon after, I noticed she stopped calling.

He told me she wanted to date other folks. I'd hear Bobby crying in his room and he was visibly down, not wanting to go out or just sitting at the piano for long stretches of time, staring into space, without playing one note. I felt helpless watching him, knowing that once again he was hurting badly, but I knew there was nothing I could do but let life take its course.

I realized that losing their relationship caused him real pain, confusion and suffering. Conditions which had consumed and controlled him since birth and I had known him to come through lots, but his maturation in dealing with serious one-on-one relationships would still have a long way to go. Through it all, we still had the music and an album to make which would fill some of those lonely moments in time but actually Bobby never got past losing Latoya.

Yet life moved on. Bobby and I wrote "You and I" in early 1978 and it sat until the right time and opportunity came to record and include in our forthcoming project. Although we finally recorded the song some 3 years after we wrote it, I have no doubt he thought about LaToya Jackson as he lay his vocals. He actually cried during the recording which is clearly heard close to the end of the recording and has left a moving and touching song for the ages.

But I also knew him well enough to know that during that vocal session he too cried out from that agony of getting no relief from his unrelenting internal struggles, which plagued him every waking moment of his life.

After the release of the first Switch album, our career instantly moved into high gear. The Motown machine stepped in and started doing the things that it had become known for throughout the entertainment community. The beginning of these various promotion efforts was, we were first introduced to a television audience on a broadcast of Hal Jackson's Talented Teens on Saturday, July 30, 1977, where we played as Jermaine's back-up band and singers on his new single, "Feel the Fire" and on "You Need to Be Loved"; then without Jermaine we performed what was to be our first single, "I Wanna Be With You" and "Somebody's Watching You". All were well-received by the house and television audience.

Right On! & Soul Magazine

Soon after came *Soul Train*, where again we backed-up Jermaine, although this time we were introduced as Switch by Jermaine and Don Cornelius and again we played our same two songs for various television performances. We were on a constant rotation of local and national radio, newspaper and magazine interviews. During this time, we did our first of many interviews with Cynthia Horner and *Right On!* magazine, photo sessions and more television, such as: *Mike Douglas, Merv Griffin, The Miss USA Pageant*, and *Don Kirshner's Rock Concert*. We were even special guest stars in the annual *Hollywood Christmas Parade of Stars* which was an annual event on major television at that time.

We would also spend lots of time in the studio, recording radio spots and station ID's for radio stations across the country. We would sing the stations call letters and say things, "Hi we're Switch; and when we're in L.A., we listen to KDAY". We would say it, sing it and sometimes do both, making the work fun and not so tedious.

Still humble and largely unaware of the impact we were having on the music industry and the world at large, we were all living and loving this life which we prayed for, played for and worked for all of our lives. We had finally arrived. Yes, Motown was serious about press and promotion with every priority record release, and at that time we and our records were a priority and Motown would certainly capitalize on the public's love of Switch and our first album release; and Switch was becoming more visible worldwide and a household name across the USA.

While my new life as the musician, entertainer and celebrity I had always dreamed of becoming began to slowly sink in, one day I was sitting in my apartment when the phone rang. I picked it up and said hello, the voice on the other end said, "Hello Greg, how you doin' boy? It's your grandfather."

I was thrown off by the call and in a bit of disbelief because as I remember, this was the first time in my entire life I had received a phone call from my grandfather, I caught my breath and excitedly responded, "I'm fine granddad. How are you?'

"I'm good thanks the lawd," he said. "Well, I just finished watching the television and I saw you with your band on that Mike Douglas show. Boy when you first told me that you were gonna play music and not get yourself a job, you remember how upset I was? You know, I ain't never known nothing but hard work, so I was against you doing your music. I guess I was worried that, if it didn't work out, you would come home with your heart and your spirit broken; and I would never want that for you or any of my children, because I've never known nothin' different. But you were so sure, and you stuck to your guns and proved me and everybody else wrong. Now you're doing it where I can see it and the whole world can see it. I just want you to know I'm proud of you son, really proud of you."

Trying to keep my emotions under control, I responded, "Thanks Granddad. You know this really means a lot coming from you."

"I'm calling this late because I just couldn't wait no longer to tell U this."

We talked a little longer, with him asking me about my life, and whether I was happy doing what I was doing, to which I responded yes, half oblivious to much of the conversation beyond granddad telling me that he was proud of me.

After hanging up that phone conversation with my grandfather, I wept. I wept because his approval really did mean the world to me. I have consciously and unconsciously sought to make him and all of my family proud and hearing his approval was a greater gift than any award I could receive in my whole musical career. I wept because he was really the only father I had known, and I lived by the standards, values and traditions he set for our family. I took the pride of this phone call, of his confirmed acceptance and approval of me as I approached my work and Motown from then onward.

Of the many fun, enlightening and adventures my new life afforded me, I can clearly remember the first time I ever saw and heard Switch's music performed live by a named act, or better yet by anyone other than us.

It was after the release of our first album and promotional tour, when Switch had some down time. I recall Bobby, Jody, Art and I hangin at my house, bored when we spontaneously decided to jump in my Lincoln and drive from L.A. to Las Vegas for an evening of fun and gambling. Once we decided to definitely make this round-trip overnight journey, we excitedly piled into my car, gassed up and hit the road. The trip took roughly five hours but seemed like much less as the four of us laughed, talked and listened to music the whole way there. After crossing California, Nevada border, from miles away, we could see the city lights get bigger and bigger as we got closer and closer and finally we reached the city.

With this being each of our first time there, we were totally overwhelmed by the tall overlit buildings down long streets. We were in total awe to be in the mega city we had heard about much of our lives, so we rode around for what seemed like another hour looking at all of the different hotel-casinos, trying to figure out where to go first. As we continued to look and talk, our car stopped at the light in front of Caesar's Palace Casino, and Art noted that this was the most famous of them all; so, we all agreed to stop there first, turned the corner, found the parking lot, parked and went in.

Mesmerized by the lights, noises, and the endless sea of people, the four of us managed to stick close together and make our way through the lobby and into and around this huge casino. In my having never seen real crap, black jack and poker tables or standard slot machines up close, I, as was each of us, was truly fascinated by what we found ourselves in the midst of! Yes, Vegas was all that and a whole lot more! As we milled about, Art was the first of us to be called from the group by a highly colorful, loud slot machine; so, Jody, Bobby and I followed, then stopped close behind him as we wanted to see just how things worked here before joining him and investing in on our own individual machines. Shortly after catching on to what I needed to do to get rich here, since I liked to play and was actually good at poker, I remembered our passing a row of poker machines, so I returned there, found an empty seat and joined the casino players.

After a few more losses than wins, I decided I would walk around, check on the fellows and absorb more of my surroundings. Over the noise of the casino patrons and the machines, I began to faintly but clearly hear music coming from somewhere behind me. As I intently listened, the song began to sound familiar, so I turned and headed in the direction of this music. As I milled through the thick crowd, closer to the sound I was able to hear the singer and his words more clearly and suddenly as it had initially caught my ear, I was totally shocked and surprised by hearing the lead vocalist sing "Please come over here and let me whisper in your ear." Yes, this group was singing "There'll Never Be".

I remembered passing Bobby and Jody while I walked around, so I quickly ran back to them, grabbing and yelling "Y'all gotta come hear this!" As Bobby, then Jody looked up at me from their machines like I was crazy or something, I continued. "Fuck those machines man. You really gotta come and here this band right now."

As we got closer and closer, I could clearly see each of their facial expressions change from confusion to delight as the could clearly recognize what we were hearing. As we inched our way further and further past the onlookers, into the doorway of this music lounge, listening to our own music being played, sang and performed by another group, I looked around at the audiences singing, swaying and loving this song which most of them seemed to know. It was clear that Bobby, Jody and I were excited and caught up in what we were witnessing.

At that moment, I know they, like me, wanted to tell everyone in the showroom "Hey, we're Switch and that's our song they just sang and played!" But we, of course, kept our elation between ourselves as we enjoyed the performance till its end. As "There'll Never Be" ended, the group on stage moved into the next song in their set; so, Jody, Bobby and I gave each other five and shared our surprise and excitement over what we had just experienced, as we headed back into the casino.

Looking over my shoulder, I then noticed the marquee over the showroom which to my surprise read, "Staring the Checkmates LTD", who were one of Las Vegas's premier, resident headlining acts. I had heard of them over many years prior to signing to Switch Motown. After seeing this, the excitement continued as we made our way back among the rows and rows of slot machines until we found where Art was still sitting and apparently winning; so, each of us then found machines, sat down and continued to play.

Within a few hours of being there, Bobby, Jody and I had gambled away all of the money we had brought with us, while Art continued to win small amounts. Once broke, the others of us borrowed from Art, only to end up losing that too. After loaning money to all three of us, Art lost what he had left, now all of us were broke. In all of the fun and excitement, all of us failed to think about our almost empty tank and we didn't have enough gas money to make it back to L.A., so we headed back to the car while discussing how much fun we had, the money we had and wondered what we could do now.

While driving away from Caesar's, trying to figure out how and where we were gonna get enough gas money to make it home, we passed this record store. It somehow caught Bobby's eye and he suggested we stop in to see if they had our album, so I turned the car around and went back. The four of us walked in and began looking through the bins and I noticed the guy behind the counter, a young black guy, was watching all of us as we milled about his store. Finally, he came over and said, "Aren't you guys Switch?"

Jody, Bobby and Art stepped over to where I was standing as I responded, "Yes we are," in response to the guys question.

"I knew it," he said.

"Look over here." And he pointed and began moving towards the back of the store where the cash register sat. As we moved further into the store, the huge wall to the right of the register was almost completely covered with Switch album covers and large posters, similar to those which were on billboards and busses throughout the country.

Of course, Bobby, Art, Jody and I were so excited we forgot about our most pressing issue and fell into the awe of this, our first experience as stars, as a group of four girls who happened to be in the store came over to where we were. As one began saying to the others, "See I told y'all it was them! I told you," she said as two of them started jumping up and down, unable to contain their excitement. The four of us and the four of them stood there in the middle of the record shop asking and answering questions for about twenty minutes or so until Art tactfully got my attention and pulled me to the side saying, "Man, it was getting late, we have a long trip home from here and we still have not resolved our gas problem."

I agreed and bowed out from the group to think with Art about what the hell we were gonna do. I must have had a worried look on my face because Bobby and Jody excused themselves from those girls and were slowly approaching me. Once they were within whisper range I looked at them and said, "Fellas, what are we gonna do to make it home? We've got to hit this road." It got real quiet in our little huddle until Jody asked, "Hey you guys, what do we have that we can pawn to this dude for some gas money?"

Looking to each other for a response and answer, I volunteered, "I'm broke. I do have checkbook in the glove compartment, but no cash."

"Me too," chimed in the others.

Then Art suggested, "Maybe they'll cash a check for us here. I'll give you the money back once we're in L.A."

In agreement I said, "It won't hurt to ask." So, all of us headed to the counter where the guy we met walking in was back working behind the counter. As we got closer to the guy, he looked up from what he was doing when he noticed us coming his way, so he was already anticipating some kind of communication; but I'm damn sure he didn't expect what came out of my mouth.

I felt a little hesitant, embarrassed to tell anyone we were all broke and had no money to get home, but something had to be done here and now, so I blurted my request. "Hey man, we have a small problem we're hoping you can help us with. See, we arrived with the intent of checking out the city, playing the tables and slots for a little while and heading back to L.A.; but as I'm sure U know, these casinos have other plans."

Bobby chimed in, "See all of us got bit, and lost all of our money, including gas money to get back home." Now, having the total picture of our dilemma, he asked, "and I can help how?" I quickly said, "Can I write you a check? Only enough so we can fill up the tank. I promise the check won't bounce," I added, with a smile.

Without hesitation he stuck his hand out for the check. As I turned and ran to my car to get it I could hear the others explaining my checkbook was in my car. In a flash I had made it to my car, grabbed the checkbook and quickly made my way back to the counter, as Art, Bobby and Jody resumed talking to the girls who were clearly hanging around the shop, hoping to get our attention again. As I began to tear out a check and bent over to write in the amount I asked, "Can I just make it out for Twenty-Five Dollars so we can also add a snack for the road?"

He smiled, let out a light chuckle and nodded his head Yes and asked, "do you think that will be enough? We can make it for a little more. I trust you guys".

"I really appreciate that my brother, but I think that's enough to get us home. Plus, we don't need to be tempted by one more casino. Home it is." I laughed. With twenty-five dollars in my hand, I thanked the guy, went over to where Bobby, Jody, Art and the girls were congregating and announced we were good to go. So, we said our goodbyes to the folks in the record store and headed for the door.

As we made our way to the car, we joked about our then situation, but were very happy that our serious problem was resolved. We stopped at the gas station across from the record store, filled up the tank, hit the road and made our way back to L.A., talking the whole way about the fun we had, the money we lost and mostly about how great it was, for the first time to hear a noted act perform our music.

In weeks to follow, Switch went on our first promotional tour with Bob Jones from Motown and Jermaine and Hazel, to Cleveland, Detroit, Philly, Baltimore and finally in New York. Switch, Jermaine and Hazel Jackson, Bob Jones and Dwight, a hair stylist who worked at a shop in Los Angeles would usually fill up the first-class section of each leg of all of our flights on the limited tour. Bobby, Tommy, Phillip and Eddie were elated to find themselves being pampered in first class, as Jody and I played it cool, trying to hide our enthusiasm over flying first class for the second time, first time being when we left Mansfield, OH headed for L.A.

All Switch members were happy and excited about this new aspect of our lives. Traveling, meeting new people who seemed to love each of us and talking about ourselves and our music was a dream come true to everyone except Bobby. He actually hated being interviewed and had no problem showing just that when he felt like it. He hated being wakened up for morning calls and though he was consistently nervous, I realized talking about himself, his life actually scared him more. Many times, when he felt forced to participate, in his over the top arrogant way he expressed his anger and contempt with radio and television hosts and even with journalists, to the surprise of all of us, including Jermaine and Hazel and even Bob Jones who had literally seen everything when it came to the actions and attitudes of artists and other creative folk.

I realized these negative responses were due to Bobby's having difficulty in separating his new life from the overwhelming aspects of his life before. He was still very guarded in what he could and would talk about and he trusted few in, and no one outside of Switch. After I initiated a couple of discussions about this with Jody, he and I decided to take this up with Bobby to keep this from becoming a big issue for anyone, especially the interviewer and/or host. When we tactfully brought this to Bobby's attention he dismissed it as nervousness and basically shut that conversation down.

Jody and I let it go until it happened again throughout the very next day; so, he and I decided to take our views, our concerns to Bob, Hazel and Jermaine who were also perplexed by this, so that all of us could help get a grip on the problem before it began to seriously hurt Switch. In our brief discussion, it was decided we would all monitor the situation and do what we could to make all parties more comfortable till we could get through the short tour.

As the coming days passed, I found that I was being pulled to the side and held back from a few outings and fun opportunities to handle the majority of the interviews. In actuality I had no real problem with the added responsibility; but I was uncomfortable with the thought that the other guys, who really did enjoy the interviews and wanted to participate in every aspect of this promotional tour were being limited to certain opportunities to speak of their newfound joy, of their accomplishments of their dreams.

When I questioned Bob as to why the change was so abrupt he responded, "Greg, don't you know that it was planned long before we left L.A. that you would always handle the majority of the interviews. Everyone that hears you speak knows that not only do you articulate things thoroughly and intelligently, you provide the history and other information better than all of the other group members. Switch is your band and who better to tell the story than you. Don't worry, it'll be fine."

So, from that point, I just let things happen as Bob Jones orchestrated. Now a promotional tour, in many cases, does not include concert or live performances; but consists of travel to major cities, visiting radio and television stations, being interviewed by local journalist, newspapers and magazines and making appearances at malls and stand-alone record stores to take photos, sign autographs and interact with fans.

In our radio show appearances, besides the normal things like talking with the DJ's, doing station id's and photo ops with the staff, before leaving we started making it a habit to sing and show off a little as to how good a vocal group we really were. At the drop of a hat, we would break into Nat King Cole's version of "When I Fall in Love", but we would do it in in five-part harmony and blow folks away. That was really our little thing to do to stay tight and keep from getting bored with it all.

I remember my having to do interviews by phone in airports upon arrivals or on layovers from one city to the next, while waiting for flights to depart, in hotel lobbies just as our party was checking in or out and even in the moments between the salad and entrée at restaurants. When duty called, I answered. I quickly came to know this promotional tour had to have cost a lot of money between the first-class flights, five-star hotels and expensive meals.

More importantly I learned that all of these charges, even down to per diems and tips were charged back to Switch, and that's the way it is when you're signed to a record label. Each morning we would all meet at breakfast. Around day three we had early interviews and meet and greets. These were to be held downstairs in the hotel restaurant in a medium-sized private room. Our entire traveling party met there and sat at a long table, full of food, with Bob, a journalist, a couple of promoters and other people connected to the music industry.

Bobby and Tommy, sitting across from each other, didn't put their napkins in their lap, wiped their mouths with the backs of their hands, threw bread and food to each other across the table and half-assed whispering started talking about doo-doo and other vile things. We could all see people were watching and listening to them and the journalists were scribbling on their pads.

Bob got up from his seat. I knew what was coming, so I got up and hurried to the bathroom just outside of our private room, where I assumed Bob would be taking Bobby. Entering the men's room, I pretended to close the door, but instead, I listened because Bob had called Bobby and they stopped just outside of where I was.

"Bobby, you and your brother can't carry on like that at the table."

Bobby started biting his lip. "What are you talking about?"

"You know what I'm talking about. Your table manners. You can't behave like that at the table in front of all these people. We're around some very important people who think you don't have any class or home training and it looks bad for all of us, okay?"

Bobby left him standing there and as I walked into the dining room, I saw him not eating and looking around at how everyone else ate. As I sat down, Bobby spoke to Tommy nastily. "Put your napkin in your lap and sit up straight."

Tommy looked around at the band and did as he was told.

Finishing with our appearances for the day, we returned to the hotel and exhausted, went to our rooms. A few hours later in the wee hours of the morning, everyone on that side of this hotel floor was awakened and startled by this loud boom, as if a bomb had gone off, followed by the cracking sound of wood splintering. Coming out of our rooms, we ran down the hall to find that Bobby and Tommy had knocked the door to their room off its hinges, fighting. They had stumbled into the middle of the hallway floor, heaving and bloodied, with fists still balled about to lunge at each other as our entire entourage, along with a few other hotel-guests on that floor appeared in corridors in our sleepwear and robes.

I looked around at Jermaine in that full-faced neon green cosmetic mask he wore every night, and at Phillip's, Eddie and Jody's hair rollers. Hotel security and front desk staff had come up to see what had happened. Embarrassed, all of us went back to our rooms and closed the doors, with me being relieved that Bob Jones was there to handle the mess instead of it, per usual, being my problem. The next morning, at breakfast, Jody, Phillip and I were sitting together, and I really didn't look up when Bobby and Tommy came in late. After seeing there was no room at our table, Bob Jones insisted that they sit with him.

Bobby stood up and shouted to me, "What's the matter with you, muthafucka. You too good to eat with us?"

"No Bobby, if you noticed, I was sitting here when you walked in, that's all." I felt bad but truth is, I was ashamed to eat with him because of his total lack of manners and more so because of what had happened yesterday and last night. I also knew Hazel, Jermaine and Bob Jones were reporting our every move back to Mr. Gordy; and involuntarily, I again, thought about what LaToya had said. After breakfast I made it a point to go to him and Tommy first to reassure them of my loyalty, to explain that much of the stuff that they were doing did reflect badly on our entire travel party, then to ease any ill feelings so that we could move forward.

After Cleveland, we boarded a flight headed for Detroit. Having been away from Grand Rapids since December 1976, I wanted to take a quick run home to see my family but that would have to wait till this promotional tour was completed. We had come here to do radio and in-store appearances with a short drop in on a local television show, The Scene, Detroit's version of *Soul Train*. Having both come from Michigan, since our early friendship, Hazel and I would sometimes talk about home.

Of the many things we shared and came to know about each other, I learned the she loved White Castle hamburgers; so even before we left L.A. for this tour, she and I made a pact that we WOULD NOT leave Detroit without hitting a White Castle. So, as our first day in Detroit wound down, she, I and I believe Phillip stole one of our limo drivers and made him take us to White Castle, where after gulping down enough of them to be full, we bought and took back to our hotel enough burgers for everyone.

Even though it was dark outside, Hazel played tour guide as we rode through her old neighborhood. Our little outing that evening turned out to be fun and informative about the Gordy family and the real beginning of Motown Records.

It was in Baltimore, during our signing autographs where two teen female fans laughing while looking at Bobby's, then Tommy's handwriting, and held up the line saying, " Gee, is this Latin? I can't read this writing."

"If you don't want the damn autograph then don't ask for it."

I angrily defended Bobby and Tommy who were embarrassed.

Everywhere we traveled, fans turned out to hear us and get our signatures. Bobby was slowly changing during this time and it really became obvious when he started cursing out fans about his signature or getting too close to him. Bob Jones always intervened and would try and calm Bobby.

After one day in Baltimore, it was on to Philadelphia, where we went to the Spectrum Arena to catch Motown's first and only band, The Commodores, in concert for the first time; but New York, which immediately followed our full day and night in Philly was the real treat because we attended a Diana Ross concert, at Radio City, which was the biggest extravaganza I'd ever seen in my life. Michael Jackson, Mr. Gordy, and many of the Motown dignitaries were there. We all went to a restaurant afterwards, which had been opened for us, and had a ball till the wee hours of the morning.

Studio 54 - Chico Ross, Eddie, Bobby, Hazel, Jermaine & Me

The next day we visited a few of New York's black radio stations and did more in-store signings with fans. This night, we were treated to an evening at Studio 54, which is where I met and became friends with Hazel's cousin, Roxanna Gordy and we hung together that whole evening. This place was exclusive, huge and bizarre. There was a long line, almost wrapped around the block, of people vying to get in. This was just one example of the many awesome people, places and things we were exposed to on our first major promotional outing.

After the end of that tour, instead of flying back to L.A. each member of Switch flew to our individual home towns for a visit, but this time we went home as stars; and to our friends and families we were a serious cut above Olympic winners and war heroes. The DeBarge boys and I had lots of family to see and that would take up most of the week we were to be there. Every time I had gone home since moving away in 1973,

406

my first couple of days were spent with my family. Coming from a big family who I dearly love, I had lots of folk to see and love on, starting with my mom and my siblings, then grandmother, then grandfather, with uncles, aunts, cousins and extended family being fit in accordingly.

Fortunately, many of the folk around my age or younger would somehow hear I was back in town and they would come and find me. Coming home a winner, a hero of sorts, was absolutely wonderful. Although I was never cocky or arrogant about my accomplishments, I exuded pride in sharing with my folks what most of them hoped for me and could now see in magazines, newspapers and on television and hear for themselves on records, cassettes and radio.

About mid-visit, while still making the rounds to see my extended family, I also made impromptu visits to a few of night spots I used to play in to see if I could catch old friends and more specifically Machen, Honeycutt and other musicians I came up playing with. I stopped by the Legion, a prominent club for Grand Rapids black folks and ran into Floyd Mayweather senior, my old friend since grade school who too had made his dream come true as a fighter. At this time, he too was known throughout the world as a high-ranking welterweight champ.

It was a joyous reunion, as years ago, we had assured each other that we would make it and both of us did! We found a table away from all the madness of friends, fans and well-wishers, ordered drinks and partied together, reminiscing about how two ghetto boys could now be on top of the world. Downing my drink, I glanced at all the people vying for attention and trying to get close. On one hand it was nice to be respected, and the center of attention; but on the other hand, this was home, and I didn't really want to be Gregory Williams of Switch, but just Greg, who's come home to see his family and friends.

With two days' left I caught up and spent a little time with Bobby, Tommy, Andre and some of their family. Being with these two, no matter how difficult at times, was more familiar and more home to me than Grand Rapids used to be because, after going through so much together, we had become family. At the end of this week and trying to say farewell to as much family as possible, Bobby, Tommy and I hooked up at the Kent County airport. Once we boarded our flight, we sat together and shared stories about our home visit and how we were suddenly adored and catered to by our big families and truckloads of old and new friends. The outcome of this trip was a big part of what we had worked for.

Returning to L.A. all members of Switch were rejuvenated and anxious to play music and with a hit record under our belt, it was time to take it to the stage. When the first opportunity came, I called Jermaine and Hazel just to talk and get caught up from the promotional tour and our trip home.

We would visit Mr. Gordy's lavish estate and he'd run, laugh, play games and talk to us. Of the various pearls of wisdom, he would share I recall him telling us, "you're only as strong as your weakest link and you have to look at your band as a long-term investment where you build your capital. I live off my interest and don't touch my money. If you approach your band the same way you'll be in for the long haul because you've built a solid investment."

Later that afternoon, when an opportunity for a private conversation opened up, I approached Berry Gordy. " Mr. Gordy, shouldn't we be going on the road soon, playing and promoting our album. The band is ready."

Switch Album Cover #1

Mr. Gordy didn't flinch. "You could, Greg; but I believe we should work to get Switch to a certain point, where we can get you guys out there starting at Twenty-Five Thousand Dollars per show, just like we did with the Jackson Five." He said, "You guys have the potential to command that type of money if we just strategize our efforts. Let's wait and then go out. What I'll do, in the interim, is raise your advance so that you can have a little more to live on."

Retrospectively, I should have pushed for our band to go on the road, but I accepted what he said as truth and I knew if anyone could, he could make that happen.

Phillip and I were riding home together, and Phillip tuned down the radio. "Greg, we're in trouble. Bobby and Tommy are our weakest links and we're in serious trouble." To which I had no choice but agree.

Yes, the success of our first album brought many other elements into our lives. On one hand, so many folks were waiting in line to shake our hands, work with us, kiss our asses and give us things, including: drugs, sex and other gifts; so, there were many normal and abnormal opportunities waiting behind every corner.

Switch members began to form outside relationships and except for Bobby who was already hanging with an altogether different group of friends due to his sexual orientation and lifestyle, we infrequently trickled out into social settings with folks other than Switch members. Of the folks we met, befriended and created life-long relationships with were Maureen Boyd, Venita Arthur, and Jimmy Levine, who actually became our family.

Shortly after our first album became a bonified hit, Motown wasted no time getting down to business, this time by way of wanting to extend our contract from five years to seven years. At this time, due to the sudden passing of our attorney and legal representative Michael Bourne, we had no one to represent the group; so Motown's legal dept used Hazel and Jermaine to lure us up to the office under false pretenses, then dropped their real intent on us once they got us into, the then head of Motown's business affairs, Lee Young Jr.'s office.

As we arrived and with all smiles and handshakes were escorted into Lee's office, I noticed on his desk was a stack of contracts waiting for our signatures. Hazel explains "Now that your record has done good, Motown wants to put a lot more money into you guys but before they do, we need you to sign these contracts which will extend your original deal by two more years. Motown has agreed to increase your bi-weekly salary by Two Hundred Fifty Dollars a pay period."

Appalled by this dirty underhanded move, I began to balk about this impromptu meeting, asking about the changes and additions to the contents of the original artist and publishing agreements. As I began to condemn the extension, Hazel asked me to step out of the room with her for a sec to discuss the publishing. Acknowledging this too was pre-planned, I hesitated but left the room anyway, thinking everything would stop till we came back in. Once outside, Hazel began speaking in this patronizing tone with, "Now what are your concerns about publishing Greg?"

"Hazel, if we're going to be writing all of these songs, I do want us to be part owner of our work."

"But you already are Greg," Hazel replies.

"As it stands we get our writers shares and Jobete gets all of the publishing. Are you telling me it says something different in this new agreement, Hazel?"

"Well I don't know because I haven't read the new contracts..."

Cutting her off I add, "Well from what I've learned so far, it won't be in there if I don't ask for it. Nor will anything else in the group's best interest, that's why we can't sign anything else without our attorney."

"Greg, you know that Jermaine and I would never hurt you guys and what you want is not unreasonable and I think it can be done. We just need to talk about it with daddy first."

"Okay, I'd like my lawyer to negotiate the contract, make the changes and then we can sign it."

When we reentered the room Lee Young, Jermaine and the fellas were laughing and talking about something else; and to my surprise, I find that everyone in the band had already signed their contracts, as they began discussing what they were going to do with their advances. I was done. Realizing that I had been set up and considering the past threats, and coercion I'd already endured I knew then I'd better join the party before it moved on without me, I never would forget being raped like this.

As we finally left that meeting, while headed to our individual cars, I remember angrily discussing how fucked up that whole scene was on everybody's part with Bobby and Jody whose primary response was, "well what else could we do?"

"Hell, you could have at least waited till I came back into the office," I said.

"Greg, they didn't give us a chance. They pounced on us to sign as soon as the door closed behind you and Hazel," Bobby stated.

"Yeah Greg," Jody interjected.

"It was clearly a sign now or it could be over for us."

"Bullshit!" I said.

"No Matter what, you guys should have waited for me. We're supposed to stick together!"

I was so incensed that I just shut down. We walked to our individual cars and went our separate ways, with me again having to swallow the fact that I had to go along to get along. If there is an upside to being repeatedly raped, after this new contract shit was behind us, we were brought more in direct contact with the folks, the Motown family and inner-workings of the company.

Soon enough it become totally clear to me that all the money Motown spent on our behalves, including our bi-monthly salaries, any advances or bonuses, managers commissions, stage costumes, our recordings, photo shoots and many other costs and fees unknown or documented would come out of our budget. It would be paid back and recouped from our record sale royalties, if we made any, before we would see dime one. This sadly enough remains the outcome to this day, with all of our record sales over the years, we have yet to see dime one from Motown artist royalties.

I learned how to itemize everything we did; but there was no way for me to even know all the ways Motown, our caring managers Jermaine and Hazel, and other Motown departments or record producers, known or unknown to us, hired to work on our music spent our money. The more I tried to learn, the more I was made to feel that I asked too many questions, but I kept pressing, knowing that above all else, Switch would have to live with the outcome. On my productions I made sure my songs were always produced and delivered ahead of time and under budget because all costs were coming out of our pockets.

I also was constantly in Hazel and Jermaine aka Mr. Gordy's ear about letting us go on the road because I had learned that money an act earns on the road is the act's money and not paid by or shared with the record company. The record company makes money from the increased record sales when an act performs and yet Switch was not permitted by our managers to go on the road.

As I later came to understand, managers are employees of the artist and therefore the artist should always have the final word on something they want to do to better their conditions. Also, in most cases the manager's income is derived from how frequently the act works; but Switch's managers were already rich and not hungry like we were, so the same things didn't matter.

At that time, the bulk of Jermaine and Hazel's money came through their loyalty to Motown and not to Switch, therefore keeping us off of the road worked to Motown's advantage. These among other negative issues and concerns about Switch's relationship with Jermaine, Hazel and Motown continued to mount inside of me but had not yet become a negative that I could not deal with. By now I was pretty much handling all business decisions concerning Switch by myself; as Jody, who was consumed with family issues, had all but removed himself from Switch's inner workings and Bobby was well into his drugs, his new lifestyle and new friends.

And factually by the finish of Switch II Motown knew, like I knew that Bobby was well on his way to self-destruction and once that happened no one would win. The powers that be at Motown knew how Bobby was now living but no one stepped up to help him or me get a grip on what was destroying him. What, as I predicted from the beginning, would ultimately be the demise of Switch. And poor Mama DeBarge was no help when Bobby's life was being destroyed as a child, so I could not even go there in thought or theory, but she could and certainly did come to me with her own unrelated request.

I remember one day during this time I received a phone call from her.

"Greg, this is Mom DeBarge."

"Hello Etterlene."

"You know Motown is thinking about starting a gospel division and they told me that I need to make a memo. Can you help me with that?"

"A what?"

"A memo Greg. They want a memo of my songs so they can hear my singing, what my voice sounds like. Can you help me?"

"I'm sorry Etterlene, I'd love to, but I really can't help you make a demo right now because they've got me swamped in preproduction for our next album. Have you asked Bobby to help? You should ask him if not."

Without answering my question, she thanked me anyway, said goodbye and hung up the phone. I never heard from her on or about that subject again, which confirmed what I already knew. Bobby had refused her long before she asked for my help.

For years, I knew that Bobby was clearly tormented by his relationship with his mother. He loved her because he, as did Bunny, knew no other way to deal, but he didn't really like her, and he didn't trust her. He would go off on her in a heartbeat if she said or did anything he didn't like or agree with and often he would curse at the mention of her name. From time to time, after a negative incident between the two of them, she would reach out to me asking, "Greg, what's wrong with Bobby?

What is he going through right now?"

"I'm not sure Etterlene, I believe only Bobby can answer that," I would say. Of course, I had too much sense and too much respect for his and my relationship to get in the middle of a dispute between them. I did not need or want him fighting with me over her repeating out of context something I may say. Plus, from years back I knew who was really at fault here, no matter what Bobby's then position and/or problem. Over the years, I was there to help him as best I could, not her.

Sadly, enough there were a few others that I wanted to help get into the business; but by then I had taken my role as leader of Switch far beyond the call of duty, foolishly thinking it was my responsibility to handle the lives and personal problems of these grown men and that role was all too consuming.

As with most of the folks I was surrounded by since my early teens, I had become known as the counselor. I was the guy with the answers, and I would help whenever asked, so when it came to Switch, I instinctively stepped into my perceived role. And as leader of these men, I was much too consumed by their issues with their home lives, their wives or ladies and their children, their friends and associates, their hopes, dreams and all other subsequent problems and concerns.

Yes, to all who knew me, knew me to be intelligent, strong, resilient and accessible to no end; so, life had come down to taking care of everyone, everyone but me. And because I didn't know how to let anyone all the way in, there's never been anyone to take care of me. Yes, members of Switch individually occupied a place in my life, and I wanted the best from them, but more so for them. I was over-protective, so I also hurt when I had to witness things that made any of them feel or look bad at the hands or in the eyes of others.

Case and point, I often remember Bobby's illiteracy putting him and me in an awkward position. On one such occasion at Motown, Switch members were riding down in the elevator with Jermaine, Hazel, Suzanne de Passe and a few other miscellaneous passengers. Bobby took and deep breath smelling Suzanne's perfume. He then looks her in the eye and says, "Suzanne, that's a nice fragment you have on."

As I looked around, everyone in the elevator had a look of shock and horror on their faces as Jermaine and Hazel immediately looked at me and Phillip, then quickly turned their heads in effort not to laugh.

I immediately thought about what LaToya had said and put my head down, afraid to look at anyone else because I knew we'd all start laughing. As the elevator stopped, Suzanne, who laid back so some of the others could go on ahead, inconspicuously pulled me beside her, "My goodness! I know you heard that. Everybody did. You know we've got to get him some English classes. We can't possibly send him out in the public sounding like that."

She walked on, showing bewilderment in her head scratching. Even though I too found that funny, I desperately wanted to defend him. By nature, and lifetime habit, I am usually the first person to instinctively correct bad diction. Not as a put-down to anyone, but in my wanting and accepting verbal as well as visual correction from those closest to me, from those who know I would definitely want to accept correction, and also make one aware of proper verbiage.

But, after my many years around the DeBarge clan and their ongoing "Debargeisms", I had long since learned the futility of such an act. Per always, it would again be interpreted as a personal attack. But bottom line, this is my brother; so later, after Bobby and I had left the building heading home, I tactfully told him what he had said versus what I knew he meant to say, to which he looked really serious and said, "Really man, fuck those people Greg!" But then he began to laugh.

Finally, I too, was free to laugh out loud and we went on about our day. Bobby was aware of some of his own disadvantages of his lack of education. One way this was apparent is how he would defer to me and later Bunny to write and or correct lyrics to the melodies and music he would create.

Chapter 12

First Base with Free-Base

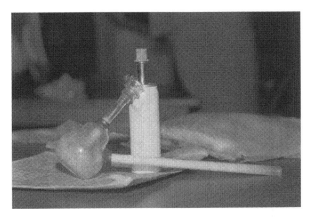

Free Base

We went into the studio to record Switch II, in 1979 and we were all alive and ready to work. All of us had fun working together during these early years.

A few days later at the studio, I was producing my song "Fallin'" and I was showing background parts to Tommy and Phillip, which didn't involve Bobby so later he walked into the studio. I was surprised because he was earlier than I expected.

While Phillip and Tommy were going over their parts Bobby pulled me away from the group. "Come to the bathroom. I got something you need to try."

I followed him into the bathroom. He pulled out some aluminum foil.

"Bobby, you know I don't like no cocaine man."

"What a minute Greg, damn."

He opened the aluminum foil and there was a solid, cream colored thing which was slightly smaller than a Quarter and resembled a chip from a bar of Ivory soap. Bobby pulled out a small glass pipe, unlike anything I had ever seen, with a small copper screen covering the hole on the end. He put a piece of the "soap" on the screen, stuck the glass up to my mouth and lit the "soap".

"Inhale this shit, Greg."

I hit the pipe, blew the smoke out, the room started to swirl, my head leapt to the ceiling and I grabbed my crotch. "What's that man?"

"Its free base, cocaine. You like it?"

"Hell yeah. Give me some more."

Within a couple of minutes, we smoked up what Bobby had put out and then returned into the studio. I threw my hands into the air when we stepped inside.

"I love everybody. All of you." Euphoric, I was happy about everything. Between trips back and forth to the bathroom, Bobby and I kept laughing at almost everything and we jammed for a few more hours working on my song.

When the session was over Bobby asked., "Do you want to get some more?"

Liking how the stuff made me feel and having nothing better to do I said, "Hell, yeah man."

"Follow me then," he said, as he hopped in his car.

As I followed, we drove to Franklin Street in Hollywood and stopped at this guy Roscoe's house. When Bobby and I arrived, we found there were others waiting for this guy to come downstairs. Soon after, Roscoe appeared and called all of the folks in sight to follow him. Bobby, me and about five other people followed as instructed and took seats around Roscoe's dining room table. Each of us were given a small glass pipe with a collection screen in it and instructed to put fifty dollars each in this large bowl in the middle of this table as we impatiently waited for him to mix and distribute this free base.

He heated and cooked up a concoction of powder cocaine, baking soda and water in a large chemistry glass vial. The mixture was first boiled by hand-torch, then cooled and allowed to harden as it stuck to the handle of a wooden spoon. Not totally understanding what was happening, we watched the concoction in the vial stick to the spoon. Roscoe then scraped off the base into a small pile for each person. Each of us smoked until Roscoe determined it was fifty dollars-worth, then we had to put in more money.

I had 200 hundred dollars in my pocket when we walked in and I was broke and zooming when I left. Smoking free base became part of my life from that moment and would last a little more than three years. Bobby and I seldom got high together after that because the album was almost finished and outside of Switch moments he hung with his new friends and I hung with mine. But the game was on and poppin' for both of us, with Tommy briefly waiting in the wings before his number came up!

Although I later realized that I was hooked from that first night, that first hit, it took more than a year before noticeable signs of addiction reared their ugly heads. Although I enjoyed the way freebase made me feel, I found myself wanting to leave it alone; and because I had such a full schedule between studio, songwriting, meetings at Motown and spending time with my then girlfriend Kathy, I barely had time to get high anyway, so I made no big deal of it and only indulged at spare intervals.

As the months moved on and most of the recording was completed, Switch would meet at Motown a little less frequently while the record was completely mixed, mastered and turned over to the label, so those spare intervals of me with a pipe in my hand came a little more often. Those early stages of freebase use, hitting the pipe was fun, considered chic and not necessarily frowned upon and my girlfriend, I, and most of our mutual friends would even smoke a little together from time to time.

Now the L.A. entertainment scene has been known for its open use of certain drugs. Marijuana, various pills and cocaine use were fairly acceptable and therefore readily available throughout events in Hollywoodland, but now Freebase was popping up at many parties and more so at folk's homes during gatherings. Now there were other less popular drugs available like Heroin, Sherm aka Angel Dust, barbiturate-based cough syrups and even various types of Acid, which had somewhat fallen from the scene over the early 70's, but at this moment in time, those and other drugs carried extreme and often negative connotations; so therefore, had to be sought out by those who partook.

I for one really didn't like any drugs with the exception of Marijuana, which I had quit smoking roughly a year or so earlier, so you could keep that other stuff away from me. Yet, being a fresh, young star, it seemed like everyone wanted to be in your company, so drugs were as plentiful and mostly free in the beginning and they were unavoidable. You didn't have to indulge but you did have to know how to say "no thanks" or "I pass, or you too would end up in the loop.

In my limited off hours away from Switch or Switch-related events, I was with my girlfriend and when we weren't alone we were mostly with our group of mutual friends, so I really didn't notice the subtle grip that freebase was taking on me, Bobby or Tommy and the three of us continued to function and make good music and very little else mattered; but in reality, once the drugs got hold of Bobby or Tommy they never let go. Though Bobby has long since passed, to this day I worry about my little brother.

Through the drug use and everything else, we had to get the Switch II album finished and we didn't miss a beat. While working towards the finish line, everything was still so new and exciting as Bobby, Jody and I were becoming confident writers, arrangers, producers, free to create and work where, when and how it suited us; while Tommy, Phillip and Eddie were also working, absorbing and learning about writing, singing and playing songs and making records. We all were making a living, we had girlfriends, we had nice apartments, we had new cars, we had new clothes and new lives.

And to top all of this off, Switch was a hit act with the number one black-owned and operated company in the world! Life then was actually as good as it gets to each of us and we all had fun working, playing and learning together. On our first album Berry Gordy was hands on in the studio teaching and overseeing every aspect of the project. For all intents and purposes, we were his new project, his babies and he made sure that album was a hit.

Now on this second album he backed off and let Jermaine, Bobby, Jody and I have the reins. Due to his personal interest and company investment, I'm sure if we were showing signs of weakness he again would have stepped in; but this time he let us go and let us grow. Now of course he was still very much involved in every selection and decision, but he oversaw the project through his niece and head of the creative department, Iris Gordy, and the few other Motown staffers who served a function in assisting Jermaine, Bobby, Jody and me in the production of this album.

This time, we were given the creative autonomy to seek out, pick and choose our own horn and string arrangers and additional musicians, like: guitarist, additional keyboard players and even percussionist, if the individual producer felt the need to add a different flavor to the song, but on this Switch II project, except for Jermaine's contribution, the songs on this album were also played and performed by Switch.

As proven producers we were now allowed to work at the recording studio of our choosing. Having been introduced to most of the high-end recording studios throughout Hollywood-land over the past year or more, Switch opted to bounce back and forth between Hitsville USA and ABC Recording through the making of this album, depending on which one had studio time available to use and our choice of engineer.

After learning who most of the top engineers were in Hollywood, we forged relationships with legendary engineers like Art Stewart and Bob Robitale, who were on staff at Hitsville, and Barney Perkins and Reggie Dozier, who were independent but worked mostly at ABC during that time. So, with Barney and Reggie being number one and two on Bobby's, Jody's and my list of favorites, most of Switch II was done at ABC Recording.

Life seemed to be very full for Switch members after signing to Motown Records. Our individual creative time suffered to a small degree from what we were used to. Those of us who were songwriters brought what we had to the table for the first Switch album and again the Switch II album project. Being new to the whole professional recording and songwriters process, we had less of our own original songs to choose from that we did on the first project, but fortunately songs from Jermaine, Bobby, Jody and I were strong enough that no additional producers were needed or allowed.

This time our song arsenal included "Best Beat in Town" and "I Call Your Name", which were released as singles and hit records for Motown's newest stars. As with the first album, the band had practiced and learned these songs too, so when we went into the studio the tracks were finished in one day. The vocals, overdubs (which is simply adding new parts) and other arrangements i.e. strings and horns would take up far more of the production time, and still for us the time passed very quickly from start to finish.

Together, including Jermaine, Hazel and Michael McGloiry we had much fun and many new experiences recording this album. I recall one day, while working over at

Hitsville USA, I and my engineer were in the studio cleaning tracks on "Fallin'", when who just walks in but Berry Gordy with Diana Ross to hear what I was working on. As this was my first time meeting her, he introduced her and then asked did I mind if they sat in for a minute to hear what I was working on. Having heard on various occasions how Mr. Gordy bragged on his new act, Switch, to his friends and his employees, I was honored to have both of them in my session; so, I of course happily said yes.

I gestured for the engineer to run the track from the top. Ms. Ross took a seat close next to me at the mixing board as the engineer stripped down, then reset up the board so the parts would play back in prospective. Once the basic track and vocals were up, the engineer motioned to me and pushed the play button. While Mr. Gordy's body language immediately showed that he was into it, Miss Ross, too, grooved to the music as she listened. As the track faded I knew they both were digging what they were hearing; but I noticed what I deemed a hint of skepticism show in her raised right eyebrow.

Waiting to get feedback Mr. Gordy immediately said, "It's a smash! It's a smash Greg," as he began to sing the background part I had placed on the vamp.

"I love that part. It's exciting."

I quickly nodded a 'thank you' while still awaiting Miss Ross's commentary that I knew was coming.

"Yes, this song is great, but I feel the music is missing something. I think this can be stronger, but I'm not sure what it needs," she added.

Being unable to display my own vanity and displeasure at her tacky outburst, "I understand your thoughts but hold on one minute," I said as I hit the stop button on the recording console and abruptly pulled down all of the faders on the recording console. I told the engineer to start again and let me make a quick mix, but this time bring all of the instruments up, including the horns and strings and play the track with everything.

This took a minute and during that time Mr. Gordy called me over to him and asked how things were going in the studios, how the other band members were doing and how I was feeling about my life in general. By now, though infrequent, I had gotten used to having conversations like this with him on the phone and face to face and I understood that I was the go-to guy for him and everyone, when they wanted the serious low-down on Switch members.

I really appreciated the respect he gave me as a musician, as band leader and as a man. The engineer had finished and stood up to let me know that he was ready when I was. I walked over to the board and hit the play button. As the song came on, Miss Ross stood up from her chair, started moving her shoulders and as it continued, danced throughout the entire song.

"Now that is a smash," she said in the way that only she can say it. She then reached out and shook my hand, then turned to Mr. Gordy as he gestured it was time to leave.

"Keep up the good work," he said to me as they made their way to the exit.

"See I told you this would be a treat!" he said to her as they walked out the studio, hand in hand. Watching them groove and the fact Mr. Gordy had brought her in to hear my music, confirmed Switch was a big part of Motown's present and history's future.

Another day, Bobby, Jody and I were working at Hitsville overseeing the mixing of "I Call Your Name" and Stevie Wonder was led into the control booth. He sat down, his head moving to multiple rhythms and when the song ended, he cocked his head to one side.

"Can I hear that again?"

Bobby and I were delighted he wanted to hear our song again and asked the engineer to play it.

Halfway through the first chorus, Stevie held up his hand. "Could you go back a bit? I hear a flat note."

The section was played again, and he stopped it at the same point. "I hear this note that's not right."

We played it three times and Bobby and I didn't hear it. Bobby leaned back in his chair, behind Stevie and shrugged his shoulders, looking at me. I know Stevie felt his movement and our bewilderment.

"Well, fellows, you know I'm blind and I hear all kinds of things others don't hear. It doesn't take away from the music though. This is a hit and you fellows are tight. Thanks for letting me listen."

He shook our hands and left. Bobby, Jody and I listened to the track four more times and still couldn't hear what Stevie heard. It wasn't until I was riding in my car one day and "I Call Your Name" was being played, that I heard that note. I stopped at a telephone booth and called Bobby.

"Bobby, I just heard "I Call Your Name" and guess what?"

"What's that?"

"I heard that note Stevie mentioned. It's in the second chorus."

Bobby held his breath. "Hold on a minute," he said.

I heard him walking, then I heard music from his cassette player. When the song reached the first chorus, the typical Bobby came out. "Muthafucka really heard that shit. I can hear it too now," he said, as he came back to the phone. "Greg, that bad muthafucka got ears beyond human."

"I told you. That's Stevie you talkin' about."

Laughing, we said goodbye and hung up the phone.

With Switch II playing on radio stations around the world, we were constantly given updates on how well the record was selling. I Call Your Name reached number 8 on the R & B charts and number 83 on the U.S. charts. The Best Beat in Town reached number 16 on the R & B charts and number 69 on the U.S. charts. These hits followed "There'll Never Be", from the first album, which reached number 6 on the R & B charts and 36 on the U. S. charts with "I Wanna Be Closer" hitting number 22 on the R & B charts. We were being confirmed as one of Motown's major acts.

By now, we were repeatedly hearing from different friends, including those who worked in Motown's sales, marketing and publicity departments, "We heard you guys are really bad live," (bad, meaning good). "We want to see you guys perform. When are you guys going out on the road?"

Concert promoters had been constantly calling and trying to get Switch performance dates but Motown, through Hazel and Jermaine, had told them no. I was pissed and puzzled because Switch had arrived, and we were being written about everywhere.

All the new hit artists across the board, including stars topping the R&B charts like Prince, Rick James, Con Funk Shun, Teddy Pendergrass and various others were taking it to the road to make money and promote their new releases, while Switch was made to sit on the sidelines and watch. Sadly enough, I did not know what to do and I had no one to help me change and get my business on the right track. Those who I thought, depended on and even paid to do so, worked for the other team which I also thought was working in my best interest; only to later find out how wrong I was to have even considered that, no matter how I was led to believe that.

On a multitude of levels, Switch was screwed from the beginning. First, due to our own inexperience in the music business, in our having to endure Bobby's ongoing psychological condition and in Motown's manipulative and unscrupulous methods.

My spirit actually knew it; but due to my lack of education, business sophistication and mostly my then naive nature, which always gave the benefit of the doubt in all situations, it took much longer for me to consciously catch on.

Now, "Fallin'" was on the B side of the single. Besides the fact that DJ's across the country were adding the song to major rotation, it was played accidentally on American bandstand's 'rate a record' and was the highest-rated record in the show's history, rating a ninety-nine. However, my spy in the marketing department told me, Motown refused to release and promote it as the next single.

One would think by now, that I would have a serious problem in coming to know that no matter what I wrote, arranged, produced for my own band, no matter how good it was to all that heard it, that Berry Gordy would push it to the side to promote his star, Bobby DeBarge. But my thoughts and sincere feelings, after acknowledging that Phillip's great talents were too being "kicked to the curb" to satisfy one man's lust for power, control and ego, were if this is what it takes to put me and my guys on top, bring it on. I can take this outcome and build on it!

The success of Switch II was a blessing, but it opened the door to a host of new problems with Bobby. First of which, by now he was dissatisfied with the bi-weekly checks we received from Motown. He wanted, demanded a bigger paycheck even though he was already being advanced an extra two thousand dollars per month from his own songwriter royalties, while he thought that me and other band members were unaware of his underhanded actions. He was paranoid of everyone in and around his life. In his mind, he could no longer trust anyone, including members of the group. Unprovoked he would have negative outbursts about even the littlest imaginary thing and was frequently enraged to the point that his whole body shook, and he would be reduced to tears.

I was often worried that he was having a breakdown of sorts; but as we could in the past, he would not let me in to discuss this or much of anything else with him. He began to blow up at and mistreat others, including band members which we would mostly just turn and walk away versus sucker punching him in his fucking face as his actions often deserved. His then psychosis made him disregard the fact that Switch was a group, my group and he consistently proclaimed to all who would listen that he was doing all the hard work.

In his mind he was writing the hits and the gold albums were solely attributable to him alone. Bobby's psychosis and ignorance had become totally overbearing, as he felt, and blatantly stated that it was he and he alone who made Switch what it was. He wanted out, to become a solo artist. And I too wanted his ass out of my band because, with all of the problems that were continuing to surface, he was actually destroying us from the inside out. But because of Motown's refusal to let the band go in separate directions, we stuck it out as best we could and on the surface continued on as if all was right with the world.

Now that sales of Switch II had begun to soar, we were again invited to Mr. Gordy's estate to celebrate, to discuss and prepare for upcoming promotional events, to review one of our Soul Train and other television appearances and to just visit and eat something, I was always impressed with the size of his mansion. We spent most of our time in the main house but there were three more full houses on the property. There was a professional tennis court, an Olympic-size pool and even a mid-sized movie theatre in the main house which was behind one of the many hidden doors that would slide open once the right place on the wall was touched.

We had spent much of the day there talking and laughing among other things, so around lunch time, we were provided menus, from which we could individually select the food of our choice. Mr. Gordy's chef and kitchen staff would fix each of us what we wanted and serve it in whatever area we were in. As with most times we were up there, the main house was filled with other guests including Berry's brothers Robert and Fuller with his wife Winnie who I also learned was Teena Marie's manager, Berry's niece Iris Gordy, Suzanne de Passe, cousin and business associate Tony Jones, and her right arm Suzanne Coston, along with Nancy Leiviska, Motown's then special projects director. Also, there was Berry Gordy's executive administrative assistant and right arm Edna Anderson, his close friend Billy Wilson, Bob Jones from publicity and a select group of others.

Of the many rooms and entertainment items throughout the estate, there was a chessboard in the primary game room and upon seeing it a couple of the guys in Switch started bragging about my chess game. Mr. Gordy challenged me to a game, and we sat down at the board. It didn't take but about three moves to realize he was nowhere near my league. With most others I know, sometimes I'd came across as arrogant and maybe even cocky when it came to my chess game, as did Mr. Gordy, but here I knew to subdue my actions and go in for the kill. I gave him a couple of breaks, thinking he might be rusty, but I soon saw, he couldn't take advantage of the openings I'd left for him. I made a couple of more moves and I had him.

The room got quiet, watching him look at the board and I happened to look up at him for the first time after the first few moves, because I always kept my eyes only on the board. The veins in his head began to stand out, he breathed heavy, his lips were tight, and I saw the same angry look he'd given de Passe, Coston, Nancy Leiviska and the others involved with the corny pictures of us for the first, unused album cover.

He made a move and I could have called checkmate, but I pulled back and gave him another opening. He saw it this time, made a move and I left an opening for him to checkmate me and win the game. He called checkmate and those in the room who stood with him laughed, congratulated him and slapped fives with him. I stood and Jody, who also played a little chess, gave me a slant-eyed curious look because he saw what had happened.

Berry IV sat down. "My turn."

Mr. Gordy pulled him from the seat. "You want to play someone else, not Greg. You can't get with him yet. Don't even think about it, son."

After the game was over, all of us continued milling about the estate, mingling with other guests or playing other games, while eating our lunch.

Both Bobby and Jody approached me, talking about the game, when Bobby said, "You had him, but you let him go. Why?"

"What makes you think I let him go?" I asked.

"Come on Greg. I saw it, so why did you let him off the hook?" Jody cut in.

"Sometimes concession is the only way to win," I answered.

We looked at each other, chuckled a little and moved on discussing various aspects of being at this place. Each of us was discreetly in awe of being there, being around these people and where our dreams had brought us. Although we had two hit albums out, all of us were still very much humbled by all of this opulence and realized that to come close we still had such a long way to go. As that afternoon moved into evening, I recall a group of eight or so guests went into the screening room to watch a new movie, which had not hit the theatres yet, while other guests played tennis.

Some folk ate or swam while the six of us and Jermaine ran with Mr. Gordy to one of the other houses on his estate so that we could listen to some of our new musical ideas on one of his stereo cassette systems. We all listened to the music and discussed our thoughts on our career. We talked about our next album and when we might get to go on the road, which the latter was quickly discouraged; so, I let it go and went with the flow. He would take a little time and share what Motown and a few of the artists like Marvin Gaye, Dianna Ross, Smokey and even Florence Ballard were like back when the company was in its infancy. I could see in his face as he talked how magical all of it was to even him. His voice became very expressive as he spoke on one person and thing or another.

Again, we were each in awe, just to be in his presence and to be privy to his sharing bits of his own history. As it began to get dark, we headed back to the main house to join the others in drinks, Hors D'oeuvres and socializing till it was time to go. As our evening there was ending, and Jermaine Hazel and Switch stood waiting in the front entryway for our stretch limo to pull up we were all saying our goodbyes when Mr. Gordy summoned me to the side and said, "Greg you've got a damn good chess game. You had me there for a while."

I smiled and listened and probably nodded involuntarily as I maintained my composure whilst thinking to myself, *You know I had you and that's all that really matters.*

Then this serious look came over his face and he said, "But don't come up here expecting to win anything!"

I was caught totally off guard by that statement and a little outdone that he would actually say that to me, but I managed to get out, "I understand you." And at that moment, I really did. Suddenly everything about my visit here in Oz and my current discussion with the Wizard became clear.

I now understood that being a member of the Motown family would be no free ride. I understood that I would have to work my ass off and still might not get what I deserved, even if I fought for it, but definitely not if I didn't fight. I further understood that Berry Gordy always chose what he and he alone deemed the most unique to reward while he equally preyed on the easiest to manipulate. And most of all, I understood that this man had to win at all cost.

He gave me the hug and hand shake I had come to receive from him and turned back to the others, as I too did, to say goodbye. The Limo was now waiting, so the eight of us piled in and drove off, verbally reliving the events of the day as we headed back to the Holiday Inn parking lot at Sunset Blvd and the 405 freeway, a few miles away from Mr. Gordy's Bel Air Estates home.

Hazel talked with Phillip, Tommy with Jermaine, and Eddie and Bobby to Jody while I sat quietly absorbing my last few moments there. Each time we'd left Mr. Gordy's home we were on a high because the infrequent visits had become a part of our lives, but this time was much more sobering to me than ever before.

Not long after that, at the directive of Berry Gordy, Hazel and Jermaine tactfully suggested Switch get away from L.A. to start our next album. Somewhere we could be to ourselves. I shortly came to know that this was Motown's unspoken effort to try and bring Bobby out of the dope houses, the gay nightclubs, off the streets and back from his road to self-destruction. And I'm hoping and praying that with this move, maybe I can pull my band back together too.

Chapter 13

Caribou Ranch

Greg & Bobby at Caribu Ranch

After discussing the idea with the fellas, all of us agreed that the idea of recording our next album outside of L.A., was a good one, so now the question was where to go! We began to speak with folks who might know something about recording facilities outside of L.A. All of us began our quest by going to few L.A. studios where we had once worked, seeking information, to find the perfect place to do our next album.

We started over at ABC Studios where Reggie Dozier was. He was now our primary engineer since working with us on Switch I and Switch II. We also went over to ask Art Stewart and Bob Robitaille at Hitsville, which was Motown's recording studio which was exclusively used for Motown artists. While there, Jody and I just happened to pick up this brochure which was about an incredible recording studio in Colorado called Caribou Ranch.

According to this brochure, Caribou Ranch was isolated in the Rocky Mountains covering more than 4,000 acres. It was owned by record producer James "Jimmy" Guercio who managed the group Chicago. When we read that John Lennon, Elton John, **Chicago and Earth, Wind, & Fire** had recorded there, this place became an easy choice; but still we had to take it to the fellas, Jermaine, Hazel and Motown.

After reading through it, we took it and waited till the group was all together again. At first glance, it was unanimously decided that this was the place we wanted to go, so we brought our choice to Jermaine, Hazel and Motown, which they easily approved; so, we immediately began planning what and how it would be done there. We talked about how much time we would need to cut our next album and how long we wanted to be away from L.A.; so, we decided to spend no less than a month to unwind and get as near completion to the album as we could over that period.

Since Reggie Dozier was our studio guy, we called, told him where we had decided to record our next album and asked if he might be interested in making that journey with us to work on our forthcoming album. With hesitation Reggie said yes, provided we would make it worth his while financially to go that far for this long. Well we agreed, , and Motown agreed and worked things out, so it was on! In discussing how we would try to work while there we also realized that we would need a guitarist; so, we asked McGloiry if he would come down there for a couple of weeks if we should call for him. He too said yes; so, another concern was now out of the way.

Switch Album Cover #2

After our rigid promotional schedule, which was roughly three weeks of constant radio, television and public appearances, after Switch II was released, because our lives had become so full with external relationships and obligations, we decided to leave for the studio resort as soon as studio and flight reservations could be booked. Over the next few days, we got word that things were locked in and our trip was a go; so, each of us packed, said our goodbyes to our folks and within another forty-eight hours, we were off again; but only this trip would include work, relaxation, adventure, recreation, peace and isolation.

Before leaving L.A., we were informed that it was decided that Mitch Canter, Jermaine and Hazel's company management assistant would accompany us on this entire outing. We were told that he was being sent to look out for and assist us, which I knew was a great idea, as specific things would need to be taken care of, not to mention the random, unexpected things that were bound to come up while we were there, even some of the things that had interrupted our workflow while in L.A. But I later found out he was actually sent in to spy and report back, which he promptly and consistently did, even though he brought along his own issues and vices, which I was to later discover.

After our two-hour flight to Denver, we arrived in the wee hours of the morning. Members of the Caribou Ranch staff met us at the airport, packed us in army jeeps, our baggage in their large van for an additional two-hour ride north to Nederland, Colorado where the ranch was located. Once off the main road we headed up into the mountains to our destination. Once there, those of us still asleep were woken up then all of us were escorted to the main cabin where we would be staying. Being totally exhausted from the long journey, once given our individual room assignments, each man hurried to his room and hit the sack.

Upon waking up on day one at Caribou, after a shave and a shower, knowing that Bobby and Tommy usually slept in, the first order of business was to find out when and where

441

we eat. So, after confirming that our bags had been placed outside of our doors while we slept, as promised. I then called Phillip, Eddie and Jody to see if they were up and at em too, which they all were; so, we decided to get dressed and meet downstairs in the large receiving room in the center of the cabin, where we had congregated last night before getting room assignments. I then called Mitch, who was booked in a smaller, one room cabin on the property. He too was up and moving around, so I invited him to join us at breakfast which he accepted.

Once there, we were again greeted and each given a pamphlet which provided a menu and guest information, which spelled out all of the available in-cabin and on-sight amenities, and stated that breakfast was served from six to eleven am, lunch was from twelve to three pm and dinner was from four pm till eight pm daily, down in this large mess hall in the main cabin. But one could also order meals and snacks and have them brought to your room throughout the day, so we opted to start our day in the mess hall.

As our hostesses prepared to take our food orders, she explained each food item on the menu was available up till eight pm, so instead of coming down for meals, we could also pre-order and it could be brought to our rooms. Since the few of us had made it down there, our orders were put in. While we waited for the food to come, she took the time to go over a different pamphlet, containing much of the property information we had initially seen in the brochure. She told us how many acres of land this place actually covered, how long the ranch had been a private recording facility and some of the named artists and producers who had visited and worked there before, among other Caribou Ranch history.

After breakfast Phillip, Jody, Eddie and I stepped outside to check out the place. The entire scenery was breathtaking. Looking around and checking out as much as we could of this huge property, among many other things we discovered, besides the main cabin, there were also individual cabins, which like the main house, they too came with daily maid and food service. Humongous, surreal and all ours for the time of our stay.

Greg at Caribu Ranch

443

Yes, we had wound up in what had to be God's country; in the middle of nowhere USA, surrounded by massive mountains, gorgeous lakes and private waterfalls and the greenest trees, so tall they blended into the sky. We were now far removed from the demands and distractions of L.A. life, which had as of late consumed each of us; and we found refuge within these elegant, peaceful surroundings. And we were here to make music which we loved.

After a couple of hours of exploration, we wound up in the incredible, state-ot-the-arts studio where Bobby, Tommy, Mitch and a few more ranch staff joined us. Although we weren't ready to begin recording that day we spent about an hour checking out the rooms, the recording equipment, the available instruments and even the external view, as much of this place had see-through walls and doors.

Yes, this place and the folks who ran it turned out to be awesome. Individually and collectively, we spent most of the day exploring and getting familiar with our surroundings and relaxing in our rooms or in the lobby before coming together in the mess hall at dinner time, where we laughed, joked and shared info we had learned throughout the day.

After dinner it was a little chilly outside, so, with the exception of those who chose to go to their rooms, the rest of us sat around this huge fireplace, listening to one of the staff tell about experiences there on the ranch with past celebrity guests until one by one each band member made his way to their rooms for the night. On the afternoon of day two, as expected, Reggie Dozier showed up there and soon after his arrival, check-in and a meal we went right to work, checking out and preparing the studio for the initial recording to begin the next morning.

From our second full day away from L.A., it became clear that all of us felt at ease and creative. Everything we desired was made available to us at the ranch, meals in bed to fishing, horseback riding, hiking, women and even drugs. Yes, I believe unknown to Jermaine and Hazel and definitely to us that Mitch was a functioning coke-head. Mitch was a young Jewish guy who was maybe a little older than Jody, recently hired by Jermaine and Hazel to work side by side with them at their company, Young Folks; so, other than the fact that he seemed like a cool guy, we too knew little about him before he was assigned to go with us. Well, it turned out that Bobby, Tommy and I had a comrade on campus, which I stumbled up on after a few days on the ranch, once my, Bobby and Tommy's stash had run out.

Jody, Phillip, Reggie and I were in the studio. When Tommy was needed for a vocal part, there was no one to go get him, so I opted to. As I began to look for Tommy, it suddenly dawned on me that Mitch, who would at least be in the studio most of each session, had not been around all day. So, after looking for Tommy at his and Bobby's rooms and throughout the main cabin to no avail, I went to Mitch's cabin to see if he knew their whereabouts.

Once there I knocked on the door for a short bit but there was no answer; so, I stopped and began to walk away, when I saw a movement past the front window. Assuming that my knocks had not be heard or he had been in the bathroom, I turned and began to knock again. It took a while and a lot more knocking and Mitch finally cracked the door asking in a shaky voice, "What's up Greg?"

Even with the door half-closed I could see that he was in his robe and sweating profusely. I could clearly see that his eyes were wide open as if he's just seen a ghost, they were bloodshot, glazed over and his mouth was twitching. Although shocked by what I was seeing, I immediately knew what was going down behind that door.

Being caught off guard, in total amazement I asked, "Are U alright Mitch? Is something wrong?"

"No, no, Greg, I was asleep," he somehow got out barely opening his twitching mouth.

"Mitch, you're high as hell. Man, I can tell you're in there getting high. Can I come in? I asked, as I began lightly forcing the door open. Without a word he stepped and made room for me to enter. Once inside, my eyes immediately saw a vial, a glass pipe, screens, a small torch lighter, baking soda, a twelve-ounce bottle of ether, and lastly a baggie filled almost half-way with cocaine on his living coffee table! Yes, all of the ingredients needed for a serious free-base party, right there.

On one hand, I wanted to and was about to ask can I join him, but on the other, I knew I had to get my ass back to work in the studio. In shock from discovering Mitch's secret, I wasn't quite sure what the hell to do; when suddenly, he pulled another, smaller pipe from his pocket with a nice sized hit already on it, which he quickly extended his hand, giving it to me. Now it was too late! The decision had been made for me. I grabbed the pipe, took that first hit and it was on.

Without many words passing between us, which honestly, I would not even remember at gunpoint, he and I sat smoking until the batch he had already cooked up disappeared. Just as he was about to cook some more, there was a knock at the door. We both looked at each other and quickly tried to clear the table, so whomever was knocking would not catch us in the act as I had done with him. The knocking continued and got louder until Mitch cracked the door to find Jody standing there, looking for both of us.

High as hell, I hurried to my feet, told Mitch to find Bobby and join us in the studio as quickly as he could and started out of the door. Jody overhearing what I said to Mitch quickly said, "Bobby is already there, man. We were just waiting for U so we can come-up with a plan of action for who and how the room would be used over the next week. So, Mitch, you can just come to the studio when you get ready.

lthough seriously buzzed, I walked and talked with Jody all the way to the studio, as if I had spent that past hour simply talking with Mitch. I'm not sure anyone knew that I was high that day, but I sure did, and I also now knew that mitch was a bigger free-base-head than me, Bobby and Tommy put together. With our secrets out, Mitch would sell and supply me, Tommy and Bobby with cocaine now and then throughout the rest of our stay at Caribou.

After becoming totally familiar with the studio equipment, the next few days were long and we were getting the recording in, coming out with probable hits but definitely great music. Each band member brought ideas and songs which we had already written, to the table; but we also came up with and recorded a few new ideas right on the spot. As our basic tracks began to take shape, as discussed back in

L.A., we knew it was time to send for McGloiry, who had already agreed and was waiting for that call from us.

Once we put Mitch on the case, Michael's flight and cabin arrangements were made and he arrived some forty-eight hours later and began to add and take our music to another level. Due to the seclusion in this very special, gorgeous place and the pampering to nearly our every wish by the staff, our heads and music began to clearly get stronger and bring us closer as a group and as brothers.

Over the first week or so, we worked hard and had big fun exploring and enjoying the amenities of this vast recording resort. When we were not resting, in the studio working, or hanging together in the main cabin, we would take total advantage of the various amenities available to us. On the vast acres of Caribou Ranch was among other awesome sights, a gorgeous, huge private waterfall which spilled into this big lake filled with fish. It so happened that Reggie and Jody loved to fish so throughout our stay, they would frequently make time to relax and enjoy themselves there, when we were not in the studio.

Surprisingly, Bobby would join them there; and Eddie and I might play chess or go horseback riding. Phillip and Tommy would also find different things to do since this incredible place offered so much. Caribou Ranch was filled with wonder, amazement and good times for each of us. Although we were having big fun in the studio and hanging together like we used to when we first became a group, a couple of us began missing our loved ones and wanting to share this beautiful place and time with them. So, one evening over dinner, Tommy brought up the subject of wishing Duck was here.

One at a time each of us chimed in and that started a discussion, ending up with the quick decision that Mitch would check the possibilities of how and if we could have our then spouses join us. Although none of us openly questioned what the fuck he was doing, but with the exception of Tommy, all of us were completely shocked and thrown off when Bobby stated that he wanted his then boyfriend Clarence, to make the trip up there, as well as the girls.

Now Clarence aka Tony was someone who Bobby had brought around the studio a few times over this past year. We learned from Tommy that he was his new boyfriend. Tony was a handsome, baby-faced, slightly buffed, brown-skinned guy who stood about five feet seven or eight inches tall which was definitely shorter than Bobby. He was a soft-spoken guy who was usually casually dressed and totally non-typical of the characters Bobby usually dated or hung with. To me he looked about fourteen or fifteen, but I believed him to be in his late teens or early twenties. He was a well-mannered, soft spoken guy with little to say most of the time. He was somewhat shy but would open up once you got to know him and if you did not know, you would not assume him to be gay at all. I just knew he was much younger than Bobby, but I never asked his age. I remember joking with Bobby about robbing the cradle, telling him, "you could go to jail for statutory rape with this one."

Of all of Bobby's past lovers and gay associates known to me, with the exception of Jermaine Stewart, I liked Tony best, as he was not overtly gay, in fact one would not even know if they weren't told and more importantly, it appeared that he loved Bobby and was actually good to and for him. But bringing Tony up here initially threw all of us off at first, but all of us went with the flow and upon confirmation that our guests would be welcome, the planning only took one afternoon. With Mitch's help, individual cabins were assigned to those who were bringing girlfriends, flights were booked, and the music continued to be made while we waited for our folks to arrive.

A few days later, our girlfriends Mary, Darlene, Duck, Audrey and even Tony flew into Denver and were picked-up by ranch staff and brought to the property and to the main cabin. Now, because Jody and his wife Maureen were the only one of us who had kids at that time, she was unable to make this trip and was really missing out on an awesome week at this ranch.

While our folk's luggage was being sent to the appropriate guest cabins, in the main cabin's receiving room, the staff had prepared, spread out and served various Hors D'oeuvres and drinks for us and our guests. After an hour or so of fun and festivity, Mary and I, Phillip and Darlene, Tommy and Duck, Eddie and Audrey and even Bobby and Tony headed to our newly assigned cabins for the evening.

fter our guests had left this awesome, dream-like place, all of us appeared happier than any of us had been for some time and began to get close to each other again. Gradually trying to mend our relationship, besides hanging in the whole group, Bobby and I hung together at the ranch, breaking bread, playing games, recording songs, not writing together though, and we were getting along a little better than I expected, considering what we had been putting each other through. I even remember us actually having fun together, riding horses, beating up on Mitch when he was off in his cabin freebasing his ass to death.

One day after recording, Bobby, Eddie and I were hanging out on the porch of the main cabin which housed the main kitchen and dining room, the game room and a huge open social area surrounded by second floor balconies, where the group would congregate daily. From a short distance, we were approached by this guy and a young girl. He came up and introduced himself as Jerry and then his cute little blond haired, blue eyed 13-year-old daughter, Jan who had this big Kool-Aid smile on her face.

Jerry proceeded to ask, "Are you guys the group Switch?" he asked.

"Yes," We all said in unison.

"See dad, I told you!" Jan chimed in.

"I know them all," She cried excitedly.

"I didn't want to bother you guys, but she told me that it was you , so I wanted to be sure if she knew what she was saying."

"Yep Jerry, she's right," Bobby stated, as he extended his hand in friendship. Eddie and I too shook hands with Jerry and Jan.

"May I have your autographs?" Jan asked.

"Do you have something for us to write it on?" Eddie asked.

"Here. Write it on my hand. No, my shirt. No, my..." Jan said.

"I'm sure we can get something better in the office Jan," I added. "Something that will last a lot longer than on your hand."

We all laughed as I headed inside to ask one of the housing staff members for a sheet of paper or something. I quickly returned with paper and pen in hand for Jan's autographs.

"She is one of you guys biggest fans and she has your album on her bedroom wall,." Jerry said.

"Both of their albums are on my wall, daddy. They have two," she blurted out.

Jan knew who each of us were and of course squealed like only teenage girls can at the thought of being this close to us. She started singing "I Call Your Name" as we all signed her paper. In talking, Jerry explained that he was a vendor who brought supplies, i.e. food, beverages, alcohol and other needed items to the ranch twice a week by helicopter, which he owned. He and Jan had just made a delivery and were about to fly down to Denver to pick up and bring back some additional items, including my fifth of Chivas Regal Scotch.

"Jan and I have to fly down to Denver for some supplies we didn't bring. Would you guys like to take a short helicopter ride? We can be back in little more than an hour." The three of us looked at each other.

"Ever been in some helicopter fellas?" Eddie asked.

"Naw man." Bobby said adding, "But I am today."

They both looked at me. "No but I wouldn't miss this for the world," I said.

"Well where do we sign?" Eddie joked.

"Yeah Jerry. We're with you," I added. "Just let me get a jacket and a few bucks from my cabin." Yeah agreed Bobby and Eddie.

Jerry and Jan headed around the big cabin towards the helicopter while the three of us ran off to our cabins, picked up a few things and quickly made it to where the helicopter was parked. While strapping in, the three of us were clearly excited to take this adventure. I thought about how nice Jerry and Jan were and about my surprise in learning that this little white girl not only knew us on sight but was actually a fan of our music.

Jerry flew over the most awesome scenery I had ever experienced in my life into Denver airport. He picked up his van and drove to the store where he would do his shopping, which happened to be inside of the big shopping mall. Jerry told us that it would take him a short while to do his shopping and offered the option of our joining him or hanging in the mall. If we wanted, Jan could be our guide and escort us around the place. We all agreed, selected a time and place to meet back up and he went his way and we went ours.

Jan was too excited as had been the three of us. She told us, "My friends are gonna just die when they find out I was with you guys."

The four of us continued to walk through the mall until a group of girls, appearing slightly older than Jan spotted us and started screaming, while running up to us. As Bobby, Eddie and I began to talk with and sign autographs for these girls the crowd grew right there in the center of the mall. Young and old, male and female, black, white, Mexican and others popped up out of nowhere. Suddenly I realized that the three of us were surrounded and signing anything these folks could get their hands on.

I grabbed Jan's hand and had her stand between Eddie and me as the commotion increased. It just so happened that we had been stopped by the girls a few stores down from a major chain record store. After various people ran in to buy Switch albums for us to sign, the record store manager was told that we were in the mall. He came out, burst through the crowd and offered us shelter in his store and an isolated area if we wanted to continue signing autographs. It suddenly dawned on me that Switch had to be pretty big in Denver to receive this kind of reaction from Jan and at this mall.

Billboard Magazine (May 1979)

454

Soul Train

Being the humble people that we were, it really didn't occur to me then that Switch was this big all over the country and in other parts of the world. In all of the ruckus, we missed our deadline to meet Jerry. While looking for us he saw and followed the still growing crowd and found us in the record store. Needless to say, the record store manager had the now assembled mall security staff handling crowd control and finally whisking Jerry, Jan, Bobby, Eddie and me out of a side door to the van so that we could make our getaway.

Back in the helicopter, we were silently all smiles the entire twenty-five or so minutes it took to reach the ranch and exit the aircraft. Back on the ground we laughed with Jan and Jerry while Caribou kitchen staffers unloaded the supplies from the helicopter. This wound up being the trip of a lifetime. Eddie, Bobby and I then said our goodbyes and went into the main cabin to see who was around as we could not wait to share with the others the details of our outing.

That day wound up being good, as comradery was the vibe of the day. Even for Bobby. During most of this outing his relationship with our side musicians, engineer Reggie Dozier and the Caribou staff was less than desirable; but from time to time I could see, he would try to shake that negative spirit. And during those times he was cool, but indiscriminately he would insult folks, curse people out, make sarcastic remarks about the studio, the ranch and its staff and the length of time that all of us had agreed to be and work there.

Sometimes he would refuse to play on songs he didn't like and acted like a real ass. When out of hearing range he would complain to no end about most things including Jody's song attempts. He looked at me and yelled in frustration, "I don't know why Motown lets him waste money in the studio on shit like that. You know that's our fucking money he's in there wasting, don't you? Greg, I can't keep singing on that shit and I won't keep my mouth shut much longer either."

Once in his zone, if Bobby wasn't complaining about Mitch, Jermaine and Hazel's assistant manager, being locked in his cabin trying to smoke up all of the cocaine in Peru, which by the way Bobby, Tommy and I were also guilty of doing, he was complaining about not having transportation to get away from the ranch when he wanted to, or the fact that the main kitchen closed at a certain hour every night, even though there was access to snacks and beverages of our choosing available twenty four seven.

Yes, he would argue, complain, cuss and fuss at everything and everyone at random. And from these random outbreaks no one was exempt as the anguish he caused escalated daily till everyone complained, including Tommy, me and a few of the Caribou staff. No one else could take any more and we were happy this trip would soon come to a close.

In our last week there, Motown sent Shelley Berger, Suzanne de Passe, Coston, Tony Jones, Nancy Leiviska and an entire film production team to Caribou Ranch to shoot a documentary of our outing. I recall there was a stylist who brought loads of clothing for each of us to try and ultimately select a couple of outfits for us to wear in the shoot. Although that day was filled with serious work it was probably the most fun day we had as a group throughout our entire time there.

We stayed at the ranch approximately one month. When our reserved time ran out, we left Caribou to complete and wrap up what we'd started there. Back in L.A., finishing the album wasn't easy. In addition, all efforts to have a photo of the band on the cover of the album failed because besides Bobby not showing up for three scheduled shoot dates, when he finally did make the fourth planned shoot, he kept trying to get in front of everyone in every photo. He refused to cooperate and even cursed out the photographer, so, eventually Mr. Gordy, on Jermaine and Hazel's advice, called it off and the album was released without a picture of the band and went nowhere.

Among other various things, it was obvious to me, Mr. Gordy had thrown in the towel on the band and didn't put the Motown machine behind it. Another indication, Motown, along with Jermaine and Hazel, had given up on Switch was a call I made to Hazel and Jermaine, one night. Rosanna the housekeeper answered the phone; "Hello, this is Greg Williams and I'd like to speak to either Jermaine or Hazel."

She asked me to please hold, then she put down the phone and I must have waited for five minutes. I heard her footsteps returning to the phone.

"Ms. Hazel told me to ask you what you want?"

Stunned at hearing this and instinctively knowing the question meant more than it asked, I struggled to respond. "I, I thought I was calling to speak with a friend, but I see I'm sadly mistaken. I don't want anything. Thank you."

I hung up the phone and sat in my living room, reeling from the shock and callousness of Hazel's directed response.

What could I have done to deserve that? Was it me or all of Switch? I asked myself. I did not understand how a supposed friend could just shut me out with such nastiness. While sitting there dumfounded and dazed, it came back to me that all communication with Jermaine, Hazel and Motown had abruptly come to a halt three years ago, when during contract negotiations, I refused to give up ownership of the group name. I thought a lot of love had grown and a bond had grown between us; but I found out, I was sadly mistaken. I sat reviewing my life, my career, my relationships with Jermaine, Hazel and Motown knowing for the later, the end was near.

Chapter 14

Beginning of The End

SWITCH

Switch Promo Pic #4

Early on, Jermaine, Hazel and Switch had been very close, always communicating and they were available or quick to get back when I called because they knew that I kept my calling infrequent and limited to pertinent issues versus

459

random, frivolous phone calling. In turn I quickly responded when they called or left a message for me, no matter the time, but that was then and suddenly no more. The communication between us had abruptly and without warning, shut down.

Various things in my life had also changed drastically over these past few short years. I remember getting antsy about things and I moved in and out of five apartments in a three-year timeframe. Although I kept my personal and business fronts up, still responsible enough to book and get to the studios on time, keeping my work ethic together, maintaining relationships with the few women I allowed in my life, always well-groomed and not exposing my drug-induced shortcomings, I had a growing addiction and I knew it, even if it was not on display to the rest of the world.

I was also feeling the lethargy of Bobby's constant psychotic behavior, Motown's games, Jermaine and Hazel's abandonment while still accepting payment and my stress over having a good band who, due to Motown's self-serving plans was still unable to tour or play live. I felt this life was strangling me. Once my abuse of drugs became obvious to me and at the very least my band mates, I would tell myself and them I was going to leave the drug alone. I could and did stop for days, even weeks at a time; but surely returned to the scene of the crime before long, which was easy to do when at almost every turn a pipe awaits.

Other than Switch and my music, during this time, the world I lived in was mostly comprised of people who partied and smoked. I had only a few non-industry friends to hang out with when not working, but most of my folks were industry insiders who liked to party. If not with one of my girls, my family, Switch or Rick James, there was a limited few which I would hang with.

I'd sometimes go to Paramount Recording Studio on Santa Monica and hang with my friend Johnny "Guitar" Watson. Most times, his mother would have cooked and brought these huge dinners, including Collard Greens with big old Ham Hocks, Fried Chicken, Mac and Cheese, Candied Yams, Potato Salad, Fried Okra, Sweet Potato Pie and other things her baby Johnny loved. There was always enough food to feed a basketball team.

John would say, "Greg, you know mama cooked for all of us."

"But John, who knew I was coming today?" I asked

"Shit nigga. I knew you was coming'. What else was you gone do. Either go to your studio or mine. Now eat muthafucka, befo I tell mama you don't like her food."

We both burst out in laughter as he'd shake his head until that gangster hat would almost fall off and his gold teeth would catch an overhead light and light up the room like a spotlight. I and whoever else was there would fix a plate, eat and we'd all talk shit while hearing the tracks John was laying. Later we would slip into the vocal booth, lock the door and light up the pipe. Often it was on at his house in the San Fernando Valley, where he lived with his woman Sasha. At the parties, which he threw frequently would be a dozen or more famous and non-famous folk who would just hang out, eating, drinking, talking, smoking weed.

Since he had a home studio filled with musical equipment, sometimes we'd have a jam session. After a while, John would call out a few of us and we would go into his special room, (a converted bathroom) just for smoking; which he called Base Station One. The invitees would sit around, fire up, pass the pipe and joke "Beam me up Scotty" a line from Star Trek. We'd take a hit and fly for a while; then rejoin the rest of the folks.

Although this was a typical party scene among various celebrities at this time, I somehow remained selective as to where and with whom I would expose my freebase use. With Hollywood entertainers forever being accused of all sorts of truth and madness, I maintained enough restraint to keep my getting high down to assumption and minor rumor versus eyewitness fact. And I also knew that other than minimal gossip and unjust speculation of Switch as a whole, my problem with cocaine was mine to assess and scrutinize, because at that time it bore no outward signs.

After those early weeks of spending money with Roscoe, just under one thousand dollars, I found out that my girlfriend's neighbor Challie' sold cocaine. I learned that he too knew how to cook up freebase; so right after he and I met, I proposed that if I spend my money with him, he would teach me how to do it. His method was different than Roscoe's. From that point, I was doing it for myself and sometimes for others.

As time went on I began to smoke nearly every day. I still managed to maintain priority, such as always handling my commitments and responsibilities for and with Switch and to myself, i.e. meetings, sessions, rehearsals, etc. I was always prompt in paying bills and maintaining my home. Personal grooming remained a first and foremost daily responsibility, and even making time for intimate, personal relationships with my girlfriend and other women close to me. *But still I made time to get high.*

I identified and accepted the fact that addiction was really upon me, when I found that I'd smoke before I went to and infrequently at parties. I'd smoke around a few select folk and at their homes but more so, I'd smoke by myself at my home. I got it down to a point that I would hit the pipe before leaving home for the studio, for rehearsal and lastly, I brought freebase with me and would hit it on break.

In the initial stages of my use, my then girlfriend and I would infrequently hit the pipe together but after a few times we backed away trying in effort to maintain our restraint from any kind of abuse or addiction. From what I know, this worked for Kathy but not too well for me. I had money and access, so I continued with sporadic use for a time longer. Strangely enough, smoking together was short-lived with Mary and me too, as I began to realize that whether I hit that pipe or not, I really didn't want my woman to do that.

Throughout my life I never cared for women who were too loose. Women who hung out too much, those who drank, smoked, cursed, flirted and partied too much I really didn't have much energy for, as I was not raised around, nor could I respect that kind of women. And here I am now in a world of sex, drugs and R&B music.

I later came to know that my views and expectations of women were misguided and too high for most of the women I allowed in life. I often tried to maintain some kind of short-term relationship; but from Valerie to now, no one got to hang out too long. Not my conscious intent but my undeniable reality; because in reality, music was my lady.

In my freebase days, after Kathy and Mary, if there was a woman I was seeing I wouldn't accept her or let her smoke because I wanted someone straight in my life, not someone with a vice like I'd developed, someone who could straight-talk and help me if I went too far. Freebase as with most Cocaine based drugs is an instant aphrodisiac to most folk. I recall more than one time I let a female friend do coke in my presence and their hands were all over me.

One in particular helped me break the cycle of getting high around women. I eased her off me. "Wait, I'm high now and I need to come down."

"Greg, you have to do something because my stuff is on fire."

I relented and I decided I'd stick with my decision not to smoke with a woman because for me, smoking and making love didn't mix. The desire is there, and most men stay ready for whatever comes while many other men's equipment, such as mine, doesn't work while using cocaine or freebase.

I had become a base-head. Yes, I was frequently chasin' Jason as some folk said of freebase addicts during that time. But somehow, as throughout my life, my conscience, my humility, my pride, my self-worth would not allow me to completely lose myself to that cigarette, that drug, that woman, that money, this music business, or anything else but the radio that constantly played in my head.

By now, I'm moving away from getting high outside of my home and only with a select few folks as, with each hit I grew more and more paranoid. In this state, I would think that someone was watching me get high. I would become intensely self-conscious about what I was doing, knowing it was wrong and so out of character for me and due to its present hold on me, a total threat to my health, my dreams, my life; but unable to stop myself from seeking hit after hit from the pipe.

I noticed the effect freebase was having on Bobby and Tommy. Through my observation of Bobby, it was clear that the combination of the small amount of fame and the drugs, unleashed the side of him I dreaded, but knew would be coming. And poor Tommy just became increasingly lost to the pipe and whatever drug he could get his hands on and though my drug use was not so overt, it was time for me to take a long, hard look at Greg also.

Now, in the mid to later stages of my drug abuse, I dated Venita, a fine Sista who worked in the sales department at Motown. Without providing information about the inner workings of Motown as it pertained to Switch and my career as an artist there, she would enlighten me and keep me abreast of what was going on around and about me the person. She was the only person to speak to me frankly about everything. I came to know and trust her with what, in my mind, had now become my secret. I exposed her to the methods and frequency of my getting high, from preparation to end result. After a year or more of use, I would take a hit and immediately sink deep into cocaine paranoia. First hit and I'd go to the window to look out, thinking someone was watching me or coming.

"Greg, sit down baby, there's no one out there." I sat down, still feeling jittery from the cocaine rush.

"Greg, you do this all of the time now. I need to talk to you. My little cousin overheard some other people were saying you've become a base-head and he asked me was it true. That's not something you want people saying about you Greg because information like that can ruin your life. You have too much going for you to throw it away behind some drugs, Greg. You need to stop smoking."

That others could see I had a problem took my sense of worth beneath the floor and tears hung on the edge of my eyes. I thanked Venita, knowing she spoke from love, but my continuance as a base-head created a growing distance between us, until she was no longer there.

Being alone, and coming down from yet another high, reality pressed itself into my face. I had always said my goal was to become a producer, writer, musician, and I had done just that; but my work was limited to Switch, Motown, and instead of using my relationships and contacts to broaden my world, I spent my free time getting high. The band suffered from incubation, not being able to travel and the drug world had forced Phillip and Eddie, the most stable members of Switch, to become somewhat distant after studio hours.

Phillip and I had been the closest from day one, sharing music and business ideas, personal thoughts and information. When we lived in the Montague house, we got up early, ate breakfast, discussed everything daily and even hung out a lot when the band wasn't practicing, meeting with Motown folk, or when we weren't hanging with our then girlfriends. Now, more than a year or so later we moved together, in yet another house and I could see, he noticed; though I never missed a rehearsal, nor a meeting, I wasn't as sharp as usual, and we'd stopped having long conversations like we used to.

Yes, all six of us were moving on, well into our new lives, while various tensions were rearing their ugly heads because of the many demands that stardom, Motown, friends and family intentionally and non-intentionally put upon us. Additional tension existed within the group after Jody had gone behind Phillip's back and hooked up with Phillip's girlfriend.

Although each of us had dealt close relationships with more than one woman, certain women were known to each member of the band as special or girlfriends and we had an unspoken understanding in this band as with most bands. There were groupies who were for anyone who wanted to partake of them freely. However, spoken or unspoken girlfriends, or even relationships which appeared serious were off limits and were to be respected at all times.

This particular lady and her young children had captured Phillip's heart, but that made no difference to Jody because what he saw and what he wanted he went for. Well Jody's actions did more damage than that of the girl because it broke a trust that could never be repaired. We were all angry about this and thought it was scandalous as we could see how much it hurt Phillip. Although I could not defend his actions when various friends would express disgust and/or call him a snake, I did what I could to stop that kind of talk in my presence.

From the night Jermaine and Hazel clarified that Switch had one leader and that was me, I felt that Jody harbored resentment against me and became angry with everyone else, but in my mind, we were still brothers. We by definition were still a group, so I was obligated to protect Switch as a whole.

I too thought the situation with the girl was an act of defiance against his ill-perceived feelings that band members had turned their backs on him. I also came to feel later that Jody was displeased about either being replaced on drums during the recordings by Bobby, which was done due to his problem in keeping the tempo steady.

Jody was a good drummer and a fantastic showman. However, no matter how close Tommy stuck to him and tried to ground his time, attempting to keep it steady, he'd often speed up or slow down and this was really noticeable on records.

Live, we could adjust, and Tommy would be holding him down as best he could. But when recording, time is money and as a producer you have no choice but hire the best musicians for the sound that you're hearing, which Bobby did.

I always wanted to get the work done as fast as possible, be under budget and get the best quality I could, and Switch members provided the sound I wanted and needed because Switch was the sound I was hearing. His actions brought him bad outcomes, and I could see Jody brooding even though he kept his feelings inside. It was clear to me that he actually resented my being the leader. His emotions, especially for me, were shown when he'd sometimes stand with Bobby against my direction when it was clear to all that I was right and acting in the best interest of the band. But I would shrug them both of and continue my task when I knew I was right.

These among many other thoughts were in heavy rotation in my head, along with my concerns about Bobby and Tommy who had become more bizarre with drugs, tearing up their cars and apartments, having frequent run-ins with the law for one reason or another, and other self-destructive behavior. Poor Tommy was frequently getting pulled over for one traffic violation or another and saying to the officer trying to give him a warning and in some cases a ticket for some infraction, "Don't you know who I am?" as if that was going to get him a pass.

And the policeman responding, "Yes, you're the guy I'm taking to jail." And off to jail he went.

Of course, I'd get the call and Upshaw was usually my go-to person to go and get Tommy and Bobby out of some of the messes they would find themselves in. With all of this going on, the other band members were growing restless and tired of the DeBarge bullshit and I was still holding on to fragments of what once was Switch while we stood on the verge of imploding.

It was like we were caught in a vacuum that was about to blow. Switch, on paper and on record was a successful band, but no one had heard us live and we hadn't gigged since playing with our former bands almost five years earlier, so in my mind we were long overdue to hit the road if we ever were again; but life moved on and each of us put forth all efforts to keep up and stay sane in the midst of our ever-changing world.

By now, family and friend migrations to California were well under way after the six of us had planted our individual and collective flags. The DeBarge siblings, as well as my brother Art had been back in L.A. for more than a year and my aunt Ruby packed up her twelve-year-old daughter and their life, and my brother Skip drove their belongings out here from Grand Rapids. Phillip's brother David had also move here.

Having family, new and old, so close brought both good and bad dynamics into play with Switch overall. Since coming to California, there had been various frequent dates; but of the girlfriends who meant more were Kathy, Mary, Venita and now Terri, and I remained happy that I and each of them were somehow able to avoid major negative fallout and walk away as friends. And that stands till this day.

Another year had come and quickly gone, and it was Nineteen Eighty, time to start on our fourth album for Motown, which would come to be titled *This is My Dream*.

While Bobby and I remained estranged, Motown and the Temptations were not, in fact there was much excitement we were told that all living members had reunited and were coming back to Motown and would kick off their return with a reunion album. Folks who know anything about my musical history can easily imagine my thrill at the possibility of meeting the main group whom I admired and emulated so well that my group, the Patterns won talent shows copying them.

Now, besides the work that Bobby, Jody and I put in for this forthcoming album, as we began pulling together song possibilities, to our surprise and honor, even Berry Gordy worked with a team of songwriters and came up with a song he thought might work for Switch called "Power". I immediately liked this song as it was reminiscent of the political songs of Marvin Gaye and Norman Whitfield in the early Nineteen Seventies. This song was written with three vocalists in mind which meant, like the song "Fever" on our first album and "Next to You" and "Fallin'" on our second album, Bobby, Phillip and I would share the lead vocals.

Instead of calling us to play this song over the phone per usual, he held on to it and in the midst of a production meeting at his home, the song was introduced, and the demo was played along with cassettes of our own few album ideas. Now, whether we thought the song was good, which I immediately did, or because it was written and presented to us by the chairman himself, Jody, I and the others showed an instant like to the song, but Bobby was clearly and blatantly disinterested, which came off offensively to all of us.

After all of the possible songs played, the group members were given cassettes of Power to learn and record at a later date. With much more to discuss about this forthcoming album, the conversation moved on to other things as we continued to enjoy time at Mr. Gordy's Beverly Hills estate. In the limo ride to our cars that evening, other than a mention of a few events of the day by Tommy, which cracked all of us up, Bobby's blatant lack of enthusiasm or energy to the song was not even brought up, then, but would be discussed the next day by individual group members.

In subsequent project discussions with Mr. Gordy, Hazel or Jermaine it never came up again, as I'm sure Mr. Gordy was again offended and felt put off by Bobby shutting down and showing no love for the song or its creator. Over the next month or so the recording process was fast, furious and in full effect with Bobby in one studio, using studio musicians for his tracks and his recently arrived brothers and sister on vocals, while Phillip and I worked closely in another; as Jody had stepped down as a producer by this time, due to song disputes with Lee Young Sr., who was now head of Motown's A&R department.

As the album continued on towards completion, although there were no more productions meetings, progress reports went back and forth between the album's current producers, including Jermaine, Hazel and Mr. Gordy. In one of many chats and inquiries, I remember asking Mr. Gordy when we were going to rehearse the song and go into the studio to record "Power" but each time, the answer was later. I knew that wasn't the truth and I knew why.

Berry Gordy was again allowed to feel Bobby's blatant disregard and disrespect, as with the time Bobby abruptly told him that he would not even consider changing the lyrics to "Power to Dance". It was the same disregard that I Jermaine, Hazel, all of Switch and various others had endured many times over past years.

One evening, in the midst of continuing on recording and producing songs for the album, I get a call from Mr. Gordy. It was once again a personal call, which of course led to us updating each other on what was being done for our project. As the updates were made and the conversation began to wear down I brought up "Power" and asked what was happening with the song, when Mr. Gordy said,

"Greg, you do know that the Temptations are back home with us?"

"Yes, I know, Carol Casano Ware asked me about writing and possibly producing songs for their forthcoming project." I was rethinking about "Power". Although we wrote this song for you guys, I think it might be a better song for the

Temps reunion album. Actually, it fits them like a glove. What are your thoughts on that?" he asked.

"I totally agree, Mr. Gordy, I'm honored that you would even bother to ask me."

"Of course, I would. Let's see what happens," he said.

"I'm sure it'll be a smash with the Temptations," I said, as we concluded our chat and hung up. As I played our conversation back in my head, I was appreciative of his call and was glad to see this song go where I knew it would be sung, produced and promoted properly. And considering that this came directly from the chairman's mouth to my ears after the way the song was ultimately treated by Bobby, I was happy for this outcome. It was now clear that he got and saw my initial effort at establishing a vocal style for Switch, using multiple male vocalists including first tenor, alto and baritone/bass leads over moving harmonies... actually, with the Temptations in mind.

Although the record was getting done, the production on "This is My Dream" was plagued by Bobby's and my diminished, if not totally non-existent communication with each other. This literally tore Switch in half with Bobby on one side, me on the other with Phillip, Tommy, Jody and Eddie caught in the middle. I opted to record in one studio, while Bobby insisted on working in another because we really needed to be away from each other if any resemblance of our friendship was to survive; and quite frankly, Bobby was so consumed by his own torment and self-destruction, it was clear he could care less what happened to me, Tommy or anyone else including himself.

It was rapidly becoming clear to all outside of the group that Bobby's mental anguish, resulting from years of abuse and distrust was now fully blown, causing him to consistently act erratically and insult me, other band members, Jermaine, Hazel, Berry Gordy and anyone else who was in sight of his neurosis déjour. By now, he was constantly spreading his negative thoughts and energy, poisoning the group's efforts to work together and enjoy where life had brought us.

Although outwardly angry, I was more so saddened, due to his growing psychosis. Saddened that I could no longer be the big brother that he once entrusted with much of his life, yet angry that I could no longer stand by, even if he'd let me, to calm his rough seas like I did when we were younger. I could no longer reach him or tolerate his intolerance.

Between Bobby's issues, Jermaine and Hazel's random availability, all the business and personal roles and responsibilities that were either dumped on me or I had voluntarily assumed on behalf of Switch and Switch members, and my escalating drug use, outwardly I was in control; but mentally and emotionally, I was approaching a serious overload, of which only I identified and endured alone because even in a crowd I was alone.

Although I've always had a woman somewhere in my life, I had become so consumed with the responsibility of trying to take care of my band and get us to the next level, I forgot how to let go and allow one woman in close enough to really love and help me take care of me. I was surrounded by women vying for my love, my attention or even just a few minutes of my time; but the wall I had put up when I was sixteen after suffering the heartbreak of losing Tracie was too high and too wide for any one of them to get around thus far, except for Kathy. For her that wall had come down though, invisible to me, it had gone back up once she too hurt me.

I could love and make love with these women, buy them cards, flowers and gifts. I could take them to movies, on trips, the theatre, parties and other social events. I could have them join me at the studios, play the piano and write songs for and with them and even cook all kinds of dinners for them, which I really loved to do, but I could not tear down the wall that kept each of these women from being my partner, my wife, the mother of my children, which the latter I so badly wanted but would only have and accept under the right circumstances.

I had a plan for my life and as long as I was in control I would live and die by that plan. I wish I knew then what I know now, the fact that life happens while you're busy making plans. So, over these years much of my life was spent like a small ship at sea, with no port should storms arise; and ultimately, they did arise.

And if my world was not crazy enough, who should try to slip back into our lives through the back door but Bernd. He had somehow maintained the rights to the White Heat masters he was given to end our joke of a business relationship. After releasing the songs on an album and an act called Hot Ice on Polygram Europe through a deal he made with the Pall Mall cigarette company he had somehow gotten them back.

Hot Ice/Smash Covers

Now Bernd resurfaced with a possible deal with Logan Westbrook and Source Records and he needed musicians to make up the band on the record, so he recruited DeBarge family members. In no time, El, Marty, Randy DeBarge and their cousins Andre Abney and Stanley Hood had moved to Cerritos, a suburb of L.A. from Grand Rapids to become Bernd's group Smash and promote the album to be released on Source Records. While they waited for work and money from the deal, instead of using Switch members Bobby had his younger siblings in the studio doing harmony and backup vocals.

On the other hand, I too was in the studio, recording and producing my songs totally separated from Bobby's sessions through which the other Switch members could work and make additional money. I did not want or like this level of separation of my band, but at the very least my sessions were prompt, productive, fun and free of negative energy, that negative energy which now Bobby seemed to interject far too frequently into everything Switch tried to do.

As his drug use began to dominate his life, his phobias, psychosis and self-destructive behavior had taken greater control, and this made life harder to and for him and unbearable for Switch. With all of the problems that were continuing to surface in and for Switch, more so due to Bobby's extensive drug abuse, ego, paranoia and negative outbursts, life had become very tense for me, as I was always trying to think and act in the best interest of the band.

Switch "Reaching For Tomorrow" Cover

Now with Motown's denial of Bobby's request to go solo and my repeated request to allow him out of his commitment to Switch, our ship was quickly beginning to sink. As Switch moved forward into making the third album, I had been wearing Mr. Gordy's, Jermaine and Hazel's ears off about the problems Bobby was having and causing;, in turn I was told that Bobby was saying the same with reference to me and Switch. They had often asked me what was wrong with Bobby, why he was so difficult, angry and aggressively determined to destroy himself.

While having some answers to their concerns, I gave as much of an honest response as I could, leaving them to face the monster they had a big role in creating. I also knew, due to Bobby's life-long psychosis, that monster would have reared its ugly head no matter what or who! Plus, in spite of all of the damage Bobby had caused and left for me to deal with, I was somehow still caught in my life-long, futile effort to be loyal and protect him.

I also know they had tired of me questioning everything they did because, though I cared about them as people, I'd stopped trusting them professionally long before this; because it had become crystal clear when I learned of their underhanded attempt to remove Bobby and Tommy from the band that they didn't have my or Switch's best interest at heart.

Because my management and record company were one and the same, I was at a loss as to how and when to properly end the management relationship as I knew I should. All of this troubled me immensely. I didn't know that Jermaine and Hazel would ultimately end the relationship before I had a chance to, simply by disappearing or better yet, by making themselves totally inaccessible to Switch without warning. They just stopped working with us all together.

As I look back, the fucked-up thing about it was, they never said we quit! They never called a meeting to tell us they were done or how they had come to feel about being our managers. They never officially told us collectively or individually that they did not want to work with is anymore. They just stopped all communication, except to have Lee Young Jr. contact us to sign off on an agreement which allowed Motown to pay them a lump sum of money as management commissions for something I called an exit fee. They just left us out there to figure it out. And with all of the shit Bobby was putting us through, I really didn't care what they did since they weren't there to help solve the problem which they helped cause.

Next thing I know, Shelly Berger gives me a call saying he is our new manager, which clearly sent the message Switch had been used up and dumped. I knew they had gotten tired, as I too had, of all the negative bullshit attached to Switch or better yet brought on by Bobby's uncaring, self-destructive antics but imposed on Switch, but to just walk away without saying anything to any of us was really saying to all of us, "Fuck you!"

Well without them Switch moved on and "Love Over and Over Again" was released as our first single from the *This is My Dream* album. It rose to number 8 on the R&B charts, but even this song wouldn't cross over to top forty of the Pop charts. All the same, it was another hit for Switch, giving us enough ammunition to win any argument about our finally going out on tour. I was finally free to engage a booking agent who arranged for us to go on our very first tour, headlined by the Bar Kays and Cameo.

Chapter 15

Let's Tour (finally)

Switch "Dream" Cover

After years of being put on hold by the Motown machine we were finally going on tour with Switch was to play in 30 cities, starting in Lake Charles, Louisiana. True to form and anticipated, Bobby, even during the planning stage, became the first problem out of the gate. Of all the things that could have been an issue, I was totally blindsided when he insisted we have to take his young boyfriend on the road with us.

"What are you saying?" I asked Bobby in a surprised voice upon hearing his demand.

"Grag, we've got to take Clarence with us."

"And do what with him Bobby? None of us are taking our girlfriends."

"Well that's on y'all but I really need him to be with me. Man, all the time I'm away from him I'll be worried about how he's doing and what he's doing," he said omitting the words "and with whom…"

"Bobby! This is really going too far, man," I insisted.

"Man, you talking about us being all over the country for weeks at a time, and I can't just leave him at home," he pleaded.

"Bobby, the rest of the guys are leaving their women behind and we won't be gone that long."

"I keep telling you, fuck them! What they do don't matter to me. I just know that if I'm going out on the road, I've got to have him with me."

"Man, if we could make this work, what is everyone else supposed to think or do?"

"I don't know, and I don't care Grag, but if he can't go, I'm not going!"

"Do you hear yourself nigga?" I yelled.

I shouldn't have been shocked at what this muthafucka just said, but I was. I struggled to find the words to say after that. I remember telling him that I'd see what could be done to make that happen saying, "Maybe we could give Tony a job doing something."

Bobby excitedly input, "He works hard, and you can trust him, Grag."

"Let me take this to the band, Bobby."

"Yeah you do that, but I'm serious."

I knew Bobby had fallen in love and was insecure about Tony's fidelity. He had also become so co-dependent that he really could not leave him behind. Bobby and I talked a little longer and I revisited the logic, but he didn't budge. In my knowing that if I couldn't make this work out, all of my hard work would end up in vain, I had to take this ultimatum back to the others. With the exception of Tommy, like me, the others were shocked, pissed and frustrated.

After discussing it thoroughly and accepting the fact that this was the only way to finally get Switch on the road, everyone reluctantly decided that we'd hire Tony to be our valet. I say reluctantly because no one had a problem with Tony, but all of us had a problem with Bobby holding another gun to our heads; but to move things forward we decided to put Tony in charge of having our stage costumes ready and waiting for us before each show; then cleaned, stored and ready for our next use. He would handle our small personal instruments and be in charge of making sure security was protecting our dressing room while we were on stage.

Once the decision was made and his role and responsibilities were defined, the whole group moved forward, planning other aspects of the upcoming tour, i.e. road manager, roadies, side musicians and stage setup. We decided on our stage costumes, our set list or song line up, which songs and who would play which instrument on what song, and even which songs would be choreographed. Putting our live performance together was really a major undertaking; but like most things we did together, we made it a fun process as we were just happy to finally get to take our show on the road.

While Switch had been busy working on the fourth album "This is My Dream", unknown to me, Bobby had also picked up another drug of choice. For years, Bobby and Tommy frequented and bought their drugs on the corner of Crenshaw and Adams Boulevard, which was a well-known drug area of Los Angeles. This is where they could buy pills, free base and other common drugs. Once signed to Motown, the other DeBarge siblings with the exception of El, followed suit where all of them also became well-known in and around this area and not just for the music they made.

But now Bobby had become strung out on cough syrup and he used it to supplement his Doors & Fours and free base addictions. He drank cough syrups named Citra Forte and Tussionnex, combined with a barbiturate, Doors and Fours. For the cough syrup Bobby found a doctor in L.A. who supplied him with the morphine-based syrup on a weekly basis. This new addiction created additional problems for Switch when we began getting ready to go on tour because by now he was seriously strung out and could not function without it.

Although he was and had been on his full-blown diva trip for some time now, he did show up for most of our rehearsals. He was always intentionally late, but in my anticipation of that I always told him rehearsal was to be an hour earlier than it actually was; and still the rest of us had time to work incorporating steps, skits and other antics into our show and with the horn section before he arrived and disrupted our peace, until Jody and I skillfully brought him back into the fold.

As I had learned throughout my previous years in entertainment, if we were finally able to take Switch on the road, there was much work to be done. So, we did a lot of working, planning and working some more until we had what we thought to be a tight stage show. Then we auditioned and hired side musicians to recreate our full sound with the exception of string players.

With eleven men onstage, our sound, look and overall performance would be full and complete. With no help or interference from Motown, we sought out and hired costume designers for our needed stage attire. After hiring Bobby's lover Tony as our valet and personal assistant, we also hired barber Pat Edmondson who, before moving to L.A. from Grand Rapids, used to do my hair from time to time when I would go home.

Pat took care of all of Switch's hair on the road. Pat now lived here in L.A. and often hung out with all of us Grand Rapids folk so I knew he would fit the needed bill. Some time back we had met and befriended Steve Altman who had been a roadie for the Jackson 5. Since Switch had never gone on the road as a group we considered having Steve go out with us; but at that time, he was owner and operator of a stage production company, working with big rock act, the Bay City Rollers, so his plate was too full; but he did advise and oversee the initial production.

At his referral and recommendation, we hired Andy Truman as our road manager, which proved to be our first and biggest error in judgment. We did not know the disaster hiring Andy would bring. Although Andy wanted to hire his own people from the start, Bobby, Jody and I were determined to remain loyal and keep our word to our guys from the White Heat days. Some time back we promised we would hire them, once Switch hit the road, so we contacted Tommy Upshaw as production assistant and David Dee and Pie as our stage crew.

The side musicians we hired were young talented L.A. professionals consisting of Gerald Albright on tenor sax, Michael Patches Stewart on trumpet, Bernard Baisden on trombone, and Danny Cortez on Trumpet. With Michael McGloiry already on the road with Cheryl Lynn, Phillip suggested and brought his college friend, guitarist Attala Zane Giles, to the table and he was so good we looked no further, Zane was our man. As we worked closer with him, his talents were so strong we later made him a group member along with Terrence Gains, as Bobby's exit was eminent.

Switch, of course, covered the rhythm section and all vocals. With all players in place now we whipped our show into shape until the day came to take this on the road. With this being Switch's first time on the road and Bobby's, Jody's and my first time out as stars, we were green and were destined to make many mistakes.

From the onset, our biggest mistake was in hiring Andy to be our road manager, but that mistake took time to surface because we did not know the right, the wrong or the indifferent about touring on this level. Bobby, Tommy and I were busy getting high while the other Switch members were mostly having fun. It's a definite that one can't do what one doesn't know how to do and in this particular case, we did not know how to cover our asses at all, so what could go wrong did go wrong. All the while Andy was taking total advantage of our ignorance.

Out of the gate, he had us traveling from city to city in Ford and Chevy rental cars instead of sleeper buses like most of the other bands; then we switched to vans and later included private airplanes. None of which were feasible or practical. This guy would run up major bills for the cars, major hotels and expensive restaurants, which began our problems. To add to the mayhem, for our first gig in Lake Charles Louisiana, our equipment didn't arrive, and we had to use the Bar Kay's stuff.

We stayed on stage beyond our scheduled twenty-minute show and the promo turned on the house lights and rushed us off of the stage without letting us finish the song we were playing. The next gig, in San Antonio, we played too long again, and they turned the lights on again. Although the Bar-Kays were sympathetic to our rough start, Cameo's members had these smirks on their faces when they saw us at breakfast the next morning; and later one or two even burst out laughing, as we headed for the stage later that night.

Our next gig in Dallas, we had equipment problems again and they turned the lights on us. After three nights of mishaps, being unprepared and downright amateurish at road protocol, we had become the joke of the tour. We tried to get things tighter and make our next night work; but the loss of our equipment, even though we cut out a song, our show was still too long, and it happened all over again in Houston Texas. So, I called a meeting of the band, our side men, our road manager and our roadies in my room after returning to the hotel that night, to discuss what the hell had gone wrong each of the prior nights.

We were all embarrassed and concerned by the outcome of each date, as we knew we were much better than we had come across to the fans, the other acts and the promoters. We determined that we would have to revamp our show as well as our entire team's way of doing things, if we were going to show these folks what and who Switch really was. We all agreed that we would find a rehearsal studio somewhere between Houston and our next date in Charleston to revamp our entire production.

With our first three days off coming up, we booked and went to SIR studios, in Nashville Tennessee, where all of our collective stage experience and fresh bruises was pooled to help us get our on-and-off-stage shit together. Once our collective years of live performance experience kicked in, we knew exactly what to do to get our show working. We had to make sure that our audience, other bands, the concert promoters and all else who would be fortunate to experience our live performance know that Switch was no joke. We came to play and were here to stay!

Over that three-day period, we rehearsed, restructured and slimmed down the show, limited the solos and even added a few dance steps for the entire eleven men on stage to participate in. We put in three eight to ten-hour days of rehearsal and restructure time; and once we knew we were ready to do the damn thing, we headed for Charleston, West

Virginia for our next performance. This time we clearly had something to prove. We hit the stage with a vengeance, with our vocals and showmanship in high gear and by the third song and the audience was ecstatic.

Just as we began singing "Girl I'll Send U Flowers Every Day," the first row of girls broke through the barriers and trampled stage security to the floor. Once it was clear that there was no security in sight, the second and third rows of girls came running. Just as this caught each of our eyes, in shock, Phillip yelled "RUN!" and every one of us fled the stage. Once safely back in our dressing room, we were all freaked out at what we had just witnessed.

"Was that all about us Eddie asked." I heard someone yell, "Hell yeah man!" The whole room was filled with excitement and everyone was speaking at the same time over each other about how awesome it was that we were having this level of effect on the audience. If I'm correct it was Norman who yelled "Hell yeah man, Switch is here!"

From that point on, Switch was turning out every performance and all promoters of all confirmed future dates were told they better triple their stage security, if they wanted a building left. By now we had also forged a bond with the entire Bar Kays entourage. They became our brothers. They mentored our first outing as live performing stars and even invited us to come and hang with them in Memphis on our off days when the tour was near Tennessee, which we did a few times.

I, as did most of my brothers, also appreciated the fan support. They clearly loved us and pretty much mobbed us at every opportunity. We were sought out and stalked at every possible opportunity. Even though, that part was so overwhelming, and we had to check into hotels, using fictitious names, we still appreciated and had respect for our fans, who by the way were no less than 90 percent female. To divert the fans from finding, stalking, mobbing and harassing us at hotels and outings we had to create an alias for our entourage. Soon after we hit the road, we traveled and booked our hotels under the name, the Steubenville Boys Gospel Choir.

Individually Jody was Sam Gucci, Bobby was Jack Daniels, Phillip was D. Pepsi, Eddie was, and Tommy was Mr. De and I was Colonel Plimmy Smith. I remember claiming the name Plimmy Smith because I played the organ but nowhere near the greatness of jazz organ legend Jimmy Smith. I explained to the fellas my playing to Jimmy's was like comparing pleather to leather, thus Plimmy versus Jimmy. The colonel part came later after Zane started calling me that.

To me, there was no joy, excitement or fulfillment that could exceed my feeling for this level of touring. Having been a performer since age five, I was now taking stage after stage, night after night, as the leader of a famous recording act with well-known hit songs, performing in theatres, arenas and concert halls filled with up to 24-thousand excited fans, yelling and screaming each band member's name.

Despite my initial resistance to hiring Tony the move quickly proved to work out because he proved to be responsible, reliable, more than efficient as Switch's valet/roadie and as my ally in keeping Bobby in line as much as was humanly possible. Just before time for us to hit the stage one night within our first two weeks out, Bobby asked

Jody and me if the three of us could have a meeting, as he had something important he needed to tell us. Having no idea what was on his mind, Jody and I agreed that the three of us should have breakfast the following morning before checkout time.

After the show, I went through that night and into the next morning trying to anticipate what he might hit us with. I thought to myself, *is he unhappy or sick, does he think somebody should be fired? He's always cussing and complaining about something,* I told myself. And then, as I began to get worked up I caught myself and realized, *just wait and see what's next, Greg.*

The morning came quick enough and the three of us met in the hotel lobby and headed into the restaurant to eat and talk. Once seated, we began to discuss how our show and the overall response of the other acts and the audience had improved by 100 percent, as the waitress approached and took our orders. As she finished and stepped away, Bobby quickly began with, "Hey you guys, I have to go back to L.A. I'm running out of my medicine and I have to go and see my doctor to get my prescription refilled."

"Prescription for what? Is it something we can get filled if we go through Memphis?" Jody asked.

"No Jody. It's for my cough syrup. My doctor makes it up specifically for me and I can only get it when I go to see him."

"Is there no over-the counter-substitute? With the cost of the three-way flight on top of the syrup, have you considered how much this stuff will cost you?" I asked.

"Yeah I have man, but I can't get the same stuff or anything close to it anywhere except from him and I get sick without it. I've got the money."

"Damn, man. This doctor has got to know that you're hooked on this stuff and he still makes it up and sells it to you and he also makes money from your office visit huh?" I added.

"Man, I just have to fly in, see him and pick up enough for the week and I fly right back. This time I'll have to meet you all in Charleston."

"Meet us in Charleston? Bobby, that's ..."

"I know, but I'm already getting sick and what would you have me do, not be able to perform at all?"

Jody and I were both upset, but again we had no choice. It was either let him go and get his drugs or have Switch leave the tour.

"Okay Bobby, meet us in DC," I said.

"But you have to come right back man," Jody added.

Our food came, so we ended that topic and resumed talking about the show and how it was too clear that we had kicked the "Came-hoes" in the ass again and how jealous they were becoming. We laughed and after breakfast we checked out of the hotel, headed for the next city, the next show. When we finished the show that night, Bobby left for Los Angeles. I became angry with myself for now making concessions to accommodate Bobby's addiction.

Making concessions had become a habit that was beginning to choke me more and more with each situation that arose through Bobby and/or Motown which held Switch, held me hostage to their demands of what had to take priority. I had been conditioned most of my life to conform to situations when demanded of me, but my capacity to justify my acceptance without revolt had worn very thin by now; and I could feel that it wouldn't be long before I blew, and folks would finally see an ugly side of Greg. And to make matters worse, little did I know this was just the beginning of a pattern for Bobby that would last throughout the entire tour.

Although the limited few times when the six of us hung together beyond rehearsal, in the dressing room or we had fun; but by now, mostly gone were the days that all of us would laugh, talk and just hang together. In the four years that had flown past, the closeness that we shared from the Holiday Inn and Montague days had all but dissipated. And even though we were still a group, at that time, it was more so in name only as everyone had all but moved on into their individual lives with their women and or children and or pets and or their mostly new friends.

But right now, that show must go on and so it did. And, so did I, with the constant hope that one day my group would be solid as friends and family, as it once was. After our second weekend out, our show had become tight, fresh and exciting to all who witnessed, and the word was being heard throughout the entertainment industry and even more loudly at the Motown offices.

Although Bob Jones would contact me and Andy to make arrangements for us to comp and or take interviews with a few press folks here and there, other than a random call from Shelly Berger to ask how things were going, we were on our own up to now.

Mr. Gordy, being kept abreast of how and what we were doing out there, surprised me with a call one morning. I happened to be in my room packing and getting ready to head for our next city when the phone rang in my room,

"Hello?"

"Hello Greg, its Berry. How are you and how's it going out there?"

Somewhat shocked at this call, having not heard from him since earlier in the year and only then, when I finally pestered him into releasing Switch from the "no live performing" hold. I managed to say, "Mr. Gordy, I'm fine and yourself?"

"I'm well Greg. I hear you're tearing it up out there on the road."

"We're trying, Mr. Gordy."

"How are the guys doing out there?"

"Everyone is hanging in there. Enjoying it for the most part." I finished.

"And Bobby?"

"Well, Mr. Gordy, you know Bobby."

"Yea Greg. That's why I asked. I'm hearing that he's being seen here in L.A. more than he is on the road. He's not missing any dates, is he?"

"None so far, thank God," I said, then holding my breath and hoping he doesn't miss any.

"Well that's good to hear. Shelly tells me our promotion team will be working with you more in every city to make sure you get our support while you're out there."

"That's good to know. A few of them have already met up with us and had us do a few radio stations, in-stores and clubs after the show."

"That's fine. Well give my best to Phillip and the guys and keep up the good work."

"I'll tell them all and we'll do our best."

That was the extent of our conversation. I appreciated the fact that he even bothered to call. The excitement we were putting down on stage made *Cashbox* and *Billboard* Magazine include our tour and box office receipts in their weekly concert report saying, "Switch-Bar Kays is the hottest R&B ticket out."

The shows and the response to Switch got bigger and better as things moved along from city to city, state to state. Bobby was sometimes late and not at his best because of the travel and the drugs; but other than the Switch members who had heard him at his best, most folks thought he sounded great.

I recall a few times, when he'd arrived in a new city early for a gig, after returning from yet another L.A. run. Bobby would be furious because he had left without or lost his travel itinerary, so he had no hotel info and couldn't find us. He'd have to go to wait at the arena until sound-check, which was always hours before the performance. The band jelled at that time and even though Bobby's weekly absence left a hole in the camaraderie of the band, every show was so good.

After that first weekend out and the revamping of our show, the next four nights of Switch was the shit! We were tight, hot and handsome and we knew it. We literally transformed overnight to the hottest act on the ticket, so much so that the Came-hoes had quit the tour after our second week on board because we'd become the attraction.

Throughout much of this tour, with the exception of my random moments with him and performance days on the bus, Switch did not see or come into contact with Bobby other than in the dressing room before or while being onstage. Other than that, he, his drug habit and his ego stayed clear of us. No more meals, outings or even grouping in the hotel lobby to go to the venue. Those days had come and gone as well as the Switch of my dreams.

As a whole, the group did a few radio stations, in stores and meet-and-greets while we toured, but mostly just the live performances. Although I could function, do my job and even keep up appearances during this short tour, drugs had also cluttered my existence; and many nights, after the show I would end up in my room with miss freebase as my date for the evening, which after I ran out, I would feel guilty about my addiction.

In fleeting moments of clarity, I repeatedly told myself, *I'm gonna stop this shit now and never do this again. I won't go out like this.* I would then proceed to break my pipe and throw it and all other paraphernalia away only to go out and buy all new stuff again and again when the urge became too strong to resist.

I remember deceiving myself into thinking, *this one time won't hurt*, but this one time came over and over and over. Yes, that freebase, that pipe was calling me, and I'd come running. Throughout this time, I somehow managed to not cross certain lines. When it came to my personal upkeep and

Switch business I was able to maintain and hold up the façade that all was ok.

As it happened, by now Switch's value to Motown had become all but nonexistent and our business as Motown artist was all but through. Without a word, Hazel and Jermaine had completely exited the picture and Shelley Berger was elected to be our so-called interim manager, in name only. On the other hand, I was alone in dealing with negative road issues, which mostly stemmed from Andy's mishandling of our business and stealing the majority of our money.

When I got tired of not seeing any money, I asked to see the expense reports, but I was never shown one; yet I was consistently given excuses why the reports weren't available for me to see. I found out he had been stealing money from us and running up tremendous bills, which Switch would then have to pay.

Jody and I had many discussions which we later took to the other Switch members before deciding that Andy was stealing and had to be fired. We kept that in the planning stage until the right time to make that move would come. As the tour and life-itself rolled on, good and bad, Switch too, continued to evolve.

Phillip, Eddie and Zane, who'd begun studying the Jehovah Witness doctrines, one after the other shortly before the tour, became Witnesses; and Jody, after marrying Maureen, also became a witness. Bobby and Tommy continued doing their thing, which the others of us were not interested in taking part. My drug use increased and so did my personal struggles and subsequent embarrassment because of it. But I had to keep moving for now and make plans to deal with my personal issues after this tour was over.

After a short holiday break, it was back to work for Switch and everyone on the tour. On this particular leg of the tour, much had changed, and Switch's first order of business was to get rid of Andy. At the suggestion of tour promoters, Darrell Brooks and Carol Kirkendall, I then contacted Norman Smith, the concert promoter out of Atlanta who Switch had met and befriended during the first leg of the tour. We offered him the job as our road manager for the balance of the tour and he accepted.

After a big dramatic blow-up confrontation about the constant theft and mis-handling of Switch's business, Andy was fired and damn near thrown out of the home that Eddie and I shared. With that out of the way, Norman flew to L.A. Together we formulated our game plan, i.e. our production and stage employees, mode of transportation, level and frequency of hotels and other details which would make this time on the road run smoother than our last outing.

This leg of the tour began on the west coast of California, playing San Diego, Oakland, Sacramento, Phoenix and even in L.A., then we moved southeastwardly across the US. Yes, it's the second leg of this tour and Switch was now seasoned pros at performing live, at knowing better what to do with our money and our time. Sadly, we also got better at knowing what to expect from and how to cover for Bobby. From city to city, the performance line up would change except, The Bar-Kays headlined, Switch held down second billing as special guest.

Switch Live - Duets

Switch Live – Eddie & Tommy

499

Switch Live – Greg & Jody

Switch Live – Phillip & Bobby

Switch Live 1981

From the start of this tour, most of the audience belonged to Switch and supporting acts, i.e. Rodger and Zapp, Kool and the Gang, The Pointer Sisters, Michael Henderson, Stacy Lattisaw, The Gap Band, Con-Funk-Shun, Slave and various other acts filled the performance roster as we moved from city to city. Unlike the first half of the tour, we traveled in a tour bus which was equipped with a folding dinner table in the game area at the front entrance, a sleeping area in the middle with six twin-sized bunks on each side of the bus and a lounge area and bathroom in the back with a couch, which opened into a queen-sized hide-a-bed.

One bus rule was to never have any women on the bus, and it was enforced by our bus driver, Big Mack, who maintained strict discipline, except for a couple of times, when the guys slipped women on and would be partying.

When the tour initially started, Cameo had second billing to the Bar-Kays but after Switch tightened up and stole the show a few times, Cameo left. Switch moved up and Rodger and Zapp opened right before Switch on most of the remaining dates, and all of us became good friends. Roger and I had this running joke, where nearly every night on his way to the stage he would stop in our dressing room and accuse me, "Man, you stole my piece of chicken!"

Of course, the room would burst into laughter. I would pretend to defend myself from his accusations, while he and I exchanged jokes for the next few minutes, then he'd leave, join the others on stage and they'd kick ass with their performance, after which, we'd do the same when it was our turn. That was the kind of camaraderie and friendship that most of Switch had with almost everyone on the tour, as egos and attitude were never a part of our make-up as a group.

I recall the night we played San Diego, many of our friends and family, including the DeBarge brothers, who were unknown at the time, came to the concert. While one of the other acts was on stage performing, Switch was in the dressing room sharing a private moment before getting dressed to go on, so we had our staff clear the room of a guest till after the show.

While waiting with the other guests backstage, El, came upon a piano which was not being used and started to play. The volume was turned off, so El playing did not disrupt anything that was happening onstage in any way, but an overzealous security guard asked him to stop playing. El, knowing he wasn't disturbing anyone continued to play as he stood up to stop. Because El didn't stop playing quick enough for the promoter, he told the security guys to physically remove El, so they picked him up and forcefully removed him, roughing him up a little in the effort.

Norman happened to catch the end of the altercation. He immediately stood up for El and made the promoter and security folk apologize for their poor handling of this minor problem. Norman then brought El into our dressing room to collect himself. Once in the room, El, crying and upset, told Bobby his version of what had happened. Without letting Norman share his handling of the problem, Bobby immediately threw a fit; yelling and cursing erratically, at the top of his lungs.

"Don't no muthafucka put they hands on a DeBarge, Greg. I'm not standing for that. I'm a man."

"Bobby, what's the matter, man? Norman's trying to say they already apologized to El and us and said it was a misunderstanding. They didn't know El was with us, he wasn't wearing his backstage pass and they had asked him to stop three times."

Bobby looked at El, noticing he wasn't wearing his pass.

"Okay, but this shit ain't over. They don't fuck with no DeBarge like that man. I ain't goin' on."

"Come on man." Jody interjected, as the look on Phillip's, Eddie's and Tommy's face turned from happy to "Aw shit. Here we go again."

"Bobby It's almost time to hit, we can't just back out now."

"Shit if we can't and that's just what I'm doing," Bobby threw in.

503

I had to walk to the other side of the room to keep from losing it. First of all, before this shit burst into our dressing room, the six of us were in there talking, laughing and having fun while getting dressed to go on. I too didn't like the fact that El was treated poorly by these idiots; but he was doing something he really shouldn't have been doing. Without visual credentials to even be back there, he got caught and paid a price after repeated requests for him to stop, so this treatment was not altogether unprovoked. Then the folks apologized to El and all of us, so this shit should have been done and over with, but not for Bobby.

"Tell them muthafuckas I'm not going on!"

"Come on man, that's taking this shit a little too far," I said from across the room.

Bobby looked me in the eye and started towards me saying, "I mean it man. If they don't straighten this out, I'm not going on!"

"How do you want them to straighten this out man?" Norman asked.

"They've already apologized."

"Tell the promoters that we want more money, or we aren't going on."

"Don't you dare do that shit!" I angrily said to Norman. Just as I began to raise my voice to tell Bobby where he could get off Norman was there to jump in front of me and cut me off saying, "Ok, ok. Colonel if that's what it's going to take to get this show done, that's what I'll do."

He turned towards me with his back to Bobby and winked his eye, which quickly defused my anger, so I bit my tongue to hold back what I had to say next, then he turned back around. "Bobby, how much am I supposed to ask for?" Norman asked seriously.

"I don't know man, just tell them what we want and see what they have to say," Bobby said without looking back at me.

"I'll handle this and come back here. Now will y'all at least get dressed while I do my thang?" Norman asked as he exited the room.

It took a minute or so but as our roadies again cleared the room, each of us began to get dressed. Taking Norman's lead, I started a conversation about how we were gonna hurt that audience tonight while Jody began to talk Bobby down from his stance. Everyone, including Bobby resumed getting dressed while we waited for Norman to return. After about ten minutes more, Tony knocked on the dressing room door and yelled, their calling for you guys.

Tommy suggested we have prayer as we usually did before going on stage, just as Norman walks back into the room. All of us jumped to attention as he gestured that we continue forming our circle. He then said, "I spoke to Darrell, and Carol is gone, but he and I will get with her and work something out as soon as she gets back here; but in the mean time we should get to work. The lights are off, the audience is getting impatient and the production folk are calling for you, so let's have prayer go do our show."

He then signaled to Bobby that they would talk after the prayer was done and then he, unexpectedly, opted to lead the Switch entourage in prayer for the first time.

"Father God bless us."

Tommy, being happy that Bobby's tantrum was over for now, could no longer contain himself or his too silly sense of humor, so before Norman could continue or get another word out, Tommy burst out laughing, causing the entire room to just fall out with laughter. Even Norman and Bobby had to break all seriousness and join in with the rest of us. This, of course, broke the tension for everyone.

As we were leaving the room to hit the stage, Norman pulled Bobby to the side and whispered something which made Bobby smile as we all stopped at the side of the stage as the night's MC introduced us. Norman later informed me that he told Bobby to let it go and he'd make sure things were made right. From that point, nothing more ever came of that incident.

The MC's introduction was met with thunderous screams and applause and we hit the stage and again kicked some serious ass. Most Switch members and our sidemen were humble, solid, considerate guys, who got along with and were courteous to the other acts, their entourages, the promoters, the fans, hotel and restaurant employees and pretty much everyone we encountered. We used to have big fun as a group on and off stage, after the gig and especially on our off days, with the exception of Bobby who quickly separated himself. Even Tony wanted to and tried to hang with us but was usually summoned away by Bobby.

In most cases, a band becomes a tighter unit and closer friends while touring, due to the large amount of time spent together on the road; but the love and closeness that I was accustomed to sharing in being a member of more than five professional bands in my years prior to Switch, did not exist here. It could not exist here because we would never again be whole, due to one person's mental and emotional fragmentation.

Although I had hope in Switch's beginning, Bobby DeBarge no longer knew trust, he no longer knew loyalty, he no longer cared what others thought; as his ego, his drug dependency and his determination to self-destruct ruled all logic, no matter how or from whom it was presented.

The years of physical, psychological, emotional and sexual abuse which Bobby had endured at the hands of his deranged father and which he subsequently forced on some of his own brothers had gradually culminated into a vicious, unrelenting cycle of self-destruction. But the rest of our band, including our side men and our road personnel partied hard on the road. And while Bobby had a Ménage a trois with his drugs and Tony, Jody, Tommy, our side musicians and I took advantage of the many women at our disposal; except for Phillip and Eddie who had serious relationships waiting at home, although one could and often did question Phillip's motives as he always had a room full of women.

But what most folk didn't know was, Phillip was always honorable in his commitments and intentions. He always made sure that of the girls he allowed to hang around, the only physical contact they might share was if she was the one he chose to do his hair that night.

I, too, was always straight with the groupies and party girls. Never promising, lying about sharing tomorrow or even the next time Switch would come through their town, so as long as she and I could have a decent conversation, I had no problems with them because we both knew what the night was about. From time to time, depending on what city we were in, I would take advantage of the limousines at our 24-hour access and would be driven on sightseeing tours, while the others were partying or sleeping.

Traveling through the south, was sometimes taxing, as many nights we'd have to leave the comfort of hotel rooms behind, climb into our bunks to sleep in an effort to make it to the next city and next performance on time. I recall being in disbelief that the Troutman brothers would travel in a couple of large vans, which they owned, and travel to the next city after almost every show. When we heard this from the Darrell and Carol most of Switch talked about how we couldn't or wouldn't travel like that because it was too hard on you.

I, too, was in total agreement till one day I learned that with the majority of the money the Troutman brothers saved on airplane and bus costs, they bought and owned apartment complexes and ran a big construction company in their home town of Dayton. From what I'd come to know they were a serious, respected business and talented music family.

Yes, road life was big fun, but it also got scary late one night. After the shows were over, per usual, female fans would somehow find us and converged on our hotel. Despite our using aliases, there were few nights without a knock at the door, or a group of girls hanging out in the hotel hallways until they found us.

One night, a man showed up at our hotel in Jackson Mississippi, screaming for his wife, who was in the room with Phillip.

"Come on out, I know you in there. I love you girl, come on out."

Eddie had come to my room and told me this fool was outside. I went to the hotel entrance. He was crying and holding his shotgun.

"Excuse me sir. There's no Betty here."

Is you one of them Switch guys?"

"Yes I am. I'm Greg and I'm the leader. I swear there's no Betty Anne in any of our rooms."

"She might be using another name, but I know she's in there because her girlfriend told me, and I'm gone kill somebody if she don't get her ass out here."

"You sure she ain't with the Bar-Kays or Kool and the Gang?"

"Naw man. She's in love with y'all Switches. And if she don't come out, I'm coming in!"

"OK man, I'll go look in all the rooms and see if anyone knows Betty. If they do, I'll have her come out. But you have to put down that gun and stop hollering before the police come and we all get in trouble."

He put down the shotgun and sat on the grass crying. I went inside the hotel and Eddie met me in the lobby. "She's in Phillips room."

By this time, Norman had shown up; so, we hurried to Phillip's room and I knocked on his door. "Phillip, man, we've got trouble. That lady in your room's husband is outside with a shotgun."

Phillip finally came to the door. "You're kidding."

"I'm not kidding man. You have to get her out of here."

"She was in here doing my hair but when she finished I told her I had to get some sleep, so she left with her girlfriend."

"OK, but if she comes back don't let her in. Tell her that a man is outside with a shotgun looking for her."

As Norman and I headed back towards my room a female voice came from somewhere behind me. "I told Roosevelt I don't want him and it's over. Damn, and now he done made a fuss. Let me go talk to him."

She was a fine little redbone, who switched past me. I stopped her. "I suggest you go out the back door, so he won't know where you came from."

She jumped up and quickly made it down the hall and out of the side exit. As she appeared outside and headed into the parking lot, Norman and I watched from the windows of my room.

"Roosevelt, what you doing here? I told you it's over, now leave me alone."

Roosevelt fell on his knees and grabbed Betty around her legs. "Betty Anne, you my wife and I want you to come home. Now don't make me have to use my gun." Crying, he let go of her and standing, picked up his shotgun. All of us who had just witnessed this situation took cover in the safety of our rooms.

When I thought it was safe, I peered out of the window again, and they were gone. A few hours later, as we were boarding the bus to leave, she appeared again and approached Phillip. All of us, close enough to see her, noticed with the right side of her face swollen and blue. Phillip backed away from her.

"Hi Phillip. I'm back."

Phillip, always the gentleman, moved her face to see the bruises better. "I see you're back, but we're leaving, and you can't come with me. I don't get involved with married women."

"I told y'all it was over between me and Roosevelt. Hell, I told him too."

"It might be over for you, but not for him and that shotgun and I don't want any trouble. I have to go now. Bye."

Phillip walked onto the bus, leaving the girl standing there waving as our bus drove off. This was just one of the many road situations many women brought and or imposed on us. And the band played on! Leaving the South, we headed to Memphis to rehearse, to get off the bus for a while and to spend our three-day break with the Bar-Kays, as we often did through this tour.

Bobby, Tommy and I got really excited when Norman told us that Grand Rapids had recently added to the performance itinerary and I quickly made sure that at least twenty tickets each were made available for us to give some of our too many family members and friends. Our date there was a couple of weeks away, but the thought of finally performing at home held all of us in anticipation until that day finally came.

In Grand Rapids, Switch was given a hero's welcome which began at the airport. My mom and my stepfather Frazier and my dad were part of the big reception we receive upon landing in Grand Rapids. I remember embracing my stepfather but being a little less enthusiastic when approached by my dad, feeling that he was more so there to be seen than in support of the son he wasn't there for.

When I thought about my actions I was saddened by the thought that I was made to feel that way by his absence from my life while I was becoming this star he now respected. In conversations with him much after that day, without knowing how I felt, he repeatedly assured me that he came because he was proud of me and yet the fact that he was sad that he was not a part of my life from the beginning showed on his face.

There was also a press and public reception at my old Alma mater, the new Ottawa Hills High School where all of Switch was given keys to the city and Bobby and Tommy were given honorary high school diplomas. Being back in Grand Rapids felt good. It was even better getting to perform as stars at home for family, friends and fans for the first time. Although in town for less than 48 hours, my family and I got together for dinner the evening before the show.

"Greg, we're really proud of you. You really represent us as a family," were just a few of the things being said by various family members throughout my brief visit. I, of course, had heard this many times before now; but after all the doubts, fears and questions of others throughout the years of my ups, downs and struggles, this was finally a well-deserved pat on the back. I would respond in return, "You all don't realize what you've given me. I carry all of you everywhere I go. I'm proud to be a Williams."

I ate, drank, hung with my family, and passed out tickets for the concert.

New cousins I'd never seen before and a few musicians I had jammed with just showed up at my mom's house, after hearing I was in town. Among other things, one of my old musician acquaintances began to tell me, "Greg, I knew I should have gone to California with you when you asked me. I'd be on stage with Switch now, just like you."

I kinda laughed with him and never called him out, but I just wondered what the hell he was talking about; all the while I'm knowing that he was straight up lying. And if he could look me in the eyes and tell that lie, I know he must have told it to anyone and everyone who would listen since Switch's music first hit the airwaves. When I thought about how he was as a musician, hell I would never have asked him to join me in anything. I did everything I could to keep from busting up laughing in his face. But I'd never step on his illusion like that anyway, especially since it cost me nothing to let him keep that thought, and possibly hope, alive.

I knew before that returning to Grand Rapids as a star would be this way. I knew that many of the folks that I knew and/or knew me, who dared not to chase dreams, those who may have been afraid or unable to leave home in pursuit of a better life, would claim a greater relationship with me than what actually existed and live vicariously through my now, well documented accomplishments. But this was still and would always be home. And the folks be it family, friends, and even acquaintances would always be my folks.

Although my moment there was just a quick pass-through I was happy to be there, to perform there and was equally happy to again leave Grand Rapids behind and continue the tour dates. After Grand Rapids we played in Minneapolis, MN where this seriously old theatre, which I believe Abraham Lincoln first saw John Wilkes Booth perform, was freezing because their heating was busted and the radiators throughout were frozen solid.

The show's opening act was a then unknown act named Flyte Time who's lead singer was a young Alexander O'Neal. This tour, although fun, was also hard work and Switch's performance appeared to get stronger as the days went on, but certain band members were beginning to show signs of wear. As we played our way across the country, I noticed Bobby's voice getting weaker; he was more agitated and becoming more irritating.

I soon discovered Phillip, again, had told both Bobby and Tommy, he wouldn't be lending them any more money. Well, Bobby probably didn't have any money for drugs and when he didn't have money for at least his cough syrup, his body suffered, his throat and singing suffered, he suffered, and then Switch suffered on and off stage.

On a date in Colorado, Bobby could only make it through four songs because he was so sick and hoarse and at another concert, he couldn't sing at all so he pretty much sat there on stage while Phillip carried most of the lead vocals as the rest of us filled in as best we could. Because Bobby's problems were now all of ours, I was almost happy this tour was coming to a close.

One day, we were preparing to leave town and get back on the road headed for the next city. While most of the guys were checking out, Norman called me outside where the bus was being packed.

"Colonel, we have a serious problem."

"What's that?"

"Actually, we have two problems."

He opened his briefcase and pulled out a stack of hotel receipts and bills and started handing specific ones to me.

"These are the bills which Motown sent this morning. They're from the last few hotels we've stayed at and they're for things Bobby either broke, but mostly stole from different rooms."

I looked at the bills. There were charges for lamps, towels, tables, sheets and pillow cases, pictures among other items, which Bobby had stolen from his and Tommy's rooms. There were also charges for broken items including wall fixtures, beds, a television and even a toilet stool. Upon discovering these broken and missing items, the hotels had done additional billing and faxed them to Motown who had them forwarded to me care of Norman at our current hotel.

Looking over the list of items, I immediately thought back to something Bobby had repeatedly told me. When they were kids, one of the DeBarge family's favorite past times was to go ally hunting. What this entailed was they would go through alleys and scrounge around in people's trash and collect and keep anything salvageable. The DeBarge children would then take these things home and use them. As that memory and vision began to dissipate and I was snapped back into the reality of the moment I asked Norman

"What's the other problem?"

He pointed to the storage space on the bus.

"We almost can't close the storage space's doors because all of this stuff Bobby has stored under this bus. We don't have room for one thing more."

Looking in the storage space, I could see where Bobby had hastily thrown various stolen hotel room items about with the intent of taking them home to furnish his apartment.

"How much of this shit can be taken back Norman?" I asked.

"How we gonna get it back Colonel?" he asked in all seriousness.

"We can't have Big Mac turn this bus around and go back to every city Bobby's done stole shit from, now can we?" With my quick wit for humor, I wanted to burst out laughing at Norman's response, but the moment was too serious and the problem at hand needed real resolution.

"Have the roadies take whatever's from this hotel back inside. They can take the rest of the small stuff and put it on Bobby's and Tony's bunks." I said, "Switch ain't gonna pay for this shit either, so I suggest that we subtract the cost of what we can't take back from Bobby's pay."

When most of the members had checked out and put their bags next to the bus where Big Mac and the roadies could pack them, Norman began to pass out pay receipts and cash to our sidemen and roadies then each Switch member. With my guys, I knew the ritual whenever we got paid. Eddie and Jody would send money home to their families, Tommy and Bobby would buy drugs and alcohol, I'd buy clothes, sometimes a little cocaine and put the rest in the bank and Phillip would put all of his in the bank.

Due to this day starting out with the discovery of Bobby's new hobby, I knew this particular payday was definitely going to be different than most others. I also knew all hell would break loose when he was informed how his pay would be minus the cost of the items he had so recklessly stolen and/or broken. As our entourage filled the bus and received their pay, I believe Bobby was among the last of us to get with Norman.

As soon as he reached Norman and saw his pay receipt, like I said, all hell broke loose. Bobby began to yell at the top of his lungs, everyone on the bus and I believe within a two-block radius could her him screaming, "Where the fuck is my money. This ain't what I'm supposed to get."

Norman began to speak as calmly as he could, trying to explain to Bobby,

"Man, this is all you've got coming. You didn't think taking all of that stuff you been hiding under the bus was gonna catch up with you? Bobby, I didn't know you were doing this, or I would have stopped you from the beginning. These hotels aren't gonna just let this slide. Here," Norman said while pulling the billing invoices from his briefcase. "Look at these bills we got from the last few hotels we stayed at. They sent this stuff to Motown and Motown sent it to us."

While snatching and glancing at one of the receipts Bobby said, "But Norman, that shit ain't worth all of this and I ain't paying for it."

"But man, you already paid for it." Norman said, "Somebody had to pay for it immediately and Motown wasn't going to pay for your stuff, besides not having the money Switch wasn't going to pay for your stuff either so just who does that leave man?"

"They can't charge all of that for that raggedy shit, man." Bobby turned and came after me as I was standing just outside of the bus. "Greg, what the fuck is this?"

I called Norman over and he said, "Colonel, he knows that he got to pay for the stuff under the bus. Bobby, it belongs to you and you have to pay for it."

Bobby glared at me, then at his pay receipt and he fell to the ground, crying, sobbing uncontrollably. His cries echoed off the bus and off the buildings near where we'd parked. Tony, who was working with Big Mac putting our wardrobe case to the bus, came over and tried to pick him up saying, "Come on Bobby, we have to get on the bus," but Bobby, balled-up into fetal position and pushed him away.

After trying again to get Bobby to his feet, Tony turned and walked away to finish loading things on the bus. After another minute, Norman managed to get Bobby off the ground, onto the bus and into a bunk. Once the last few members piled onto the bus, we drove off, headed for the next city and the next hotel. It was midday when we arrived and checked into our hotel.

Everyone exited the bus without a word, waited to get their room keys from Norman, and immediately went to their rooms.

I, too, went straight to my room and waited till I thought everyone would be situated, then I called Norman and the other four Switch members and asked them to come to my room, which they did.

"Guys, I think this is the end of the road. I think Bobby's having a nervous breakdown and he's not going to make it."

Looking around, Phillip leaned against the wall and looked out of the window. Eddie and Jody looked worried and Tommy, who had taken a seat, shook his head in agreement. I actually felt relieved. "You don't think he can make it through this last week or so Greg?" Jody asked. "There's nothing else we can do?"

"Between the drugs, the losing his voice and his attitude with all of us, I don't know if any of us can keep going," I replied.

Norman chimed in, "If things don't get better with him after our next three off days, I don't think we gonna have much of a choice."

With nothing else to be said, everyone left my room to eat and get some rest before duty called that evening. After traveling to perform one-nighters for more than three months without returning, through America's south, mid-west and east coast, by car, van, airplane and bus, this tour was about to end. We had one more gig, before heading home and by now, the band was tired, physically, mentally and emotionally.

On the day of our last performance for this tour came, a few of us had picked up colds due to the constantly changing weather and our entire entourage was exhausted. We played the Omni in Atlanta, Georgia. To the audience our performance didn't suffer at all, but we knew that the concert sucked that night because the band had lost its energy and once again Bobby had killed everyone else's joy.

Due to a cold and fatigue, during that performance, Eddie fell off the side of the stage, which was six feet off the ground, and he was taken to the hospital by ambulance. While playing the last song of our set, Jody who earlier that day had complained of flu-like symptoms fainted and he too was taken to the hospital by ambulance. The signs were too obvious, that for Switch, this tour was over. My intuition was confirmed when Bobby told me after we finished our last gig that he was through with Switch. I assumed that to mean that he was finally going solo.

This time, all I could feel was relief. No sadness, no anger, no concern about my group. While talking with Shelly and other Motown execs from the road, both Bobby and I had finally convinced them that, after this tour, we would no longer work together. By now, I was really glad to see him go; because, among the obvious reasons I could no longer watch him suffer; and he saw no way out, causing others to suffer, especially me. The writing was on the wall as his and my friendship had seen its last day, for now. I still love him; but now I had to even put that love on hold. Enough already! Uno mas!

Upon our return to Los Angeles each member of our entourage retreated back into our personal lives. As more than a month had passed, I had been in contact in one form or another with each member of Switch with the obvious exception of Bobby.

In speaking with Tommy, I was told that Bobby was outraged and constantly making aggrieved accusations against Motown and me. His drug-ridden state of mind had escalated to the point where his psychosis had everyone he knew doing things to hurt him. His complaint about Motown was the typical "I'm a superstar and them muthafuckas are ripping me off," while his main complaint about me was mean and totally unfounded.

In his mind I had become an enemy who supposedly had gone behind his back and got money from promoters and didn't share with him, as he had accused me of doing the same with Motown a year or so back, when nothing could have been farther from the truth then and at any time. Bobby also felt that he should be in control of Switch and all aspects of the group's business since he was the group's lead singer. In fact, according to him, "Grag, people know my voice and your hat, the other muthafuckas don't matter".

But besides the fact that he in no way, shape or form was ever responsible enough or even sober enough to handle his own business and with the exception of Tommy, no member of Switch had enough respect for him, other than musically to follow him in anywhere. After he realized his thoughts and actions were getting him nowhere, he simply stopped taking my calls and showing up for meetings and rehearsals. By now he was living in a completely distorted reality.

Ultimately and sadly, his arrogance accompanied by his out-of-control drug use destroyed all hopes he'd had in becoming a solo artist. Motown had no choice but drop him soon after Switch left the label. Once dropped from Motown, I came to know that through relationships he had with James Mason of the Bar-Kays, Larry Blackman, founder/leader of Cameo signed Bobby to a short-lived production deal, which also yielded no fruit due to Bobby's life of drugs and overt sexual proclivities.

Not long after the Switch tour was over, I did, however have to reach out to Bobby with the intent to get our stage costumes so that I could have them cleaned and stored. Bobby was nowhere to be found which led me to accept the fact that he really didn't want to see me and was in hiding out from me. This was truly fine by me, but only if I got me hands on

Switch's and my property, which Bobby was holding somewhere.

In my quest to get our stage costumes back, I did find out that he and Clarence were now living as a couple and had been evicted from their apartment, due to nonpayment of rent and destruction of property. I didn't know till later that he had moved back into Howard Weekly Hotel in Hollywood, which was the first place Bobby and I ever stayed in California, as members of White Heat. Bobby was a star and yet he and Tony were living in that dive, paying for a room by the week.

In trying to find Switch's belongings, I tracked down the apartment manager where Bobby and Tony had been evicted. I was told that rent had not been paid for four months and all of their belongings, including Switch's costumes, Bobby's and my ASCAP awards for R&B songwriter of the year, which had been awarded to us for co-writing "I Call Your Name," had also been left and locked in the apartment and was not the property of the apartment owner. This really increased my anxiety as, in picking up an advance check from ASCAP, Bobby was given both plaques but never turned mine over to me.

I offered to pay the past due money to get back what belonged to me, Switch and possibly Bobby's possessions; but the building manager had been too badly injured by the destruction of the apartment and Bobby's promises to make payments that never came. The apartment manager got down-right nasty with me, abruptly said no to my offer to pay the debt and told me to get the hell out of his building.

I consulted my lawyer that day to see if there was anything that I could do to retrieve my belongings; but was told that I had no recourse because Bobby's irresponsibility made the building manager's actions legal. So again, Switch lost more than forty-thousand dollars in stage costumes and miscellaneous stage equipment and I never even got to see my ASCAP award.

Chapter 16

Switch V

"Switch V" Album Cover

After a few weeks of shaking off the road weariness and getting my life back in full swing, it was time to gear up for the next Switch album. Preparing to record the new "Switch V" for Motown was bittersweet because my problems with Bobby and vice-versa were finally over, but I had a big void to try and fill.

Switch was free to replace him as we saw fit. I knew before I made the move that replacing him, replacing his sound would almost be as big a detriment as it was dealing with the person he had become over the past few years, but we had to try.

After putting out the call, meeting and auditioning many singers, although Phillip, Eddie, Jody and I auditioned many great vocalists, I could not believe some of the guys who walked through our door thinking they could replace Bobby DeBarge. Besides not having the look we needed, there were bass vocalists, operatic vocalists, vocalists who didn't sing but creaked out the words like an old door, and there were even vocalists who couldn't carry a tune in a fork lift. Please note that I didn't call them singers and after hearing them I didn't call them back either.

Over the years I have learned there is no replacing Bobby DeBarge, because to me Bobby DeBarge was among the greatest talents God allowed to come down and visit this planet. Because Bobby DeBarge, as tortured and tormented a soul he was, he could bring a song to life from a gust of wind, from a flicker of light, from a smile, from a tear and anything else within his grasp. And mostly because Bobby DeBarge was my friend, my brother, my child and I loved him as God commanded me to.

Of the vocalists I continued to audition there were two who impressed me enough to call back and a guy by the name of Terrance Gaines who was my first choice, ended up being the guy we hired. By stature, Terrance was a little shorter than the rest of us, but he was attractive, had a very pleasant personality and most of all he could really sing. From my opinion, his vocal sound and range was more like that of Blue Magic or like Harry Ray of The Moments, who later became

Ray, Goodman and Brown; but we liked him just the same and in my mind, since our group had changed and our sound was evolving, the difference he brought would bring Switch closer to my original vision when Arnie was the co-lead vocalist opposite Phillip.

So, Terrance was it and we signed him along with our friend and live guitarist Zane Giles. We groomed Terrance, taught him all of the lead and background parts of our hit songs, among other songs we performed. We also introduced him to and rehearsed him on new songs we planned to record for our next album. After working so hard at rehearsal, teaching Terrance and Zane getting ready for the studio, most of us found ways individually and collectively to play hard also.

Now and then I would attend parties or go to clubs along with my non-Switch friends. The L.A. Party scene, was always waiting for me and on occasion I would pop up at upscale places like Osco's Disco, the Speak Easy, Carlos and Charlie's, where I'd run into and hang out with then peers like my brother Rick James, or Jeffery Daniel of the R&B group Shalamar who had once again become a close friend, after accidently discovering we had both moved to L.A. from Grand Rapids.

Jeffery and I had met years before after becoming close as costars of the Grand Rapids production of the play "The Me Nobody Knows." Along with well-known, well established stars in Hollywood, you were likely to run into or hang out with other fresh music and television stars, i.e., Stoney Jackson who was a friend and my first management clients a few years later: Kevin Hooks, Richard Dimples

Fields, Jimmy Jam and Terry Lewis, Grand Master Flash and the Furious Five, Klymaxx, actors TK Carter, Tina Andrews, Miguel Nunez, Reggie Dorsey, Ernest Thomas, Eddie Murphy, Eric Laneuville, Ron Glass and a host of other young, black Hollywood stars.

Me, Cynthia Horner, Stoney Jackson, Todd Bridges & Jeffery Daniel

These were the folks and that was a big part of my life during those days. Although the clubs were big fun, I was most comfortable at private parties, jazz clubs and more intimate settings with small groups of personal friends. Yes, during the time I did big things and had big fun, as did most members of Switch; but beyond that, I spent the majority of my time making music and taking care of Switch business.

Once again, it's time to get back in the studio to work on our fifth album for the Gordy label. Little did any of us know or assume at that time our days at Motown were about to come to an end. With Bobby, Jody and Jermaine no longer involved with Switch's music, the bulk of production for his album was thrust upon my shoulders. Phillip, Eddie, Zane and I wrote and arranged most of the songs for the album and I inherited three other incomplete songs which Bobby had started for the Switch album but was unable to complete.

No matter what state he was in, out of my respect for him and more so his creative rights, I initially refused to touch his work without him giving me the go ahead; but due to his ongoing use of drugs he had abandoned his work and was nowhere to be found. So, after being told by Lee Young Sr., Motown's then vice president of creative that finished or not, the cost of these tracks would come out of Switch's current recording budget, I agreed to work to complete the tracks, add arrangements and vocals to turn in completed songs.

Due to all of the changes in my life including my now drug addition, this time I went into the studio with the weight of the world on my shoulders. See, there was never a question of if I could produce this album by myself because this moment I had been grooming myself for, since conceiving the group that would become known as Switch. But with all of the life and career changes I now had to endure and contend with, there was a question of whether I really wanted to take on all of this, but that question too diminished like a candle in the wind, the day the first song was written.

Soon after we began recording our final album for Motown, I got a call from home. In the midst of catching me up on the goings on with my family, mom tells me that my granddad's health had gone down so much that the family had to place him in a nursing home.

"Besides being physically sick, his mind is going from dementia and he's forgotten many things and most people," she said. When that update was done, we talked about a few things before saying our goodbyes. After hanging up the phone, I decided I really needed to get there to see him before he slipped away all together; so, within a few days I made the time and headed home on another of my surprise visits.

Once I got to Grand Rapids that evening, I picked up a rental car, made it to my mom's house and remained there until the next day; enjoying mom's company, her cooking and getting caught up on what had been going on with much of the Williams family. Early the next morning, I'm out making a few family rounds before visiting hours at the nursing home where my grandfather was. The scenery in Grand Rapids, per always, had not really changed since I first left home for Arizona and ultimately California to sign with Barry White and White Heat.

The morning was cold and gray, the traffic was all but nonexistent and most of the streets were desolate, but I did see a few folk that I knew going here and there as I made my way to my grandmother's home. Of course, she was excited and happy at my surprise visit. Per usual I joined her, having a morning cup of coffee and she and I talked for what seemed like hours.

I so enjoyed exchanging ideas and personal history with my grandmother. The woman had always been wise and insightful; but for me and my dreams, she remained forever affirming and optimistic that all I had to do was try and I'd make it happen. So, for me to come home successful in the profession of my choosing and be able to share my stories and victories with one who believed in and supported me from the word go, this was the victory I reveled in and cherished above most.

As our conversation began to wind down, I let her know that next on my agenda for the day was to see granddad. She then changed gears and began to share what she knew about my grandfather's current mental and medical state. She let me know that his overall health was failing him and because of the dementia he was gradually slipping away, and he really wouldn't be with us much longer. She told me that it was good that I came home to check on all of them. I wanted to catch him before lunch time, so I told her I'd better get going, to which see agreed was a good idea. I told her I'd be back either later or the next day, and I was on my way.

I would later find that there was nothing she or anyone else could have said to really prepare me for what I would find. With most of my family living in close proximity, the nursing home too was close and within ten minutes I had parked the car and was standing at the front desk signing the nursing home's guest list to see my grandfather.

I recall that I couldn't stand still from the nervous tapping of my feet as the anxiousness consumed me. I was excited, I was worried, I was happy, and I was little Greg all over again as I got closer to my primary reason for coming home. Upon making my way through the corridors and finally upon his room, I was taken aback at first sight of this man, my granddad as he lay in his bed looking up at his younger brother, my uncle Ivory "Toad" Jennings.

The small but full-chested man I came looking for was no longer there. Instead, I saw a frail, much older man deep into dementia. My uncle Toad was at his bedside when I arrived. I stood at the door listening to their verbal exchange as I fought to get my bearings before entering the room.

"Toad, we've got to get back home before Poppa gets back and I need your help. If you can get them chickens, I'll get the pigs and we can make it back and won't get a whipping."

Uncle Toad slowly bowed his head and wiped his eyes.

"Shoat, you know poppa's been dead too many years and we don't live on the farm no more. We're in Michigan now." At that moment uncle Toad looked up, saw me standing in the doorway to Granddad's room, he quickly stood up and stretched out his arms to greet me with a hug. "Boy, ain't you a sight for sore eyes?" He asked as I got close to receive the big bear hug he planted on me.

"How are you uncle Toad." I asked, just as he was saying. "Shoat, here's your grandson, Greg, who done come all the way from California to see you."

"Toad, we got to get back home, now are you going to help me, or not?"

I approached my grandfather, grabbed his hand as he had mine so many times in my life, and said, "Hi Granddad. I finally made it in."

He looked up at me with this confused expression across his face, then turned to my uncle and asked, "Toad, ain't this the man from the farm down the road?"

Uncle Toad looked at me sadly, then at my grandfather and replied, "Shoat, this is your grandson Greg. I know you remember him. He's Mattie's boy. He come up here from California to see bout you"

At first my grandfather remained silent, while looking me up and down. Then he chuckled a little, turned to uncle Toad and said, "don't be playing with me. You know papa's gone get us if we take much longer."

My heart dropped as I struggled to accept the fact that my grandfather could no longer recognize me. The fact that my grandfather was gone, that he no longer had any idea who I was, hit me like a Mac truck.

I was so dumbstruck and hurt I began to gasp for breath, and I stumbled to a chair resting against a nearby wall to break free of that moment. I tried to sit and pull myself together but wound up stepping out of the room to lean up against a desk, a wall or anything to support my legs which seemed determined to collapse under me. I seriously fought to keep from crying out loud in front of staff and few guests moving about in that hallway. In short time, Uncle Toad emerged from the room and silently gestured for me to follow him to the outside patient area where he pulled up two chairs and sat at a round picnic table.

"Boy try not to feel bad, he don't really know nobody for long but Mattie. He's slipping away a little more every day. Don't let that stop you from coming by here to see him while you're here."

"I won't, Uncle Toad, but it's such a shock that he don't know me."

"Yeah Greg, I tell you that's the way it is with everybody. One day he knows me and the next minute he don't; but as much as he loves you, he just might know who you are next time you walk in the room, so keep trying long as you're here.

Tell me, how is it out there in California? We all saw you on, on,.. What that boy name on the television?"

"Mike Douglas, I asked?"

"Naw, naw the other boy with the car commercial too..."

"Oh, you mean Merv Griffin, the Merv Griffin Show."

"Yeah that's him. We all saw you and your group on the show. Now boy, you done made it to the big time, huh?" as he chuckled proudly.

Everybody over there knows you and we all proud of you boy. Just remember to put God first, cause' only what you do for Christ gone last. You know that, don't cha?"

"Yes, Uncle Toad. As long as Granddad, Mother, You, Aunt Mary and everybody else been drilling that into our heads, yes sir I betta know that."

"You sho got that right," he said with a hearty laugh. It was that moment which would set the tone for my all too brief stay in Grand Rapids this time. Yes, this particular visit was all about checking on and spending time with the elders in my family; as in my first visit with my Grandfather I was hit right between the eyes with the fact that any one of them might not be there next time I came through.

As children, the Williams, Jennings, and Edwards children were taught to respect their elders. Honor thy mother and thy father and we did, and on top of that we loved them too. From the big to the small, from the young to the old, we learned and live by that. Uncle Toad and I spent nearly an hour at that table getting caught up on each other's lives. He filled me in on most of my cousins, his children's lives, especially my cousin David who was in the Patterns with me, as best he could; and I shared with him aspects of my life that I knew would make him happy and proud.

Once we abruptly became aware of the time, we wrapped up the chat and made our way back into granddad's room. He lay there fast asleep so my uncle decided he would head home, and I decided to walk out with him and return later that day before it got too late. As we made it to his car I hugged him, and we said goodbye after I promised to drop by his house and see everyone before I headed back to California.

I made it to my car and left the nursing home with my heart and spirit broken. I had just left the shell of the one man who had been the definitive example of what a man is throughout my life. Right, wrong or indifferent I knew my granddad to be a strong, caring honorable man who may not have been the smartest men I'd encountered on my journey, but certainly the wisest and biggest contributor in me becoming the man I was constantly on my way to be.

Yes, even though breathing, he was gone, never to return as the man I knew and loved. I went back to see granddad twice more during my week at home but both visits yielded the same result as the first. My grandfather was no longer there and would never make it back, for any of us. When the day came to catch my plane home, I boarded knowing this trip would probably be the last time I'd see my grandfather alive and it was. He held on a few months more, but died later in 1982.

Due to my having no training when it came to money matters and saving, on top of my frequent drug use, I was living from paycheck to paycheck and didn't have the money to go to the funeral and nowhere to get it from. Still being under contract to Motown, I reluctantly decided to go to the record company to request a small advance.

At this time the label was being run by Jay Lasker who, behind his back, everyone, including some of Motown's top executives, was called "cock eyed Junior" because he was cross-eyed. The name was a reference of a Richard Prior character and comedy routine. I had to keep myself from looking around the room, when he spoke, wondering if he was talking to me or someone else, because of his eyes, but when he pulled out the accounting book, he looked down.

"Greg, I see that the last Switch record isn't selling."

"But, Mr. Lasker, the *This is My Dream* album did well, I should have some producer royalties building up and I'm not asking for much, just enough to go home to my grandfather's funeral."

"I'm sorry, but if I don't see sales in this book, they don't exist. I can't give you an advance."

I tried a little harder to convince him that I was not the risk he was trying to make me out to be, by reminding him that since coming to Motown I had always delivered and including my contributions, Switch had sold millions of records and would continue to do so; but that fell on deaf ears and my pride was not about to let me beg him or anyone else for anything.

Pissed off, I walked out of his office trying to make sense of what I had just experienced. On every song I had written, arranged and produced since I signed with Motown, my projects were always submitted ahead of schedule and under budget, not like most recordings done by some producers at

Motown who spent excessive amounts of money on one song which was rarely completed and turned in by its due date.

I also had just learned that producers, whether signed to a Motown producer contract or not, were paid a per song producer fee, which my so-called managers failed to tell me or request on my behalf because when it came down to it, they worked for Motown and really didn't work for me at all.

On my way from Lasker's I walked past Bob Jones' office, who usually had his door closed, but this time it was open; and I didn't look up to even know if he was in there. Bob saw me walk by, got up and came to the door and called out to me.

"You just gonna walk on by Mr. Williams?" he asked in his gruff voice.

Slightly stunned, I looked back, trying to smile and responded, "Hi Bob. How are you?" I asked.

"If you bring your ass on in here, I can tell you," he said in a low joking tone.

I followed Bob into his office and took a seat. Trying to be upbeat, we began to get caught up on how things were going. Bob, of course, filled me in on what was being said about Switch's professional and nonprofessional behavior.

Then he said, "Word is, you finally solved one of your problems. Bobby' finally left the group."

"Now Bob…" I began, but he quickly cut me off saying," "I know, I know! You don't have to tell me you guys wanted him out as much as he wanted to leave."

I chimed in… "Bob if no one else knew, you know I've been trying to have the cancer cut out for little more than a year now, but the powers that be around here…"

"Well he's so strung out on that shit that they don't know if they're ever gonna get a record out of him, anyway. But at least he doesn't get to drag you guys down any further. You know it just makes me sad. I feel for him, but more so you because I know how hard it is to love somebody and not be able to get through to them. Anyway, what are you doing up here?"

I really didn't want to tell him that I had just been turned down for an advance, the only advance that I had ever asked for since signing with Motown, but this was Bob and he knew each of us well. He really cared about Switch, especially Bobby. Under Bob's gruff, stand-offish exterior was really a sweet, caring person, but most folk were not allowed close enough to know this about him.

Well, I ended up letting Bob in on my dilemma, to which, without a word he opened his desk, pulled out his personal check book, began to write and then asked, "How much do you need?"

Caught off guard by his immediate action, I stumbled for words while sincerely trying to refuse his offer; but again, he cut me off saying, "Don't back up now. You need it and I've got it, so just tell me how much and I can finish this check and put this damn book away."

Even though I knew that I could and would pay Bob back from my next bi-weekly pay and that he was doing this out of a real love for me, in my forever need of being self-reliant, I usually don't ask or take money or gifts from others, including family members and I am therefore unintentionally awkward and not too gracious when accepting the kindness of others. But in this situation as he said, I really did need it and he was offering, in fact insisting that I take it, so I accepted this act of pure consideration and kindness and took the money to go home.

Granddad's death added to the haze which surrounded me. During this period, financial instability, emotional upheaval, career uncertainty accompanied by a growing drug addiction was consuming me as I tried optimistically to stay in control and keep things moving.

As it stood, the world, especially my immediate world was counting on me to continue to assure them that all in life was well, even though in reality it was falling apart a little at a time. I had to keep things tight here in L.A., but I really needed to get to Grand Rapids to say goodbye to someone that I loved, admired and respected with all of my heart throughout my life, so within the next few days

Art, Ruby and I flew back to L.A. together. Once there, we too were swept up by the goings on with family and friends, which included the good, bad and sad emotionalism of the occasion.

Chapter 17

Leaving Motown

Greg Williams (Right On! Magazine)

Once back from my adventure in Michigan, Switch continued to evolve as did our relationship with Motown. I learned more valuable information about Motown at that time, all too late to do a damn thing to keep the snowfall from turning into an avalanche. By now Shelly Berger's short-term involvement with Switch was over and I had enlisted possible management with Joe Jackson and even Tony Jones as Motown was tossing Switch around like used up hoes.

Bobby was gone and Switch had a gig in San Diego. Everyone was ready to go, but we couldn't find Tommy. Now bear in mind that Tommy had made all of the rehearsals, so we had no indication that he wasn't going to show up, so I held the bus and went to three dope houses where I knew Tommy bought his base. Each house that I went to, I was told that Tommy wasn't there, so I had no choice but leave it alone.

Fortunately, on short notice we were fortunate enough to find and hire a friend, Mike McKinney who played bass for the Jacksons. Mike learned the entire show and songs on the bus as we drove to San Diego. This was also the show where we introduced Terrance Gaines to the stage. Terrance, having never performed before this many people before, roughly, ten thousand, froze up and could not remember when he was supposed to sing lead, when he was supposed to sing background, he forgot the limited dance routines, the brother was all together lost.

Now my keyboards are positioned front stage left, Eddie is positioned front stage right with Phillip and Terrance both singing center stage. We began to play "Love Me Over and Over", and Phillip and Terrance took the microphones from the stands and began to sing the song. As the song gets to the chorus I hear Phillip sing his lead as Zane and I sing the background, but I notice Terrance's voice is missing. Just as I raise my head to look up he had danced his way to my immediate right, so close I was startled, and he bends over to me and says, "Hey Greg, I'm fuckin' up, ain't I?"

If it hadn't been such a serious moment I would have laughed my ass off, but my show was falling apart because this brother got stage fright, in the middle of a song at that! I looked at him angrily and trying not to give the audience a clue as to what was going on I said, "Do your show man. Do your show!"

He danced his way back center stage, still not knowing how or where to pick up, yet he continues. Now I'm dealing with a new bass player who really wound up doing a great job and a singer who was not a performer. And I have to find this out, not in rehearsals, but on stage in front of ten thousand people. Needless to say, everyone else on stage caught on to Terrance's dilemma and tried to cover for his inability to pull it together. As the show ended I saw Terrance leave the stage but to this day I haven't seen him since.

I spoke to him by phone twenty-four years later, in 2005, and again in 2017 but sill I haven't seen him. Not back stage. Not in the dressing room. Not at the hotel. Nowhere. I would have taught him how not to be afraid. Switch would have taught him how to hold his own during a performance. We believed in him. Hell, that's why we hired him, but he never gave me the opportunity to help him live his dream. I was sad about that. I was sad about Tommy and even missed Bobby, although I knew our finally going in separate directions was for the best. I knew then that the journey downhill had begun and that recording for Motown would soon be a memory.

Returning to L.A. after the gig, a friend from Grand Rapids, James Long, whose house I had gone to looking for Tommy and was told that Tommy was not there, called me and said Tommy had been in his house all of the time I was there looking for him. He was hiding under the bed. I was hurt because, as close as I thought we'd been for all those years, he didn't have the decency to tell me he was leaving the band.

Tommy, with his misguided sense of loyalty, was leaving to follow Bobby who was going nowhere fast. Everyone but Tommy could see that Bobby had no real loyalty to Tommy, or anyone else for that matter, because in his present state of mind, he was incapable of being loyal to himself. But just the same, Tommy left Switch and waited for Bobby.

Once his recording budget became available, Bobby recruited Tommy to play bass on his tracks and be a part of his band, but he never got his shit together, and his promises to Tommy never came through. So later, after leaving Switch, Billy Preston helped Tommy by taking him on tour with him to Australia, and after that brief tour ended that was it for Tommy. With nowhere else to go and no way to feed his wife and children, Tommy packed up his belongings and his family and headed back to Grand Rapids.

As our time and even some of our personal relationships at Motown continued to dwindle, the remaining Switch members tried to remain creative. Me, Phillip, Jody, Eddie, Zane and our newest member Terrance Gaines put forth our best efforts to move on past the ghost of Bobby and Tommy

DeBarge quickly. We wrote and arranged new material and diligently dove right back into the studio.

While getting it in with positive progress, we were called by Motown to schedule another of our post-DeBarge A&R meetings with then Vice President of Creative, Lee Young Sr., who was younger brother to jazz great Lester Young and father to Motown's chief attorney and then Vice President of Legal, Lee Young Jr. Because Lee Sr. was a noted musician himself and was Nat King Cole's drummer for many years, Lee understood the creative process, concerns and issues better than anyone who sat in his seat throughout our entire five years at Motown.

Being faced with Bobby's and now Jermaine's absence, writing, producing and working side-by-side with the rest of Switch, the bulk of this album's production fell into my lap, which I had to accept and embrace like no time or role before. Still, from time to time, individually and collectively we had and welcomed infrequent update meetings with Lee. Within a few months into Switch V, Suzanne de Passe who, as with The Jackson Five stepped into Lee's job and role.

Motown legal sent then A&R director Simone Sheffield to the session with an addendum to our existing contract, which still had Switch bound for another three years. The addendum to resign with the same money, but without a signing bonus and after serious discussion with Jody, Phillip, Eddie and I, we agreed to decline Motown's bullshit offer and look elsewhere for a deal.

You signed as an artist, a songwriter and producer; however, your advance moneys, in Switch, DeBarge and various other Motown artists' cases was our bi-weekly salary; the studio-time to record your music, the musicians payments, the producers being paid as well as unrelated promotional expenses, i.e. internal and external promotional and publicity costs, equipment, stage props and costumes and other applicable expenses related to artist's career, which are advanced and or paid by record company on artist's behalf has to be covered and recouped before you get a dime. Therefore, you can and often will always be in debt because even the money you are supposed to be paid for records sold goes to cover all moneys provided and/or spent on your behalf, so in the final analysis, you have nothing. Artists make the bulk of their money from going on the road. After meeting and discussing this with the remaining members of Switch, I let Motown know that we would pass on their offer and we would be leaving upon completion of the album.

Phillip left the band, in 1983. He said that his brother James had set up meetings for him and Zane with Ed Eckstein who was to head up Quincy Jones' new label, Quest Records.

I asked Phillip, "well what about Switch? Might there be some interest for us over there?"

He was quick to respond, "Quincy don't deal with cats who do drugs."

I remember becoming real quiet. I was first shocked to feel that Phillip, Zane and James had conspired to make this move and kept me in the dark, confirming again that there really is no loyalty in the music business. Just me and my antiquated ideas that *do unto others as you would have them do unto you* still meant something in the hearts and minds of a chosen few, especially people who I had handpicked to take this journey with me.

Reacting through my own guilt and paranoia and knowing that not to be true, I took it personal. But instead of arguing and or fighting which I really felt like doing, I just dropped the subject all together and moved on.

I was left further in the midst of my fog. Now Switch was over, and all was left was my going through the motions. See, in retrospect I knew the second I accepted Bobby into my band it would not last long because I knew that either he would have to leave or be thrown out because he had problems that nothing and no one could resolve, but I didn't consider the possibility that Tommy would leave me. I had no idea that one-day Phillip would leave me, but once those three members were gone, Switch was finally gone. In my heart I knew that I had left Switch at Motown.

As I moved on to what would be a Total Experience, the final reality was so far from where my band began, there was no resemblance of my initial dream with shattered memories of Switch, DeBarge Motown & me!!

ABOUT THE AUTHOR

Gregory Williams is the founder/leader of late 70's Motown Records multi-platinum selling artist Switch and the author of his first published book, *Switch, DeBarge, Motown & Me!*

A "play by ear" musician/singer/arranger/producer, Gregory's fifty-plus-years journey through life, love and the entertainment industry is the backdrop for this insightful, factual telling of his "how I did it" autobiography.

Gregory has an Associate's degree in English and better than equivalence of a master's degree in making magic through music and entertainment. Over the years, he has won various accolades and awards as a performer, including: gold and platinum album awards as artist/songwriter/producer for Switch and Switch II; Gold Album Awards for Best of Switch; and Multi-Platinum Album Awards (more than 15 Million records sold to date) as a producer on Boyz II Men II.

Gregory is a winner of ASCAP's Top 100 R&B Songwriters for the years of 1979 and 1980 and winner of two (2) ASCAP "Rhythm and Soul Music Awards" for top Hip-Hop/Rap Writers and top Music Publisher for 2007.

Gregory currently makes his home in the Los Angeles area while he continues to perform with Switch and remains active as a recording artist, musician and record producer.

According to Gregory, "Music and Entertainment have Always Been My Life!" From his beginning as a solo vocalist in his kindergarten Christmas play and being the trumpet blowing leader of his first band at age seven, to a not-too-short stint in acting, singing and playing through his teens; and even through his successful years as the founder/leader of former Motown Recording group "SWITCH", Gregory stays on task and continues to live each day as if it's his last, by asking, "What else can I do?"

On top of all that Gregory loves to make folks laugh, is a serious cook and is known from coast to coast for his incredible home-made popcorn.

Made in the USA
Columbia, SC
01 January 2020